Achieving Excellence in the Management of Human Service Organizations

Peter M. Kettner

Arizona State University

Allyn and Bacon

Boston ∎ London ∎ Toronto ∎ Sydney ∎ Tokyo ∎ Singapore

Series Editor, Social Work and Family Therapy: Patricia Quinlin
Editor-in-Chief, Social Sciences: Karen Hanson
Series Editorial Assistant: Alyssa Pratt
Marketing Manager: Jackie Aaron
Editorial-Production Service: Omegatype Typography, Inc.
Composition and Prepress Buyer: Linda Cox
Manufacturing Buyer: Suzanne Lareau
Cover Administrator: Kristina Mose-Libon
Electronic Composition: Omegatype Typography, Inc.

Copyright © 2002 by Allyn & Bacon
A Pearson Education Company
75 Arlington Street
Boston, MA 02116

Internet: www.ablongman.com

Library of Congress Cataloging-in-Publication Data

Kettner, Peter M.
  Achieving excellence in the management of human service organizations / Peter M. Kettner.
    p.   cm.
  Includes bibliographical references and index.
  ISBN 0-205-31878-9 (alk. paper)
  1. Human services–Management. I. Title.
 HV41.K46 2001
 361'.0068–dc21

2001018856

Printed in the United States of America
10   9   8   7   6   5   4   3   2   1   06   05   04   03   02   01

CONTENTS

5   Using Job and Work Design Creatively to Achieve Maximum Employee Performance   110

10   Using Job Analysis as a Basis for Ensuring Consistency within the Human Resources System   250

11   Strengthening the Organization through Excellent Recruitment, Selection, and Hiring Practices   276

12 Maximizing Employee Potential through Staff Training and Development   300

13 Supervision, Performance Appraisal, Rewards, and Termination   326

We refer to it by a variety of names: *work, the office, the agency,* and various other names or acronyms, some of which are probably not particularly endearing. What we're referring to is the organization where we are employed. We spend a great part of our lives dealing with organizations. An employee who works for 40 years spends more than 80,000 hours working within the context of an organization. And in addition to our place of employment, there are the organizations where we make our purchases, where we come together for social purposes, where we worship, and where we fulfill many other needs and wants. Renowned sociologist Amatai Etzioni (1964) stated it this way:

> We are born in organizations, educated by organizations, and most of us spend much of our lives working for organizations. We spend much of our leisure time paying, playing, and praying in organizations. Most of us will die in an organization, and when the time comes for burial, the largest organization of all—the state—must grant official permission. (p. 1)

However, in spite of the prominent role that organizations play in our lives, few entities are taken as much for granted as the organization. Most likely the vast majority of employees recognize that they have a job to do and approach it with varying degrees of conscientiousness. But the organization is more than a roster of individuals carrying out their duties. The whole, in this case, is much greater than the sum of its parts. The workplace is made up of systems and subsystems, resources, technology, people, interpersonal dynamics, power, authority, democracy, participation, and many other complex interacting factors. Whether a person feels like getting out of bed in the morning to go to work depends on how the organization is able to blend these interacting factors in a way that makes the organization truly productive, while motivating its employees and making the organization a desirable place to work.

Whose job is it to ensure that everything blends well and the organization performs at the highest possible level? Everyone in the organization must contribute something toward an organization's achievement of excellence, but the persons who must create the environment in which employees want the organization to succeed are the managers. It's an enormous responsibility and one that cannot be taken for granted. I have met hundreds of managers who believe that their professional training in psychology, social work, law, nursing, or other discipline is enough—that it is not necessary that they become experts in the field of management as well. On-the-job training, they believe, should suffice. Findings from studies of successful organizations and successful leaders do not support this position. Management knowledge and skill are critical to success, in addition to the knowledge, skill, and values developed in professional study.

For more than thirty years I have practiced, taught, and provided consultation to others on many topics associated with the administration and management of social service agencies—primarily nonprofit organizations but also a good share of government agencies. As a result of these experiences, I have learned to appreciate the important and unique role managers play in influencing the success of their organizations. It is a highly complex role and one that must be approached and carried out with great understanding of and respect for the special contributions that management theory, knowledge, and skill have to offer.

Management theory and research have been focused primarily on for-profit business and industrial organizations. Perhaps for this reason management theory often receives only a cursory overview in management and administration courses in professional programs such as social work and other human service professions. The major focus in programs that specialize in nonprofit administration or social service administration seems to be on understanding the unique characteristics of nonprofit or social service organizations and on value considerations established by professional associations. As a result, many agency administrators and managers trained in professional schools identify with their professional knowledge and values (which is good) but fail to recognize that there is an extensive and well-developed body of knowledge about management theory and practice that is highly relevant to the ways in which they carry out their day-to-day responsibilities.

Professional preparation as a social worker, lawyer, clergyperson, psychologist, teacher, counselor, or other discipline is important and highly relevant for those who choose to apply what they have learned to their work with individuals, groups, and families. However, for those who choose to go into management or administration, not all of this professional preparation translates directly into the knowledge and skills needed for day-to-day management of an organization. Some knowledge about the organization and its personnel, understood within the context of management theory, is also necessary. It is for this reason that I have compiled this book on management knowledge and skill as applied to human service organizations.

In creating the outline for this book, I have attempted to develop something that, in very general terms, might be called a practice model. Practice models, of course, never function precisely in the ways in which they are designed. Yet they provide the budding manager, and especially the student preparing for a career in human services management, with some guidelines for practice.

The practice model for the management of human service organizations is built around the concepts of organizational excellence and internal consistency. *Excellence* is a term that appears periodically in management literature, but it is often left undefined. Part of my intent in this book is to begin to identify some of the components that make up organizational life that, when planned and implemented in harmony with other systems and subsystems, contribute to maximizing organizational productivity. The working hypothesis associated with this model is that if all of the systems are designed in a way that they are internally consistent and compatible, if they are designed in a way that supports consistent pursuit of the mission and philosophy of the organization, and if employees are encouraged to perform at their highest levels and supported and rewarded for their performance, then the organization will achieve excellence as measured by consistent progress toward its stated strategic, long-range, and program goals and objectives.

The model is grounded in management theory. In Part I, Developing a Theory and Philosophy of Management, classical and contemporary theories are discussed and principles extracted that hold potential for providing a framework for the management of human service organizations. Although a framework is prescribed for a theory of human service management, flexibility is allowed for the student and practitioner to adapt theoretical underpinnings to the unique characteristics and needs of the organization, its managers, and other factors.

Components of the organization are presented in a way that is intended to guide the manager toward building an organization that is internally consistent and supports high levels of performance. An age-old concern expressed about social service agencies is that they do not have the resources necessary to succeed. Part II, Managing the Organization, explores strategies such as restructuring the organization, redesigning jobs, and reconfiguring the motivation and reward system to achieve maximum productivity. These are strategies that do not necessarily require significant additional resources. Part III, Managing Data, Information, and Finances, focuses on making the best use of existing resources by designing systems that promote cost-efficiency, cost-effectiveness, and lend themselves to a practice/research orientation.

Part IV, Managing Human Resources, examines ways to recruit, select, train, develop, nurture, and evaluate each employee in a way that encourages mutually supportive teamwork and generates a synergy that keeps the organization functioning at high levels. Part V, Monitoring and Evaluating Organizational Effectiveness, discusses ways to identify organizational strengths and weaknesses in the interest of preventing any deterioration or decline while supporting improvements in levels of functioning.

A set of exercises is proposed at the end of each chapter. These exercises are designed to produce a policy and procedures manual that the student or practitioner can keep as a resource document, use as a model, and adapt for any organization. Well-designed policies and procedures that are mindful of the agency's mission and philosophy can go a long way toward promoting organizational excellence.

It is my sincere hope that this book will provide many students and managers with a resource that will guide them toward the kinds of practices that will not only maximize levels of achievement for the organization but will also provide great job satisfaction for the manager.

Many people deserve thanks for their contributions to the completion of this project. First, I want to express my great appreciation to the many students with inquiring minds who have challenged ideas over the years and caused me to sharpen my thinking to make the concepts and principles consistent and compatible. In the technical preparation of the manuscript, an author would be overwhelmed were it not for the great patience and attention to detail provided by those skilled in computer graphics and editing. For these contributions I am deeply indebted to the staff at the Publications Assistance Center of the College of Public Programs at Arizona State University including Janet Soper, Director, Mary Fran Draisker, Victor Garman, and Roisan Rubio. Many thanks to Karen Hanson, senior editor at Allyn and Bacon, to Alyssa Pratt, who were always ready with a prompt answer to my many questions, and to the reviewers, Arturo Acosta, El Paso Community College, and Francisco Villarruel, Michigan State University, for their helpful suggestions.

Finally, I come to the dedication of this book. Frankly, I have never really seen the point of dedications. Feelings for loved ones have always been a private matter, and I have chosen to dedicate all my previous books to those students and practitioners who struggle every day with ways to alleviate social problems and reduce human suffering, and who take learning seriously and attempt to master and apply new concepts and ideas. However, in this instance I have written a book alone for the first time and found it a very different experience from collaborating with colleagues. My sole source of support and strength throughout the project was my wife, Judy. She read every chapter at least three times, made valuable suggestions, identified hundreds of necessary corrections, tracked down elusive references, guided me through the use of some of the special features of WordPerfect, and provided great moral support. So it is to her that I dedicate this book. Honorable mention also to my children Tim, Rick, and Becky who have taught me more about management than they will ever know.

CHAPTER 1

Perspectives on Excellence in Management

CHAPTER OBJECTIVES

Upon completion of this chapter, the reader will be able to:

- Explain the role of a manager in a human service organization.
- Summarize research findings on the criteria that contribute to excellence in the management of organizations.
- Summarize research findings on what qualities make for an outstanding leader.
- Explain the meaning of being knowledge and value centered as a manager.

Assumptions

- That human services management is a professional discipline with a body of knowledge, skills, and values.
- That there are things that can be done by managers and administrators to achieve excellence in an organization; it's not accidental.
- That the major responsibilities of managers have to do with finding ways to get staff to feel a sense of achievement and success, thereby enhancing productivity.
- That management knowledge and professional ethics form the foundation for achievement of excellence in the practice of management.

■ Understanding the Manager's Role

In a column in *Newsweek,* Robert Samuelson (1999) reflects on the topic "Why I Am Not a Manager." By way of explanation he states that managers face two contradictory demands: (1) they are expected to get results, and (2) they must motivate their workers. As a result, he says, they get pressure from above and resentment from below. He confesses a grudging admiration for those who are able to do the job well but says he prefers a position in which he has no responsibility for managing anyone or anything.

Given the choice, why would anyone want a management position in an organization? Setting aside the many possible psychological, power-oriented, need-meeting, status-seeking, Maslow-framed explanations, there are many potentially fulfilling and rewarding components to the role of manager or administrator and many potential, tangible accomplishments for the good of the organization, the community, and the population served. There are also many challenges, and it is clear from more than a hundred years of experience that the role of manager is not for everyone, and that simply having the ambition to manage is not enough to do the job successfully.

What, then, does it take to excel as a manager or administrator? Before we get into the substantive content of the manager's job, let's briefly examine the expectations of the position. For many activities that we encounter during our lifetimes, there are clear practice routines that, if undertaken systematically and in a disciplined way, will lead to excellence. Golf and tennis are good examples. We can break down the motions necessary for the "perfect" swing or stroke, and if we devote enough time to practice and feedback, we can work toward a tangible goal. The same might be said of such functions as mastering the use of various types of software, becoming an outstanding therapist, or excelling in the practice of surgery.

The key difference for managers and administrators is that, for them to excel, they must achieve their accomplishments indirectly. Success for the manager comes through managing people in a way that motivates and enables them to work at their highest levels of productivity and in harmony with one another so that the total organization demonstrates success in terms of efficiency, effectiveness, quality, and productivity. Many managers have expressed the sentiment that it would be so much easier if only they could do a task directly rather than assigning it to a staff member! Getting the staff member to do the task in a positive way and producing a quality piece of work, however, is what the manager's job is all about. Nobody cares whether or not the manager could do a better job by doing it him- or herself.

■ Defining Management and Administration

There is a tendency to use the terms *management* and *administration* interchangeably, yet there are some subtle differences described in the literature and demonstrated in practice. Sheldon (1966) distinguished the functions in this way:

> *Administration* is the function of industry concerned in the determination of corporate policy, the co-ordination of finance, production, and distribution, the settlement of the compass of the organization, and the ultimate control of the executive.

> *Management* is the function in industry concerned in the execution of policy, within the limits set up by administration, and the employment of the organization for the particular objects set before it. (p. 32)

One management scholar who focused on defining management was Henri Fayol (1949). He indicated that all management activity is made up of five components: planning, organizing, commanding, coordinating, and controlling. His definitions support the notion that management is involved primarily in the execution of policy and the supervision of subordinates in achieving the goals of the organization. Weinbach (1994) sums up the role of the human services manager as follows:

> Management can be thought of as those specific functions performed by persons within the work setting that are intended to promote productivity and organizational goal attainment. (p. 11)

The critical difference between administrators and managers has to do with distinguishing between the executive level, policy-making, decision-making functions of the administrator and the implementation of policy and decisions designed to achieve a mutually agreed-upon set of goals and objectives, all guided by a mission and a shared vision about the organization's direction. It is intended that this book will focus on the functions of the implementer (the manager), the person whose job it is to make the organization run in a productive and harmonious way. Job titles vary and can include supervisor, program manager, director, or other such title, depending on the level of management.

The focus on the role of management is adopted for a number of reasons. First, much is expected from human service organizations today, and organizational effectiveness is highly dependent on good management. Second, a manager's role and responsibilities can be categorized and broken down into components so that they can be better understood and practiced. Finally, many organization-related functions overlap the domains of both management and administration, so the body of knowledge and range of skills have wide applicability. In the field of human services there are often positions that require the dual role of manager/administrator.

■ Creating a Positive Work Environment

Getting staff to perform at high levels has a lot to do with finding out exactly what motivates high performance. Have you ever held a job that you absolutely loved? A job in which you couldn't wait to get to work? A job in which you didn't watch the clock, but if you did happen to notice it, you were constantly amazed at how the time flew by? What about the other end of the scale? Have you ever had a job you hated? A job in which you worked only because you had to, because you needed the money? A job in which you spent the absolute minimum amount of time and energy that was necessary to keep the job?

What do you think makes the difference between those two types of jobs? Is it salary or the way people are treated? Is it the type of work employees do or the ways in which employees are rewarded (or not rewarded) for good work?

The pursuit of answers to these questions will form the major theme of this book. These are some of the most important questions in all of management, because if you can create an organization in which people understand the job to be done, are committed to the organization's mission, are competent to do the jobs to which they are assigned, love their work, and work well together, you will have put your organization in a position in which you can achieve maximum efficiency, effectiveness, quality, and productivity. On the other hand, if the drive to achieve excellence does not come from the collective efforts and motivation of the employees, no amount of close supervision, monitoring, evaluating, or threats will bring about an excellent organization.

◾ Establishing Criteria for Organizational Excellence

In a sense, it might be said that the history of management thought is a story of the search for the correct formula that, when applied to the management of an organization, will ensure maximum performance. Management theorists, then, can be distinguished from one another by understanding their concepts of the "correct formula."

For the proponents of scientific management theory in the early twentieth century, for example, the formula involved an assembly-line approach to manufacturing in which motion and energy were focused on certain limited tasks. If those who performed and supervised the tasks could perfect the motions and find the one best way, the production lines and, therefore, the organization would have achieved excellence.

For the proponents of human relations management in the 1940s and 1950s, employees needed positive attention and feedback from supervisors and others in the organization. If supervisors understood human behavior and motivation and would take the time to provide feedback and personalize the work environment, employees would perform at their highest levels and the organization would achieve excellence.

Douglas McGregor (1969), the author of the Theory X and Theory Y framework, presented a different argument. People were productive or unproductive, he believed, because of the assumptions management held about them—assumptions that then were translated into how employees were treated. If managers understood that people were capable of investing themselves and their creative abilities in the job, and if managers saw their responsibilities as getting barriers out of the way and unleashing the potential of a creative and energetic workforce, employees would perform at their highest levels and the organization would achieve excellence.

Other management scholars have proposed that the formula for achieving maximum productivity can be understood from the perspective of employee participation in decision making (Likert, 1967), careful planning and establishment of objectives (Drucker, 1954), having a form and structure that is in harmony with organizational purpose (Burns & Stalker, 1961), or establishing quality control standards for organizational processes, products, and services (Deming, 1982).

Research on Excellence

A number of researchers and authors in the field of management have addressed the question of what contributes to excellence in management. Peters and Waterman (1982) entitled their book *In Search of Excellence*. Their research led them to examine about 75 companies (some in greater detail, some in less). Companies were selected only if they fit their definition of excellence by meeting certain performance criteria over a previous twenty-year period. Through careful scrutiny of data and information from a sample of these successful companies, the authors identified eight basic principles that characterized excellent companies. The eight principles were:

1. *A bias for action:* preferring to do something—anything—rather than sending a question through cycles and cycles of analyses and committee reports
2. *Staying close to the customer:* learning the customer's preferences and catering to them
3. *Autonomy and entrepreneurship:* breaking the corporation into small companies and encouraging them to think independently and competitively
4. *Productivity through people:* creating in all employees the awareness that their best efforts are essential and that they will share in the rewards of the company's success
5. *Hands-on, value driven:* insisting that executives keep in touch with the firm's essential business
6. *Stick to the knitting:* remaining with the business the company knows best
7. *Simple form, lean staff:* having few administrative layers with few people at the upper levels
8. *Simultaneous loose-tight properties:* fostering a climate in which there is dedication to the central values of the company combined with tolerance for all employees who accept those values

Although some of the subsequent research on high-performing organizations did not completely support these eight principles as those that will consistently lead to high performance, the Peters and Waterman principles did contribute to early thinking on the subject of organizational excellence. Some of the themes that run through their eight principles still appear twenty years later in literature on high-performing organizations. For example, their findings support a recognition, on the part of management, that employees bring a wealth of talent to the job and will perform at higher levels when there is a respect for their abilities to make positive contributions without constant direction and supervision. A second theme has to do with developing a niche or area of expertise and building on it rather than promoting continuous diversification. Another theme focuses on a commitment to the customer. We will revisit Peters and Waterman's findings in the next chapter, but at this point we simply want to explore the various ways in which excellence in management has been defined.

Excellence as Defined by Accreditation Standards

Accrediting bodies also have ideas about what constitutes a range of performance from minimally acceptable to excellent. The Council on Accreditation (COA) is an organization whose purpose is to establish accreditation standards and evaluate social service agencies in relation to those standards. COA states that its accreditation gives assurance to various constituents that the agency meets rigorous standards and demonstrates that it (1) has effective management, (2) is fiscally sound, (3) designs programs to meet community needs, (4) continually monitors and evaluates service quality, (5) has qualified personnel, and

(6) has safe, accessible facilities (Council on Accreditation of Services for Families and Children, Inc., n.d.). These six criteria provide a very general framework for understanding what a professional accrediting body might look for when evaluating an organization and making a judgment about its performance.

The National Committee for Quality Assurance (NCQA) is a private, not-for-profit organization that assesses and reports on the quality of managed health care plans. Since 1991 NCQA has reviewed plans against more than fifty different standards, which fall into one of six categories that lead to an overall accreditation score:

1. Quality Improvement (40 percent)
2. Physician Credentials (20 percent)
3. Preventive Health Services (15 percent)
4. Members' Rights and Responsibilities (10 percent)
5. Utilization Management (10 percent)
6. Medical Records (5 percent)

Organizations are scored within each of the six dimensions. Standards are used to determine scores. A high score would represent excellence in managed health care.

Another body concerned with excellence in organizational functioning is the U.S. Department of Commerce. Every year the president of the United States presents the Malcolm Baldrige National Quality Award to recognize U.S. companies for performance excellence. The point system used in judging applicants for the annual award uses seven criteria, with varying points allocated to each as follows:

Criteria	Points
1. Leadership	100
2. Information and Analysis	70
3. Strategic Quality Planning	60
4. Human Resource Development and Utilization	150
5. Management of Process Quality	140
6. Quality and Operational Results	180
7. Customer Focus and Satisfaction	300
Total points	1,000

Curt W. Reimann, director of the awarding organization, lists eight critical factors that the examiners and judges look for:

1. A plan to keep improving all operations continuously
2. A system for measuring these improvements accurately
3. A strategic plan based on benchmarks that compare the company's performance with the world's best
4. A close partnership with suppliers and customers that feeds improvements back into the operation

5. A deep understanding of the customers so that their wants can be translated into products
6. A long-lasting relationship with customers, going beyond the delivery of the product to include sales, service, and ease of maintenance
7. A focus on preventing mistakes rather than merely correcting them
8. A commitment to improving quality that runs from the top of the organization to the bottom (Main, 1990)

The Baldrige Award is given to business organizations. Not all criteria are equally applicable to human service organizations. However, the emphasis is on continuously improving the quality of the product or service, and positive relationships with satisfied customers or clients are important criteria for defining excellence regardless of the type of organization.

The Opinions of Managers

Harvey (1998) interviewed fifty-one persons in management positions in human service organizations, thirty-one of whom were at the highest level and the rest at lower levels in very large organizations. She identified eight excellence dimensions, with several subcategories to one of the dimensions, as follows:

Excellence Dimension	*Definition*
1. Purpose	Having a very clear sense of purpose, direction, mission, or vision, and a focus on its accomplishment.
2. Serving Client Needs	Attentiveness and responsiveness to the needs and feedback of the people that it serves.
3. Commitments to Staff	Commitment to provide a positive organizational climate where people feel trusted, valued, and respected.
4. Commitments from Staff	Demonstrated personal characteristics or attributes such as integrity, loyalty, and a sense of responsibility.
5. Flexibility and Adaptability	Constant examination of the organization's need to change, awareness of organizational environment, making changes proactively.
6. Internal Processes	Responsible financial management, program evaluation, sound policies and procedures, an effective board of directors, strategic planning, a relatively flat structure, and nonantagonistic relationships with employee unions.
7. Congruence	All components of the organization are internalized and valued by staff and are well integrated and noncontradictory.
8. Striving	Excellence is not a static state; it requires that all employees have an internalized commitment to and actually do excellent work. (p. 38)

Some Themes Emerging from a Study of Organizational Excellence

In summary, there are many different perspectives on a definition of excellence in organizational functioning. Themes that emerge from studies of excellence include (1) establishing a purpose and mission for the organization and ensuring that all systems are consistent with the mission; (2) creating an organizational structure that is consistent with organizational purpose and maximizes flexibility; (3) designing jobs in a way that will permit staff to use their expertise and creativity; (4) demonstrating commitment to high performance by rewarding productive staff; (5) collecting data and information about services that will permit evaluation and continuous program improvement; (6) budgeting and financing the organization in a way that is consistent with the mission; (7) recruiting and retaining the best qualified and most productive staff; and (8) monitoring, evaluating, and providing feedback about staff performance in a way that leads to continuous improvement and high levels of productivity.

These themes will form the basis of many of the following chapters. The focus of this book is on ways to organize the many dimensions of social service organizations so that a framework for excellence can be created and systematically pursued by those committed to its achievement.

■ Establishing Criteria for Excellence in Leadership

In order for human service organizations to achieve excellence, the sine qua non is outstanding leadership. Many who have studied administration and management wish that it were not so—that the quality of organizational life was not so dependent on the quality of leadership. But, like it or not, it is! Agency executives and top management personnel set the tone for life in the organization. They strongly influence the performance of staff. They decide who will receive and who will be denied rewards. They profoundly affect morale. The bottom line is that it is simply not possible to maximize the potential of an organization with mediocre or poor leadership.

Therefore, it behooves students of organizational life to learn to recognize qualities of good organizational leaders and to become skillful in enabling an organization and its employees and other stakeholders to maximize organizational potential. Let's begin by exploring the criteria that have been used by researchers and scholars to define excellence in leadership.

Examining the Qualities of Outstanding Leaders

Warren Bennis, a professor of management and former university president, is a person with a long-standing interest in the qualities of leaders. During the 1980s, Dr. Bennis attempted to determine what makes a "superleader." He interviewed ninety top corporate executives, university presidents, public officials, newspaper publishers, and the coaches of consistently winning athletic teams. From this research, Bennis (1984) identified five traits his superleaders had in common:

- *Vision:* the capacity to create a compelling picture of the desired state of affairs that inspires people to perform
- *Communication:* the ability to portray the vision clearly and in a way that enlists the support of constituencies
- *Persistence:* the ability to stay on course regardless of the obstacles encountered
- *Empowerment:* the ability to create a structure that harnesses the energies of others to achieve the desired result
- *Organizational ability:* the capacity to monitor the activities of the group, learn from mistakes, and use the resulting knowledge to improve the performance of the organization

In a later analysis, Bennis (1989) described four traits of competence in leaders as the management of:

1. *Attention:* the ability to capture the attention of others because of a compelling vision and a clear sense of purpose and direction
2. *Meaning:* the ability to align people with them by communicating a sense of excitement about their vision
3. *Trust:* the qualities of constancy and reliability; holding to a consistent philosophy or theme regardless of its popularity so that there is a sense of predictability without rigidity
4. *Self:* knowing one's skills and using them effectively

Bennis (1989) notes, "There is a term—*iatrogenic*—for illnesses caused by doctors and hospitals. There should be one for illnesses caused by leaders, too. Some give themselves heart attacks and nervous breakdowns; still worse, many are 'carriers,' causing their employees to be ill" (pp. 21–22).

In another study undertaken by Kouzes and Posner (1987), subordinates were asked what they expect from their superiors. The four responses to appear most frequently were honesty, competence, vision, and inspiration.

Clearly, there are some special qualities that set an excellent manager apart, and they involve (1) vision: the ability to define and generate enthusiasm for the organization's future direction; (2) knowledge: being well grounded in understanding how an organization ought to function in its ideal state; (3) people skills: getting the highest levels of productivity out of personnel; (4) analytical skills: using data and information in a way that institutionalizes the concept of continuous improvement in efficiency, effectiveness, quality, and productivity; and (5) personal qualities: honesty, trustworthiness, integrity, and ability to inspire others.

On Being Knowledge and Value Centered

In his internationally acclaimed best seller, *The Seven Habits of Highly Effective People*, Steven Covey (1989) introduces the concept of being "centered." He describes the many ways in which one's life can become centered, including being spouse centered, family centered, money centered, work centered, possession centered, pleasure centered, enemy centered, church centered, or self-centered. He goes on to point out the futility and emptiness achieved in one's life if any of these choices are made. In their place, he recommends becoming *principle centered.* "Principles are," he says, "deep fundamental truths, classic truths, generic common denominators. They are tightly interwoven threads running with exactness, consistency, beauty, and strength through the fabric of life" (p. 122). Principles are timeless and do not change from one personal encounter to another.

In establishing the meaning of excellence, we will build on a foundation or "center" of a solid grounding in management theory as depicted in Figure 1.1. In defining a foundation for managerial growth and development, the excellent manager will first have the highest respect for the theoretical- and research-based foundation upon which good management practices today are based. Many managers in human service organizations have been trained in fields other than management and have not been exposed to much of this important liter-

FIGURE 1.1

Knowledge, Skill, and Values Foundation for Human Services Management

Managing the organization

Commitment to the organization's mission and philosophy

Managing personnel

Commitment to professional values and ethical practices

Ongoing development of management knowledge and leadership skills

Solid grounding in management theory

Managing information

Managing finances

ature. And although some become fine leaders because of their good instincts and ability to learn quickly on the job, they would undoubtedly be even better if grounded in sound knowledge of the various themes that have developed throughout the history of management.

Some may question the usefulness of management and organizational theory (much of which has been developed essentially for U.S. corporate, for-profit enterprises) to the nonprofit world of human services. The history of management thought has centered on maximizing productivity and profit. There have been many different perspectives on what makes people work hard for a company, but every perspective ultimately has increased productivity and profit at its core. It is, therefore, a perfectly logical and legitimate question to ask whether principles and concepts can be extracted from a competitive, profit-oriented environment and adapted to a noncompetitive, nonprofit organization. It is important that the reader keep an open mind on this question and use good critical thinking skills to evaluate and reevaluate constantly the usefulness of business-oriented concepts for human services management. Understanding how to adapt the best and most useful managerial themes to meet the unique needs of human service organizations and honing leadership skills are fundamental to excellence in management.

The next level in building a core or foundation for pursuit of excellence in management is a commitment to values and ethical practice. Value considerations in management include a commitment to behave in accordance with certain principles. Social work in particular and the broader field of human services in general will function with greater consistency and integrity if its managers are clear on questions of values and ethics. The major professional organization for social work, the National Association of Social Workers (NASW), has a code of ethics that proposes appropriate conduct as a professional person as well as responsibilities to clients, to colleagues, to employing organizations, to the profession and to society. Good managers will not only be able to articulate their values but will incorporate them into the roots from which their day-to-day practice flows.

Once grounded in management and organizational theory, in continuous and ongoing knowledge building, and in values, the manager in pursuit of excellence will carry out responsibilities in a way that is consistent with the organization's mission and philosophy. It is mission and philosophy that provide a shared vision and sense of commitment and serve as a compass in planning and decision making.

Day-to-day practice for the manager involves the guidance of several organizational components. Managing the organization requires constant monitoring to ensure that all systems within the organization are functioning appropriately and in harmony with each other. Managing information requires attention to detail to ensure that data and information are collected and processed in a way that permits ongoing monitoring and evaluation and meets the needs of all stakeholders for information and reporting. Managing the budget requires carefully thought-out decisions about allocations to ensure that they are consistent with mission and philosophy and regular monitoring to ensure that expenditures support budget planning. Finally, managing personnel requires conscientious attention to every element of the human resources system to ensure that employee recruitment, selection, hiring, appraisal, and development are carried out with integrity throughout the system. When these guidelines for knowledge, skill, and value foundations are followed, managers of human service organizations will be providing themselves, their staff members, and their agencies with the very best opportunity to achieve excellence.

The Manager as Maestro

If you are among the many millions who have enjoyed Meredith Willson's *The Music Man,* you will no doubt remember the scene in which "Professor" Harold Hill (a known fraud and charlatan), after having sold band instruments and uniforms to all of the families with elementary school children in a small Iowa town, proceeds to direct them in the "Minuet in G," using the "think system." The result is a cacophony of uncoordinated and unpleasant sound, funny in this particular context but unacceptable if you paid top dollar for a ticket and were expecting to hear a polished philharmonic orchestra.

In many ways, the role of the maestro is a good analogy for the role of the manager. Leading an orchestra looks easy, and many people are convinced they could step right into the role with no advance knowledge or preparation. Likewise, many who have been successful at lower levels in the organization believe that they can move from the role of clinician to manager without missing a beat, simply because they have observed other managers for many years.

Most of us are aware of organizations that, in the ways that they go about their business, seemingly make beautiful music while others emit only noise. Those managers who are guided by their knowledge of good management theory and practice, their knowledge of the organization, who make good use of data and information for continuous quality improvement, and who manage personnel in a way that elicits the highest levels of motivation and productivity will achieve excellence. Those who attempt to fulfill their responsibilities based on their instincts alone are less likely to do so.

In the following chapters we will develop a knowledge base on which a foundation can be built. We will identify the critical organizational principles that must be understood and appropriately applied to make the organization run smoothly. We will identify the elements of a comprehensive plan for the optimum utilization of human resources. If all of these components can be applied by a visionary and innovative leader in a way that achieves maximum internal consistency and integrity while remaining continuously responsive and relevant to external needs and demands, then we can say with conviction that excellence will ultimately be achieved in the management of that organization.

SUMMARY

1. **Understanding the Manager's Role.** An excellent manager is one who excels in getting others to do their best work to achieve the goals of the organization.
2. **Defining Management and Administration.** Administration determines policy and sets the direction for the organization. Management carries out policies and promotes goal attainment.
3. **Creating a Positive Work Environment.** An excellent manager coordinates all the complex organizational variables in a way that employees identify their own success with the success of the organization.
4. **Establishing Criteria for Organizational Excellence.**
   - *Research on Excellence.* A number of researchers have focused on the subject of excellence. Peters and Waterman identify eight criteria for excellent organizations.

- *Excellence as Defined by Accreditation Standards.* Accrediting bodies establish standards that can be used to define excellence.
- *The Opinions of Managers.* Harvey interviewed fifty-one managers and defined eight excellence dimensions.
- *Some Themes Emerging from a Study of Organizational Excellence.* A review of literature on organizational excellence produces eight themes.

5. **Establishing Criteria for Excellence in Leadership.** A number of researchers have explored the question of what makes a great leader.
   - *Examining the Qualities of Outstanding Leaders.* A summary of the literature identifies the qualities of vision, knowledge, people skills, analytical skills, and selected personal qualities as important for leadership.
   - *On Being Knowledge and Value Centered.* The core around which excellent managers are centered is a solid grounding in management theory and professional values.
   - *The Manager as Maestro.* The role of the manager can best be described as one who orchestrates many variables to produce harmonic functioning.

■ Overview of All Chapter Exercises

The exercises at the end of each chapter are designed to have the user develop a model, comprehensive manual that can serve as a reference document for all future responsibilities and assignments as a manager or administrator. Completion of the assignments will require that a specific agency or organization (either real or created for these assignments) be used as a basis for completing the policies and other documents.

At the end of each chapter the reader will be asked to develop a section of a policy manual, resulting in fourteen sections in all. These sections should be separated by a divider and placed in a three-ring binder. In some cases the assignment will ask for the creation of a policy. In these instances it is recommended that the policy statements follow a consistent format including the following standards: (1) they are assigned a number, (2) they are given a title that is printed in bold at the beginning of the policy statement, and (3) they are written in policy language. This means that they are written as short statements with no long, descriptive narratives. If new thoughts or ideas are introduced, they should be numbered as a subcategory of the policy and written as a separate section. An example follows:

Section 1: Organizational Philosophy

1.1 Statement on Excellence. It is the philosophy of this organization that all efforts will be consistently performed in a way that contributes toward overall organizational excellence (and so on).

1.1.1 Definition of Excellence. The term *excellence* as applied to this organization shall be defined as. . . .

When an attachment is required, a notation should be made in the policy statement that an example or an attachment is included. The attachment should be numbered in a way that associates it with the policy statement (e.g., Attachment 1.1a).

EXERCISES

Develop a brief description of the organization you will be using in these exercises. Include the types of clients and problems served, the types of programs and services offered, number and types of staff, and other relevant factors. Complete "Section 1: Organizational Philosophy" in relation to the organization you will be using throughout the fourteen chapters of the book.

Section 1: Organizational Philosophy

1.1 Statement on Excellence. Write a statement that expresses your organization's commitment to excellence. Make it brief and to the point. Explain what the term *excellence* means as applied to your organization.

1.2 Statement on Leadership. Write a statement that expresses your organization's criteria for defining outstanding leadership.

1.3 Philosophy on Management. Write a statement that expresses your organization's philosophy on the role of management.

REFERENCES

Bennis, W. (1984). The 4 competencies of leadership. *Training and Development Journal,* (August), 15–19.

Bennis, W. (1989). *Why leaders can't lead.* San Francisco: Jossey-Bass.

Burns, T., & Stalker, G. (1961). *The management of innovation.* London: Tavistock.

Council on Accreditation of Services for Families and Children, Inc. (n.d.). Brochure. New York: Author.

Covey, S. (1989). *The seven habits of highly effective people.* New York: Simon & Schuster.

Deming, W. (1982). *Quality, productivity, and competitive position.* Cambridge: MIT Center for Advanced Engineering Study.

Drucker, P. (1954). *The practice of management.* New York: Harper.

Fayol, H. (1949). *General and industrial management.* London: Pitman.

Harvey, C. (1998). Defining excellence in human service organizations. *Administration in Social Work, 22* (1), 33–45.

Kouzes, M., & Posner, B. (1987). *The leadership challenge.* San Francisco: Jossey-Bass.

Likert, R. (1967). *New patterns of management.* New York: McGraw-Hill.

Main, J. (1990, April 23). How to win the Baldrige award. *Fortune,* pp. 101–116.

McGregor, D. (1969). The human side of enterprise. In W. Eddy, W. Burke, V. Dupre, & O. South (Eds.), *Behavioral science and the manager's role* (pp. 157–166). Washington, D.C.: NTL Institute for Applied Behavioral Science.

Peters, T., & Waterman, R. (1982). *In search of excellence: Lessons from America's best-run companies.* New York: Harper & Row.

Samuelson, R. (1999, March 22). Why I am not a manager. *Newsweek, 133*(12), 47.

Sheldon, O. (1966). *The philosophy of management.* New York: Pittman.

Weinbach, R. (1994). *The social worker as manager: Theory and practice.* Boston: Allyn & Bacon.

CHAPTER 2

Developing a Theory for the Management of Human Service Organizations

CHAPTER OBJECTIVES

Upon completion of this chapter, the reader will be able to:

- Identify the major themes presented in each of the ten management or organizational theories or frameworks introduced in this chapter.
- Identify principles from each theory or framework that are useful in developing a theoretical framework for the management of human service organizations.
- Identify the organizational variables that define the parameters within which achievement of excellence will be determined.
- Identify the human variables that must be addressed by management in order to achieve excellence.
- Explain how the manager serves as integrator of organizational and human variables in achieving excellence.

Assumptions

- That management theory represents an important body of knowledge for managers; knowledge of the theory of one's professional discipline is not sufficient for those who take on the role of manager.
- That management theories, although created for for-profit businesses and industries, have much to offer as a theoretical foundation for the management of human service organizations.
- That no one theory can encompass the complexities involved in managing human service organizations, but certain principles and themes can be extracted from each to form an integrated, eclectic theoretical framework useful for human services management.
- That a manager's theoretical and philosophical framework forms the basis for consistency and integrity in practice.

The Usefulness of Early Management Theory

Although literature on the field of business management dates back to the late nineteenth century, the study of social service management and administration is relatively recent. Most of the literature has come either from the field of social work or from the field of nonprofit management (the arts, education, research, science, religion, philanthropy, and other such activities). In social work, the major focus of attention was on clinical practice until the 1960s. During this period of social unrest, the field began to shift its emphasis to policy, community, and organizational level interventions. However, in spite of the significant increase in the body of literature devoted to social work management and administration, to date there is little consensus within the profession about the appropriateness of any particular theoretical framework applicable to the management of human service agencies (Au, 1996).

Managers and administrators in practice may argue that a well-developed theoretical or conceptual framework for human services management is not possible, given the tremendous variability among social service organizations. Others suggest that it is management skill, not theoretical knowledge, that is needed. However, as we explore a range of organizational and management theories, it will become evident that well-grounded theory and philosophy are critical to the internal consistency and integrity of day-to-day organizational life.

If this is true, then it is of vital importance that the human service manager of the twenty-first century be well grounded in some of the major theories of management, their principles, and their basic concepts. The successful manager must also have an understanding of how these basic concepts might be adapted or used to promote excellence in overall organizational functioning. Indicators of excellence include high levels of productivity, high quality of services provided, and optimum achievement of outcomes, all while operating at the lowest possible cost.

The History of Management Thought

Although one might, in retrospect, be able to identify a management role as far back as biblical times, and certainly in the construction of such wonders as the pyramids, management as a formally recognized role dates back only about one hundred years. But in those one hundred years, the role of management has evolved from a vaguely defined role in the running of business and industrial organizations to being recognized as having a central place in our economy and our society. Very few professional fields produce literature that makes the best-seller lists; management literature regularly appears there. People are fascinated with the subject of how to make organizations more productive. In 1997, the Labor Department reported that there were 18 million executives, managers, and administrators in the United States and probably double or triple that number in aspiring executives, managers, and administrators.

So it should not be surprising that new ideas and innovations about management sell. Management has a role in the success of both large and small business, in achieving effective government, in maximizing the quality of education for our children, in strengthening the national defense, and in maximizing the potential good that can be accomplished within the nonprofit sector. Good management, however, is not driven by gimmicks. To be in a position to offer ideas and innovations for organizations that are meaningful and have staying power, one must understand the thinking that has gone into organizational effectiveness to date.

Application of Management Concepts to Human Service Organizations

What can we learn from the theoretical framework and the concepts generated by management theories since the early 1900s? In creating an eclectic theoretical framework for human services management, it is important to remember that historically management theories have been created for industry and the corporate world. The focus of management is productivity and profit. For-profit organizations operate in an arena in which ignoring innovations in management can mean the loss of a competitive edge. For this reason, as we trace the history of management thought, we must remember that business and industry bought into and adopted certain practices many years ago. As innovations were proposed, they typically were implemented in the workplace. Where they increased efficiency, effectiveness, and productivity, they were permanently installed. Where they did not contribute, they were eliminated.

Human services management has no such history. Human service agencies historically have had neither the commitment nor the resources to sponsor research and development units, as has business and industry. Consequently, there has not been a sense of building a sound theoretical framework for human services management, and adding to it over the years as new management techniques emerge. It is, therefore, incumbent upon scholars and practitioners in the field of human services today to identify those concepts and principles that may be useful in crafting a modern-day conceptual framework for good management practice. In the following sections we will explore some of the basic principles of both classical theories as well as some contemporary theories and frameworks that may have contributions to make to human services management. Those to be discussed will include (1) scientific management, (2) bureaucracy, (3) human relations management, (4) Theory X and Theory Y, (5) management by objectives, (6) systems theory, (7) contingency theory, (8) organizational culture, (9) Theory Z and total quality management, and (10) managing diversity and incorporating issues of ethnicity and gender. This list is by no means comprehensive, but it provides a range of concepts that can be used as building blocks toward the construction of an integrated theoretical framework for the management of human service organizations.

Scientific Management

Although extensive conceptualizing and writing about the functions of management did not occur until after 1900, the groundwork for scientific thinking about management was laid in the post–Civil War period. This era was marked by the expansion of mechanical industries and by the abolition of slave labor. During this period, the railroads gained a central role in shaping the growth and development of the country. After a period of time devoted to start-up considerations, U.S. industries began to attempt to streamline in the interest of maximizing profits. Issues of organization, structure, communication, and control began to emerge and to initiate a rethinking about how to manipulate these variables in the interest of increasing productivity and profit.

In these early years of emerging thought about the proper role of management, leaders in industry read papers and shared their ideas with colleagues in associations such as the American Society of Mechanical Engineers. Academics were increasingly recognizing the importance of research in the workplace. For example, W. S. Jevons, a lecturer at Queens College, in his principal work, *The Theory of Political Economy* (1888), poses some interesting questions about the intensity of labor and fatigue:

> Let us take such a simple kind of work as digging. A spade may be made of any size, and if the same number of strokes be made in the hour, the requisite exertion will vary nearly as the cube of the length of the blade. If the spade be small, the fatigue will be slight, but the work done will also be slight. A very large spade, on the other hand, will do a great quantity of work at each stroke, but the fatigue will be so great the labourer cannot long continue at his work. Accordingly, a certain medium-sized spade is adopted, which does not overtax a labourer and prevent him doing a full day's work, but enables him to accomplish as much as possible. The size of a spade should depend partly upon the tenacity and weight of the material, and partly upon the strength of the labourer. (p. 204)

The attempt was to bring a more disciplined type of study and data collection into the workplace in the interest of finding ways to reduce wasted motion and inefficiency. It was this environment that stimulated the thinking of Frederick Taylor and led to the creation of scientific management.

Taylor was born in Germantown, Pennsylvania, in 1856. He was educated in France and Germany. He worked for a number of industrial organizations in Pennsylvania, the most notable of which was the Midvale Steel Company where he became chief engineer in 1884. In 1890 he became general manager of the paper mills of the Manufacturing Investment Company in Maine, and in 1893 he opened an office in New York as a consulting engineer. During his career, he was credited with a number of inventions and received a number of awards. He died in Philadelphia in 1915 (Matteson & Ivancevich, 1981).

Taylor recognized the need to view the production process as a system and to focus on the elements of planning, organizing, and controlling. From his perspective, the workplace was somewhat chaotic. Management had no clear concept of responsibilities; work standards had not been developed, so there were no agreed-upon expectations. There were no incentives for workers to work up to the limits of their capacities. Managerial decisions were based on hunch and intuition. Virtually no studies were done of overall flow within the workplace, and workers were required to perform tasks for which they had little or no aptitude (George, 1968).

Taylor presented a paper in 1903 to the American Society of Mechanical Engineers entitled "Shop Management," in which he made the following points:

- *Wages.* The objective of good management was to pay high wages and have low unit production costs.
- *Research.* To achieve this objective management had to apply scientific methods of research and experiment to its overall problem in order to formulate principles and standard processes that would allow for control of the manufacturing operations.
- *Selection and Placement.* Employees had to be scientifically placed on jobs in which materials and working conditions were scientifically selected so that standards could be met.
- *Training.* Employees should be scientifically and precisely trained to improve their skill in performing a job so that the standard of output could be met.
- *Management/Worker Relationships.* An air of close and friendly cooperation would have to be cultivated between management and workers in order to ensure the continuance of this psychological environment that would make possible the application of the other principles he had mentioned (George, 1968, p. 89).

Taylor often referred to scientific management as requiring a complete mental revolution on the part of both management and employees. Managers, he felt, needed to recognize their partnership relationship with employees, and employees needed to develop a new attitude toward their work and their fellow employees, as well as toward their managers. Suspiciousness and watchfulness, he said, needed to be replaced with mutual confidence. Taylor's (1911) principles of management included these four:

First: Develop a science for each element of a man's* work, which replaces the old rule-of-thumb method.

Second: Scientifically select and then train, teach, and develop the workman, whereas in the past he chose his own work and trained himself as best he could.

Third: Heartily cooperate with the men so as to ensure all of the work is being done in accordance with the principles of the science which has been developed.

Fourth: There is an almost equal division of the work, and the responsibility between the management and the workmen. The management take overall work for which they are better fitted than the workmen, while in the past almost all of the work and the greater part of the responsibility were thrown upon the men. (pp. 36–37)

Taylor developed a variety of tools to assist in the precise description of motions and activities that went into developing a science for each element of work. He placed a great deal of emphasis on getting the right person into the job and developing collaborative relationships between management and workers.

[*Early writers consistently used the noun *man* and the pronouns *him* or *his* in their writing. Although it is recognized in a contemporary context that this terminology is sexist, the words of the original authors will be retained in the interest of accuracy and will not be followed in each instance by *sic* indicating inappropriate use, in the interest of not interrupting the flow of the thoughts presented.]

■ APPLICATION

To the Management of Human Services

Some useful concepts and principles that can be drawn from scientific management include the following:

- The concept of management as a specialized role
- Recognition of the importance of training and preparation for the job
- Attention to precision in the development of technology
- A research orientation to improve organizational efficiency, effectiveness, and productivity

Management as a Specialized Role   Because of the high levels of expectations of managers of nonprofit agencies today, there can be little doubt that management needs to be seen as a specialized role with its own body of knowledge and skills. It has been clearly demonstrated in other fields that people who are proficient in entry-level technical skills do not necessarily have the aptitude or the knowledge and skills needed to function as managers. Laurence Peter (1977) wrote a revealing treatise on what he referred to as the "Peter Principle." Briefly summarized, his position was that a person who performs competently at one level often receives a promotion, and if the person again performs competently he or she receives another promotion. This continues until finally the employee reaches a level where he or she is not able to perform competently; Peter calls this reaching their level of incompetence. He says they then remain in these positions and perform incompetently, perhaps until retirement.

It is not uncommon to find that those with the power to hire managers do not recognize the special expertise needed to achieve excellence in management. Good clinical skills may be valuable but are not sufficient to address the full range of demands of management and administration. A business background may provide some applicable experience, but it encompasses neither the values nor the professional and community context of social service management. For social service managers to be competently prepared to assume their responsibilities, the role of the manager must be conceptualized and defined as a specialized role.

Training and Preparation for the Job   If social service management is conceptualized as a specialized role, then clearly there must be education and training in preparation for that role. Many universities have centers for the training of nonprofit managers. National conferences, workshops, and seminars are provided on management topics of interest and relevance to managers and administrators of social service agencies. A program of continuous professional development as a manager should be planned and adopted by any manager committed to excellence.

Precision in the Development of Technology   A third principle of scientific management that is useful is the emphasis on precision in the development of technology. Social work is typically the primary discipline at the casework or case management level in social service agencies. Historically, the technology used by social workers has been far from precise. The approach to defining casework has been to provide general guidelines for a process and to encourage each individual to develop, in conjunction with the client, a plan for intervention. Thus, ten families with the same problem could conceivably have ten different plans, and if the caseworker changes, the plan may change also. Although there are good arguments for some degree of individuality, greater precision in defining the technology could lead to less trial and error, to greater efficiency, and to better results for clients.

A Research Orientation   It is clear that a lack of research on the effectiveness of interventions has limited the ability to streamline the helping process and make the technology more precise. For this reason, Taylor's on-the-job research orientation deserves serious consideration if social service organizations expect to achieve excellence. The more data and information collected about the helping process and its results, the more likely it is that the technology will be improved, resulting in better and more permanent positive outcomes for clients. On-the-job research, data collection, data aggregation, and data analysis probably offer the best hope for social service agencies to achieve the kind of research and development capacity that has enabled many corporations to achieve excellence.

So as human service managers today consider what is relevant for the agency of the twenty-first century, some of the concepts and principles associated with scientific management, even though they are over one hundred years old, should be recognized for what they potentially can bring to the creation of an eclectic theoretical framework for human services management.

Bureaucratic Theory

Many managers and others with experience in different types of organizations would argue that bureaucracy is one of the least popular approaches to organizational structure and design among practitioners. The simple use of the term *bureaucracy* brings to mind red tape, dehumanized interpersonal relationships with consumers and between coworkers, limits imposed by policy manuals, and a host of other negative stereotypes. We should be careful, however, not to allow the problems of implementation to overshadow the contributions of many of the theoretical concepts and principles of bureaucracy. Many professional social work and other human service practitioners, including many managers, will spend a good part of their professional lives working within bureaucratic organizations. It is, therefore, useful to attempt to understand the basic concepts and principles of bureaucratic theory and to weigh their value in the light of the realities of twenty-first-century practice.

The theoretical framework for bureaucratic management was created by Max Weber. Weber was born in 1864 in Thuringia, in Germany, and grew up in a highly intellectual atmosphere in Berlin. Beginning in 1882 he attended the University of Heidelberg to study law, and at the same time studied economics, philosophy, and history. Much of his career was spent as a professor of economics at various universities in Germany. His greatest contribution was *The Theory of Social and Economic Organizations* (1947). Weber died in 1920 in Munich (Matteson & Ivancevich, 1981).

Weber was looking for a way to bring orderliness and predictability to the workplace, to minimize chaotic, random behavior, and to resolve problems of authority and decision making, all worthy objectives, most would agree. It is important to remember that he proposed his principles at a time when (1) lines of authority were not always clear,

(2) people were appointed to positions based not on their expertise but on their connections, (3) neither job expectations nor the rules of operation were in writing, and (4) much of the work environment was managed from day to day. A careful analysis of Weber's contributions reveals that he did much to promote written policies and procedures, written job descriptions, requirements for education and expertise to qualify for positions, and other positive contributions. His basic premise underlying what he referred to as the ideal bureaucracy can be summed up in the following ten principles as applied to officials who are appointed to positions within the organization:

- *Authority.* They are personally free and subject to authority only with respect to their impersonal official obligations.
- *Hierarchy.* They are organized in a clearly defined hierarchy of offices.
- *Competence.* Each office has a clearly defined sphere of competence in the legal sense.
- *Contractual Relationship.* The office is filled by a free contractual relationship. Thus, in principle, there is free selection.
- *Qualifications.* Candidates are selected on the basis of technical qualifications. In the most rational case, this is tested by examination or guaranteed by diplomas certifying technical training, or both. They are appointed, not elected.
- *Compensation.* They are remunerated by fixed salaries in money, for the most part with a right to pensions. Only under certain circumstances does the employing authority, especially in private organizations, have a right to terminate the appointment, but the official is always free to resign. The salary scale is primarily graded according to rank in the hierarchy; but in addition to this criterion, the responsibility of the position and the requirements of the incumbent's social status may be taken into account.
- *Sole Occupation.* The office is treated as the sole, or at least the primary, occupation of the incumbent.
- *Career Ladder.* It constitutes a career. There is a system of "promotion" according to seniority or to achievement, or both. Promotion is dependent on the judgment of superiors.
- *Separation from Ownership.* The official works entirely separated from ownership of the means of administration and without appropriation of his position.
- *Discipline.* He is subject to strict and systematic discipline and control in the conduct of the office (Weber, 1947).

It is interesting to note that so many of the rights and privileges that are taken for granted in the workplace today find their roots in bureaucratic theory. Separating one's personal life and personal time from any obligation to an employer is one of these commonly accepted principles. Having a clearly defined set of expectations for a job, and hiring an employee because of his or her qualifications and ability to meet these expectations are others. Large organizations would find it extremely difficult to carry out the work of the organization, to communicate effectively, or to hold employees accountable without the concept of hierarchy. And the concept of a career ladder, providing avenues for promotion, has served to provide stability for organizations by allowing employees to stay with the same organization rather than having to move on to advance.

Weber himself stated that the primary reason that the bureaucratic form of organization advanced so quickly was its technical superiority over any other form of organization. All functions within the organization, he believed, are raised to the optimum point in a bureaucracy.

■ APPLICATION

To the Management of Human Services

Probably the greatest and most lasting criticism of bureaucracy comes from Robert Merton (1952) when he defines the concept of *trained incompetence.* By this he means that employees who focus so intently on policies as defined in a manual often lose their capacity to listen and to understand problems and needs as they are presented by consumers and users of the organization's services. It has certainly been true in some public agencies that the structure and uniformity required in a bureaucracy can overwhelm an organization's ability to be responsive to the sometimes highly individualized needs of clients of social service agencies. Furthermore, bureaucracies have not had a great deal of success in accommodating the application of knowledge and skill that is such an important part of professional practice. Even physicians are finding that, within the context of managed care, there are limits on the exercise of their professional judgments and the application of their knowledge and skill.

These limiting factors having been acknowledged, there are still some lessons that we can learn from bureaucratic theory that can make a contribution to a theory of human services management, including some of the following considerations:

■ Accountability
■ Defining jobs and placing them within a hierarchy
■ Valuing competence and preparation for the job

Accountability   If there is one feature that stands out in a bureaucracy it is that of accountability. One of the reasons that governments so often opt for a bureaucratic structure is that within this structure it is possible to pinpoint responsibility for decision making. Other models may offer more in terms of flexible work arrangements and productivity, but in organizations in which accountability for decision making is highly valued, bureaucracy becomes one of the more practical options. Given considerations of organizational liability for worker performance, it is perhaps not surprising that many government organizations continue to operate under bureaucratic structures even when other options offer promise of higher levels of productivity.

Hierarchy and Definition of Responsibility   Another important characteristic of well-run bureaucracies is an orderly workplace. Drawing on the principles that all jobs should be clearly defined and should fit within a hierarchy, we find that bureaucratic organizations tend to establish clear domains for their departments, programs, and units as well as for each employee. Ideally, this should mean that employees are able to function with a certain degree of independence without having to rely on direction from others to perform routine daily tasks. By the same token, however, defining the parameters for the functioning of departments, programs, units, and individuals can also be limiting when it comes to applying professional knowledge and skill to decision making. Although not useful in all human service organizations, some form of hierarchical structure is indispensable in large agencies.

Preparation for the Job   Like Taylor, Weber supports the idea that competence and preparation for the job must be a qualification for hiring and retention. For many years in the field of social services, positions have been downgraded in terms of their expectations for professional education, with years of experience substituting for years in school. Successful agencies today recognize that a carefully constructed job analysis can provide a sound framework for hiring decisions, and that these decisions should be based on demonstrated preparation for the job, not on impressionistic data. As we develop a theoretical framework for human services management and administration, it will become clear that the notion of competence and preparation for the job has an important place in that framework.

There are undoubtedly other principles that are useful, but the principles of accountability, clearly defined organizational subdivisions, clearly defined job functions, as well as competence and preparation for the job stand out as useful principles for the management of human service organizations.

Human Relations Theory

One of the more interesting stories that emerges in a review of the history of management thought is the story behind human relations theory. Elton Mayo is generally acknowledged to be the discoverer of the concepts and principles that form human relations theory. Mayo was a Harvard professor who conducted experiments from 1927 to 1947 at the Department of Industrial Research at Harvard.

The story is well known, but is worth repeating here, how Mayo undertook a study of attitudes and reactions of groups under varying conditions. Conducted at the Western Electric Company's Hawthorne Works in Chicago from 1927 to 1932, the original study was designed to learn the effects of illumination on productivity and output. The hypothesis to be tested was grounded in principles of scientific management that better illumination would result in increased productivity. As expected, productivity rose when illumination was increased for the experimental group, but surprisingly it also rose for the control group for which no increase in illumination was provided. In fact, productivity continued to rise in both groups even when illumination was decreased to a bare minimum for the experimental group (George, 1968, pp. 128–129).

In another experiment, conditions of work were changed so that experimental groups were given rest periods of varying lengths to test the effects of rest on the rate of productivity. While the rate of production showed a consistent increase, it was not related to the length of the rest periods and, therefore, could not be attributed to them. When the rest breaks were abolished and the longer day was restored, productivity continued at a high level in the experimental group (Etzioni, 1964, p. 33). What Mayo and his associates were able to demonstrate from these experiments was that it was not, in fact, the manipulation of the physical environment that led to higher productivity but rather the fact that the workers knew they were being watched and that the products of their teamwork were being monitored and compared. This factor, since referred to as the Hawthorne effect, led to the discovery that social and interpersonal effects were much more powerful predictors of productivity than were factors relating to the physical environment. Etzioni (1964) summed up the findings of these experiments in these five points:

> *Productivity.* The level of production is set by social norms, not by physiological capacities. In order to understand the productivity of a given worker or unit, one would have to understand the social environment as well as the demands of the job.

Rewards. Noneconomic rewards and sanctions significantly affect the behavior of the workers and largely limit the effect of economic incentive plans. The amount of work done by a worker will be greatly influenced by the worker's need for acceptance and approval by his or her coworkers. The establishment of informal norms and sanctions for "rate-busting," have given further credibility to this principle.

Group Behavior. Often workers do not act or react as individuals but as members of groups. This is similar to the foregoing principle, and explains why management rewards and sanctions sometimes do not change behavior if the group in the workplace has established its own set of norms. The behavior of members of labor unions is a good example.

Group Support of Leaders. Leadership is important for setting and enforcing group norms and it is important to recognize the difference between informal and formal leadership. Groups are most effective when they are led by those who are accepted and acknowledged as leaders by the group members themselves. Management imposed leaders will be less effective in setting and enforcing group norms.

Inclusion through Communication. Communication between the ranks and participation throughout the ranks in organizational decision making are important factors in any attempt to understand worker behavior and productivity. Workers who feel included, especially in decisions that affect them directly, are likely to participate in the life of the organization in a more positive way than those who feel left out. (pp. 34–38)

The major contributions of Mayo and his colleagues centered around the attitudes and reactions of workers under varying conditions. They discovered that there is a culture or perhaps several subcultures in the workplace that can be observed and analyzed. They also discovered that for productivity to be maximized, attention must be given to both the personal needs for a feeling of belonging in the workplace as well as to the company's needs for high levels of output. Managers trained using the findings and conclusions of human relations theorists were taught about how to generate cooperation and teamwork, and how to increase an employee's feelings of belonging in the workplace. They did not, however, lose sight of the fact that these tactics were used for a purpose: to encourage the worker to work at high levels of productivity, thereby adding value to the organization.

■ APPLICATION

To the Management of Human Services

A number of useful principles can be extracted from a study of human relations theory as applied to the management of human service organizations, including the following:

- Recognition of the importance of cultures and subcultures within organizations
- The influence of the group on individual performance
- Understanding the nature of meaningful rewards

Organizational Culture   The notion of a *culture* or *subculture* within the social service agency is an important one. For example, typically professionals in the human services see themselves as being committed to a value system that focuses on the needs of clients and view it as the organization's responsibility to develop the necessary resources to meet client needs. Informal leadership may support an attitude among staff that managers are merely "bean counters," or people who can't see beyond the resource limitations of the agency, and don't share the same level of compassion or concern for those in need as the staff. These attitudes and commitments can create a subculture that sets itself in opposition to management and can lead to low morale and low levels of productivity. Conversely, understanding the nature of organizational culture and keeping open lines of communication can strengthen and enhance performance.

The Influence of the Group   Recognition of the importance of social norms and group behavior in the workplace can help the manager of a human service agency to avoid the pitfalls inherent when a subculture is created. Employees tend to behave as members of groups, and productivity is set by social norms. Building on these understandings, a manager can design communication and decision-making systems, for example, that provide staff with the necessary budget and regulatory information to make informed decisions. Armed with this information, staff can then participate in the decision-making process in a meaningful way.

Understanding and Utilizing Meaningful Rewards   The issue of rewards is addressed in several theoretical frameworks. Early assumptions focused on monetary rewards; later efforts focused on such issues as wages, hours, and working conditions. Mayo was one of the first to recognize that noneconomic rewards significantly influenced behavior. Within the human relations framework, those noneconomic rewards tended to focus on such factors as group acceptance and approval. For others, as we will see, they had to do with the nature of the work itself.

Theory X and Theory Y

Douglas McGregor's essay, "The Human Side of Enterprise," provided an interesting perspective on organizational effectiveness and efficiency. In this essay, McGregor identified two different ways of looking at employees and motivation, and he referred to these perspectives as Theory X and Theory Y (McGregor, 1969). An interesting note is that neither framework is considered by scholars to be a theory, and most likely even McGregor did not intend to make such a claim. He was simply writing an essay and making some observations about the attitudes of management; yet the names *Theory X* and *Theory Y* have survived, and even been expanded upon, as management literature has been developed over the years.

McGregor referred to one perspective as the conventional view of management and called it *Theory X*. This view, he said, can be summed up in three propositions:

- *Management's role in the organization.* Management is responsible for organizing the elements of productive enterprise—money, materials, equipment, people—in the interest of economic ends.
- *Management's role with employees.* With respect to people, this is a process of directing their efforts, motivating them, controlling their actions, and modifying their behavior to fit the needs of the organization.

■ *Stimulating employee performance.* Without this active intervention by management, people would be passive—even resistant—to organizational needs. They must, therefore, be persuaded, rewarded, punished, controlled—their activities must be directed. This is management's task. We often sum it up by saying that management consists of getting things done through other people. (pp. 157–158)

McGregor (1969) went on to state that there are additional beliefs implied, as follows:

- The average man is by nature indolent—he works as little as possible.
- He lacks ambition, dislikes responsibility, prefers to be led.
- He is inherently self-centered, indifferent to organizational needs.
- He is by nature resistant to change.
- He is gullible, not very bright, the ready dupe of the charlatan and the demagogue. (p. 158)

McGregor criticized existing management theories and philosophies as being unaware of human factors. He characterized management approaches as falling within a range of possibilities from coercion and threat, close supervision and tight controls at one extreme and weakness, permissiveness, and a focus on worker satisfaction at the other. Neither extreme, he believed, was effective because neither took into consideration the realities of human behavior and factors associated with motivation.

A more realistic approach, he believed, could be characterized in four propositions, which McGregor (1969) referred to as *Theory Y:*

- *Management's role in the organization.* Management is responsible for organizing the elements of productive enterprise—money, materials, equipment, people—in the interest of economic ends.
- *Employee commitment.* People are *not* by nature passive or resistant to organizational needs. They have become so as a result of experience in organizations.
- *Employee motivation and capacity.* The motivation, the potential for development, the capacity for assuming responsibility, the readiness to direct behavior toward organizational goals are all present in people. Management does not put them there. It is a responsibility of management to make it possible for people to recognize and develop these human characteristics for themselves.
- *New management role.* The essential task of management is to arrange organizational conditions and methods of operation so that people can achieve their own goals *best* by directing *their own* efforts toward organizational objectives. (pp. 163–164)

In short, McGregor was attempting to establish the premise that management attitudes toward employees and the ways in which managers behaved toward employees on the job were important factors in the levels of productivity achieved within organizations. If, on the one hand, managers believed that workers wanted to be told what to do and did not want to have to make decisions, then managers would respond with close supervision and controlling behavior. If, on the other hand, managers believed that workers were talented and energetic people who were prepared to invest high levels of energy and commitment in their work, managers would respond by creating a work environment that allowed workers to perform at their highest levels. The differences in these two approaches, he believed, did not require vastly different resources; they could be accounted for simply in the way the manager approached the relationship with workers and the amount of creativity and responsibility workers were allowed to exercise. A Theory Y approach, he believed, had the potential to yield much higher levels of productivity.

■ **APPLICATION**

To the Management of Human Services

Though McGregor's ideas about management are clearly dated as seen in a twenty-first-century context, there are a few ideas that can be drawn from Theory X and Y concepts that may well be relevant to human services management today, including:

■ The nature of motivation in the workplace
■ The role of the manager in stimulating and capturing that motivation

Motivation in the Workplace   A great deal of research since McGregor's time has, in fact, supported the idea that many people come to the workplace highly motivated to work for the good of the organization and want the feeling of satisfaction for a job well done. This is especially true in human services where people select their careers not because of the financial or material gains they expect to make but because they hope to find fulfillment in helping others. When management creates an oppressive environment or fails to organize the elements of productive enterprise in a way that will allow for creative and effective use of energies, employee enthusiasm becomes stifled, and a potentially productive worker can be turned into a clock watcher. McGregor also recognized that not all employees approach work with a sense of excitement and interest. However, he believed that it was much more common to find that management has squelched employee enthusiasm than it was to find that employees did not measure up to management challenges.

Stimulating Employee Motivation   Management inherently holds a great share of the power in an organization, including the power to create, mold, shape, and influence organizational culture. Used creatively, this power can become a resource that brings a high level of energy into the workplace by establishing meaningful challenges and ensuring that the structure and the resources are appropriate to allow for meeting expectations. Instead of using the role in a positive way, some managers succumb to the temptation to exercise their power directly by giving orders rather than by finding ways to motivate. As we will see, there are many opportunities in a well-designed personnel system to track employee performance and to ensure that high performers are rewarded and low performers are not. But it takes a disciplined, skillful manager to design and use these systems in a way that maximizes productivity.

Although these ideas have been further developed over the years, we should credit McGregor with introducing the important principles that employees are most productive when they are challenged and allowed to use their abilities, and management functions best when it understands how to motivate and challenge employees.

Management by Objectives

In concluding his article on Theory X and Theory Y, McGregor commented that the principles underlying Theory Y were consistent with what Peter Drucker called *management by objectives* as contrasted to *management by control*. Management by objectives is a theoretical framework created by Drucker (1954), which proposes an approach to planning in which management makes clear its goals and expectations, employees understand and identify their own talents and interests, and together management and staff create a plan that meets organizational expectations and needs while also meeting worker goals and achieving employee job satisfaction. In this way, management promotes the Theory Y principles of motivating the workforce by structuring work in a manner that enhances worker productivity toward the achievement of organizational goals.

Drucker (1959) summarized some of the principles of management by objectives in his discussion of decision making. "Risk-taking entrepreneurial decisions," he said, "always embody the same eight elements:"

- *Objectives.* The part of a long-range plan that organizes future activities toward the achievement of hoped-for results.
- *Assumptions.* Beliefs held by people who make and carry out decisions about the realities of the organization and its environment.
- *Expectations.* The results considered likely to be achieved.
- *Alternative courses of action.* Since there is never one right decision, it is incumbent upon planners to evaluate other viable courses of action, including no action.
- *The decision.* For planning to move ahead, someone, ultimately, must select a course of action.
- *The decision structure.* Carrying out the plan will have implications for allocation of resources, requiring a series of decisions and commitments.
- *The impact stage.* In order for a plan to be implemented, effort must be focused in a particular area by selected employees. This, in turn, may shift certain burdens to other employees. This impact must be carefully structured and implemented.
- *The results.* Expected results are clearly specified. Progress toward achievement is monitored, and results are measured. (pp. 101–102)

These concepts have contributed to the development of program planning and strategic planning models in which goals, objectives, and activities are specified, written out in detail, implemented, monitored, and used as a basis for an evaluation of effectiveness as illustrated in Figure 2.1.

Probably the major contributions of management by objectives (MBO) have been the introduction of a focus on expectations and results and the introduction of precision and measurement into the planning process. Management theories developed prior to MBO tended to focus on the past and the present. Scientific management brought research and a scientific approach into the workplace, but its focus was on efficient functioning for the present. Bureaucratic theory introduced a rational structure and policies that supported consistency and objectivity in decision making, but its focus was also on efficient functioning in the present. Human relations efforts were devoted to maximizing productivity in the present. None of these theories questioned the direction of the organization. Organizational expectations were a given.

Management by objectives had an important impact on management thinking. If competitors are thinking about direction and future expectations, it becomes incumbent upon the organization that hopes to thrive to develop and translate into a plan its own visions for the future. In addition, the planning orientation has the potential to take some of the drudgery out of necessary, routine, daily work. It brings to mind the responses of the three stonemasons who, when asked what they were doing, the first replied, "I am cutting stones."

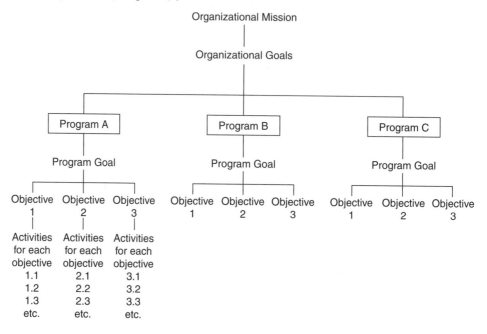

FIGURE 2.1

Hierarchy of Goals, Objectives, and Activities

The second answered that he was shaping and preparing some of the raw materials for a construction project. The third said, "I am building a cathedral." People who work within an organization that has a vision and a plan for an exciting and challenging future can more easily overlook the unpleasant and tedious parts of work because they focus on the organization's vision of the "cathedral."

Adapting to Change   Human service agencies have a special need for looking ahead, predicting future problems and needs, and translating them into goals and objectives. An agency that focuses on the present only and sees its function as serving existing clients and

■ APPLICATION

To the Management of Human Services

Many of the benefits of MBO realized within the business and corporate sector are also applicable to nonprofit human service agencies. However, they may be applicable in a special or unique way.

In general, it can be said that selected MBO principles, adopted as part of a theory for human service management, have the potential to make some of the following contributions:

- Remaining current with changing needs
- Strengthening of selected management practices
- Enhancement of employee motivation
- Bringing greater precision to performance appraisal

community needs often becomes insensitive to changing community economic and social conditions and falls into the rut of providing business as usual. Many social service programs were originally conceptualized and planned many years ago. They may or may not be designed and structured in a way that they are able to meet contemporary needs. Introducing a future orientation into program and organizational planning can help ensure that services are consistent with current and changing client needs, not just those of the past.

Strengthening Management Practices   Management practices in the absence of a sound and consistent application of management theories and techniques can become inconsistent and counterproductive. In the complex world in which organizations attempt to meet changing human needs, coupled with increasing demands for accountability, management by objectives provides a conceptual framework and a format for carefully laying out organizational, program, unit, and individual expectations that can allow an organization to run much more smoothly and efficiently than it would without a plan. The framework and format have the further advantage that the plan, if properly developed and produced, carries a sense of ownership among workers, supervisors, and managers that contributes momentum toward achievement of commonly agreed-upon goals and objectives.

Enhancing Employee Motivation   The employee motivation factor is an important one. Provision of direct services can be difficult, emotionally stressful, and can leave workers with a lonely feeling. If, on the other hand, management can successfully structure and implement a team concept in which employees see themselves as working together toward goals and objectives about which there is a shared commitment and around which there are advance agreements, stress and feelings of isolation can be significantly reduced. In a team environment, the synergy produced can become perpetually reinforcing to employee and team motivation.

More Precise Performance Appraisals   A final advantage of MBO for human services is that the system contributes to more precise performance appraisals. We will discuss the role of performance appraisal in more detail in Chapter 13, but perhaps we can summarize the issues by simply stating at this point that the ability to reward exceptional performance and to avoid rewarding poor performance is among the most powerful tools available to a manager in achieving excellence in organizational and program performance. MBO provides a very precise format in which goals, objectives, and activities are identified and responsibilities assigned to specific individuals. A system is then designed to monitor completion of tasks and activities and to evaluate quality of performance and results achieved. This, then, becomes the basis for performance appraisal, a documented chronology of completions and accomplishments rather than a vague reconstruction of past performance. Building incentives into a precisely planned and monitored MBO system can go a long way toward improving overall organizational and program performance.

Systems Theory

Daniel Katz and Robert Kahn (1966) were among the first authors to recognize the applicability of systems concepts to organizations. Systems theory was originally conceptualized and developed by a biologist, Ludwig von Bertalanffy (1950), who recognized that certain principles that applied to the interdependence of parts in living organisms also applied to other systems as well. Katz and Kahn took selected systems concepts a step further and applied them to organizations. They state, "System theory is basically concerned with problems of relationships, of structure, and of interdependence rather than with the constant attributes of objects." They go on to state, "Living systems, whether biological organisms or social organizations, are acutely dependent upon their external environment and so must be conceived of as open systems" (Katz & Kahn, 1966, pp. 17–18). They believed that the following characteristics seemed to define all open systems:

Importation of energy. No social structure is self-sufficient or self-contained. All need resources and raw materials from the environment to survive. This importation of energy is typically referred to as input. In human service organizations, input refers to clients to be served and the resources available to serve them.

The throughput. Open systems use the energy available to them to transform or reorganize raw materials received as input. Clients represent the raw materials that (hopefully) become transformed from individuals or families with problems to individuals or families in which problems have been alleviated or resolved.

The output. Open systems export some product into the environment. A client who has completed all the services prescribed represents this product in human service organizations.

Systems as cycles of events. The pattern of activities defined by input, throughput, and output has a cyclic character; that is, successful completion of the cycle provides sources of energy and resources for repetition of the cycle. This is more easily recognized in organizations in which products are produced and sold and the profits used to regenerate the cycle. Successful resolution of client problems, in the same way, contributes to the generation of resources that allows the cycle to continue.

Negative entropy. Entropy is a universal law of nature in which all forms of organization move toward disorganization and death. To survive, open systems must interrupt and arrest the process of entropy. This is accomplished by acquiring more energy or resources than needed and retaining as comfortable a margin of operation as possible.

Information input, negative feedback, and the coding process. In addition to receiving energy and resources from the environment, open systems also receive information. Some of this information comes in the form of negative feedback and allows the system to correct its deviations from course. This helps to keep the system in what is called a steady state. Consumer and client satisfaction and service effectiveness typically define the types of feedback received by human service organizations.

The steady state and dynamic homeostasis. Homeostasis is a self-regulating process whereby open systems maintain a continuous inflow of energy from the external environment and a continuous export of the products of the system in the interest of preservation of the basic character of the system. As organizational inputs increase or decrease, within certain limits, one can expect to see outputs increase or decrease, while the basic character of the system remains the same.

Differentiation. Open systems naturally move in the direction of differentiation and elaboration. In organizations this results in increased specialization of function. As more is learned about the process of converting raw materials into finished products, knowledge is applied to refinements of services provided.

Equifinality. Open systems can reach the same final state from differing initial conditions and by a variety of paths. It is not necessary to regulate all process in a search for uniformity in order to achieve desired results. Different methodologies can be equally effective while arriving at essentially the same destination. (pp. 19–26)

FIGURE 2.2

The Systems Model: A Framework for Understanding Organizational Functioning

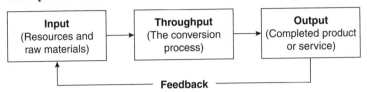

These are some of the concepts that help define the organization as a living system in which inputs, including raw materials, are imported from the environment, are converted in the throughput process, are exported back into the environment as output, and provide information in the form of feedback that helps correct the process and keep the organization stable. This process is depicted in Figure 2.2.

A second set of concepts that contributes to our understanding of organizations as systems comes from the work of James Thompson (1967). Thompson argued that a key element of understanding organizations as open systems was the uncertainty of the environment. Because of the natural tendency toward a steady state and survival, organizations seek predictability. However, the environment is never perfectly predictable, so the organization needs to structure itself to be able to respond to environmental changes in order to survive.

Thompson's work is primarily descriptive rather than prescriptive; that is, he explains how organizations behave rather than to suggest ways they should behave. In describing how organizations deal with an unpredictable and sometimes turbulent environment, he conceptualizes three different systems within each organization, which he calls (1) the technical core, (2) the managerial system, and (3) the institutional system. These are depicted in Figure 2.3.

FIGURE 2.3

Thompson's Framework for Understanding Organizational Functioning

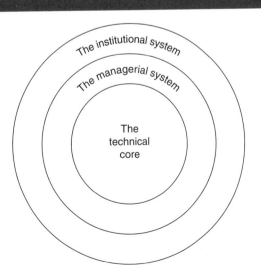

The technical core is made up of those parts of the organization that do the work for which the organization was created. These are the people that are often referred to in the literature as *line* workers. They serve on the "front lines" in terms of producing the product or providing the service that is central to the organization's reason for existence. In schools they are the teachers. In social service agencies they are the social workers. Line workers are often distinguished from staff workers. Staff refers to supportive personnel such as business managers, secretarial staff, and the like.

The second level in Thompson's scheme is the managerial system and includes those structures and processes that manage the work of the technical core. We often refer to the individuals who occupy these positions as first-line supervisors or program managers. They carry the largest share of the responsibility for managing the internal workings of organizations.

The third level is referred to as the institutional system. This level includes those structures and processes that deal with interactions between the organization and the environment. People who occupy positions in this system may be, for example, chief executive officers, executive directors, public relations directors, or lobbyists.

The significance of this particular conceptualization of an organization is that it emphasizes the importance of an organization structuring and designing roles and responsibilities to deal with the demands of the environment. Thompson argues that organizations behave in a way that is designed to protect the technical core. For example, when there are budget cuts, organizations attempt to maintain services at a continuing level and to avoid program cuts as long as they possibly can, directing their cuts to supportive services first. He goes on to describe how organizations adapt to environmental demands in a three-part sequence of strategies, which he describes as (1) actions to protect the technical core, (2) actions to acquire power over the task environment, and (3) actions to absorb important elements of the environment by changing or expanding organizational domains.

In short, if efforts to absorb environmentally imposed changes internally without affecting services are not enough to protect the basic programs and services, the organization will attempt to acquire power over the environment. This is done through attempts, such as lobbying, to coopt the decision makers and funding sources. If these efforts are not effective, organizations will next attempt to unite with competitors or enlarge their boundaries in the interest of positioning themselves to become indispensable to those who are in need of their products or services.

■ APPLICATION

To the Management of Human Services

Two major constructs taken from systems theory contribute to the understanding of human service organizations and to predicting how they will behave under conditions of environmental stress, which frequently means reductions in funding:

- The input-throughput-output construct
- The ways in which human service organizations deal with an uncertain environment

good

Understanding Organizational Inputs, Throughputs, and Outputs   Human service organizations are continuously under pressure to be accountable for the resources expended. And it should be recognized that human service agencies are not all small operations involving a few staff and a few hundred thousand dollars a year in the budget. Some social service agencies have become conglomerates with budgets of over $100 million. Furthermore, programs initiated at the federal level and funneled through state administration to local service delivery agencies often involve multibillion-dollar nationwide efforts. It is certainly legitimate that questions are asked about what happened to the money and what results were achieved.

The systems model contributes a great deal to our understanding of organizational efficiency and effectiveness. Using systems concepts—inputs, throughput, outputs, and outcomes—programs and services can be defined, implemented, tracked, monitored, and evaluated. Without these analytical tools, organizations and systems would have great difficulty meeting accountability expectations. The systems model has been applied successfully to program planning in the human services (Kettner, Moroney, & Martin, 1999) and to performance measurement (Martin & Kettner, 1996). The importance of understanding the interrelationships among various system components both in programs and in overall agency functioning cannot be overstated. The ability to collect and use data and information effectively to improve the efficiency, effectiveness, and quality of services is greatly enhanced by the systems model.

Developing and Maintaining Relations with Critical Elements of an Organization's Environment   The second major contribution of systems theory to human services management has to do with the importance of organizational-environment relationships. Organizations need an active, ongoing relationship with a number of elements in their environment in order to ensure their relevance and survival. Thompson (1967) notes that, as originally defined by Dill (1958), an organization's task environment consists of four key components: (1) customers (both distributors and users); (2) suppliers of materials, labor, capital, equipment, and work space; (3) competitors for both markets and resources; and (4) regulatory groups, including governmental agencies, unions, and interorganizational associations (pp. 27–28).

For a human service organization, the message is, first, that in order to maintain its steady state, an organization must tend to issues affecting clients and consumers, including accurate assessment of changing needs, and service effectiveness. Second, there must be working relationships with those who provide the financial resources, the personnel, the space, and other resources in order to ensure that future needs are met. Third, there must be an awareness of activities and efforts undertaken by competitors. This usually means other agencies that serve the same population and provide the same service. Competition is usually for both clients and grants or contracts. Fourth, there must be a good working relationship with accrediting bodies, government regulating bodies, and other such organizations that establish the parameters within which human service agencies function. The foregoing represent four components of an organization's environment that are critical to its success and sometimes even to its survival.

Well-run agencies have a strategy for dealing with these external entities. An agency executive once observed that she probably knew more about what was going to happen to her agency in three to five years than she did about what was going on today. If the agency executive understands her responsibility as a part of the institutional system (the system that deals with the external environment), that is exactly where the executive should be placing her priorities. This external focus gives recognition to the agency's dependence on positive interactions with these external entities. Competent and reliable people must continue to fulfill the functions of the managerial system (the system that manages internal operations), so that the executive is freed to deal with these most important external components.

Although the concepts and constructs drawn from systems theory may not be extensive, their value as conceptual tools used to develop a sound theoretical framework for human services management is significant.

Contingency Theory

During a period in the 1950s when Theory Y assumptions about worker motivation were popular and management by objectives was becoming the theory of choice as the underpinning framework for managing many organizations, a number of researchers were exploring the limits of these approaches to management. Beginning in the 1960s and continuing through the 1970s, research findings were published on a number of projects that challenged the premise that loose structures and maximum flexibility for employees led to the highest levels of productivity.

Prominent among these were the findings of Burns and Stalker (1961), who examined at least twenty firms in the United Kingdom. The companies studied were drawn from a variety of industries; the focus was on what types of management methods and procedures produced the highest levels of productivity. What they found was that demands from organizational environments varied, and these, in turn, influenced the predictability of tasks and functions to be performed in the process of producing products and/or services. For example, consumer demand for household appliances might require one type of structure and process (assembly line), whereas law enforcement may require another type (community policing teams). The determining factor is the nature of each organization's demands from the environment and the types of tasks and functions necessary to meet those demands.

These findings resulted in the development of a typology of organizations, which Burns and Stalker referred to as (1) mechanistic organizations (at one end of the continuum) and (2) organic organizations (at the other). A mechanistic organization was defined as one that tended to be fixed and somewhat rigid, with predictable tasks and a relatively stable environment. Despite McGregor's assertion that this Theory X approach was outdated and counterproductive, certain types of organizations were found to function better when employees were told what to do and supervised in the process of carrying out their tasks and responsibilities.

An organic organization was defined as one that is more loosely structured, that provides consultation rather than supervision, and that establishes outcome expectations for workers rather than tasks. These organizations function best in an unstable environment in which inputs are unpredictable and the organization is expected to respond to changing environmental conditions.

Although some human service organizations may find themselves in a steady or predictable environment, it is much more likely that they will need to learn to survive in an unsteady or turbulent environment, given the nature of the social and economic problems agencies are expected to address. If this is the case, then an organic-type structure will lead

---

TABLE 2.1
Factors Descriptive of Mechanistic and Organic Organizations

	Characteristics of Mechanistic Organizations	Characteristics of Organic Organizations
Focus of work	Jobs tend to be highly specialized; separated into discrete tasks	Jobs are less well defined; focus is on results
Locus of responsibility	Decisions are made high in the organization	Delegation and decentralization
Supervision	Supervisor assigns and directs work; supervisor integrates work performed	Peers and superiors act as consultants to one another; teams integrate their work
Structure	Hierarchy	Fluid; project teams; adapt to current needs
Communication	Tends to be top-down; information is seen as power	Information is shared; everyone who needs it should have it
Basis of prestige	Seniority; experience; knowledge of the organization; best interests of the organization	Knowledge of theory, concepts, principles; commitment to values and ethics and to vision and mission

---

to higher levels of productivity and better results. Table 2.1 summarizes the elements of an organization and how they would be structured or designed in a mechanistic organization versus an organic organization.

There were several additional studies designed to explore the relationship among organizational structure, efficiency, and effectiveness. One is particularly worth mentioning. In 1970, two researchers published an article based on some of the findings of Burns and Stalker and others (Morse & Lorsch, 1970). They selected two different types of organizations, one with a predictable manufacturing task and one with an unpredictable research and development task. For each type, they selected one that had been evaluated as performing at a highly effective level and one low performer. The design is depicted in Table 2.2.

TABLE 2.2
Summary of Research Findings by Morse and Lorsch in Testing Hypotheses of Contingency Theory

	Higher-Performing Organization	Lower-Performing Organization
Manufacturing	Mechanistic	Organic
Research and development	Organic	Mechanistic

In exploring internal structure, climate, and tasks, they discovered that the high-performing manufacturing plant was structured along the lines of a mechanistic organization, whereas the high-performing research and development laboratory followed the organic model. Conversely, the low-performing manufacturing plant tended more toward organic, loosely defined structure whereas the low-performing research lab leaned toward a rigid, mechanistic model. Clearly there was a relationship here among task, structure, climate, and overall productivity and effectiveness. Interestingly, Morse and Lorsch (1970) entitled their article "Beyond Theory Y," implying that McGregor's notion that Theory Y was the one best way for all didn't go far enough in explaining optimal organizational structure and job design.

These findings led to a new set of assumptions, which they called contingency theory. Morse and Lorsch (1970) included the following:

- Human beings bring varying patterns of needs and motives into the work organization but one central need is to achieve a sense of competence.
- The sense of competence motive, while it exists in all human beings, may be fulfilled in different ways by different people depending on how this need interacts with the strengths of the individual's other needs—such as those for power, independence, structure, achievement, and affiliation.
- Competence motivation is most likely to be fulfilled when there is a fit between task and organization.
- Sense of competence continues to motivate even when a competence goal is achieved; once one goal is reached, a new, higher one is set. (p. 67)

Contingency theory has essentially put to rest the notion that there is one best way to structure and design an organization. In response to the question "What is the best structure and design for an organization?" the correct answer is "It depends." The challenge among contemporary management researchers and consultants is to answer the question, "On what does it depend?" The answer tends to be that it depends on the mission, purpose, and function of the organization and the ways in which existing technologies are capable of producing products and services to meet organizational and environmental expectations.

Providing Structure and Design Options   One contribution of contingency theory to human services management is the recognition that there is not only one way to structure and design an organization. It may be that within certain types of agencies there are depart-

■ APPLICATION

To the Management of Human Services

Contingency theory makes several contributions that are potentially useful in developing an eclectic theory for social service management, including the following:

- Providing alternative structure and design options
- Focusing on results rather than process as the primary consideration
- Recognizing the importance of a feeling of competence to workers

ments or units that function better and more effectively with a mechanistic design, whereas others achieve maximum productivity following the organic model. For example, it is possible that such functions as the processing of eligibility or certain screening and assessment functions are better performed following specified tasks. Or within a residential treatment center, clinical staff may need to operate flexibly as a team, whereas clerical or maintenance staff may function better when tasks are defined and specific responsibilities assigned.

A careful examination of the conditions under which mechanistic or organic designs are preferable raises a number of questions. Can some programs and services operate efficiently following a mechanistic design? Or, given the turbulent environment within which many social service agencies and programs operate, are they always better served by opting for an organic model? Social service agencies and programs typically address such problems as violence, abuse of drugs and alcohol, or child abuse, for example. For most social service agencies, inputs, including client problems, are unpredictable. Throughputs can be translated into routine tasks only in a very general sense. The key to effectiveness, at least for some types of organizations, seems to be the kind of flexibility described as fitting within the organic model.

Improving Effectiveness through Result-Oriented Team Interaction   It is the organic model within contingency theory that provides the legitimization for specifying results expected rather than tasks to be performed; for establishing a climate of team cooperation toward the achievement of shared goals; for defining supervision in terms of consultation rather than giving orders; for shared accountability; and for valuing professional knowledge and skill over knowledge of internal organizational functioning. Mechanistic systems essentially manage the process; organic systems manage the results.

This is not to say that an organic structure eliminates the need for following certain expectations for accountability or bureaucratic procedures. Those requirements remain in effect in all types and sizes of agencies. The important issue is that they need not drive either structure or decision making. They can exist comfortably within an organic organization, department, or unit.

The Importance of a Sense of Competence   The recognition of the importance of a sense of competence is also of value in human service organizations. If undertrained and unprepared workers are presented with challenges beyond their capacity, they are unlikely to enjoy their work or to perform at high levels of productivity because they will not feel a sense of competence. Conversely, if highly educated and well-prepared professionals are asked to do only routine eligibility work, they, too, are likely to feel negatively toward the job, perform at low levels, and to lack a sense of competence. Recognizing the importance of a sense of competence, the skilled manager will match employees to work responsibilities that neither exceed nor fail to rise to the level of their abilities to do the job.

Contemporary Theories

Since the 1980s, management literature has tended to focus on a number of themes, each of which promises either to help in the understanding of organizational behavior or, if translated into practice, to increase productivity, efficiency, effectiveness, or quality. For the sake of this discussion, these themes are divided into three categories: (1) decision making and the influence of organizational culture, (2) quality, and (3) diversity. Each of these themes is supported by a number of authors and perspectives.

Decision Making and the Influence of Organizational Culture

Understanding Organizational Culture   Edgar Schein (1985) introduced the concept of organizational culture, which he defines as:

> a pattern of basic assumptions—invented, discovered, or developed by a given group as it learns to cope with its problems of external adaptation and internal integration—that has worked well enough to be considered valid and therefore, to be taught to new members as the correct way to perceive, think, and feel in relation to the problems. (p. 9)

Organizations, Schein argues, have their own highly individualized ways of perceiving and understanding the meaning of experiences and events that occur in the course of daily as well as cumulative organizational life. Perceptions and understandings come through a long shared history of experiences; it is typically the longtime employees that frame the organization's culture and influence new members to perceive, think, and feel in the same way. New members often find it difficult to introduce change because longtime employees must first be convinced that the change is workable within the existing culture. Understanding an organization requires that one understand what assumptions leaders bring to the decision-making process.

In some ways it might be argued that Mayo's (1945) research led to some discoveries about the concept of organizational culture. Mayo demonstrated the influence of the group on individual performance. However, Mayo and his colleagues focused exclusively on the ways in which people relate to each other in relation to their work. Schein has developed a more elaborate framework for understanding the full range of employee behaviors. He emphasizes the importance of understanding attitudes and perspectives toward management and toward the overall organization, and he explains how new employees are coopted into the existing culture. Culture can have a profound effect on productivity and other factors, and it is vital that managers understand its impact on their organization.

Understanding the Culture of Excellent Organizations   As discussed in Chapter 1, Peters and Waterman (1982), management consultants for McKinsey and Company, published their findings from a study of a number of organizations that met their definition of excellence. From their extensive interviews and examination of documents, they distilled their eight basic principles that contribute to a culture of excellence within organizations. As discussed in Chapter 1, these principles include (1) a bias for action, (2) staying close to the customer, (3) autonomy and entrepreneurship, (4) productivity through people, (5) hands-on, value driven, (6) stick to the knitting, (7) simple form, lean staff, and (8) simultaneously loose/tight properties.

When examined collectively, these eight principles can be summarized as issues relating to:

- *Structure*—simple form, lean staff; simultaneously loose-tight properties
- *Job Design*—autonomy and entrepreneurship; productivity through people
- *Philosophy and Values*—a bias for action; staying close to the customer; hands on, value driven; stick to the knitting

---

■ APPLICATION

To the Management of Human Services

The common theme of the foregoing perspectives on decision making and the influence of organizational culture is that they introduce the importance of understanding internal dynamics to
accurately assess organizational functioning and productivity. The major theoretical formulations
tend to assume a culture of rationality, in which the rules are clear and collective commitment is
powerful enough to control behavior.

The foregoing contemporary theories help in our understanding of management principles by
contributing the following ideas:

- Influencing employee behavior requires an understanding of culture and informal leadership.
- Shared vision is critical to organizational harmony and productivity.
- Achieving a shared vision requires openness to a wide range of perspectives represented in a
  diverse organization.

In many ways, the system described by Peters and Waterman captures a sort of organizational culture, in which organizational and program designs and structures work in a
way that maximizes productivity, and in which, in return, employees are committed to a
shared vision and demonstrate their commitment through high levels of productivity. Such
an organization might be said to be centered around an organic structure and design, while
practicing a Theory Y culture, in which management respects employees and sees its role
as removing barriers to productivity.

Understanding Organizational Cultures and Subcultures   Schein (1985) helps
us to recognize that individuals within organizations, especially longtime employees, contribute to a certain perspective that influences the way that activities, events, and decisions
are perceived. Within human service agencies there is likely to be, among staff, a strong
commitment to a particular set of values and perspectives focused on meeting client needs.
These beliefs and the solidarity they generate among staff can influence staff perceptions
of management and management decisions. Because it is overwhelmingly acknowledged
in the management literature that employee support and commitment are necessary ingre-
dients to productivity, it becomes incumbent upon management to understand the culture,
its leaders, its values, and how communication between staff and management can best be
facilitated in the interest of maximizing productivity.

Recognizing the Importance of Shared Vision   Peters and Waterman are a bit
more prescriptive, but their approach can also be described as focusing on organizational
culture. A central theme of their work is the concept of shared vision—a situation in
which employees understand and are committed to the organization's mission and vision.
If the shared vision and commitment are present, then the other principles leading to
excellence can be put into practice. Without taking into consideration where employees—
both long and short term—stand on mission and vision, it will be difficult to maximize
productivity. It is often the case that human service organizations tend to take for granted
their employees' commitments, without exploring the extent to which they are commonly
shared among staff.

All of these perspectives argue for a systematic approach to soliciting employee input into the decision-making process. Some form of individual or group participation, polling, surveying, or other approach to incorporating employee ideas into the running of the organization is essential in well-run human service organizations.

Incorporating Diverse Perspectives into the Organizational Culture   Green (1999) points out the importance of openness and receptivity to the views and perspectives of others in his discussion of a study conducted in a nursing home:

> In an ethnographic study of labor in a nursing home, Foner (1994) wanted to know if the frustrations of care giving, for both givers and receivers, are an inevitable feature of institutions. She found that what she called the "hidden injuries of bureaucracy" came from a number of sources including legal mandates, regulatory demands and procedures, limitations of funding, inadequate training, internal hierarchies, office politics, policies, and reward structures. Race and gender occasionally figured into these dimensions. When conflicts occurred, among staff or between staff and patients, services to the residents deteriorated and relations between employees soured. The "work culture" of the institution was the arena where conflicts often played out, sometimes in subtle ways. By looking at that culture, Foner determined, among other things, that one of the constant sources of conflict was the need of the institution to be efficient and accountable (expressed through managers and supervisors) and the desire of many of the direct service staff to give quality care with only secondary interest in time or financial constraints. Different agendas, formal and informal, were operating in different parts of the organization, and all were influenced by the personalities of the participants and the history of their relationships in the home. (p. 109)

Perspectives of employees emerge around issues related to culture, gender, position in the organization, length of service in the organization, and many other factors. Rodwell (1995) argues that evaluation of organizational performance must be based on several assumptions, including the assumption that "All services and sites have multiple realities. They are different events and places for different people (the 'stakeholders'), and each of their perspectives has to be made explicit in the evaluation" (p. 192). Understanding the full range of perspectives represented in an organization does not come easily or quickly. It takes time, effort, and openness. The evidence suggests that the investment is worth the time, and it is a prerequisite for developing a shared vision.

The Issue of Quality

Classical theories tend to focus primarily on productivity; the concept of quality does not receive as much attention. However, as organizations, including human service agencies, have responded over the years to demands for increased productivity, it was recognized that productivity is often increased at the expense of quality. Increasing productivity in a counseling agency, for example, can be a relatively simple matter of putting individuals into groups for group therapy, thereby increasing the number of people treated by one worker in one hour from one to as many as six or eight. But is it sound in terms of the quality of treatment received? Another example is day care. Productivity in a day care center can easily be increased by doubling the number of children cared for without increasing staff. But will each child receive the quality of care needed for healthy development? It was these types of questions and issues that prompted a focus on quality as an important concern.

Theory Z   In his book entitled *Theory Z: How American Business Can Meet the Japanese Challenge,* William Ouchi (1981) describes the following scene:

> A team of engineers and managers from the Buick Division of General Motors Corporation recently visited their dealer in Tokyo, who imports Buick automobiles and sells them to the Japanese. The operation appeared to be a massive repair facility, so they asked how he had built up such a large service business. He explained with some embarrassment that this was not a repair facility at all but rather a re-assembly operation where newly delivered cars were disassembled and rebuilt to Japanese standards. While many Japanese admire the American automobile, he noted, they would never accept the low quality with which they are put together. (pp. 3–4)

For many years U.S. industrial and technological superiority was taken for granted, and it was only when the automobile and electronics industries were challenged by Japanese companies beginning in the 1970s that U.S. corporations began to take notice of Japanese management practices.

In many ways, Japanese-style management could be categorized under the previous heading of organizational culture. Much of what happens in Japanese corporations that makes them effective has to do with the dynamics of the relationships between management and staff and among the employees themselves. But the central theme and shared vision are focused on the quality of the product(s) produced.

Ouchi (1981) characterizes the contrasts between Japanese and U.S. organizations as follows:

Japanese Organizations	*American Organizations*
Lifetime Employment	Short-Term Employment
Slow Evaluation and Promotion	Rapid Evaluation and Promotion
Nonspecialized Career Paths	Specialized Career Paths
Implicit Control Mechanisms	Explicit Control Mechanisms
Collective Decision Making	Individual Decision Making
Collective Responsibility	Individual Responsibility
Wholistic Concern	Segmented Concern (p. 58)

The characteristics of Japanese organizations support the principle that employees and employee opinions are vital to organizational success. The organization shows loyalty to the employee, and the employee reciprocates. Decisions are made by consensus; a process ensures that each employee will have input, and employees ultimately support decisions with which they may disagree because they respect the process. Collectively they hold themselves accountable, and their focus is on their common concerns and commitments, not their individual interests and agendas.

These values and commitments clearly create a culture, and Ouchi (1981) describes "A 'Z' Culture" (pp. 195–218). However, none of these principles and practices would have attracted worldwide attention had it not been for Japan's ability to capture a significant portion of market share in selected industries. The factor that enabled them to make these inroads into the global market was their commitment to quality. Martin (1993) notes that the idea of quality management caught on and flourished in Japan and is considered to be part of the explanation for Japan's economic prowess today.

Unlike the U.S. philosophy with its commitments to competition in terms of productivity and profit, Japanese philosophy focused on long-term loyalty between producer and consumer. Japanese employees recognize that producing products of high quality is critical to the long-term survival of the organization. Employees also recognize that they must focus on identifying problems and proposing solutions if they are to remain competitive. These contributions are seen as shared responsibilities, not solely the responsibilities of management. The results have been remarkable, and much of Japan's concern for quality has been incorporated into management philosophies around the world.

Total Quality Management (TQM)   A number of scholars have contributed to the concepts and principles that form the basis of TQM, the most prominent of these being W. Edwards Deming (1982). His focus on quality dates back to the 1920s, when he worked at Western Electric's Hawthorne plant in Chicago, the same plant where Mayo conducted his studies that led to the formulation of human relations theory. For many years, Deming's ideas were largely ignored in the United States, but in post–World War II Japan they were welcomed. Much of the turnaround in the Japanese economy was credited to the work of Deming. *Kaizen,* the Japanese term for quality management, is based to a great extent on Deming's ideas (Imai, 1986).

According to Martin (1993), key elements of TQM as a philosophy of management include:

- *Quality*—is a primary organizational goal.
- *Customers*—determine what quality is.
- *Customer Satisfaction*—drives the organization.
- *Variation*—in processes must be understood and reduced.
- *Change*—is continuous and is accomplished by teams and teamwork.
- *Top Management Commitment*—to promoting a culture of quality, employee empowerment, and a long-term perspective. (p. 24)

In many ways, this philosophy is reflective of Japanese-style management as described in Theory Z. TQM, however, is designed to be adaptable to U.S. organizations that are willing to make the internal changes necessary to achieve total quality in their processes and products or services.

One concern central to any discussion of TQM is what is meant by the term *quality.* It is common to find among practitioners the expectation that quality is a one-dimensional concept, and that fine quality, like good art or music, is defined as being in the eye (or the ear) of the beholder. The research of Zeithaml, Parasuraman, and Berry (1990) helps to broaden the understanding of the meaning of quality. The research was based on focus group interviews with nearly two thousand customers and was designed to determine how customers perceived quality. Zeithaml, Parasuraman, and Berry (1990) were able to reduce their findings down to five dimensions of quality, as follows:

Reliability:	Consistency and predictability in the product or service.
Responsiveness:	Timeliness in provision of the product or service.
Assurance:	Sense of competence and support conveyed by staff.

Empathy: Feelings that customer needs are understood by staff and that they receive individualized attention from staff.

Tangibles: Aesthetics or appearance of the buildings and equipment used in the production of products or the provision of service. (p. 27)

Martin (1993) has summarized the research on quality and lists fourteen different dimensions that can be used when applying the term to human service programs, including (1) Accessibility, (2) Assurance, (3) Communication, (4) Competence, (5) Conformity, (6) Courtesy, (7) Deficiency, (8) Durability, (9) Humaneness, (10) Performance, (11) Reliability, (12) Responsiveness, (13) Security, and (14) Tangibles (p. 28). From these and other works on TQM, it is clear that the concept is multidimensional and that it can be understood only by learning what it means to customers or clients.

Defining Quality in Practice   Provision of social or mental health services to people in need involves what is sometimes referred to as a "soft technology." As a result, much of what transpires between helper and person-in-need is determined on a case-by-case basis. Because of the unique needs of individuals and families, and because of the idiosyncratic ways in which people deal with their problems, it is difficult to establish uniform approaches to what appear, on the surface, to be similar problems. However, inroads are being made into developing more precise technologies by testing various models that have demonstrated effectiveness with certain types of problems. As this type of research increases, there will be more tangible ways to deal with the issue of quality in practice.

Developing Systems for Continuous Quality Improvement   If organizations are to define and monitor service quality, human service professionals must begin to survey consumers and clients on a regular basis to determine how they define quality: what factors are important to them in the course of receiving services? Accrediting organizations have introduced the concept of continuous quality improvement. What this means is that organizations providing health and human services, in order to be accredited, must demonstrate that they have in place a system to collect data on quality of services provided. Then, having determined a level of service quality in measurable terms, the organization must demonstrate that it has in place mechanisms to make use of its findings by improving the quality of services provided in the next and subsequent years. Quality can no longer be treated as a vague concept to which agencies give tacit support.

■ APPLICATION

To the Management of Human Services

Quality is an issue of utmost importance in the management and delivery of social services. The foregoing theories highlight the following principles:

- Quality is difficult to define and establish in the absence of a uniform technology.
- Systems for continuous quality improvement can be designed and implemented.

Concerns about service quality have received increasing attention in the provision of health and human services. The issue of quality is emerging as a prominent focus among managers and clinicians alike, along with efficiency, effectiveness, and productivity.

The Issue of Diversity

Putting together a workforce that is representative of a community in terms of culture, ethnicity, and gender is yet another important challenge to the human services administrator or manager. Green (1995) brings into focus an important perspective:

> Cultural differences reflect not only a history but also fundamental variations in what people hold to be worthwhile. As long as variations persist, they will invite comparison and questioning of the practices and preferences of others. It may be disconcerting to have to acknowledge that members of historically stigmatized racial and ethnic groups often do things their way, not just because they have been excluded from mainstream institutions by prejudice and discrimination, but because they find the values and institutions of the larger society inferior to their own. (p. 4)

The primary reason for existence of social service organizations is to address individual, family, neighborhood, community, and social problems and needs. Given this purpose, it is critical that the voices that help shape organizational and programmatic approaches to problem solving be representative of diverse community perspectives. Effectiveness in meeting community and client needs depends on bringing together a diverse staff and developing the kind of openness to alternative perspectives that fosters growth among all staff and enhances the quality and relevance of services provided.

Beyond Race and Gender   In his book, *Beyond Race and Gender,* Thomas (1991) states that affirmative action grew out of a number of premises:

1. The mainstream in U.S. business is made up of white males.
2. Women and minorities are excluded from this mainstream because of widespread racial, ethnic, and sexual prejudices.
3. Such exclusion is unnecessary, given the strength of the U.S. economic edifice.
4. Furthermore, it is contrary to both good public policy and common decency.
5. Therefore, legal and social coercion is necessary to bring about change.

These premises, he argues, do not hold up in the long run and need to be reexamined in the light of current realities. Thomas conceptualizes three levels of organizational diversity, which he entitles (1) affirmative action, (2) valuing differences, and (3) managing diversity.

Thomas argues that affirmative action should be understood merely as a first level of change. Although affirmative action made an important contribution toward bringing ethnic minorities and women into entry-level positions, it is time, he says, to recognize these policies as a minimalist approach and move toward more progressive and productive management techniques.

Thomas suggests that there are higher levels to which organizations can move when they are ready to progress beyond the first level of affirmative action. The second level he calls valuing differences. Organizations using this approach focus on individual and interpersonal growth in terms of mutual understandings of cultural and gender issues. Such techniques as staff development, training, and group discussion foster a climate of mutual respect and learning to appreciate and value differences, rather than equating difference to inferiority.

The third and highest level Thomas refers to as managing diversity. Organizations adopting this approach review their overall culture and their core values and ask themselves questions about whether they are achieving maximum productivity. Are they allowing the diversity represented among employees to work to its highest advantage in terms of achieving organizational goals? Where it is not, all dimensions of the organization need to be reevaluated to ensure that employees are being used to the full extent of their talents and abilities, including the diverse perspectives that bring richness to the organization. The three approaches can be summarized as follows:

Affirmative Action	*Valuing Differences*	*Managing Diversity*
Focus is on bringing people in protected classes into the workforce	Focus is on achieving greater mutual understanding of and respect for ethnic and gender perspectives other than one's own	Focus is on full utilization of talents and abilities that all employees bring to the workplace
Achieved through attention to recruitment and retention practices	Achieved through staff development, workshops, and improved internal communication across ethnic and gender lines	Achieved through management's understanding of the positive role that ethnic, gender, and other diverse perspectives can play in enhancing organizational productivity

Gender Issues in Human Services Management   In her examination of the role of gender in practice knowledge, Figueira-McDonough (1998) discusses the systematic exclusion of women from participation in the construction of knowledge. She makes the following observation:

> The history of women's everyday life demonstrates how it has been experienced differently from men's and how it may have produced different types of knowledge and understanding. It is this dissociation between women's experience and traditional knowledge that is conducive to interpretative distortions of women's reality. Since men and women have different experiences and men are predominantly the insiders in knowledge construction, men tend to study women as outsiders. The standard assumptions they use will shape the questions they ask, and this, in turn, will condition the data they collect. (p. 6)

The significance of this observation for organizations is that women's conceptual contributions to the management of organizations have, in many ways, been absent from consideration in developing the major theoretical themes in the field of management. To remedy this deficit, Netting and Rodwell (1998) explore gender concerns as they apply to the knowledge base for management and administration. The authors apply the work of Weick (1995), who proposes that people within organizations attempt to make sense of their experiences by applying seven "sensemaking" properties (explanations are paraphrased):

Identity. Individuals find an identity as they rethink their understandings based on their changing experiences. Making sense of an organization is tied to an identity, which changes over time.

Retrospection. Understanding of organizations is based on experiences and reflection. Organizational activities to be meaningful must be tied to one's reality.

Enactment. Organizations are understood through participation in meaningful activities.

Social. Social interaction influences how a person perceives and understands an organization.

Ongoing. Understanding an organization is an ongoing process. Experiences and interests change, so sensemaking is never really complete.

Extracted cues. People form perceptions about an organization from information that is shared with them. Conclusions drawn from cues depend on the person's experiences and the context within which the cue was received.

Plausibility. Truth in understanding organizations is not an absolute. Rather, it is the piecing together of extracted cues. Plausibility, therefore, takes precedence over accuracy.

Netting and Rodwell (1998) use these seven properties to create a lens through which organizations can be understood in a way that incorporates and values gender. This exploration leads to questions about (1) the fit of theory to women's identity, (2) shaping perspectives from the context of women's history, (3) what constitutes meaningful participation for women, and (4) what information influences the way women understand the organization and its activities.

Women form the numerical majority of both staff and clients in human service organizations. It is critical that the full range of gender perspectives be fully incorporated and integrated into management philosophy, theories, and practices.

■ APPLICATION

To the Management of Human Services

Incorporation of ethnic and gender perspectives is fundamental to the relevance of human service organizations. In organizations in which the majority of clients are either women or persons from a nondominant cultural or ethnic group, or both, incorporating ethnic and gender considerations into the management of programs and services is critical.

The major issues confronting human service management include the following:

- Standards of cultural competence should be established for human service agencies.
- Management theories should be evaluated and applied in the light of contemporary concerns about their fit to gender issues.

Cultural Competence   Green (1995) makes an extremely powerful point about the provision of social services. Racial and ethnic groups, he says, often do things their way not just because they have been excluded but also because they prefer their own ways and find them, in many instances, superior to the values and institutions of the larger society. How can an agency be effective in serving clients from varying ethnic groups without its staff members understanding the traditions, values, beliefs, and practices of cultures that are different from their own?

Cross, Bazron, Dennis, and Isaacs (1989) view cultural competence as falling on a continuum and define the culturally competent social service agency by applying the following definitions:

Cultural Destructiveness. This negative end of the continuum is represented by attitudes, policies, and practices that are destructive to cultures and, consequently, to individuals within cultures.

Cultural Incapacity. This occurs when the system or agency does not intentionally seek cultural destructiveness through policies or practices but lacks the capacity to help minority clients or communities.

Cultural Blindness. This is the belief that color or cultures make no difference, that all people are the same, and that traditional helping approaches are universally applicable.

Cultural Precompetence. This is an agency's recognition that it has weaknesses in terms of its cultural relevance in service to its clients, and the agency makes attempts to strengthen and improve its cultural competence.

Cultural Competence. Agencies are characterized by respect for cultural differences and continuous expansion of cultural knowledge and resources.

Cultural Proficiency. Agencies hold culture in high esteem. Research and therapeutic approaches are based on understandings of culture, and findings are disseminated through professional channels.

Thomas (1991) points out that cultural competence is equally important in the management of organizations. When people of color are employed as part of a strategy to achieve organizational diversity but are excluded from important decision-making roles, opportunities are lost and programs lose their relevance over time. The same basic arguments can be made in relation to gender considerations. Historically, women have been excluded from contributing a perspective that has potential value in the management of organizations. As human service organizations move into a new era of diversity, there must be assurances that programs and services are designed and managed by those who have clearly established their credentials as having cultural and gender competence. The kind of dialogue that can emerge from negotiations around such issues as program design, job design, and measurements of quality and effectiveness can enrich an agency and help to retain its relevance and vitality.

Incorporating Gender Issues into Management Practices   Netting and Rodwell (1998) argue that theories and practice models need to be reexamined from a perspective of relevance to gender. They propose a "reconstruction of the assumptions that have been part of organizational theory so that gender sensitivity can occur" (p. 302). Their reformulation proposes five new assumptions, as follows:

> *Interdependence.* Organizations and environments are interdependent, are not always distinctive, and are mutually influential. Organizations should avoid overly rigid distinctions between their own elements and those of their environment.

> *Constant Change.* Organizations are constantly changing within a changing global community. Decisions and actions to effect change occur in multiple ways. Uncertainty presents possibilities and challenges. Attempts to control uncertainty are not the only logical responses. Change processes should be engaged in a positive way.

> *Politics and Decision Making.* Every decision made and every action taken is political and represents a choice among values. Decision making cannot always be linear and technically clear. Sometimes it is necessarily tentative and incremental and requires frequent reformulation.

> *Use of Language.* Language is political and symbolically communicates power. Selection of terms used in management should be done with sensitivity to gender differences.

> *Incorporation of Multiple Rationalities and Realities.* Organization cultures are distinctive, and organizations are comprised of diverse persons with different realities. There are multiple rationalities and realities. Managers should take care to acknowledge voices that have been traditionally ignored.

These new assumptions should be given careful consideration in developing an integrated theoretical framework for human services management. Issues of culture, gender, and diversity will be critical in defining what approaches hold promise for human service agencies in the twenty-first century.

■ Toward an Integrated Theoretical Framework for Human Services Management

The Importance of System Integrity

As we have seen, there are many perspectives on how organizations maximize productivity, efficiency, effectiveness, and quality. Over the years it has become increasingly clear that there is no one best way, as Taylor had hoped, yet there are many right ways to manage an organization and its personnel. Organizational life, as we have observed, is a complex, multidimensional phenomenon. Developing an eclectic theoretical framework for the management of human service organizations, therefore, requires that we, first, identify the dimensions; second, identify the theories and principles that help us to understand each dimension; and, third, examine the overall framework in terms of its internal consistency and integrity.

Following the very sound and practical framework developed by Miles (1975), the text will examine the organizational and human variables that contribute to the understanding of organizational behavior. Following this the text will propose a framework for understanding the role of the manager. The manager is responsible for integrating organizational and human variables both vertically (over time) and horizontally (across all components of the organization) in a way that promotes optimal productivity. The combination of (1) anchoring a framework firmly in established theoretical principles and (2) applying these principles in a consistent manner provides a sound approach to management that has the potential for remaining practical and relevant, and leading to the achievement of organizational excellence.

Neither theory nor the realities of practice alone should drive decision making in management. Rather, in making decisions, managers should have one foot firmly anchored in an understanding of the history of management thought and the other fully immersed in a knowledge of contemporary practice issues. As decisions are required, no assumptions need be made that theoretical principles always be followed regardless of their current relevance. Neither is it assumed that the current situation alone should always dictate the parameters for problem solving. Rather, both theory and current realities should be seen as having something to offer. Drawing from both in an interactive and dynamic way, new and constantly relevant approaches are derived and new theoretical principles are conceptualized and established for testing. This relationship is depicted in Figure 2.4.

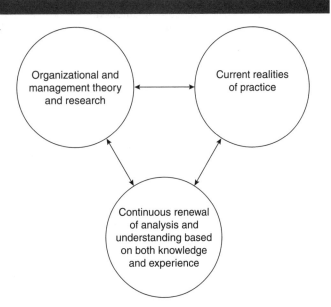

FIGURE 2.4

Drawing on Both Theory and Practice to Keep Applications Current and Relevant

Organizational and management theory and research

Current realities of practice

Continuous renewal of analysis and understanding based on both knowledge and experience

Selecting the Organizational Variables to Be Considered

With the approach to theory and practice depicted in Figure 2.4 in mind, the following organizational and human variables are presented as key components of a theory for management of human service organizations.

For each variable, a theoretical connection is proposed. Principles drawn from these theories are intended to help inform managers about how they should attempt to understand each of the organizational and human variables that defines organizations in action. The theories and principles proposed are not intended as final, definitive ending points. Rather they are intended as a beginning.

Organizational Variables	*Theoretical Base*
Understanding the organization as a system; input, throughput, output, and outcome; subsystems	Systems theory
Mission, goals, and objectives	Management by objectives
Flexibility and appropriateness of structure	Bureaucratic theory, Theory Y, contingency theory, excellence framework
The significance of the environment	Systems theory
The importance of quality	Theory Z, total quality management
Job design/technology; autonomy and entrepreneurship; productivity through people	Scientific management, bureaucratic theory, human relations theory, Theory Y, contingency theory, excellence framework
Motivation and reward systems; the importance of internal consistency	Scientific management, human relations, Theory Y, management by objectives, contingency theory
Monitoring, evaluation, and research	Scientific management, management by objectives
The importance of communication and control	Contingency theory, excellence framework

Selecting the Human Variables to Be Considered

Research on organizations and their productivity has provided a great deal of insight into motivation. Contemporary authors have also contributed much to our understanding of such issues as organizational culture, ethnicity, gender, and the need for a sense of competence in the workplace. Drawing on these works, the following human variables have been selected, along with some of the theoretical frameworks and conceptual pieces that help inform a manager's understanding of human factors.

Human Variables	*Theoretical Base*
The importance of diversity; incorporation of multiple perspectives into all aspects of organizational life	Affirmative action, valuing differences, and managing diversity in organizations; cultural competence; "sensemaking" concepts and questions
Employee need for attention and recognition; personalization; finding a niche; developing an identity	Human relations, organizational culture, excellence framework, literature on culture and gender in organizations
The importance of the social group	Human relations, Theory Z, excellence framework
Employee need to use knowledge, skills, and creativity; need for a sense of competence	Theory Y, contingency theory
Rewarding for performance; the importance of internal consistency	Management by objectives, contingency theory, total quality management

Both organizational and human variables need to be addressed as the organization goes about its day-to-day business. Integrating these variables in a way that maximizes performance and productivity is the job of the manager. This role is depicted in Figure 2.5.

FIGURE 2.5

Management's Role: Integration of Organizational and Human Variables

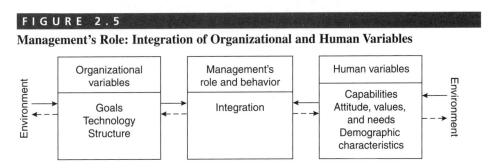

Source: Miles, R. (1975). *Theories of management: Implications for organizational behavior and development.* New York: McGraw Hill, p. 21. Reproduced with the permission of The McGraw-Hill Companies.

The Manager as Integrator

The foregoing organizational and human variables can best be understood as falling on a continuum that is roughly contiguous with the mechanistic-organic continuum as defined by Burns and Stalker (1961). Organizational structure, for example, can range from a traditional, hierarchical, bureaucratic structure to a loosely designed project team. Job design can range from highly detailed specification of tasks to general statements of areas of responsibility. Reward systems can be rigidly structured along the lines of seniority and preestablished performance criteria, or they can establish annual team objectives and take peer evaluation into consideration, revising criteria on an annual basis. A general framework depicting these options is presented in Figure 2.6.

Miles (1975) points out that it is not implementation of a highly structured versus flexible system that enhances or discourages productivity as much as it is consistency or inconsistency within the system. For example, an organization's goals and objectives may promote high levels of performance in relation to achieving results with and for populations served. The job design, however, may be so rigid that workers find themselves severely limited in their attempts to help clients to achieve results. This inconsistency leads to low levels of morale and, consequently, to low levels of performance.

Who, then, decides where on the continuum from structured, mechanistic to fluid, organic a particular organization ought to fall? The answer is that it is the responsibility of the management team, with appropriate input and participation from staff, board, clients, and other constituencies. Managers and administrators are the people who are held accountable for overall organizational and program performance. These are the people who have an overview of all of the organizational components and the extent to which they are integrated. These are the people who are in a position to act as go-between from the policy-making board to program-implementing staff. In short, the role of the management team is to design and implement a system that will ensure internal consistency and integrity in organizational performance.

FIGURE 2.6

**Selected Factors in Applying Management Theory and Their Position
on the Mechanistic-Organic Continuum**

Mechanistic, highly structured, closely supervised work environment

Organic, loosely structured, team-oriented, consultative work environment

├───────────────── Appropriateness of organizational structure ─────────────────┤

├───────────────── Appropriateness of job design, use of technology ─────────────────┤

├───────────────── Fit of motivation philosophy to rewards ─────────────────┤

├───────────────── Philosophy on data collection and dissemination ─────────────────┤

├───────────────── Effective utilization of a diverse workforce ─────────────────┤

├───────────────── Recognizing and meeting employee needs ─────────────────┤

Management Roles and Responsibilities

The following list of management responsibilities and roles represents the ways in which managers define, design, and establish subsystems of the organization in a way that ensures that they are internally consistent and support efficiency, effectiveness, quality, and productivity. The remaining chapters of this book are organized around these responsibilities and roles in an attempt to direct managers of human services organizations toward organizational integrity.

Management Responsibility	The Role of the Manager
Analysis of the Entire System	Assess purpose of the organization, expected outcomes, needed technologies, state of the art. Define organizational and program inputs, throughput, outputs, and outcomes. Use as an overarching framework of the concept of system integrity.
Establishment of Mission and Goals	Ensure consensus on shared vision. Create a process for ongoing development and refinement of organizational and program goals, objectives, and activities, with input from all stakeholders. Structure the organization and allocate resources to meet goals and objectives. Examine mission, goals, and objectives from the perspective of system integrity.
Creation of Ideal Structure	Assess existing structure and reporting and control systems. Create "ideal" structure for maximizing efficiency, productivity, effectiveness, and quality in terms of the organic/mechanistic continuum. Consider how the structure is organized to protect the technical core, ensure high quality and competent management, and attend to the needs and demands of the task environment. Examine all components from the perspective of system integrity.
Creation of Ideal Job Design	Develop a job analysis for each position within the organization. Create "ideal" job designs for maximizing efficiency, productivity, effectiveness, and quality recognizing employee need to use knowledge, skills, and creativity. Evaluate all positions from the perspective of how they fit into the overall system to accomplish stated mission, goals, and objectives. Ensure system integrity.
Design of Motivation and Reward System	Understand what motivates employees. Design a system that ensures that those who work the hardest and demonstrate the highest levels of commitment to organizational mission, goals, and objectives—and achieve the best results—receive the highest rewards. Incorporate both intrinsic and extrinsic rewards into the system. Check the system against all other components to ensure internal consistency.

(continued)

Management Responsibility	The Role of the Manager
Design of a Data Collection and Reporting System	Design a system that will permit collection of data on all phases of implementation and achievement for monitoring, evaluation, and research purposes. Ensure that data and information collected and aggregated are useful in tracking stated goals, objectives, and activities; are used in refining structure and design; and are consistent with the motivation and reward system.
Establishment of a Budgeting and Financial Management System	Design a system that accounts for and tracks all resources included as agency inputs. Allocate all resources into standard budget formats. Calculate unit costs in a variety of formats in order to track efficiency factors. Ensure that budget priorities are consistent with mission, goals, and objectives as well as with principles of the motivation and reward system.
Establishment of a Human Resources Plan	Prepare a plan that is grounded in an analysis of the needs of the organization for professional and technological expertise. The plan should include a complete job analysis for each position, together with a plan for recruitment and selection of personnel that is grounded in human resources law and meets the diverse needs of the organization and its clientele.
Design of a Recruitment, Screening, and Selection System	Establish a system for recruiting a broad and diverse pool of applicants. Design a screening system that will ensure selection and hiring decisions that are consistent with the expectations established in the job analysis for the position. Check against organizational variables to ensure system integrity.
Establishment of Principles for Supervision, Training, and Staff Development	Ensure that supervision is appropriate to the needs of the employee, taking into consideration what is known about employee needs and motivation in the interest of maximizing performance. Provide training that is appropriate to the employee's need for knowledge and skill. Encourage the employee to focus on his or her career goals and to prepare for advancement toward them.
Design of a Performance Appraisal System	Design a system for performance appraisal that is consistent with the goals and objectives of the organization and with the job analysis. Ensure that the system accurately measures performance in a way that is comparable to other employees. Reward high levels of performance; do not reward low levels of performance. Check against mission, goals, and objectives and against reward policies to determine consistency.
Establishment of Policies for Termination	Design a system that will ensure that low-level performers, nonperformers, nonproductive employees, and those who commit acts of misfeasance or malfeasance are evaluated in terms of whether they should be continued in employment. Terminate those whose performances do not warrant continuation. Termination policies should be consistent with mission, goals, and objectives and with the performance appraisal system.

Management Responsibility	**The Role of the Manager**
Evaluation of Organizational Performance	Compile data and information that will permit stakeholders to understand and review organizational performance on a regular basis and to make informed decisions about changes or continuation of existing programs and practices. Evaluate organizational performance in terms of system integrity.

These roles and responsibilities, then, help to define the meaning of excellence in the management of human service organizations. Each can be carried out in a manner that is consistent with a mechanistic, highly structured organizational theory and philosophy or with an organic, flexible approach. The decision should be made based on what form is optimum, given the purpose and function of the organization. Consistency is the key to success and is a step in the direction toward achievement of excellence. The following chapters are designed to interpret management expectations in greater detail for each of the roles specified.

SUMMARY

1. **The Usefulness of Early Management Theory.** Theory drawn from business and corporate management can be useful in the management of human service organizations.

2. **The History of Management Thought.** Various management themes have emerged from the study of management over the last one hundred years.
   - *Application of Management Concepts to Human Service Organizations.* Certain principles can be extracted from theories and used to create an eclectic management theory for human service organizations.
   - *Scientific Management.* Taylor focused on attention to precision and efficiency in the workplace.

     Application to the Management of Human Services
       • *Management as a Specialized Role.* Specialized management knowledge and skills are needed.
       • *Training and Preparation for the Job.* Employees should be prepared before beginning a job.
       • *Precision in the Development of Technology.* Procedures should be made more precise.
       • *A Research Orientation.* Work performance should be studied to make it more efficient and effective.
   - *Bureaucratic Theory.* Weber developed a highly organized, hierarchical system.

     Application to the Management of Human Services
       • *Accountability.* Bureaucratic structure supports pinpointing of responsibility.
       • *Hierarchy and Definition of Responsibility.* Responsibilities are defined. This creates benefits and limitations.
       • *Preparation for the Job.* Demonstrated competence should be a prerequisite for hiring.
   - *Human Relations Theory.* Mayo discovered the human elements that affect productivity.

Application to the Management of Human Services
- *Organizational Culture.* Social relationships can affect organizational philosophy and culture.
- *The Influence of the Group.* Employees tend to behave as members of groups.
- *Understanding and Utilizing Meaningful Rewards.* Noneconomic rewards can be important to employees.

■ *Theory X and Theory Y.* McGregor characterized an old philosophy of management as well as one that he believed could lead to higher productivity.

Application to the Management of Human Services
- *Motivation in the Workplace.* Most employees come to the organization wanting to be productive.
- *Stimulating Employee Motivation.* Managerial styles often determine whether employee motivation can be captured for the good of the organization.

■ *Management by Objectives.* Drucker introduced the idea of planning and projecting organizational expectations.

Application to the Management of Human Services
- *Adapting to Change.* Planning ahead can help an organization adapt to change.
- *Strengthening Management Practices.* Objectives establish organizational, departmental, and unit expectations.
- *Enhancing Employee Motivation.* Working as a team toward the achievement of goals and objectives can be a motivator.
- *More Precise Performance Appraisals.* Advance specifications help focus performance appraisal.

■ *Systems Theory.* Katz and Kahn defined systems concepts. Thompson helped our understanding of how they affect organizations in action.

Application to the Management of Human Services
- *Understanding Organizational Inputs, Throughputs, and Outputs.* These systems concepts have made a great contribution to the understanding of efficiency, effectiveness, productivity, and quality in human service organizations.
- *Developing and Maintaining Relations with Critical Elements of an Organization's Environment.* Environmental factors can have a significant impact on the life of a human service organization.

■ *Contingency Theory.* Burns and Stalker and others conducted research that demonstrated that there was no one best way to structure and design an organization. The mechanistic-organic continuum presents options.

Application to the Management of Human Services
- *Providing Structure and Design Options.* Human service organizations need to carefully consider mechanistic versus organic options.
- *Improving Effectiveness through Result-Oriented Team Interaction.* The team approach offered by the organic model coupled with a focus on results rather than process may be more applicable to many human service organizations than the mechanistic mode.

- *The Importance of a Sense of Competence.* Workers tend to perform at their highest levels when they feel a sense of competence about what they are able to accomplish.

■ *Contemporary Theories.* Three themes emerge: organizational culture, quality, and diversity.

■ *Decision Making and the Influence of Organizational Culture.*
  - *Understanding Organizational Culture.* Employee perceptions will be greatly influenced by the ways in which long time employees have shaped the organizational culture through a long, shared history of experiences.
  - *Understanding the Culture of Excellent Organizations.* Peters and Waterman defined eight principles that contribute to excellence in organizations.

  Application to the Management of Human Services
  - *Understanding Organizational Cultures and Subcultures.* It is important for managers to understand the predominant values of an organization's culture and subcultures.
  - *Recognizing the Importance of Shared Vision.* Excellent organizations are able to focus employee effort around a shared vision of where the organization is going.
  - *Incorporating Diverse Perspectives into the Organizational Culture.* Organizations have multiple realities; time should be invested in sharing and learning diverse perspectives.

■ *The Issue of Quality.* This is an important issue for human service organizations because productivity can be increased at the expense of quality.
  - *Theory Z.* Ouchi established principles that lead to quality in the organization's products or services.
  - *Total Quality Management (TQM).* Deming and others defined basic principles to which organizations must be committed if they hope to achieve total quality management.

  Application to the Management of Human Services
  - *Defining Quality in Practice.* Professions serving people in need should focus on defining quality.
  - *Developing Systems for Continuous Quality Improvement.* Improving quality needs to become part of a system of service delivery, not an isolated value or concept.

■ *The Issue of Diversity.* Human service organizations serve people in need. Culture and gender are extremely important components of one's identity. To be effective in serving people, human service professionals must understand cultures, gender issues, and how they affect practice.
  - *Beyond Race and Gender.* Thomas defined three levels of organizational commitment and involvement in dealing with issues of diversity.
  - *Gender Issues in Human Services Management.* Weick proposed seven "sense-making" properties that can be used to help interpret experiences within organizations.

Application to the Management of Human Services

- *Cultural Competence.* Cross et al. developed a continuum of cultural competence.
- *Incorporating Gender Issues into Management Practices.* Netting and Rodwell proposed a set of new assumptions designed to support gender sensitivity in organizations.

3. **Toward an Integrated Theoretical Framework for Human Services Management.** Selected theoretical principles are used to support a number of themes that are important to the achievement of excellence in the management of human service organizations.

   - *The Importance of System Integrity.* No single organizational philosophy, theory, or design is correct for all organizations. What is important is that organizational mission and philosophy carry throughout the organization in a way that promotes and supports consistency in decision making and other actions.

   - *Selecting the Organizational Variables to Be Considered.* Nine organizational variables help to define the parameters within which organizational consistency and integrity will be practiced.

   - *Selecting the Human Variables to Be Considered.* Five human variables help to define the parameters within which employees will be nurtured and productivity maximized.

4. **The Manager as Integrator.** The person responsible for integrating organizational variables and human variables in a way that supports maximum productivity is the manager.

   - *Management Roles and Responsibilities.* Thirteen management roles are defined that, if performed with consistency and integrity, will lead to organizational excellence.

EXERCISES

Please complete the following sections of your manual based on the content covered in Chapter 2:

Section 2: Theoretical Framework for Agency Decisions and Actions

2.1 Major Theoretical Themes. Identify the major themes drawn from management theory that represent the important factors to be addressed in bringing consistency into the practices of your organization.

2.2 Organizational Variables. Identify the organizational variables that need to be examined periodically to ensure that they are functioning in a way that is compatible with the rest of the organization.

2.3 Expectations for Managers. Identify those parts of the role and responsibility of managers that are to be established as expectations for all managers and those parts are discretionary and left to the style of each manager.

REFERENCES

Au, C. (1996). Rethinking organizational effectiveness: Theoretical and methodological issues in the study of organizational effectiveness for social welfare organizations. *Administration in Social Work 20*(4), 1–21.

Burns, T., & Stalker, G. (1961). *The management of innovation.* London: Tavistock.

Cross, T., Bazron, B., Dennis, K., & Isaacs, M. (1989). *Towards a culturally competent system of care.* Washington, DC: Georgetown University Child Development Center, Technical Assistance Center.

Deming, W. (1982). *Quality, productivity and competitive position.* Cambridge: MIT Center for Advanced Engineering Study.

Dill, W. (1958). Environment as an influence on managerial autonomy. *Administrative Science Quarterly, 2* (March), 409–443.

Drucker, P. (1954). *The practice of management.* New York: Harper.

Drucker, P. (1959). Long-range planning: Challenge to management science. *Management Science, 5*(3), 238–249.

Etzioni, A. (1964). *Modern organizations.* Englewood Cliffs, NJ: Prentice-Hall.

Figueira-McDonough, J. (1998). Toward a gender-integrated knowledge in social work. In J. Figueira-McDonough, F. Netting, & A. Casebolt (Eds.), *The role of gender in practice knowledge. Claiming half the human experience* (pp. 3–40). New York: Garland.

Foner, N. (1994). *The caregiving dilemma: Work in an American nursing home.* Berkeley: University of California Press.

George, C. (1968). *The history of management thought.* Englewood Cliffs, NJ: Prentice-Hall.

Green, J. (1999). *Cultural awareness in the human services: A multi-ethnic approach* (3rd ed.). Boston: Allyn and Bacon.

Green, J. (1995). *Cultural awareness in the human services: A multi-ethnic approach.* Boston: Allyn & Bacon.

Imai, M. (1986). *Kaizen.* New York: Random House.

Jevons, W. (1888). *The theory of political economy.* New York: Macmillan.

Katz, D., & Kahn, R. (1966). *The social psychology of organizations.* New York: Wiley.

Kettner, P., Moroney, R., & Martin, L. (1999). *Designing and managing programs: An effectiveness-based approach* (2nd ed.). Thousand Oaks, CA: Sage.

Martin, L. (1993). *Total quality management in human service organizations.* Thousand Oaks, CA: Sage.

Martin, L., & Kettner, P. (1996). *Measuring the performance of human service programs.* Thousand Oaks, CA: Sage.

Matteson, M., & Ivancevich, J. (1981), *Management classics* (2nd ed.). Glenview, IL: Scott-Foresman.

Mayo, E. (1945). *The social problems of an industrial civilization.* Boston: Division of Research, Harvard Graduate School of Business Administration.

McGregor, D. (1969). The human side of enterprise. In W. Eddy, W. Burke, V. Dupre, & O. South (Eds.), *Behavioral science and the manager's role* (pp. 157–166). Washington, DC: NTL Institute for Applied Behavioral Science.

Merton, R. (1952). Bureaucratic structure and personality. In R. Merton, A. Gray, B. Hockey, & H. Selvin (Eds.), *Reader in bureaucracy* (pp. 261–372). Glencoe, IL: Free Press.

Miles, R. (1975). *Theories of management: Implications for organizational behavior and development.* New York: McGraw-Hill.

Morse, J., & Lorsch, J. (1970). Beyond Theory Y. *Harvard Business Review 45,* May–June 61–68.

Netting, F. E., & Rodwell, M. K. (1998). Integrating gender into human service organization, administration and planning curricula. In J. Figueira-McDonough, F. Netting, & A. Casebolt (Eds.), *The role of gender in practice knowledge. Claiming half the human experience* (pp. 287–321). New York: Garland.

Ouchi, W. (1981). *Theory Z: How American business can meet the Japanese challenge.* Reading, MA: Addison-Wesley.

Peter, L. (1977). *Peter's quotations: Ideas for our time.* New York: Morrow.

Peters, T., & Waterman, R. (1982). *In search of excellence: Lessons from America's best-run companies.* New York: Harper & Row.

Rodwell, M. (1995). Constructivist research: A qualitative approach. In P. Pecora, M. Fraser, K. Nelson, J. McCroskey, & W. Meezan (Eds.), *Evaluating family-based services* (pp. 192–193). New York: Aldine de Gruyter.

Schein, E. (1985). *Organizational culture and leadership.* San Francisco: Jossey-Bass.

Taylor, F. (1911). *Principles of scientific management.* New York: Harper.

Thomas, R., Jr. (1991). *Beyond race and gender: Unleashing the power of your total work force by managing diversity.* New York: AMACOM.

Thompson, J. (1967). *Organizations in action.* New York: McGraw-Hill.

von Bertalanffy, L. (1950). An outline of general system theory. *British Journal for the Philosophy of Science, 1*(2), 493–512.

Weber, M. (1947) *The theory of social and economic organizations* (A. M. Henderson & T. Parsons, Trans.). New York: Macmillan. (Original work published 1924).

Weick, K. (1995). *Sensemaking in organizations.* Thousand Oaks, CA: Sage.

Zeithaml, V., Parasuraman, A., & Berry, L. (1990). *Delivering quality services.* New York: Free Press.

CHAPTER 3

Understanding the Organization from a Systems Perspective

CHAPTER OBJECTIVES

Upon completion of this chapter, the reader will be able to:

- Explain why managers need to understand the organization as a system of subsystems.
- List factors in an organization's external or task environment and explain how they affect organizational functioning.
- List important organizational components and explain how they work together to achieve optimum organizational functioning.
- Write a mission statement for a human service organization.
- Explain how organizational mission and purpose serve as the standard for organizational consistency and integrity.

Assumptions

- That decisions and actions in one part of the organization affect many parts.
- That factors external to the organization affect the organization.
- That compatibility among organizational components is an important feature in well-run organizations.
- That the mission statement can serve as a goal or beacon to help guide decisions and actions.

What Is a Systems Perspective?

Elements or components of organizations do not act in isolation. What happens in one department or unit often affects, and is affected by, what happens in other parts of the organization. If, for example, an employee behaves inappropriately toward a client and the client brings a lawsuit against the agency, ultimately this single act may affect a number of personnel and programs within the agency. The executive would have to be notified and make arrangements to respond to the suit. The board of directors would be expected to take a position on the issue. The business manager may have to review insurance policies and finances. The employee's supervisor would have to be involved in fact-finding. The other workers in the unit may have to be consulted about their perspectives on the alleged offense. The director of staff training and development may be expected to design a training session to deal with the problem. The public information officer may need to develop press releases and deal with public perceptions if the matter becomes a public issue. A variety of interests in the community may be affected in some way.

To address the issue appropriately, all efforts by affected personnel should be coordinated. That is to say, the components of the agency should function as a system. If the employee denies the charge and client advocacy groups threaten a boycott while the executive prepares an apology and the business manager pursues a settlement, activities will work at cross-purposes and the incident will inflict serious damage to the agency's reputation, regardless of guilt or innocence.

These same coordinated efforts should apply not only to isolated incidents but also to day-to-day functioning. Very few things that happen in the day-to-day activities of an organization happen in isolation. When things are operating smoothly and efficiently, it is easy to forget the interrelationships. But when attempting to understand, assess the effectiveness of, or problem solve within an organization, recognizing the significance of these relationships is critical.

Take, for example, an agency that provides detoxification and rehabilitation services to drug and alcohol abusers. The executive is informed that one of the agency's funding sources will not be contracting with the agency next year because it has not adequately demonstrated the effectiveness of its programs in helping clients to overcome their addictions. This action would most likely trigger the following, and perhaps more, actions on the part of persons involved with the agency:

Board	A review of funding sources; assessment of financial stability of the agency. Assessment of impact of loss of a funding source.
Executive	An examination of how effectiveness is defined, and how the agency's programs are designed, in an attempt to determine why program objectives are not being achieved. Is there a good fit between services provided and outcomes expected?
Program Staff	An examination of how client progress is defined and documented; what are they doing with clients to help them overcome their addictions? Is it possible that they are getting good results but not properly documenting them? Or have they failed to define what they mean by success? Where is the problem located?

Human Resources Director	An examination of staff competence to carry out the tasks and responsibilities specified in the job description. What knowledge and skills do employees need? Is the agency hiring people with the appropriate background education and experience?
Monitoring and Evaluation Personnel	An examination of data collection and aggregation practices. Are the data elements collected framed in a way that permits accurate assessment of effectiveness? Are staff providing accurate and complete data? Are reports aggregated in a way that allows for evaluation of effectiveness?
Supervisors	An examination of performance evaluation criteria. Do annual performance evaluations accurately assess and identify workers who excel in achieving expected outcomes with clients? Are these workers being properly rewarded? Are there incentives for high levels of performance? Do employees receive appropriate feedback on their performance?
Business Manager	An examination of the adequacy of funding for the support services needed in order to increase success with clients. What support services (such as day care and transportation) have caseworkers been requesting? Have these services been made available? If not, why not? Do we know that providing them would make a difference in terms of effectiveness with clients?

Another way to look at who and what are affected by this situation is as follows:

External Entities Affected	*Internal Entities Affected*
Funding sources	Board
Clients and their families	Management and administration
Potential employees	Direct service staff
Educational institutions	Human resources
Other agencies	Business management
	Data management and reporting

These are just a few of the individuals, units, and components of the organization that would be affected by such an event as losing funding for nonperformance on a contract. An important starting point for understanding an organization is to understand the ways in which the organization functions internally as well as how it relates to significant elements in its environment. This knowledge is essential to moving the organization toward excellence in its overall achievements as well as its day-to-day management and level of functioning.

■ Understanding the External Environment

Without further refinement, an agency's external environment refers to everything outside the boundaries of the agency or organization itself. Attempting to understand everything outside is not realistic, possible, or necessary. Fortunately, a number of authors have helped

FIGURE 3.1

**Factors in an Organization's
Environment That Affect
Organizational Functioning**

us to understand what parts of the external environment are important to organizations. Thompson (1967) uses the term *task environment* to refer to elements outside an organization that enable it to operate and that set the basic context for these operations. Drawing on the work of Dill (1958), he includes four key components in the task environment: (1) customers (both distributors and users); (2) suppliers of materials, labor, capital, equipment, and work space; (3) competitors for both markets and resources; and (4) regulatory groups, including governmental agencies, unions, and interfirm associations.

Martin (1980), writing specifically about human service organizations, identifies a number of external elements that affect agencies, including (1) funding sources, (2) sources of noncash revenues, (3) clients and client sources, and (4) other constituents. Montana and Charnov (1993) describe the external environment in terms of economic, sociological, political, and technological domains. The text will attempt here to synthesize these three different ways of conceptualizing the external environment, using the categories of (1) economic factors, (2) sociological factors, (3) political/professional factors, and (4) technological factors as organizing themes. Figure 3.1 illustrates the four external domains.

Economic Factors

When exploring economic factors in the environment that have significance for the organization, five components drawn from a number of the foregoing frameworks include (1) funding sources, (2) noncash revenues, (3) clients or consumers, (4) suppliers, and (5) competitors.

Funding sources are an important part of the task environment. Social service funding is generally drawn from the following sources (Netting, Kettner, & McMurtry, 1998, p. 242):

Government Funds
- Direct government appropriation
- Government purchase-of-service contract funds
- Government grants
- Matching funds
- Tax benefits

Donated Funds
- Direct charitable contributions
- Indirect contributions (e.g., through United Way)
- Private grants
- Endowments

Fees for Service
- Direct payments from clients
- Payments from third parties (e.g., insurance)

Other Agency Income
- Investments
- Profit-making subsidiaries
- Funding-raising events and appeals

As funding resources are secured through grants, contracts, and other sources, each funding source becomes an important part of the agency's relationship with the external environment. All funding should be coordinated and expectations understood. Funds should be carefully tracked to ensure that they are achieving their purpose.

Noncash revenues or resources may include volunteers, in-kind contributions (such as food, clothing, equipment, or facilities), and tax benefits. Achieving excellence in resource management requires a good working knowledge of current funding sources and noncash revenues. This includes the agency's past history with each as well as each source's likely dependability in the future. A list of potential, currently untapped resources both in terms of funding and noncash revenues may prove to be helpful in economic and fiscal planning.

The availability of and demand from customers, clients, or consumers have an economic impact on a human service agency and are critical components of the task environment. Human service organizations are built on the assumption or on the knowledge that there is a need, and that the need can be translated into a demand for services. As long as demand for service exists, the agency will continue. If client demand declines or stops altogether, the need for the organization ceases to exist.

One of the ways in which nonprofit organizations differ from the for-profits is that high demand from potential clients or consumers does not always translate into higher levels of income or revenue. In commercial enterprises, more customers are almost universally seen as a good thing. More customers bring in more income, which in turn allows for growth and development of the business. In nonprofit organizations, clients do not always pay the full cost of service. From the standpoint of fiscal analysis, an agency's clients can be categorized in four different ways: (1) high pay or break even: those that pay the full cost or even more than the full cost of services through self-pay or insurance; (2) low pay: those that pay on a sliding scale, but pay less than the full cost of services; (3) no pay: those who pay nothing; and (4) contract-eligible clients: those whose services are paid for through a contract awarded to the agency (Netting et al., 1998). A profile of the agency's client population from this service reimbursement perspective can be informative in terms of attempting to understand the agency's fiscal soundness.

In translating the concept of suppliers from a business context to a nonprofit context, we need to look at two different components of the task environment: referral sources for clients and the institutions that prepare workers for positions within the agency. Martin (1980) points out that an important external element for human service providers is the various sources of referrals such as government agencies, teachers and school administrators, physicians and medical personnel, and other such sources.

In addition, an assessment of the labor pool is important. What educational institutions in the community prepare the workers who will fill the various positions within the agency? What is the nature of the job market currently, and how has it changed over the years? What are the projections for the short term and long term for personnel needs and availability? These and other questions should be addressed in an attempt to better understand the task environment. Many agencies that employ child care workers, for example, experience more than 100 percent turnover during the course of the year. This represents an expense to the agency and argues for more analysis of the supply of and demand for these employees.

The final economic factor to be assessed is an analysis of competitors. Competition within the human services was relatively unknown prior to the introduction of purchase of service contracting in the 1970s (Kettner & Martin, 1987). As the concept of privatization has gained momentum over the last few decades, government entities have been less inclined to attempt to provide a full array of services and more likely to contract with either for-profit or nonprofit agencies to provide selected services. Day care, mental health services, drug and alcohol treatment, and residential treatment are examples of the kinds of services typically purchased from private for-profit and nonprofit agencies.

What this means for agencies, then, is that if they hope to keep a steady stream of clients coming through their doors, they must compete with other agencies that offer the same type of service. Increasingly, funds have come with strings attached requiring data collection about costs of service, quality of service, and client outcomes. Data are used to develop indicators about an agency's success rates, which are then used in the subsequent round of contract awards. It is important that a manager understand not only who the competitors are, but also where the agencies stand in terms of reputation and past records of service costs, quality, and outcomes.

Sociological Factors

In exploring the sociological dimensions of the task environment, a manager should attempt to understand community demographics, both in terms of the client and community problem and need profile as well as in terms of the available labor pool. At issue here is the importance of understanding the socioeconomic, ethnic, gender, and age profiles of the community to be served. Community mapping, using census data, can help depict the community's makeup in terms of income, education, ethnicity, gender, age, and other demographic factors. Identifying high concentrations and their location in relation to the agency can be helpful for planning purposes. These findings should lead to an exploration of the extent to which the agency is meeting the diverse needs of all groups represented. Some review of census data together with past and current needs assessments and key informant interviews may be helpful in understanding the priorities and needs as seen by community members.

In addition to an examination of overall community demographics, it is also useful to look at the ethnic and gender makeup of the staff and to determine the extent to which it is reflective of the available pool of workers and the demographic profile of clients. This is not, of course, to imply that staff members cannot be effective working across ethnic and gender lines. However, any staff that is reflective of only one ethnic or gender perspective severely limits itself in terms of the richness that cross-cultural and cross-gender perspectives, including those of gays and lesbians, can bring to staff discussions and problem-solving efforts.

Political/Professional Factors

In examining the task environment of the nonprofit organization, there is some logic to combining both political and professional factors. Political factors include laws and regulations imposed from a federal, state, or local level as well as what might be described as a political climate. The term *climate* refers to values and attitudes of community and state leaders as well as those of the general public toward the services being provided and the consumers of those services.

Professional factors also involve a type of regulation, referred to as accreditation, as well as consideration of working relationships with any of the relevant professional organizations that may be represented within the community.

Laws and Regulations   Most human service agencies and programs operate within an environment in which there are a number of laws or regulations that govern service provision. Jansson (1994) notes that social services became more complex after funding changes from the 1960s through the 1980s. Public funding and purchase of service contracting transformed a relatively simple pattern of funding and regulation into a system in which social services were:

> increasingly influenced by interorganizational relationships in their work; they had to ask which clients "belonged" to whom, which ones should be retained or referred elsewhere, and whether to develop collaborative services, such as joint programs. (p. 14)
>
> Federal and local governments gave so much money to social services in the 1960s and 1970s that the nature of human services fundamentally changed and the role of private donors and federated fundraising diminished. Many nonprofit agencies received the bulk of their funds from public authorities, who saddled the agencies with rules and regulations about how to use their funds. (p. 15)

A worker in a residential treatment center once commented that the center received forty-four different site visits during the course of any given year. These visits included contract monitors from state departments of child welfare, juvenile corrections, developmental disabilities, and education, as well as from county health and other departments responsible for the health, hygiene, and safety of its citizens. Although forty-four site visits in one year seems rather excessive, given the amount of staff time that must be devoted to preparing for each visit, it does illustrate the kind of environment within which an agency operates when government funding and service to the public is involved. It is important to be aware of what kinds of regulations govern service provision and the organizations to which the agency is accountable.

Political Climate   There is also that elusive issue of political climate. If someone decides to open up a grocery store in a community, it is unlikely that the storekeeper needs to give a great deal of thought to how people feel about grocery stores in general. Politics and value considerations do not enter into such a decision. However, when dealing with the provision of social services, the attitudes of community leaders and citizens are important. Some who have attempted to open up halfway houses or transitional living centers for various populations (e.g., recovering alcoholics or homeless) have discovered the NIMBY factor ("not in my back yard"). Community value systems tend to be supportive of vulnerable groups such as abused and neglected children or women who are victims of family violence. Other populations raise concerns. This, of course, is not to suggest that people in need of services be abandoned if the community objects to providing services. It is simply one more variable within the task environment that a good manager needs to take into consideration in attempting to understand the dynamics of interaction between agency and community.

Professional Considerations   In addition, human service agencies are increasingly becoming part of an accrediting network. Accreditation involves having a team of site visitors conduct a thorough study of the agency and make a determination as to whether the agency measures up to a set of standards. In some instances government contracting agencies require that their contractors be accredited. In other instances, agencies find that fund-raising is more successful if they can advertise their accredited status. In an era when there are so many fund-raising efforts and so many worthy causes, accreditation by a body qualified to evaluate agency performance and standards can provide a valuable edge.

Finally, there is the issue of relationship to professional organizations. The American Psychological Association (APA), the National Association of Social Workers (NASW), and other such organizations have divisions that license or certify professionals within their disciplines. They may also have procedures for sanctioning individuals or organizations that violate professional standards. Human service agencies should be aware of the licensing or certification standards and should promote good working relationships with these organizations.

Technological Factors

The final domain to be considered in the attempt to understand the task environment is that of technology. For human service agencies, technology can refer to the use of equipment, including computer hardware and software, as well as the development of new treatment approaches. The kinds of monitoring and evaluation responsibilities that are being imposed on social service agencies today require data-processing capability. It is likely that agencies are expected to report cost per unit of service, cost per successful outcome, successful outcomes per FTE staff, and other such indicators of performance (Martin & Kettner, 1996). It is important, therefore, that managers be knowledgeable about software that will track dollars as well as services provided and outcomes, so that the appropriate and necessary data and information can be generated.

In addition, a thorough analysis of the latest technology requires attention to the professional literature in order to ensure that innovations developed and proved effective in other settings can be tried and adopted if they prove to be successful. The provision of human services is a dynamic enterprise. Social, community, and individual problems change, needs change, and practice approaches must change to keep pace. For example, in dealing with violence in the schools, a peer counseling approach may be effective with some segments of the population, yet may not address the full range of problems and needs for all who have a potential for violence. Knowing what is working in other school districts within the area or around the country can add valuable information to the planning, delivery, and effectiveness of services provided.

In summary, then, understanding the organization from a systems perspective requires a knowledge of the important and relevant economic, sociological, political, professional, and technological factors in the environment.

■ Understanding the Internal Environment

Understanding agency operations requires an identification of the significant components of the organization, as well as an analysis of the extent to which they work in harmony with each other. As with examination of the external environment, we will begin our look at the internal environment by exploring some of the frameworks commonly used by leaders in the field of organizational analysis.

Miles (1975) describes the organization as a coming together of organizational variables and human variables. Successful organizations, he points out, are those in which managers are able to integrate these two sets of variables in a way that is internally consistent and responsive to organizational mission and goals (see Figure 2.6, p. 54).

According to Miles (1975), organizational variables include goals, technology, and structure. Human variables include capabilities, attitudes, values, needs, and demographic characteristics. The role of management is to design the organizational variables in a way that is internally consistent with a particular philosophy of management and then to blend human variables in a way that maximizes productivity.

Montana and Charnov (1993) use five factors as an organizing framework for understanding the internal environment: (1) financial resources, (2) physical resources, (3) human resources, (4) technological resources, and (5) corporate culture/ethics. Netting, Kettner, and McMurtry (1998), synthesizing from a number of sources and applying them specifically to human service organizations, identify the variables of (1) corporate authority and mission, (2) leadership style, (3) organizational and program structure, (4) programs and services, (5) personnel policies, and (6) technical resources. Again, in the interest of drawing the best from each list of organizational variables, an eclectic framework for organizational analysis is proposed, utilizing the following six components:

- Organizational purpose, mission, and philosophy
- Organizational planning
- Organizational operations
- Human resources
- Technological resources
- Financial resources

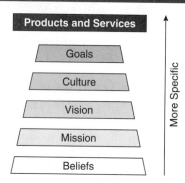

FIGURE 3.2

Diagram of the Organizational Platform

Source: The National Network for Social Work Managers. (1994). *The organizational platform.* Washington, DC: Author. Reproduced with the permission of the National Network for Social Work Managers.

Organizational Purpose, Mission, and Philosophy

Of all the variables that make up the internal environment, organizational purpose, mission, and philosophy should be examined first because it is here that one gains an understanding of the mission and vision that is intended to provide the logic and the organizing theme for all the other variables. Brody (1993) describes a mission statement as follows:

> A good mission statement should be lofty and inspiring, concise, capable of being easily understood and remembered, should reflect the organization's fundamental purpose, and should indicate what the organization wants to accomplish in relation to the beneficiaries of its work. (pp. 46–47)

Mission statements should be stated in terms of the agency's projected ideal outcomes for the populations served. For example, an adoption agency may state that its mission is that every child who comes for service will achieve his or her fullest potential in a loving and nurturing adoptive home. As an inspirational statement, the mission provides the basis for the shared vision that Peters and Waterman (1982) found to be a necessary ingredient for excellent organizations.

Organizations sometimes attempt to accomplish too much with a mission statement and incorporate program description as well. When a mission statement includes the term *provide* or some synonym, the statement goes beyond the definition of mission to program description.

The National Network for Social Work Managers (1994) presents what it calls the organization platform, depicted in Figure 3.2.

The National Network for Social Work Managers (1994) defines each of the terms as follows:

Beliefs: Your credo, the philosophical underpinnings, values that motivate your organization to action.

Mission: Historic, philosophical statement of your general, global purpose. What you hope to do for whom.

Vision: A specific, usually emotional, view of a preferred future; the primary goals or accomplishments of the organization.

Culture: Description of values and attitudes that describe how the organization will pursue and execute its vision.

Goals: The broad objectives that drive product line and strategic planning. (Long- and short-term plans, strategies, and tactics are designed to achieve goals.)

Products: The products and services offered to reach the vision. (p. 2)

This organizational platform offers a great deal of promise in clarifying, in a concise manner, what a human service agency believes in, what it hopes to achieve, and what services it plans to provide in order to achieve its mission, vision, and goals.

Organizational Planning

Montana and Charnov (1993) describe three levels of planning: strategic planning, long-range planning, and operational planning. Strategic planning takes the longest view and attempts to identify where the organization, ideally, would like to be in a time frame of five years or more.

■ CONSIDERATIONS

For Strategic Planning

Basic Questions: What are our current goals, objectives, programs, and services? Should we broaden or shrink our size and scope?

Time Frame: Usually five years or more.

Process: Extensive self-study, development of graphs and charts depicting current operation. Environmental scanning to determine projected future community problems and needs. A series of group meetings and retreats involving board, executive, management, staff representatives, community leaders, and clients. Possible use of management consultants.

Analysis: Variables relating to both external and internal environments are assessed in terms of strengths, weaknesses, and opportunities.

Report: A brief report sets in writing the agreements reached, including a reevaluation of existing mission, goals, programs, and services, with recommendations for future directions.

In summary, strategic planning attempts to use available data to project future needs and resources and to create a visioning process. Study and brainstorming among stakeholders become translated into a loosely defined set of agreements intended to keep the organization on course and relevant to changing problems and needs.

Long-range planning involves an examination of what actions are necessary to achieve the expectations specified in the strategic plan. The time frame for implementation and accomplishment is usually one to five years, and details for implementation should be spelled out as goals, objectives, and activities.

■ CONSIDERATIONS

For Long-Range Planning

Basic Questions: On what programs and services must we concentrate our attention in order to achieve the expectations of the strategic plan? Will new programs and services be added?

Time Frame: One to five years.

Process: Representatives of top management who understand the strategic plan should be involved; program managers, supervisors, staff, and clients from affected programs should also be involved. Data and information on current status of programs and services should be examined as well as current and projected community problems and needs.

Analysis: The impact of increasing or shrinking the size and scope of programs and services should be carefully analyzed in terms of effects on clients, community, staff, and the organization.

Report: Written guidelines should cover at least the following areas:
1. A precise description of programs and services to be expanded or reduced.
2. Financial implications of the change; source(s) of new funding, if needed.
3. A description of the target population and potential referral sources.
4. Additional personnel and other resources needed.
5. Additional physical facilities needed.
6. A plan for monitoring and evaluating progress.

In long-range planning, goals express a broad intention of outcome expectations. For example, a long-range organizational goal in a women's domestic violence shelter might be "to enable at least 50 percent more women who have been victims of domestic violence to achieve an independent and safe status over the next three years." Objectives would then spell out shorter-term processes such as acquiring property, beginning construction, refining programs and services, and hiring staff. Activities then become the specific tasks that must be carried out, including the time frames, for achieving long-range objectives. Implementation of activities is closely monitored, as is the success in terms of achieving objectives. The relationship of goals, objectives, and activities is depicted in Figure 2.1 (p. 30). Not all human service organizations engage in both strategic and long-range planning. Elements of both types may be incorporated into one planning process focused on future directions.

Operational planning, translated into human service terms, is better described as program planning. Program planning involves an analysis of the social or community problem to be addressed and a detailed planning of all the elements of the program. As defined by Kettner, Moroney, and Martin (1999), program planning in human services includes the following components:

- Conducting problem analysis and needs assessment
- Selecting an appropriate intervention strategy
- Setting goals and objectives
- Designing programs
- Building a management information system
- Developing a budget
- Evaluating program effectiveness

In examining homelessness in Center City, for example, planners would want to know what types of problems and needs were present as well as how many people were experiencing each type of need. How many homeless are there? How many have drug and alcohol problems? How many have problems with mental illness? How many need job skills training? Based on the findings, planners would then develop a working hypothesis about planned interventions and expected results. Working from this hypothesis, a plan is developed that includes goals, objectives, and activities; program design; data collection and aggregation; a budget; program monitoring and evaluation; and feedback of findings into the next generation of service provision. The process is depicted in the flowchart in Figure 3.3.

FIGURE 3.3

Flowchart of the Program Planning Process

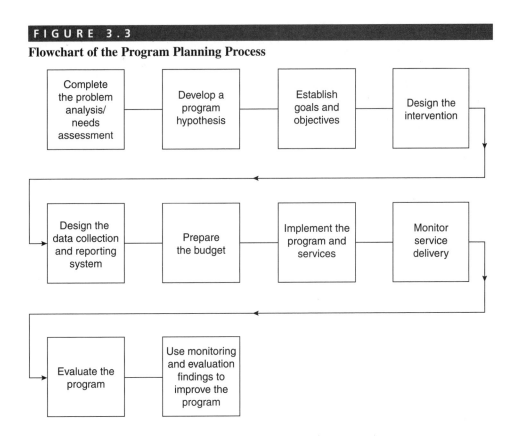

■ CONSIDERATIONS

For Program Planning

Basic Questions: What problems and needs are being experienced by the target population? What interventions are needed, and what results are expected from these interventions?

Time Frame: Usually one year or less; can be more, depending on the problem, population, and funding.

Process: Staff with knowledge and expertise on the population and the problem review the literature and develop a working hypothesis. Broader review and comment by staff, management, outside experts, and clients may be appropriate.

Analysis: The goodness of fit between the proposed intervention and the expected results is examined, as well as the expected impact on the size and scope of the community problem or need. Resources needed to produce the expected results are identified and itemized.

Report: A detailed program plan includes a brief problem analysis and needs assessment, program hypothesis, goals and objectives, elements of program design, a plan for data collection and aggregation, a budget, and a plan for evaluation.

The three levels of strategic, long-range, and program planning are not separate, stand-alone processes. Their interrelationships are depicted in Figure 3.4.

Organizational Operations

The third internal variable, organizational operations, requires regular review and examination of the programs and services offered as well as all support functions. Expectations for productivity, efficiency, effectiveness, and quality are established for each unit within the organization. Indicators are used to monitor each unit, division, or department to ensure that

FIGURE 3.4

Hierarchy of Planning

Source: Montana, P., & Charnov, B. (1993) *Management.* Hauppauge, NY: Barron's Educational Series. Adapted with permission from Barron's Educational Series, Inc.

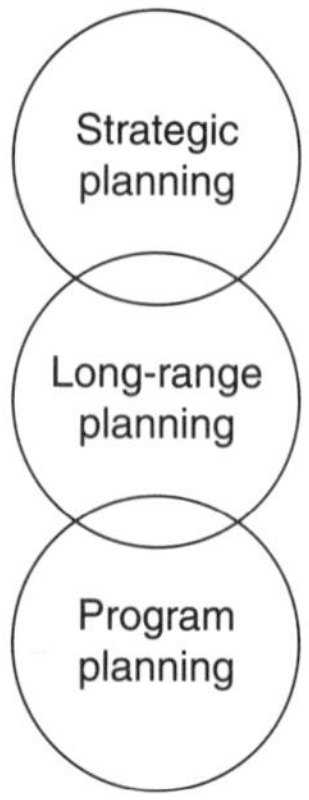

overall organizational performance is measuring up to expectations. This examination differs from program planning, discussed previously, in that it involves a monitoring of past and current activities rather than planning for the future. Program planning focuses on designing new or revising existing interventions. A review of program operations may examine such factors as program achievements in relation to program objectives, the adequacy of the data collection, reporting and evaluation systems, or efficient use of support staff.

■ CONSIDERATIONS

For Reviewing Organizational Operations

Basic Questions: What are the expected accomplishments of each unit within the organization, and to what extent is each unit achieving them?

Time Frame: Annual, with possible monthly, quarterly, or semiannual reports feeding into the review system.

Process: Supervisory and management personnel regularly review reports to ensure that all units are performing at acceptable levels. Possible management team meetings are periodically devoted to the review of all findings and a discussion of strengths and weaknesses. Summary report is made to the board.

Analysis: Depends on the department or unit. For programs, data analysis should focus on service provision and results achieved in relation to the plan. For human resources, data analysis should focus on compliance with the human resources plan. Similar criteria should be used from other departments or units.

Report: A detailed report should be prepared for management use. A summary report should be prepared for the executive and board. This may become part of the agency's annual report.

A sample outline for a program review report is included as Figure 3.5.

Human Resources

The term *human resources* has replaced the term *personnel* over the years and refers to the many functions that are involved in the supervision and management of the organization's employees and volunteers. Sound planning for the recruitment, hiring, and retention of staff requires a working knowledge of human resources law. Agency employees responsible for supervision, management, and administration must at least understand the general parameters of laws governing affirmative action and equal employment opportunity to ensure that agency policies, procedures, and practices operate in compliance with the law. For a more detailed and current understanding of day-to-day changes in the law, in policy, or in legal precedent, it is advisable to retain a consulting attorney who specializes in human resources law. Agency policies and practices should be reviewed periodically by an expert in human resources law in order to ensure that they are responsive to the ever-changing legal requirements.

The human resources planning process begins at the point of examining organizational operations and determining what job functions are needed to accomplish long-range and program goals and objectives. This analysis enables the manager to determine what types

FIGURE 3.5

Sample Program Review Report

Program Review Report		
Program _____	Quarter _____	
	This Quarter	To Date This Fiscal Year
1. Dollars expended	_____	_____
2. Percentage of dollars expended	_____	_____
3. Number of clients served	_____	_____
4. Number of units of service provided	_____	_____
5. Mean number of units of service per client	_____	_____
6. Cost per unit of service	_____	_____
Additional items might focus on achievement of program objectives, number of clients completing service, number of successful client outcomes, and other program-related issues.		

of staff with what types of education and experiences are needed to meet expectations. The human resources planning process then continues by having a job analysis (a document that requires specification of responsibilities and tasks, knowledge and skills required, and results expected) prepared for each position. Working from the job analysis, job descriptions are written. Policies and procedures are then prepared for the recruitment, selection, and hiring of employees and volunteers; for supervision, training, and development of employees and volunteers; for performance appraisal, promotion, retention; and, if necessary, termination. Each of these elements of the human resources planning process will be discussed in detail in later chapters in this book.

■ CONSIDERATIONS

For Reviewing Human Services Planning

Basic Questions: What job functions are necessary to achieve organizational and program goals and objectives? Are positions filled with people qualified to carry out these functions? Are personnel policies and procedures in compliance with the law? Does staff reflect ethnic, gender, and age diversity?

Time Frame: This review should be conducted on an annual basis.

Process: The person(s) responsible for human resources functions within the agency should lead the review. Input and participation should come from the executive, the board's personnel committee, managers, supervisors, and staff.

Analysis: Profiles of staff should be prepared that reflect the ideal in terms of education, experience, demographics, knowledge, skills, and personal characteristics. A profile of currently employed staff should be compared to the ideal.

Report: A report should be prepared for the executive and the board, including an assessment of strengths, weaknesses, and opportunities in human resources planning for the agency, together with recommendations about how to move toward the ideal overall staff profile. Parts of this report could also become part of the agency's annual report.

Technological Resources

Technological resources include the equipment and expertise needed to carry out the professional and technical work of the organization. In the field of human services professional work generally includes all of the therapeutic interventions used within the agency. Technological resources can include support and consulting services, computer resources, financial management expertise, marketing and public relations expertise, and other technologies that may be used to support the work of the organization. Because of the wide variety of disciplines often represented, it is advisable to involve staff in identifying and planning for the use of technology. Professional staff, for example, should be expected to keep up with all the changes in scaling devices for measuring client progress. They should also be current on research in the field as published in professional journals and made available on the Internet. Staff responsible for program evaluation should be aware of software available that can be used to aggregate and analyze data.

A successful manager will keep a current inventory of technological resources needed and compare it to those on hand. Facilities and equipment should be monitored in terms of their age and condition. Purchase or lease of new facilities and equipment should be a regular part of the budget planning process. Staff development and training may also be considered a part of the process of updating technological resources. It is also useful to follow up after new equipment has been purchased or leased, or training has been completed, to determine whether it is being used and meets expectations. Where possible, technological resources should be evaluated in terms of their impact on the workload and achievement of program goals and objectives.

■ C O N S I D E R A T I O N S

For Assessing Technological Resources

Basic Questions: Is the agency using state-of-the-art technology? Does it need state-of-the-art technology? Does the use of outdated technology impact the productivity, efficiency, effectiveness, or quality of services provided? Can the agency afford new technology? Will it be used?

Time Frame: This process should be ongoing, with a running log or tally of existing technological equipment and other resources available to compare to newly emerging technologies.

Process: The business manager or other designated person should regularly survey all levels of staff to determine what problems, if any, are created by outdated equipment and what new equipment is recommended.

Analysis: The business manager and other management staff should evaluate how new equipment will be used to improve the productivity, efficiency, effectiveness, or quality of services.

Report: Requests for new equipment determined by management staff to be needed should be submitted to the executive for consideration, along with all the necessary specifications and costs associated with its purchase and use.

Financial Resources

An assessment of financial resources requires a careful examination of budget documents to determine where the funding is coming from and what obligations the agency assumes in accepting funding from each of the various sources. Budget documents produced by the business manager will regularly report the status of income and expenditures so that the executive, the board, and agency managers are current on available financial resources. It is useful to know, for example, for each line item, what proportion of the budget has been spent as compared to the proportion of the fiscal year that has elapsed.

It is also important to utilize details of program performance, such as the number of units of service provided, the number of clients who completed the program, and the number of clients who achieved outcome objectives. These factors can be tied into program cost dollars and used to calculate costs per unit of service and other useful cost-efficiency and cost-effectiveness factors. A variety of indicators have been developed over the years that help to measure efficiency, effectiveness, and productivity, and regular monitoring throughout the year can provide early warning indicators that problems may be emerging. These measures will be discussed in detail in a later chapter on budgeting.

■ C O N S I D E R A T I O N S

For Examining Financial Resources

Basic Questions: What are the sources of financial support for the agency? What untapped sources exist? To what extent are resources being used in cost-efficient and cost-effective ways?

Time Frame: Financial resources should be monitored on a regular basis by the business or financial manager.

Process: Financial and other useful data should be fed into the office of the business manager on a regular basis. Data should be compiled in a way that is useful to management, executive, and board.

Analysis: Performance indicators should be combined with financial data to calculate cost per unit, cost per client completion, and cost per outcome for all programs.

Report: Comparative data should be provided to managers, executive, and board on a monthly basis, with a more detailed annual report that is used to compare financial and performance data to preceding years.

Figure 3.6 illustrates the components of the internal environment and the ways in which they interact with each other.

■ System Integrity and the Fit of Internal Environment to External Environment

The value and importance to managers of understanding these systems cannot be overstated. For a newly appointed manager, understanding where the agency stands in relation to all the components discussed is similar in some ways to a wilderness guide getting his or her bearings before taking a group of tourists into the wild. In both instances decisions

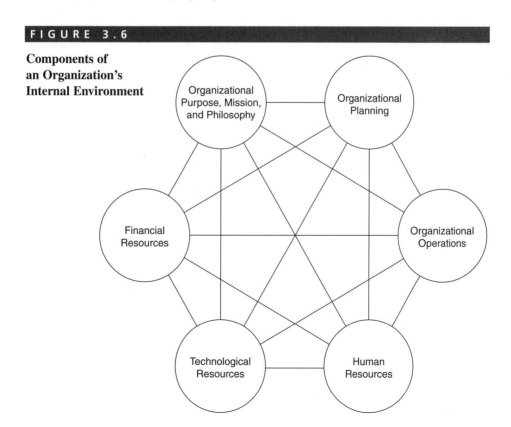

FIGURE 3.6

Components of an Organization's Internal Environment

are complex and should be based on knowledge and information. In both instances people are dependent on their leader to provide informed guidance. And in both instances, a successful journey will require a team effort and full participation under the guidance of a trusted and knowledgeable leader or guide.

Knowledge about external and internal environments of an organization is basic to good management. An understanding of the external environment, including the economic, sociological, political, and technological domains, will enable a manager to work skillfully with funders, clients, referral sources, community representatives and decision makers, and those with technical expertise to put the agency in the best possible position to succeed. Understanding the internal components, including organizational purpose, planning, operations, human resources, technological resources, and financial resources, will put a manager in the best position to make informed decisions that will strengthen agency performance.

Once these systems are understood, the next challenge is to ensure that they are all operating in a way that is, first, consistent within the organization and, second, consistent in interactions between the organization and its environment. Internally, the agency's mission and purpose are the organizing theme. All internal systems should reflect the agency's commitment to its mission and purpose.

A family counseling agency, for example, may have as its mission "To strengthen families in a way that family members individually are able to achieve their potential in their physical, intellectual, emotional, and social growth and development, and that the family as a whole behaves in a way that is mutually supportive." If the agency is to maintain an internal consistency, then its strategic plan will focus on ways to strengthen individuals and families. Current programs will be designed to enhance individual functioning as well as to promote the family as a nurturing resource. The human resource system will focus on recruiting, selecting, hiring, rewarding, and promoting those staff members who perform at the highest levels in a way that is consistent with the mission. The technological and financial resources will be allocated in a way that reflects a commitment to the mission. If all of these subsystems are working in harmony, then the agency will have taken its first step toward the achievement of excellence.

The second step will involve ensuring that the organization is well synchronized with its external environment. Ongoing assessments of community needs and client satisfaction will help the agency to determine whether its services continue to be relevant to individual and family needs. A thorough examination of priorities for funding sources and political decision-making bodies will help the agency to understand the fit of its mission, purpose, and goals to what community leaders say they need and expect. Staying on the cutting edge of developing technology and professional expertise will keep the agency in a leadership position in the provision of services.

The focus of these efforts for the manager is consistency, or what might be called system integrity. The work of human service agencies is so important and so physically and intellectually demanding that they cannot afford to expend energy and resources working at cross-purposes.

Funding and community support can fluctuate greatly over time. Someone within the organization needs to be designated to keep a finger on the pulse of local, state, and federal agendas to determine what the program and funding priorities will be over the next three to five years. Agency priorities and plans need to be reviewed to ensure that the agency's plans are consistent with community needs. All systems must be examined for consistency with the external environment.

It should also be noted, however, that setting policy, program, and funding priorities is not a one-way street. Staff of social service agencies who work with clients are well positioned to observe the needs and problems of clients and community members. When programs and services are poorly designed, when there are critical gaps in a continuum of services, or when services have a detrimental effect on clients, decision makers will not necessarily be aware of these factors if there is no advocacy from human service agencies. Jansson (1994) argues that advocating for vulnerable populations not only offers a more relevant and realistic approach to the resolution of certain types of problems, but it is also a moral obligation for professionals, for the following reasons:

> First, all professionals are morally obligated to advance clients' beneficence. Second, they cannot do so without policy-sensitive and policy-related practice. Third, we can make moral judgments about all professionals' work on the basis of acts of commission (such as lying to a client) and omission (such as not using policy-sensitive and policy-related practice). (p. 38)

A forum for systematic feedback from all levels of staff, combined with training in policy practice and organizing community-wide task forces around issues, can help to ensure that appropriate advocacy is taking place and important feedback destined for community, state, or federal-level decision makers is not being ignored.

Internally, all components of the organization need to be constantly reevaluated for their internal consistency among planning, programs, services, human resources, and support services. In an ideal organizational world, frontline staff will be in harmony with supervisors on the design and functioning of all these components. Supervisors, in turn, will be in harmony with managers, executives, and board. There will be shared vision, commitment to resolution of the problems faced by the target populations served, and support for high levels of productivity, efficiency, effectiveness, and quality. If that harmony does not exist within and among these subsystems, points of conflict need to be addressed. If it does exist, the organization has at least the fundamental qualities necessary for achieving excellence. Finding ways to promote internal consistency and integrity will be the subject of the remaining chapters of this book.

SUMMARY

1. **What Is a Systems Perspective?** A single action can affect many parts of the organization. Awareness and anticipation of potential impact of actions are important.

2. **Understanding the External Environment.** Factors in an organization's immediate or task environment should be assessed.
   - *Economic Factors.* Funding sources, noncash revenues, clients and consumers, supplies, and competitors should all be assessed.

- *Sociological Factors.* Community demographics, community problems and needs, and the available labor pool should all be assessed.
- *Political/Professional Factors.* Regulations, political climate, and professional expectations should all be assessed.
- *Technological Factors.* New technology and new practice models should be explored.

3. **Understanding the Internal Environment.** A number of internal components need to be understood, as well as their fit with other components and their impact on each other and the whole organization.
   - *Organizational Purpose, Mission, and Philosophy.* Well-run organizations should have a mission and philosophy that permeate all aspects of the organization.
   - *Organizational Planning.* Strategic, long-range, and program planning overlap and interact.
   - *Organizational Operations.* The functioning of each department, program, and unit should be periodically reviewed.
   - *Human Resources.* Human resources functions should be summarized and reported on annually and assessed for their internal consistency.
   - *Technological Resources.* All departments, programs, and units within the organization should stay on top of and incorporate the latest technology.
   - *Financial Resources.* Financial data should be compiled and used to create performance indicators.

4. **System Integrity and the Fit of Internal Environment to External Environment.** All systems should be designed to fit well with each other and with the external environment.

EXERCISES

Please complete the following sections of your manual based on the content covered in Chapter 3.

Section 3: Organizational Systems and Subsystems

3.1 Mission Statement. Write a mission statement for your organization.

3.2 Internal Consistency. Write a statement of philosophy about the organization's commitment to internal consistency and compatibility of its systems and subsystems. Include a statement about the use of the mission statement as the standard by which consistency will be determined.

3.3 The External (Task) Environment. Identify those elements of the task environment that the agency will track in some way in order for the agency to be able to monitor current developments and issues.

3.4 Internal Components. Identify the major internal components of the agency and specify the ways in which compatibility will be ensured in their interactions.

REFERENCES

Brody, R. (1993). *Effectively managing human service organizations.* Newbury Park, CA: Sage.

Dill, W. (1958). Environment as an influence on managerial autonomy. *Administrative Science Quarterly, 2* (March), 409–443.

Jansson, B. (1994). *Social policy: From theory to policy practice* (2nd ed.). Pacific Grove, CA: Brooks-Cole.

Kettner, P., & Martin, L. (1987). *Purchase of service contracting.* Newbury Park, CA: Sage.

Kettner, P., Moroney, R., & Martin, L. (1999). *Designing and managing programs: An effectiveness-based approach* (2nd ed.). Thousand Oaks, CA: Sage.

Martin, L., & Kettner, P. (1996). *Measuring the performance of human service programs.* Thousand Oaks, CA: Sage.

Martin, P. (1980). Multiple constituencies, dominant societal values, and the human service administrator. *Administration in Social Work, 4*(2), 15–27.

Miles, R. (1975). *Theories of management: Implications for organizational behavior and development.* New York: McGraw-Hill.

Montana, P., & Charnov, B. (1993). *Management.* Hauppauge, NY: Barron's Educational Series.

National Network for Social Work Managers. (1994). *Platform.* Washington, DC: Author.

Netting, F., Kettner, P., & McMurtry, S. (1998). *Social work macro practice* (2nd ed.). New York: Longman.

Peters, T., & Waterman, R. (1982). *In search of excellence: Lessons for America's best-run companies.* New York: Harper & Row.

Thompson, J. (1967). *Organizations in action.* New York: McGraw-Hill.

CHAPTER 4

Using Structure to Facilitate and Support Achievement of the Agency's Mission

CHAPTER OBJECTIVES

Upon completion of this chapter, the reader will be able to:

- Give examples of how structure affects the day-to-day work of the organization.
- Present options for the formal structure of an organization and provide a rationale for a proposed optimum structure.
- Present options for an informal structure of an organization, select an option for a specific organization, and provide a rationale for the proposed informal structure.
- Explain the role of a board of directors and how the board works with the executive.
- Develop a board matrix for an organization.

Assumptions

- That structure can be adapted to the function of an organization, and an optimum structure can be determined.
- That a formal, hierarchical structure is necessary to clarify formal relationships.
- That options are available for an informal structure, and creating informal working relationships can improve overall organizational functioning.
- That planned selection of a diverse board of directors can contribute to both board and organizational effectiveness.

FIGURE 4.1

Organizational Chart for a Human Service Agency

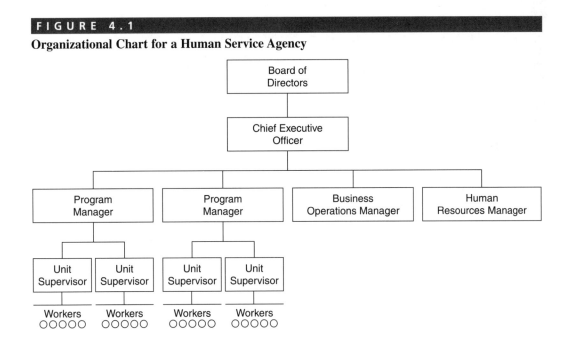

The Importance of Structure

It is almost a given that when an organization sets out to develop a structure through which it will conduct its business, the organizational chart will reflect some form of hierarchical structure, with boxes depicting positions and lines indicating channels for reporting and supervision. The box at the top designates the board or policy-making group. The next level represents the chief executive officer (CEO) or president. The third level from the top depicts the ways in which the organization subdivides itself, and program managers or persons with some comparable title occupy those positions. The program level typically includes programs that provide services to clients but may also include such departments as business operations or human resources. Under the programs that provide services there may be a number of units under each program manager, with each unit headed by a supervisor who is responsible for anywhere from five to ten line workers. Figure 4.1 illustrates such an organizational chart.

As we have seen from our review of the management literature, structure is an extremely important variable in determining the tone and substance of day-to-day functioning and, ultimately, has a lot to do with organizational progress toward the achievement of mission and goals. Once the structural framework for an organization is established, it defines the ways in which other functions will be carried out. For example, organizational structure can determine any or all of these factors:

- The focus of work and the extent to which an employee can use his or her independent expertise and judgment.
- Locus of responsibility; who is responsible and who will be held accountable for what types of accomplishments.

- Supervision and direction, including who will do performance appraisals and determine such factors as merit increases and promotions.
- The lines of communication; who communicates with whom about what issues.
- The extent of participation in agency planning and decision making.
- The extent to which a particular employee or unit can have an impact on organizational mission and goals.

In the following sections the ways in which structure affects each of these areas of organizational life are explored.

The Focus of Work

Many who have graduated from professional programs and have received an advanced degree often go into the workplace with the expectation that they will be able to make extensive use of their newly gained knowledge and skill. However, some discover that workloads are structured in such a way that the newly hired employee finds herself in a unit that focuses exclusively on intake or some other area of specialization. This may mean that, instead of using counseling skills, she finds that the focus of her work is on helping clients to complete applications, reviewing documentation that establishes eligibility, and entering data into the agency's computerized information system. Or another worker, determined to hold out for a position in which he will work more intensively with troubled families finds that he is in a unit in which the focus of the work is case management. Perhaps the counseling is contracted out to community professionals in private practice. The ways in which these agencies choose to structure themselves may be perfectly logical and efficient. The point is that structure will affect the focus of the work.

The Locus of Responsibility

When Weber (1947) created the fundamental principles of bureaucracy, he conceptualized what he called an "office." His use of the term did not refer to a place with a desk, a telephone, and a file cabinet but rather to a collection of responsibilities that belong to a position within the organization, regardless of who occupies that position. Within most organizations today, there is an expectation that the person who holds a position will be held accountable for performing the functions that accompany that position in a way that is legally, ethically, and professionally responsible. The lines in the organizational chart make clear the superceding levels of responsibility and authority. Structure often determines what responsibilities are to be allocated to what units and positions, and the extent of the authority and resources available to fulfill assigned functions.

Take, for example, a professional social worker working in a unit that provides case management services to children with mental health problems and needs. The case manager assesses and screens client families and then refers them as needed to a managed care system that allows a maximum of six visits with a psychiatrist or psychologist. Few mental health problems can be effectively resolved within that time frame, and the case manager finds that client families are often worse after treatment than they were before because they are discouraged about the lack of progress. Who is held accountable for ensuring appropriate and adequate services to clients? Clearly, responsibility belongs with the source(s) of funding and allocation of resources, but in many instances, the case manager's work is monitored and evaluated in terms of his or her "success rate" with clients. In this example, however, there is little control over the resources necessary for success. This is not entirely an issue of structure, but it does play a role in allocating responsibility and establishing expectations for accountability.

Supervision

Almost everyone who has been employed knows something about the importance of one's immediate supervisor to the quality of work life. A supervisor who is interested in his or her employees' growth and development and is supportive and positive can make life at work a pleasant experience. On the other hand, a supervisor who is threatened by a subordinate's competence and blocks movement or promotion within the organization can make life at work miserable. Although much of supervision has to do with style and personal competence, some is determined by structure. Some organizations are structured in a way that the supervisor has almost dictatorial powers over his or her subordinates. Under this type of structure there are few meaningful avenues of appeal. There are, however, alternative ways of structuring that do more to ensure that employees' talents and energies are focused on accomplishing the job and working toward the achievement of mission and goals. Creative use of structure can help to ensure that staff are not limited in their effectiveness by an overly controlling and possibly vindictive supervisor.

Lines of Communication

Ask most top-level executives for their opinions about the effectiveness of communication in their organizations and many will respond that they think that it's great—they send out many memos and notices every day in the interest of keeping their employees informed. Ask lower-level line staff, and they may well have a very different opinion.

Many studies have explored the relationship between organizational structure and the flow of communication (Kahn & Kram, 1994; Marsden, Cook, & Kalleberg, 1996). It is not unusual to find that much information gets filtered out of the system before it gets from top to bottom or bottom to top. In many cases little of the original message reaches its intended destination. The greater the number of levels in the structure, the more likely that information will be filtered out. Staff concerns about communication tend not so much to be about top-down information but rather about bottom-up communication. When organizations are rigidly structured with many levels, a number of individuals occupying supervisory and management positions will have the opportunity to decide that a message is not important enough to be passed on up the chain of command. If not designed with communication in mind, structure can act as a major barrier to intraorganizational communication.

Extent of Participation

Structure can also either limit or facilitate participation in decision making. At one extreme, decisions can be made at the top and passed down the chain of command for implementation without soliciting staff input. A second option is to send out written descriptions of decisions being considered and provide an opportunity for written feedback from anyone who wishes to provide it, within a certain time frame. A third option is to encourage staff to initiate ideas and send them upward through the system. In instances in which there is little or no direct contact between management and line staff, it is not unusual to find that there is little staff input into the creation of policies and procedures or into the decisions made by the organization.

Organizations committed to high levels of productivity, efficiency, effectiveness, and quality will attempt to structure themselves in a way that facilitates full participation in decision making on those decisions that affect the quality or quantity of work performed. Agency structure can make a difference in terms of the opportunities that are provided for full staff interaction around important work-related and productivity-related issues.

Impact on Accomplishment of Organizational Goals

Finally, structure can influence the extent to which individuals and units feel that they have an important role in working toward the achievement of mission and goals. For example, an agency provides services to individuals with the goal of helping them to become economically self-sufficient. In its early efforts to help clients, the agency structured itself around process: one unit for intake and screening, a second unit for locating temporary shelter, a third unit handled referrals for substance abuse, and a fourth dealt with job placement. Over time, it was discovered that worker productivity and morale were low because it was difficult for workers to see a relationship between their daily tasks and the achievement of program goals and objectives.

In this type of situation a restructuring effort might allow each worker to participate in offering the full range of services from intake through training and ultimately job placement to clients in his or her caseload. Under the initial structure, workers felt only marginally involved in helping the clients move toward self-sufficiency. After the restructuring, each worker had the opportunity to work with clients from beginning to end, ultimately being responsible for placing them in jobs and helping them to achieve a stable, self-sufficient lifestyle.

The point in examining structure is that decisions about structure are critical to organizational functioning. Structure can affect a wide range of issues that have an impact on day-to-day work life as well as on progress toward the achievement of mission and goals. There are many structural options available. Decisions should be based on a knowledge of alternatives examined in the light of what type of structure will provide the best opportunity to achieve the agency's mission, goals, and objectives.

■ Structural Alternatives

A number of options are available to managers contemplating decisions about structure or restructure. One of the first questions to be answered is how the work is to be divided and subdivided. Once the work is conceptually separated into divisions, these divisions then can be used to create an organizational structure. This structure is typically depicted as a formal organizational chart with boxes that establish offices and lines that establish hierarchy and chain of command. A second set of questions has to do with the actual working relationships of units and staff members. These can be depicted in an informal organizational chart that may use a variety of symbols to define work relationships, areas of responsibility, and lines of accountability. Ways of depicting both formal and informal organizational charts will be addressed in the following sections.

■ The Formal Organizational Chart

The formal organizational chart as adapted to human service agencies can be used to divide the work of the agency in a number of ways. A variety of terms has been used to describe the various divisions within an organization (e.g., *division, department, program, unit*). To describe the first set of subdivisions we will use the term *department* and will consider the options of departmentalization by (1) program, (2) function, (3) process, (4) market, (5) consumer/client, or (6) geographical area (Montana & Charnov, 1993).

Each of these will be discussed in the following sections. The reader should bear in mind that departmentalization does not apply only to large organizations. A small agency with only five or six employees could have several departments, with each person devoting a portion of time to two or more departments. Departmentalization is a conceptual tool, not simply a way of depicting the number of positions within an organization. Decisions about how to subdivide the work of an agency will depend on the nature of services provided, populations served, location of the agency, and other factors.

Departmentalization by Program

One of the most common organizational structures in human service agencies is departmentalization by program. The term *program* refers to services clustered around a special population and problem, such as a teen-pregnancy program, a drug-counseling program, or an adoptions program. When specialized knowledge and skill about a particular type of problem or client are needed, departmentalization by program is often the option of choice. Family service agencies typically divide the work into a foster-care program, an adoption program, and a family-counseling program. Foster care may be further subdivided into units that focus on recruitment of foster homes, casework with children in foster care, and perhaps training and supportive services for foster parents. Behavioral health agencies likewise are often divided into programs dealing with drugs, alcohol, and mental health. This type of division allows staff to specialize in selected interventions and to become knowledgeable about other community services and resources available to this population. Departmentalization by program is illustrated in Figure 4.2.

Departmentalization by Function

When departmentalization by function is selected as the structural option, technical expertise provides the rationale for division of labor. Departments typically include operations, marketing, finance, and human resources. Operations has responsibility for producing the product

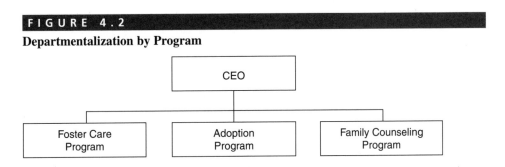

FIGURE 4.2

Departmentalization by Program

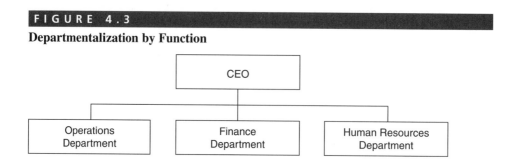

FIGURE 4.3
Departmentalization by Function

or delivering the service for which the organization was created. The other departments market and distribute the product or provide support services to employees and to operations.

Applied to human services, this concept of departmentalization by function might be used in some very large agencies in which an operations department would be responsible for clinical services, a business management department would oversee all financial matters including contract compliance, and a human resources department would deal with all matters relating to staff development, training, certification, and other such responsibilities. It is also possible to subdivide the operations department function. An agency, for example, that focused on workforce development for long-term unemployed people might divide the services into outreach, transportation, child care, counseling, prejob training, skills training, and job placement, even though all these services fall under the heading of one department. Departmentalization by function is depicted in Figure 4.3.

Departmentalization by Process

A third structural alternative is to divide the work by process. This is used when special skills or technical expertise are organized in terms of the chronology of the helping process. In child protection work, for example, the first contact with the client family often comes unsolicited when a worker informs the family that a child abuse report has been filed against the family. This position requires a great deal of tact as well as the ability to inform and educate the parents as to their rights and obligations under the law. This is a very different kind of relationship from that of the worker who then attempts to help the family to deal with its problems. For this reason, many child protection agencies divide the work by process, with one unit taking responsibility for intake, a second unit for ongoing clinical and court-related work, and perhaps a third unit of specialists who focus on termination and transition to community-based resources. Departmentalization by process is also often used when there is a fairly elaborate admission and screening process that requires a good deal of professional and technical knowledge and skill. One department focuses on intake and screening, others on various types of counseling services. The strength of this model is that each phase of the helping process has its own set of experts. The weakness is that clients change workers and lose continuity in their relationships with workers. Departmentalization by process is depicted in Figure 4.4.

Departmentalization by Market

When the need is to provide better services to selected markets, departmentalization by market is the option of choice. Some types of human service agencies, such as residential

FIGURE 4.4

Departmentalization by Process

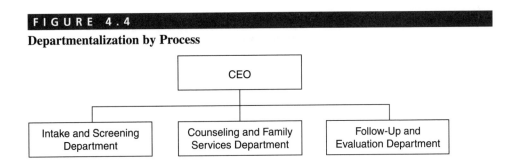

treatment centers, for example, rely heavily on referrals from various entities within the community. Because keeping beds full is critical to the survival of the centers, they often find that it is in their interest to structure themselves in a way that caters, to some extent, to their referral sources. The bulk of referrals may come from the state department of social services, from the state department of juvenile corrections, and various school districts. Each referral source may have a complex set of criteria, procedures, and funding sources that require specialized knowledge and expertise on the part of the admitting and treatment staff of the residential treatment center.

Referral agencies may find it frustrating if they have to deal each time with a different worker who is unfamiliar with their policies, procedures, and expectations. To prevent this problem, and to provide workers who are knowledgeable about each referral source, the center may elect to allocate certain beds and to designate certain staff to work exclusively with selected referral sources and the clients who are referred. This type of departmentalization might also be used by a health plan that markets its products to corporations, to universities, and to government agencies. Division of work by specializing in certain types of organizations is called departmentalization by market and is illustrated in Figure 4.5.

Departmentalization by Consumer/Client

Sometimes the types of clients served and the problems they are experiencing are different enough in nature that it makes sense to divide the departments by client. Many who provide services for the homeless, for example, have discovered that the needs of single men and single women are more effectively addressed in separate programs, and that homeless families represent a third client group with unique needs. This structure might also be used in a program that serves the elderly, in which one department might deal with victims of Alzheimer's

FIGURE 4.5

Departmentalization by Market

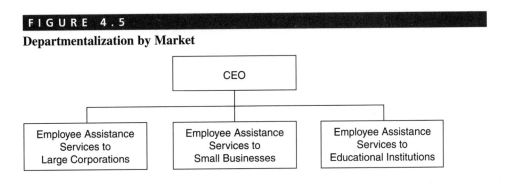

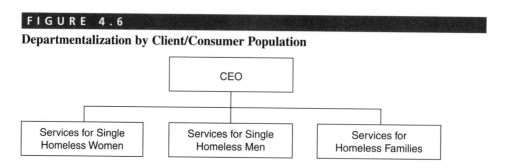

FIGURE 4.6

Departmentalization by Client/Consumer Population

disease who need constant care and supervision, one department might deal with those clients who have health care or nutrition needs, and a third department might deal with those interested in socialization and recreation. This type of division of work has the advantage of clustering similar types of clients with similar types of problems and needs and lends itself to logical group and community types of interventions. This approach to structure is referred to as departmentalization by consumer or client and is illustrated in Figure 4.6.

Departmentalization by Geographic Area

A sixth option, departmentalization by geographic area, is used when the area served is large enough that access to services is an important issue. This structure is commonly used by large agencies with branch offices. Responsibility is divided by establishing geographic boundaries for each office, and having each branch office provide all the services available within those boundaries. Following this model, branch or district offices often have their own budgets, staff, facilities, and equipment. They may also have the flexibility to determine needs within their boundaries and design services that are responsive to the local community. The primary advantage of departmentalization by geographic area is that it improves access to services. People in need are often not in a position to travel great distances to a central office. A local office in which the staff know the neighborhood is often in a position to provide more personalized and better-quality service. When departmentalization by geographic area is used by a parent organization, all the smaller local offices still must choose a structural option as they divide the work within their boundaries. Departmentalization by geographic area is illustrated in Figure 4.7.

Creative use of structure can be one of the most powerful tools available to the manager and administrator. When a unit or an employee is unproductive, there can be many causes, but one cause could be boredom with performing the same routines over and over

FIGURE 4.7

Departmentalization by Geographic Area

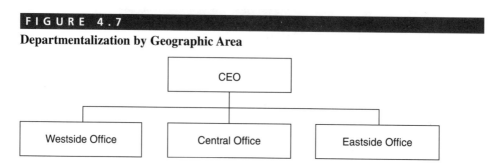

for many years. Hackman and Suttle (1977) point out that restructuring work alters the basic relationship between a person and what he or she does on the job. "When all the outer layers are stripped away," they say, "many organizational problems come to rest at the interface between people and the tasks they do" (p. 100).

Terminating unproductive employees is a time-consuming and emotionally trying undertaking. Hiring and training employees is expensive. Restructuring is a tool that can be used to put employees in new and different relationships to each other and to their work and has the potential to reenergize the whole organization.

The Informal Organizational Chart: Introducing Flexibility into the Organizational Structure

As we have seen throughout the development of management theory and research, many of the most productive organizations have been able to find creative alternatives to traditional structures that allow for more flexibility and teamwork. In some types of organizations, we have learned, the highest levels of productivity have been achieved when workers and/or teams are held accountable for results, when information is widely shared, and when structure is fluid and responds to organizational mission and program purpose.

Matrix Organizations

The kinds of structures that are flexible and responsive can all be categorized under the heading of matrix organizations. Matrix organizations are characterized by employees having more than one immediate supervisor. The structural innovation is based on the premise that in order to perform at an optimal level of productivity, employees often need expertise that comes from more than one person or discipline.

A frequent example used to illustrate the logic of a matrix structure comes from a medical or state mental hospital. Hospitals typically are divided into wards. In a medical hospital it may be by illness (e.g., oncology) or by age grouping (e.g., pediatrics). Likewise a state hospital may be divided by age or gender. Each ward in a state hospital typically includes a number of professional disciplines: psychiatry, nursing, psychology, social work, and psychiatric technicians. Because it is important that all staff on each ward work as a team, a team leader is commonly appointed who carries the administrative responsibilities, including supervision of the work of the staff on the ward. However, for most professional disciplines, there is an expectation that people with the same education and professional knowledge, skill, and values will provide supervision and/or consultation for those within their profession (e.g., physicians supervising physicians, psychologists supervising psychologists, etc.).

The solution to this dilemma is the matrix organization, in which the work that affects the patients and other team members on the ward is supervised (although usually in a consultative manner) by the team leader on the ward. This person organizes patient staffings and ensures that administrative directives from hospital management are promulgated throughout the ward. However, for each employee, professional growth and development, including performance appraisal, are the responsibilities of a designated person within the hospital system who is from the same profession. This type of structure is illustrated in Figure 4.8.

FIGURE 4.8

Matrix Management Model as Applied to a Psychiatric Hospital

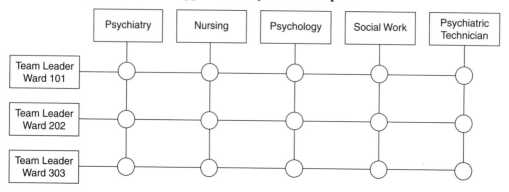

No organizational structure is perfect. The strict bureaucratic, hierarchical design has the strength and simplicity of one and only one supervisor and a clear chain of command but lacks flexibility. Matrix designs introduce flexibility but introduce the complexity of multiple supervisors, each of whom could conceivably make conflicting demands on an employee.

Davis and Lawrence (1978) describe some of the problems that emerge in matrix organizations. One of the most common problems has to do with the use of power and authority. Optimum use of matrix structures requires an attitude of collaboration. If one or more supervisors are determined to exercise their power and authority to their limits, the organization will consume a great deal of valuable energy in resolving internal conflicts. Another problem they describe by using the term *groupitis*. Some supervisors and managers see the essence of matrix management as being group decision making. This can lead to attempts to ensure that everyone affected has full and complete information on every issue, resulting in extended time lines before decisions can be reached. The nature of human services, including funding processes, is such that quick decisions must sometimes be made. Extensive pondering of all the variables and attempts to continuously extend the circle of involvement can lead to what Davis and Lawrence describe as decision strangulation, and they explain that it can make matrix management an expensive model of management. In short, introducing flexibility into the structure runs the risk of making the organization more complex, requiring more input for decisions, requiring more collaboration between and among supervisors, and in general adding time and costs to many day-to-day procedures. However, the benefits may well outweigh the costs if better decisions are made, if they are more widely supported throughout the organization, and if they prevent the alienation that so often accompanies a rigid, bureaucratic structure.

Raymond Miles (1975) introduced a number of matrix alternatives designed to provide greater flexibility in structuring an organization. He called them (1) the linking-pin structure, (2) the project team, and (3) the collegial model.

The Linking Pin

The linking pin is the most conservative departure from the traditional hierarchical structure. A linking pin allows the basic hierarchical structure to remain intact, while providing an overlay that depicts relationships that link selected positions. The linking pin is illustrated in Figure 4.9.

F I G U R E   4 . 9

The Linking-Pin Structure

(a) Vertical linkages

From: To:

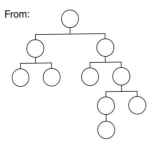
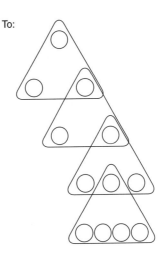

(b) Horizontal linkages

From: To:

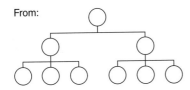
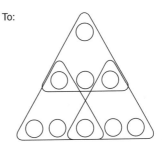

(c) Cross-departmental linkages

And finally to:

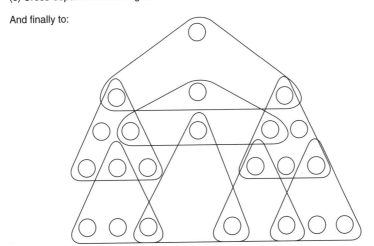

Source: Miles, R. (1975). *Theories of management.* New York: McGraw-Hill, p. 87. Reproduced with the permission of the McGraw-Hill Companies.

What this model does is to design into the structure a number of teams or units and to build in points at which the teams or units overlap. The triangle at the top represents a top-level management team. This team has responsibility for establishing organizational goals, objectives, and strategies and for monitoring and evaluating performance. The next level of triangles represents middle management in which program-level goals, objectives, and strategies are the focus of attention. Middle-level managers have the advantage of having been part of the team that deals with top-management concerns, thereby becoming the "linking pin" to the next level and ensuring that program goals are compatible with organizational goals and vice versa.

In addition, there are lateral linkages. A woman's shelter may have two major programs: residential and community. A staff member in the residential program who holds a linking-pin position would participate in all the discussions and decisions that affect the residential program and would be a full participant in the community program's meetings as well. This staff member is assigned responsibility to communicate between both programs, to ensure that policies, procedures, and practices are compatible and working collaboratively for the best interests of clients. Linking-pin structures work best in situations in which day-to-day communication between units and between levels of staff is necessary to optimum functioning.

The Project Team

The project team is designed to facilitate maximum independence in group or team performance within the organization while ensuring coordination and accountability. Project teams typically carry part of a responsibility for a larger whole. The process of putting a rocket into space, for example, might involve a design team, a manufacturing team, a quality-control team, and a documentation team. Each team has its own distinct responsibilities and can, at least to some extent, work independently of the other, as long as there is regular coordination in areas of overlap. Each team has a lead person who serves as a member of the overall project management team. This group functions as a sort of steering committee to ensure that all the phases of design, production, and implementation are coordinated. Contrast this very flexible structure to a hierarchical model in which each individual works for, reports to, and must get permission from a supervisor in order to move the project along. Rockets would rarely get off their launching pads if such a structure were used.

Project teams can be equally effective in human service organizations. A program designed to prepare unskilled and unemployed people for the job market might be subdivided into the following four teams:

- A screening, assessment, and skill-development team is made up of workers who do the initial intake; gather education, training, and employment history; and get applicants into appropriate skills training programs.
- A job-finding team is made up of workers who develop contacts with employers and take responsibility for job placement once the trainees are job-ready.
- An employment-skills-training team is made up of workers who teach basic job skills including résumé preparation and how to complete a job application, and who secure donations for such necessities as clothing and alarm clocks for trainees who are job-ready.

- An evaluation and problem-solving team is made up of workers who do periodic follow-up with employers to collect data for evaluation purposes. This team also helps the new employees to accommodate to their new work environment and to manage the pressure of work and home responsibilities.

The project team is illustrated in Figure 4.10.

What the project team structure does is to subdivide the overall program responsibility and create groups of people who can specialize in more narrowly focused areas. Each of these teams works relatively independently. The lead person from each team has responsibility for assuring that the overall program is being coordinated and that activities are monitored.

The Collegial Model

In organizations in which the collegial model is used, each person who is a part of the group or team holds the status of peer or colleague. All share management responsibilities equally or work out some type of rotation. This model is used to achieve maximum freedom and flexibility for individual partners or team members. For the collegial model to work effectively, each member must be able to operate independently and come together with other members to deal with matters that affect the entire group or team. Ideally, in the collegial model, each member should be able to generate his or her own income, so that primary responsibility is to one's clients or customers.

FIGURE 4.10

The Project Team Organizational Structure

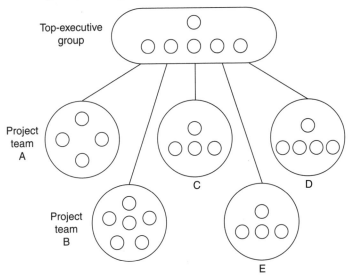

Source: Miles, R. (1975). *Theories of management.* New York: McGraw-Hill, p. 88. Reproduced with the permission of the McGraw-Hill Companies.

This model is most commonly used in situations in which a group of professionals (e.g., psychiatrist(s), psychologist(s), and/or social worker(s) in private practice) comes together for the purpose of setting up a clinic and sharing facilities and clerical staff. Each member is equally responsible to every other member to ensure that the overall work of the clinic is well run and no one has leadership or management responsibility. The primary advantage of the collegial model is that it permits independent functioning and decision making while supporting collaboration when it is needed.

The major drawback is that there is no individual accountability to ensure that the collective work of the organization is accomplished. Each person operates essentially as an entrepreneur. This is not compatible with the expectation of most human service organizations in which employees receive a salary and are expected to carry out tasks and responsibilities assigned by the agency. The collegial model is illustrated in Figure 4.11.

This model, although it provides a maximum of flexibility for the members, runs the highest risk in terms of performance and accountability. The model can be used in a university department, for example, in which each faculty member on the team carries a fair share of the workload. However, when one or more members choose not to participate in faculty meetings or carry their share of the organizational maintenance workload, the collegial model fails for lack of authority among peers to deal with deviant behavior.

The collegial model may work effectively in a human service organization under special circumstances. In an organization in which professional personnel are employed and each member carries her or his own caseload, for example, a modified collegial design could be utilized. Responsibility for working out the details of collaboration is assigned to a team of professionals. The unit or team, then, is given a set of responsibilities, including assigning cases to the team and holding team members accountable for assessment and

---

FIGURE 4.11

The Collegial Form of Organizational Structure

Source: Miles, R. (1975). *Theories of management.* New York: McGraw-Hill, p. 89. Reproduced with the permission of the McGraw-Hill Companies.

Manager or professional

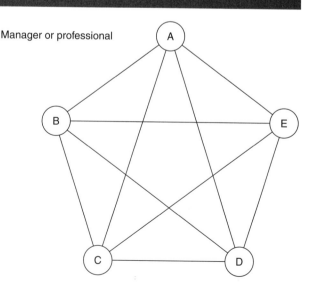

screening, treatment, monitoring, evaluation, and termination. Work is assigned in accordance with the system designed by the team.

The accountability issue can be addressed by having the team conduct peer evaluations, which are then used as a basis for decisions about salary increases, promotions, and other personnel actions. If used within an organization, a lead person is designated, but functions primarily as a consultant or facilitator to ensure that the team carries out its responsibilities.

Mixed-Matrix Options

Any of the foregoing models can be used in conjunction with others. Even within a hierarchical, bureaucratic structure, it is possible to introduce elements of linking pin, project team, or collegial models. There may be instances in which one department or division is set up as a project team while another division in the same organization must, for purposes of accountability, operate according to highly structured rules with specific tasks assigned to each employee.

As more and more agencies respond to demands for program evaluation, for example, it is not unusual to find various forms of matrix management techniques used to facilitate evaluation design and implementation. Workers are assigned for part of their time to regular clinical responsibilities. For several hours each week, however, they serve on a project team to design and implement a plan for data collection and ongoing evaluation of program effectiveness. For the clinical responsibilities the worker has a clinical supervisor. For the evaluation responsibilities, the worker may be part of a unit that is structured around the project team or collegial models. The mixed-matrix option depicted in Figure 4.12 is built around a project team structure, in which each team uses a different team structure, and interteam linkages are represented by dotted lines.

FIGURE 4.12

A Mixed Matrix Operating within the Framework of a Project Team

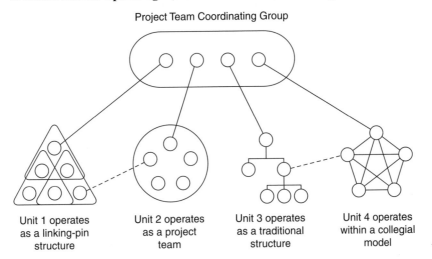

Project Team Coordinating Group

Unit 1 operates as a linking-pin structure

Unit 2 operates as a project team

Unit 3 operates as a traditional structure

Unit 4 operates within a collegial model

■ Working with Both Formal and Informal Structures

The mixed-matrix models discussed in the foregoing sections rarely, if ever, appear on a formal organizational chart. Formal charts are used to depict to interested groups and individuals the formal chain of command within the organization. Formal charts are typically a part of contract or grant applications. They are made available to funding sources and other interested parties on demand. These individuals or organizations usually are not interested in the details of day-to-day organizational functioning and communication. Understanding levels of management and administration, division of labor through departmentalization, and unit structure within programs will usually satisfy those who have an interest in an organizational chart.

The informal chart is a tool that can be used internally to increase the flexibility of how staff relate to and work with each other in the interest of achieving organizational and program mission, goals, and objectives in the most efficient and effective way possible. Organizations should be structured in a way that ensures that form will follow function. Primary consideration should be given to the work to be done. Structures should be created to provide the best possible opportunities to achieve success in terms of productivity, efficiency, effectiveness, and quality. Alternative, creative structures should be used when they offer a design for working relationships that is superior to the traditional, hierarchical model.

Achieving excellence is a complex process. Creating optimum structures requires that managers be skilled in translating mission and goals into practice expectations and determining what kinds of freedom, flexibility, consultation, supervision, and accountability systems are necessary to achieve success. Finally, it is the manager's responsibility to instill in all employees a commitment to work within the structure toward overall program and organizational excellence.

■ The Role of the Board of Directors

Organizational structure represents one of the components that establish the framework and parameters for organizational functioning. But there is a second component that also establishes important ground rules and guidelines for the ways in which the organization carries out its responsibilities. The second component is the framework of constitution, bylaws, policies, and procedures that set in place the rules within which the organization conducts its business. Constitution, bylaws, and policies for the nonprofit organization are approved by and under the control of a board of directors.

In this position of control, the board holds a great deal of power over decisions that affect agency functioning. In considering ways to optimize structural and functional creativity, therefore, it is critical that managers within human service organizations have a thorough understanding of how a voluntary board of directors contributes to the achievement of excellence in organizational performance.

General Responsibilities of the Board

The board of directors of a nonprofit agency is an entity that has legal status as specified in the articles of incorporation. A nonprofit agency is typically incorporated as a charitable corporation. Its powers, capabilities, and liabilities are set by state law. Unlike the private corporation, there are no stockholders and no profits are distributed to owners (*Revised Model Nonprofit Corporation Act,* 1987). The activities of incorporated nonprofit agencies are monitored by the attorney general of the state in which they are incorporated.

Boards have a fiduciary responsibility to act as trustees of the agency on behalf of its donors and funding sources (Siciliano & Spiro, 1992). They are legally accountable for all aspects of agency operation. They have a role in determining the agency's strategic planning directions, and they establish policies and other general rules, regulations, and guidelines for agency operation. They hire, evaluate, and have the authority to fire the agency's chief executive officer. They provide formal authorization for the agency's programs, and they have a responsibility to evaluate program performance.

Selection of Board Members

Board members are selected by means of a process that is formally established in the organization's bylaws and approved by the board. The process usually involves a nominating committee, which submits names of nominees to the board for approval. The nominating committee is expected to determine what types of skills and expertise are needed on the board. Some boards specify qualifications that must be met in order to be considered. For example, a community center may establish a requirement that at least 60 percent of its board members must be residents of the community.

Over the last few decades, the issue of representativeness of board members has emerged. For many years members were selected for their area of expertise and willingness to serve. This selection process produced boards filled with attorneys, accountants, real estate brokers, and others representing various business and professional disciplines. Although this expertise was useful to the nonprofit agency, the selection process often produced boards in which the members were almost exclusively white males and had little familiarity with communities and populations served. This raised the question of representativeness. It was recognized that a board should represent the various groups the agency serves, including ethnic, cultural, gender, age, socioeconomic, and other considerations.

Daley and Angulo (1994) note that "nonprofit boards are responsible for developing policy. Their decisions bind organizations in legal matters. They are often expected to represent diverse perspectives reflecting the community in general, consumers, and other groups of special concern to the nonprofit organization" (p. 175). Yet their research demonstrates that, although nonprofit boards have made progress in selecting people from diverse ethnic, gender, and other demographic groups, diverse voices have not necessarily emerged, and many boards continue with business as usual. For this reason, the authors distinguish between demographic diversity (having a diverse board composition) and functional diversity (incorporating the diverse voices or perspectives into the policy-making process). Clearly the spirit and purpose of bringing diversity to nonprofit boards cannot be achieved without hearing the voices or perspectives in determining policies or approving or evaluating programs. Daley and Angulo (1994) propose a number of strategies to enable a board to be more inclusive, including (1) framing issues in a language that avoids in-group jargon and ensures understanding for all, (2) providing incentives and rewards for active participation, and (3) attending to the socialization and acculturation of board members. Carefully planned board orientation, training, and ongoing planning should take these issues into consideration.

Creating a Board Matrix

The issues of diversity and representativeness have led some agencies to think through, in a proactive way, what mix of interests, perspectives, skills, and expertise is most likely to support positions that reflect those of the agency's major constituents. Agencies that serve people with AIDS struggle with concerns about whether all board members should be people with AIDS. Agencies serving ethnic communities try to find a balance that will ensure that ethnic perspectives are represented while also ensuring that necessary areas of expertise are also available.

In determining the best interests of the agency and its constituents, two factors must be considered. One is the demographic diversity previously described. This includes the human richness as defined by gender, age, ability, socioeconomic class, ideology, cohort history, status as a service client or person to be impacted by a policy decision, length of time a person has served on a board or lived in the community, political influence or connections, and so on (Houle, 1989). The second is area of expertise. The Southern California Center for Nonprofit Management (1985) proposes a wealth, wisdom, work philosophy of board composition. Under each of these headings, special areas of expertise are needed, as follows:

Wealth	*Wisdom*	*Work*
Resource Development	Legal	Program
Fund-Raising	Finance/Accounting	Evaluation
Special Events	Personnel	Planning
Marketing	Facility Management	

These areas of expertise represent a range of the types of knowledge and skills that a human service agency will need in the course of conducting the business of the agency and the board over the years.

It is much more likely that an agency will achieve the optimum mix of demographic diversity and expertise on its board of directors if selection of board members is carefully planned. Some organizations accomplish this planning through use of a board matrix. This document lists, as column headings, the various demographic and expertise areas that have been selected as important to the agency. Rows are used to fill in the names of board members. Some rows may also be used to list potential board members. Columns are then checked in accordance with the characteristics represented by each board member. An example of a board matrix is illustrated in Figure 4.13.

A board matrix can be useful in highlighting for a board what constituencies, perspectives, or areas of expertise are missing, and in guiding a board in selecting future members.

FIGURE 4.13
Board Matrix

Current Board Members	Ethnicity					Gender		Age					Area of Expertise									
	African American	Asian American	Caucasian	Hispanic/Latino	Native American	Male	Female	20–29	30–39	40–49	50–59	60 and older	Resource Development	Fund-Raising	Marketing	Legal	Finance	Personnel	Program	Planning	Client	Community Member
1																						
2																						
3																						
4																						
etc.																						
Potential Board Members																						
1																						
2																						
3																						
etc.																						

■ Developing a Constitution and Bylaws

The constitution and bylaws are important documents for governing the work of the organization. The constitution specifies the very general framework for governance. The bylaws establish detailed rules with which the board must comply in all its operations. Both are considered to be foundation documents on which the board and other organizational entities base their actions and as such should be difficult to amend. Amendments must be proposed at one meeting and adopted at a subsequent meeting to allow time for full consideration. Something more than a simple majority (51 percent) vote is required for adoption of amendments. Some agencies specify a two-thirds majority; some three-fourths.

Language used in a constitution or a set of bylaws is important. The term *shall* refers to actions that are intended to be mandatory. The term *may* refers to discretionary or permissive actions. *Robert's Rules of Order* (Patnode, 1989) is often specified as the reference document that will be used in conducting the business of the board of directors.

A typical constitution will include the following articles:

1. *Name.* The name of the organization.
2. *Purpose.* Purposes, powers, and scope of the organization.
3. *Members.* Qualifications of members of the organization, if applicable.
4. *Board of Directors.* Provision for a board of directors; qualifications of members; number of members constituting a quorum.
5. *Officers.* Identification of officers of the board.

6. *Meetings.* Specification of the time and place for regular meetings; procedure for calling special meetings.
7. *Amendments.* Method of amending the constitution and the vote required.

Bylaws cover some of the same items as those included in the constitution, but the specifications are spelled out in much greater detail. Bylaws may include sections covering any or all of the following topics:

1. *Membership of the Board.* Qualifications, number of members, how selected, provision for filling vacancies, provision for removing board members.
2. *Committees of the Board.* A list of standing committees; scope of work; method of selection of members and chair; establishment of agendas; rights and responsibilities of members.
3. *Duties and Powers of the Board.* Responsibility and process for policy determination. Specification of expectations in terms of planning, financing, public relations, personnel, program evaluation, and other areas.
4. *Officers of the Board.* Specification of offices; term of office; duties and powers; provisions for filling vacancies and removing officers who do not perform their duties.
5. *Election of Board Members and Officers.* Method of nomination, election, and voting.
6. *Notice of Meetings.* Requirements for sending out notices, drawing up the agenda, and maintaining attendance records.
7. *Order of Business for Meetings.* Order of agenda items including director's report, committee reports, old business, new business, announcements, and adjournment.
8. *Amendment of Bylaws.* Procedures for proposing an amendment, dissemination to members, time frames for consideration, and votes required for passage.
9. *Quorum.* Specification of the votes required in order for actions taken to be legal.

Board/Executive Relationships

Achieving an appropriate balance in the ways in which organizational matters are addressed requires a good deal of knowledge and understanding both on the part of the board and the executive. Both have responsibilities for dealing with many of the same concerns. Each, however, maintains responsibility for a specific perspective and domain. When lines are crossed, agency functioning can be disrupted. When the executive attempts to establish policy or the board gets involved in decisions about personnel, potential problems emerge. The Southern California Center for Nonprofit Management (1985) has developed a framework that is helpful in sorting out roles and responsibilities. The center identifies seven areas in which both executive and board have responsibilities: (1) legal, (2) finance/accounting, (3) planning, (4) policy, (5) personnel, (6) resource development, and (7) board governance.

In each area the policy/planning perspective of the board is described. For example, in the area of finance and accounting the board approves the annual budget, reviews reports, and ensures that proper internal controls are in place. The executive also has responsibilities in each of the seven areas. They typically include provision of information to the board, overseeing the preparation of reports for the board, preparation of plans for submission to the board, and implementation of policies passed by the board. For example, in the area of finance and accounting the executive prepares the annual budget, oversees preparation of monthly financial reports, and implements proper financial controls. When both board and executive understand and respect each other's boundaries, a foundation is established for the type of cooperative and collaborative functioning that can lead to achievement of organizational excellence.

S U M M A R Y

1. **The Importance of Structure.** The way an organization is structured can influence many factors in the workplace.
   - *The Focus of Work.* The way workloads are designed is affected by overall organizational structure.
   - *The Locus of Responsibility.* Hierarchical structure places responsibility in a chain of command. Sometimes those with responsibility do not control resources.
   - *Supervision.* Supervisors can allow freedom or tightly control performance.
   - *Lines of Communication.* The flow of communication is influenced by hierarchy and chain of command.
   - *Extent of Participation.* Structure can either limit or facilitate employee participation.
   - *Impact on Accomplishment of Organizational Goals.* Achieving organizational goals may be affected by the extent to which employees see their work as affecting goal attainment.

2. **Structural Alternatives.** The organizational chart depicts formal, hierarchical relationships. Alternative charts can depict actual working relationships.

3. **The Formal Organizational Chart.** Organizations can be structured in a number of ways to address their own unique populations, problems, needs, and staffing patterns.
   - *Departmentalization by Program.* Services provided determine structure.
   - *Departmentalization by Function.* Specialized areas of expertise determine structure.
   - *Departmentalization by Process.* The chronological process designed to serve clients determines structure.
   - *Departmentalization by Market.* Referral sources determine structure.
   - *Departmentalization by Consumer/Client.* Types of clients served determine structure.
   - *Departmentalization by Geographic Area.* Access to services determines structure.

4. **The Informal Organizational Chart: Introducing Flexibility into the Organizational Structure.** Alternative working relationships can be depicted in a chart designed for internal use only.
   - *Matrix Organizations.* Structures that include more than one reporting and supervisory relationship and support teamwork.
   - *The Linking Pin.* A structure that uses overlapping boundaries to include selected staff on different teams or in multiple units.
   - *The Project Team.* A structure that permits teams to function independently while a leadership team ensures coordination.
   - *The Collegial Model.* A structure that permits each individual to work independently while coordinating efforts with other team members.
   - *Mixed-Matrix Options.* More than one alternative structure can be used within the same department or program.

5. **Working with Both Formal and Informal Structures.** Formal organizational charts are necessary to depict the chain of command; informal charts depict more flexible working relationships.

6. **The Role of the Board of Directors.** The board holds significant power and authority over organizational functioning.
   - *General Responsibilities of the Board.* The board has fiduciary, legal, and planning responsibility. It also establishes policies, regulations, and guidelines.

- *Selection of Board Members.* Both demographic and functional diversity is important to the optimal functioning of a board.
- *Creating a Board Matrix.* Demographic diversity and desired areas of expertise should be identified in planning for recruitment of board members.

7. **Developing a Constitution and Bylaws.** These are important documents that govern the work of the organization.
   - *Board/Executive Relationships.* Areas of responsibility overlap but roles differ.

EXERCISES

Please complete the following sections of your manual based on the content covered in Chapter 4.

Section 4: Organizational Structure

4.1 Formal structure. Select an option for the formal structure of the organization and provide a rationale for your selection. Attach a copy of the organizational chart and label it Document 4.1a.

4.2 Informal structure. Select an option for the informal structure of the organization and provide a rationale for your selection. Attach a copy of the informal organizational chart and label it Document 4.2a.

Section 4A: Constitution and Bylaws

4A.1 Constitution. Prepare a constitution for the organization. (Use *Robert's Rules of Order* and other references.)

4A.2 Bylaws. Prepare a set of bylaws for the organization. (Use *Robert's Rules of Order* and other references, including copies of existing agency bylaws.)

4A.3 Board Matrix. Prepare a matrix that depicts demographic and expertise diversity that is appropriate for the organization and can be used for planning purposes and for recruiting board members.

REFERENCES

Daley, J. M., & Angulo, J. (1994). Understanding the dynamics of diversity within nonprofit boards. *Journal of the Community Development Society, 25*(2), 172–188.

Davis, S., & Lawrence, P. (1978). Problems of matrix organizations. *Harvard Business Review, 55* (May–June), 131–142.

Hackman, R., & Suttle, J. (1977). *Improving life at work: Behavioral science approaches to organizational change.* Santa Monica, CA: Goodyear.

Houle, C. (1989). *Governing boards: Their nature and nurture.* San Francisco: Jossey-Bass.

Kahn, W., & Kram, K. (1994). Authority at work: Internal models and their organizational consequences. *Academy of Management Review, 19*(1), 17–50.

Marsden, P., Cook, C., & Kalleberg, A. (1996). Bureaucratic structures for coordination and control. In A. Kalleberg, D. Knoke, P. Marsden, & J. Spaeth (Eds.), *Organizations in America* (pp. 69–86). Thousand Oaks, CA: Sage.

Miles, R. (1975). *Theories of management: Implications for organizational behavior and development.* New York: McGraw-Hill.

Montana, P., & Charnov, B. (1993). *Management.* Hauppauge, NY: Barron's Educational Series.

Patnode, D. (1989). *Robert's rules of order: The modern edition.* New York: Berkley Books. Revised from H. Robert. (1876). *Robert's rules of order.* Copyright by Major Henry M. Robert.

Revised Model Nonprofit Corporation Act. (1987). Clifton, NJ: Prentice-Hall Law and Business, Section 8.01, 171.

Siciliano, J., & Spiro, G. (1992). The unclear status of nonprofit directors: An empirical survey of director liability. *Administration in Social Work, 16*(1), 69–80.

Southern California Center for Nonprofit Management. (1985). *Building an effective board of directors.* Los Angeles: Author.

Weber, M. (1947). *The theory of social and economic organizations* (A. M. Henderson & T. Parsons, Trans.). New York: Macmillan. (Original work published 1924).

CHAPTER 5

Using Job and Work Design Creatively to Achieve Maximum Employee Performance

CHAPTER OUTLINE

- What Is Job and Work Design?
- Analyzing Job Responsibilities
- Job- and Work-Design Strategies
- Toward a "Jobless" Work Environment

CHAPTER OBJECTIVES

Upon completion of this chapter, the reader will be able to:

- Explain the concepts of job and work design and redesign.
- Identify six job-design strategies.
- Apply job-design concepts to a specific organization and job.
- Discuss three trends that will influence future work environments.

Assumptions

- That what a person does on the job has a profound influence on job satisfaction and productivity.
- That jobs can be designed and redesigned in ways that will stimulate motivation and productivity.
- That there is an optimum fit between person and job, and it is the responsibility of managers to help find that fit.

■ What Is Job and Work Design?

Job design or redesign involves changing or reorganizing the tasks and responsibilities assigned to employees. The purposes of job design are to maximize the fit between employee skills and responsibilities and to introduce variability into the work environment. Improving the fit between a worker's knowledge, skills, and interests and the worker's responsibilities is intended to increase efficiency and productivity. Introducing variability into the work environment is intended to improve the quality of the employee's overall work experience. Davis (1976) refers to this type of strategy as "work system redesign" in recognition of the fact that it involves more than the simple changing of a job. Here both the terms *job design* and *work design* are used in recognition that there are really two levels of involvement when dealing with employees' work experiences—individual jobs and the total work environment. The terms *design* and *redesign* are also used here in recognition that, although some new jobs are being created, many existing jobs need to be reorganized in order to achieve maximum effectiveness from this strategy.

Any work environment, even one in which employees are dealing with complex individual and family problems, can become routine and stagnant without attention to issues of job design and redesign. As Hackman (1977) points out, "highly repetitive jobs have been found to diminish worker alertness, to decrease sensitivity to sensory input, and in some situations to impair muscular coordination" (p. 105). Data collection and data entry are examples of the types of responsibilities that can lead to boredom and understimulation. On the other hand, some job responsibilities may be so complex that they cannot be resolved regardless of the amount of time and conscientious attention devoted to them. For example, when a caseworker is expected to help a long-term unemployed person become self-sufficient with severely limited resources and within unrealistic time limits, job responsibilities become overstimulating and frustration and burnout often set in.

Ouchi (1981) describes another value of job redesign when he compares career specialization in the United States to job rotation in Japan. In the typical U.S. firm, he points out, one employee will spend an entire career in manufacturing, another in sales, another in engineering, and a fourth in accounting. "When people spend their entire careers within one specialty," he says, "they tend to develop sub-goals devoted to that specialty rather than to the whole firm" (pp. 31–32). Employees of Japanese firms, on the other hand, experience lifelong job rotation. Research on management effectiveness suggests that workers who continually face new challenges and redesigned jobs bring more energy to the job, are more productive, and are more satisfied with their work than those who continue in the same set of routines (Ouchi, 1981).

When Can Job Design and Redesign Be Effective?

Not all situations of low productivity or morale can be remedied through job design or redesign. It is quite common to find that low productivity stems from a morale problem rooted in leadership or personnel issues. For example, there are some situations in which employees work extremely hard, yet the management team focuses only on criticism and negative feedback. Lack of positive feedback or recognition for a job well done ultimately leads to low morale. Personnel and leadership issues are not likely to be resolved through job redesign. Situations of low productivity and low morale require some investment in problem analysis in order to ensure that the proposed solution will resolve the problem.

Problem analysis should involve examination of program goals and objectives, together with the ways in which the work responsibilities have been allocated in order to achieve them. Is there a logical fit between (1) the way workloads have been defined and (2) the objectives to be achieved? For example, a program objective may establish an expectation of self-sufficiency for clients, whereas workloads are structured around resolving clients' personal and emotional problems. Or perhaps workers were hired who did not have the proper training, education, and experience to handle the complex responsibilities that come with helping clients to achieve self-sufficiency. So the fit of goals and objectives to workload design should be examined. Problem analysis should also focus on understanding not only what has been done in the past but also why it was done that way, the consequences of changing the way work is designed, and how work redesign is expected to solve the problems that need to be addressed. To understand the effects of job redesign, there should be some exploration of the possible impact on (1) the organizational environment, (2) the internal functioning of the organization, (3) the technologies affected, and (4) employees, including (5) their possible need for training and new skills.

In attempting to understand the impact on the organizational environment, there must be an understanding of the degree of stability or turbulence that exists or may exist at any given time. A time of funding instability, for example, is not a good time to attempt a redesign of the work environment. Nor is accreditation time a good time. Although there is probably no perfect time, the more stable the organizational environment, the better the chance that work redesign will achieve its objectives.

The same comments can be made about the internal functioning of the organization. It is possible that intraorganizational turbulence, such as disruptive personal or professional conflicts, may negate the positive effects of job redesign. A time of relative stability is usually preferable to one of turbulence.

In redesigning work and workloads, there will typically be issues of technology to be addressed, including consideration of practice models and techniques used in the helping process with clients. Part of the objective should be to ensure that complex responsibilities and tasks are assigned to those with the most advanced education, experience, or demonstrated skills and abilities. Routine, standardized responsibilities and tasks should be packaged in a way that makes their completion manageable and efficient, and should be assigned ideally to employees who prefer these types of tasks, but at least to employees who understand the expectations and are willing to focus on task completion. Employees who are expected to carry out complex tasks should be comfortable with self-direction and self-control. Employees who will carry out routine tasks should be comfortable with a workload that is very specifically defined. It is desirable that all affected employees have input into, accept, and support the newly designed work responsibilities.

The need for training for employees is also a consideration. Some will need new knowledge and skills. Others will need to learn new routines, including the completion of forms and other paperwork, and possibly the use of new software. Analysis should be focused on whether existing skills and interests are transferable to newly designed work expectations and how much training and preparation will be necessary to perform the newly designed jobs.

In summary, job design and redesign, although valuable tools, are not universally effective in solving problems within the work environment. A number of published case studies demonstrate that job redesign can be an effective tool for improving both the quality of the work experience as well as productivity (Hackman, 1977). Numerous failures are also reported, and it may well be that the effectiveness of job design or redesign as a technique for stimulating productivity is only as good as the analytical work that was done in attempting to understand the problem and design an appropriate solution. When it works, it can be very effective. When it fails, it can cause a serious setback in terms of resolving the real problems.

■ CONSIDERATIONS

For Job Design and Redesign

Basic Questions: Is there a problem with low productivity, inefficiency, ineffectiveness, or poor quality of services provided? Is it possible that job design in this unit or program causes either understimulation leading to boredom or overstimulation leading to burnout?

Time Frame: This activity should be undertaken whenever available data and information indicate that there is a problem in any part of the organization.

Process: Program managers and supervisors should review available data in an attempt to pinpoint as accurately as possible the nature of the problem. They should then survey employees to get their perspectives on the problem.

Analysis: The problem(s) should be isolated to as few positions as possible. A job analysis (see Chapter 10) should be initiated (or if one exists, it should be reviewed). Tasks, knowledge, and skill required and results expected should be reevaluated to determine if they are realistic or are contributing to the problems of understimulation or overstimulation.

Documentation: A new job analysis should be prepared, using any of the techniques described in Chapter 10.

What Can Work Design and Redesign Accomplish?

Hackman (1977) identifies four ways that work redesign changes life in an organization, which make this particular strategy different from others:

> *Work redesign alters the basic relationship between a person and what he or she does on the job.* Many organizational problems, Hackman argues, can be pinpointed to the place at which people interface with the tasks that they carry out. Jobs may be designed in a very routine and standardized way in order to satisfy issues of accountability.

Although this design may achieve accountability objectives, it may not promote maximum productivity. Redesign focused on quality of service to clients, for example, may require a different attitude toward and approach to job responsibilities. This changed relationship to the job can bring about significant improvements in terms of services to clients, thereby demonstrating improvements in achievement of program objectives.

Work redesign directly changes behavior—and it tends to stay changed. Many workshop hours have been devoted to attempting to change attitudes in the hope that they will bring about changed behavior. Often there is little carryover to behavior. The value of work redesign is that it begins at the point of changing behavior, and invariably, if the experience is successful, changed attitude follows. For example, a unit of workers may raise questions about the quality and availability of supervision, pointing out that they often need timely input on difficult cases when the unit supervisor is not available. In such a situation work responsibilities might be redesigned to provide for peer consultation instead of supervision. This places the issue more under the workers' control and changes their role to active participants in the problem-solving process.

Work redesign offers—and sometimes places into worker's hands—numerous opportunities for initiating other organizational changes. Continuing with the foregoing example of peer consultation, it is possible that putting coworkers in a position to find solutions in relation to their cases might also lead to problem solving in relation to the flow of work. Because they have been given the authority to find and implement solutions, it is possible that they might also find ways to streamline the intake and assessment processes and reduce the time on the waiting list for clients. This may further evolve into forums in which coworkers find constructive ways to resolve interpersonal problems among peers.

Work redesign, in the long term, can result in organizations that rehumanize rather than dehumanize the people who work in them. When the focus of work is changed from the routine processing of cases to a collegial analysis of problems and solutions, employees may feel a much greater sense of satisfaction in the knowledge that they are providing the best that the synergistic efforts of the organization have to offer. These types of changed attitudes in turn can reignite an interest in and commitment to professional growth and development. The outcome can be a work environment that is much richer in terms of its supportive and nurturing qualities.

■ Analyzing Job Responsibilities

Miles (1975) presents three different frameworks for understanding job design: (1) the traditional model, (2) the human relations model, and (3) the human resources model. These three models correspond roughly with the organic-mechanistic continuum as conceptualized in contingency theory. The relationship is depicted in Figure 5.1.

Job design under the traditional model is based on the assumption that workers want and need to be told what to do. Supervisors and managers translate responsibilities into tasks and procedures. Short-term assignments are given, and close supervision is provided. Workers are able to learn fairly routine tasks quickly and follow precise instructions through to completion. When help is needed, the worker is expected to seek it from the designated supervisor. In human services, such tasks as completion of forms or data entry

FIGURE 5.1

Three Models of Management as Conceptualized by Miles

Mechanistic ◄───► Organic

The Traditional Model	The Human Relations Model	The Human Resources Model
Manager's role is close supervision and control	Manager's role is to make each worker feel useful and important	Manager's role is to make use of the creative energy and abilities of staff

might fit this description. Consistent with the findings in support of contingency theory, this job design would be appropriate only in situations that require a mechanistic structure in order to maximize productivity and when workers are able to achieve a sense of competence through conscientious completion of assigned tasks. Job design under the traditional model of management is depicted in Figure 5.2.

A second framework for use in guiding job design is the human relations model. Job design following the human relations model (as with the traditional model) also specifies tasks to be carried out under close supervision. However, in the human relations model there is more of a focus on human needs for nurturing and socialization. Planning and evaluating are still carried out by the supervisor, but the supervisor's responsibilities are broadened to encompass consideration of employee needs to feel that he or she is an important part of the unit and of the organization. Achieving a positive sense of identity is accomplished at two levels. First, the supervisor attends to the employee's needs for esteem and belonging by identifying ways in which the employee meets unique needs of the organization and by reinforcing the significance of the employee's status and role. Second, the supervisor provides opportunities among employees to develop relationships and form a cohesive, supportive work group. Neither of these emphases, however, is expected to interfere with the completion of the tasks assigned. As in the traditional model, task completion is the primary focus.

This approach to job design might be appropriate in human services among certain types of paraprofessional staff such as child care workers in a residential treatment center.

FIGURE 5.2

Job Design under the Traditional Model of Management

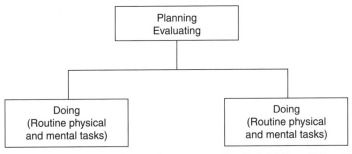

Source: Miles, R. (1975). *Theories of management.* New York: McGraw-Hill, p. 53. Reproduced with the permission of The McGraw-Hill Companies.

Although their responsibilities are clearly defined and not open to individual interpretation, their morale and job satisfaction may well depend on nurturing supervision. Close, supportive supervision is typically available to help with problem situations. Workers may be sent to workshops to learn how to deal with disruptive behavior. Members of a cohesive work group provide backup for each other as stressful situations with difficult children require more intensive involvement from time to time. These types of positions tend to be low-paid, high-stress jobs, and without a nurturing, learning, and supportive environment, burnout and turnover would be even higher than typically found among child care workers. Figure 5.3 illustrates job design under the human relations model.

The third approach to job design is called the human resources model. This model is used in situations in which supervisors expect to achieve high levels of performance by tapping the knowledge, skill, and creative potential of workers. The model is built on the assumption that maximizing freedom for self-direction and self-control will lead to optimum use of abilities, including full participation in planning and evaluating work responsibilities and performance. The supervisor's role, under this model, is to eliminate the barriers to optimum performance and to create ways for workers to contribute directly to overall unit, departmental, and organizational performance. Job satisfaction, under this model, is achieved through employees' sense of participation, competence, and contribution.

Managers and workers plan jointly to define work objectives and time frames. The goals and objectives of the organization and the program are important and frame the context within which employee objectives are defined. However, employee interests, needs, and talents are also taken into consideration in the interest of finding a synergy that will be mutually beneficial to employee, unit, and organization. A substantial investment is made on the part of the organization in terms of development and training for the employee so that knowledge and skills are current.

FIGURE 5.3

Job Design under the Human Relations Model

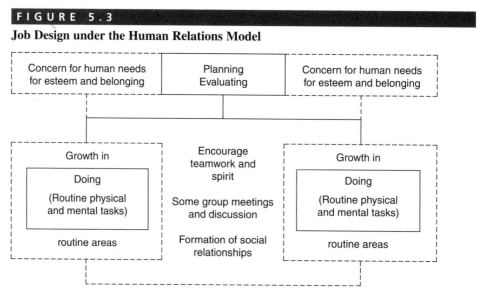

Source: Miles, R. (1975). *Theories of management.* New York: McGraw-Hill, p. 54. Reproduced with the permission of The McGraw-Hill Companies.

FIGURE   5.4

Job Design under the Human Resources Model

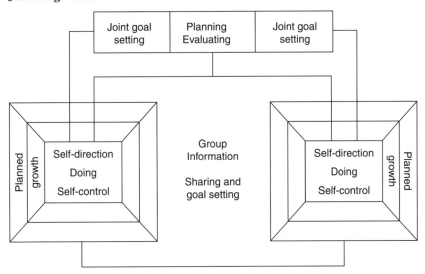

Source: Miles, R. (1975). *Theories of management.* New York: McGraw-Hill, p. 56. Reproduced with the permission of The McGraw-Hill Companies.

The human resources model is applicable in human services in units that employ people with advanced degrees and in which there is an expectation that they can rely on a body of professional knowledge and skill rather than on policy and procedural directives. Those counseling victims of domestic violence, for example, need a foundation of knowledge, skill, and values in order to perform effectively in this role. It is expected that workers will find ways to help their clients achieve a sense of inner strength and self-esteem so that they need not return to the violent situation that brought them into treatment. Workers need a great deal of flexibility and creativity to accomplish these objectives with their clients, and a consultative relationship with a supervisor can be important to successful performance. Job design under the human resources model is depicted in Figure 5.4.

■ Job- and Work-Design Strategies

The literature on job and work design covers a wide variety of approaches and strategies. Because the focus of this book is on application to human service organizations, strategies that seem to be most applicable and relevant to these organizations will be explored, including (1) job enlargement, (2) job enrichment, (3) job rotation, (4) creating teams, (5) varying working conditions, and (6) using technology.

Job Enlargement

Job enlargement refers to manipulating and varying job characteristics in a way that makes the job more complex and challenging in the interest of increasing motivation and productivity. Job enlargement begins with a review of the job analysis, identifying duties and responsibilities, knowledge and skills required, and results expected. Enlargement is not a simple matter of adding or subtracting tasks but rather a reconceptualizing of ways to achieve the same or better results with a different, perhaps more streamlined, approach or method.

This approach focuses on what Kossen (1978) refers to as the "whole job concept," in which workers are given more complete or whole jobs to perform. It is built on the principle that workers will achieve more job satisfaction if they see their roles as part of a whole and if they are able to see the completed product or the results of a completed service.

Job Enlargement Example

A unit within an adoptions program has responsibility for reviewing applications and approving couples for adoption. Over the years the work has become routine, with each couple attending an orientation session, participating in two joint interviews as a couple and each of the partners completing an individual interview. Potential parenting problems have not been picked up by the workers, and extensive counseling time is needed postadoption to address problems that should have been prevented.

Job enlargement might focus on taking cohorts of three or four couples through the process together and approach the process from a perspective of teaching parenting skills and developing mutually supportive relationships among the adopting couples so that they could form an ongoing support group after the adoptions are complete. This type of redesign calls for a new approach to the job with the expectation of achieving better results in a more efficient way. It very likely would involve learning new skills, and it would not be unreasonable to have existing employees apply for and be screened for their ability to handle the newly designed job functions.

■ CONSIDERATIONS

For Job Enlargement

Basic Questions: Is there a factual or data-based reason that supports low levels of productivity, efficiency, effectiveness, or quality in a particular program, unit, or individual worker? Is there a reason to believe that job redesign will solve the problem?

Time Frame: Whenever existing performance indicates problems.

Process: Supervisor and worker together reexamine the job analysis and review existing literature on the subject to learn if other approaches have been tried elsewhere. Small, pilot projects to test out concepts may be appropriate.

Analysis: Begin with a review of the results or outcomes that workers are expected to achieve with their clients. Revise as needed. Identify which methods are achieving positive results and which are not. Redesign so that all methods fit together to achieve overall positive results.

Documentation: The result of this effort should be a rewritten job analysis and job description.

Job Enrichment

Job enrichment refers to redesigning the job in a way that workers assume more responsibility for their own work, often including some of the responsibilities formerly assigned to supervisory staff. The focus of job enrichment is on removing barriers to motivation and streamlining the work flow. It is not uncommon, for example, in highly structured, bureaucratic organizations to find that getting permission to take a particular action may take so long that the action may no longer be relevant. Job enrichment would permit workers to make their own decisions about taking an action and would also hold them accountable for the results of the action taken. Job enrichment is intended, in addition to increasing motivation, to improve the quality of decision making, to reduce interpersonal friction between workers and supervisors, and to reduce burnout.

Job Enrichment Example

Workers in a rural program that serves developmentally disabled children and their families attempted to provide parents with information and education to secure respite care resources and to find sheltered employment for those capable of meeting job expectations. Resources were limited and the approval process through county offices was cumbersome. Because it was a small community, matches had to be made carefully and with great discretion. When individuals and families were found who were willing to provide respite care, or when sheltered employment opportunities were identified, the approval process required two levels of decision making in the local office and then approval from the county office. By the time the decision was made, families and employers had often moved on to other interests, the opportunity for the client and family was missed, and the process had to begin all over. Moving decision making about use of resources down to the unit and worker level required more work from the workers. They had to learn budgeting techniques, and job descriptions were changed to reflect increased accountability for judicious use of resources. In spite of this, the workers welcomed the job enrichment approach because it contributed greatly to successful stabilization of family situations and at the same time contributed to job satisfaction.

■ CONSIDERATIONS

For Job Enrichment

Basic Questions: Are workers prevented from performing their jobs efficiently and effectively by limiting their realm of responsibility and decision making? What are the consequences of adding responsibilities? How would workers and others affected feel about a change?

Time Frame: Whenever it is recognized that limited authority is affecting the ability to serve clients effectively.

Process: Review job analysis. Interview or use focus groups with workers, supervisors, and others affected.

Analysis: Flowchart the decision-making process as it exists and as it would be if changed. Identify possible problems. Consider pilot testing with a small number of workers in order to debug the system if necessary.

Documentation: This process should result in new policies and procedures and revised job descriptions.

Job Rotation

Job rotation refers to a planned exchange of job responsibilities in the interest of having employees understand the work of the organization from a broader perspective and also in the interest of reducing boredom. Lifelong job rotation is one of the features of Japanese-style management described by Ouchi (1981). When considering the total workload of a particular unit, or even of the entire organization, there are many ways to divide responsibilities. One factor to be taken into consideration is the part of the workload that involves monotonous, tedious work. If, for example, a particular agency has been cited by its funding source for a high error rate in its reports, someone in the agency will have to take responsibility for checking data-collection forms and processes on an ongoing basis to reduce errors. This work may be assigned to a supervisor, to a specialized worker, or it may be made a part of the job for an entry-level worker. If the responsibility for checking the accuracy of forms is placed on one worker only, there is a good chance that the worker will tire of the job and move on to other employment. In such a unit, workers might agree to rotate so that everyone takes a turn at the tedious work. A side benefit of job rotation is that everyone gets an opportunity to see firsthand the consequences of careless paperwork or careless data entry. This may have the effect of improving performance for each worker who rotates through the position. Job rotation can also enhance mutual understanding and collaboration among workers.

Job Rotation Example

The Midwest Behavioral Health Center contracted with the state to provide services to people with problems in the areas of drugs, alcohol, and mental health. Its program structure and design (specified by funding source requirements) included an intake and screening unit, with subsequent referrals to units specializing in the treatment of problems in mental health, in use and abuse of drugs, and in use and abuse of alcohol. Although each specialized unit had workers who were highly skilled in treatment of problems in their specialized area, they were not familiar with symptoms, needs, and treatment options in the other two areas. It was not uncommon for clients who were referred to the agency to have problems that cut across two and sometimes all three specialized units.

It was only a matter of time until units were squabbling with each other and criticizing the intake, screening, and referral unit for what they considered inappropriate and uninformed referral decisions. Service quality deteriorated and clients suffered. The management team decided that the solution was job rotation. Within the next year, one worker in each unit rotated every three months. Consultation was provided by the other workers in the unit. Rotation was continued on a regular basis until all workers had completed the full cycle. Subsequently, job rotation was built into the system for newly hired employees. Although the problems of overlapping specializations were not entirely solved, each worker developed a greater appreciation of the other disciplines, a spirit of greater collaboration was fostered, and clients were better served.

■ C O N S I D E R A T I O N S

For Job Rotation

Basic Questions:	Would workers benefit from knowing more about the jobs of others in the unit or organization? Would the benefits likely result in improved performance, higher job satisfaction, and better client services?
Time Frame:	Whenever it is recognized that focus on specialization is generating conflict or stress that results in lower job satisfaction and poor client services.
Process:	Examine worker knowledge, skills, education, and experience against job descriptions and job expectations. Examine the complexities of entering and exiting a job and transferring cases to another worker.
Analysis:	Identify critical knowledge and skills required for each position to be included in the job rotation. Determine if workers will bring necessary knowledge and skill or if consultation with other workers can compensate for lack of knowledge and skill.
Documentation:	A plan for job rotation should be prepared, reviewed by all staff affected, and presented to the management team for approval. The plan should identify eligible staff, establish a process for rotation and training, and identify the tasks to be completed prior to leaving one position and assuming another.

Creating Teams

Creating teams refers to reallocating collective responsibilities from individuals to a group of workers and subdividing the workload in a way that allows each to contribute to the team from an area of strength and specialization. This principle was promoted in the organic model proposed by Burns and Stalker (1961) in their initial conceptualization of contingency theory. The use of teams attempts to benefit from the adage that "none of us is as smart as all of us." When organizational structure permits delegation of responsibility, and when teams or units are able to take responsibility for decisions, both worker and unit performance can be enhanced. In working with complex problems, it can be useful to get input from many perspectives rather than having only one person assume decision-making authority.

Use of Teams Example

In a child welfare agency a unit of workers was responsible for working with troubled families to prevent and reduce the incidence of child abuse and neglect. Each worker carried a caseload and had full responsibility, together with the supervisor, for all decision making regarding families in that caseload. When workers were able to find community resources to support client families, they were able to help families achieve some level of stability. However, in many cases problems associated with child care, transportation, or the clients' work schedules interfered with successful resolution of problems.

The management team decided that work could be done more effectively and better results achieved with clients through the use of teams. The work unit was redesigned so that all cases for the unit were assigned to the supervisor rather than to individual workers. A case manager was transferred to another unit, and in her place two paraprofessionals were hired, one for transportation and one for child care. When cases were assigned to the unit, they were staffed and a decision was made about who would take responsibility for what aspects of family problems and needs. A lead worker was assigned to keep track of all case participants. Families in crisis received intensive team attention. Transportation and child care were made available to all families either directly from staff or through subcontractors. The shared responsibility and decision making proved to be helpful with many families when a single case manager alone was unable to achieve family stabilization.

■ CONSIDERATIONS

For Creating Teams

Basic Questions: Are jobs designed and responsibilities allocated in a way that unrealistic expectations are placed on a single worker? Would specialized areas of knowledge and skill be useful in achieving improved client outcomes? Is joint, collegial decision making possible without encumbering the timeliness and responsiveness of the helping process?

Time Frame: Any time it is recognized that workers alone are expected to achieve outcomes with their clients that are not possible without a support infrastructure, specialized resources, and consultation.

Process: Workers and supervisor would need to prepare data on cases, identifying basic demographics of families, types and severity of problems, barriers to problem resolution, and some common resources needed.

Analysis: A flowchart should be prepared, which depicts the current flow for clients from entry to exit. A second flowchart should depict the newly proposed model. Impact on workers, clients, workloads, and work flow should be analyzed. The capabilities of existing workers to fulfill new responsibilities should be considered and decisions made about new positions and workers needed.

Documentation: New job analyses should be prepared, followed by new job descriptions.

Varying Working Conditions

Varying working conditions refers to increasing the flexibility in the ways in which jobs are carried out in the interest of adapting to the personal and family demands of employees, while retaining their energy, commitment, and high level of performance. This technique may also involve changing the location in which the work is performed. Like job rotation, varying working conditions can also be used to alleviate boredom or monotony. Even some of the techniques tested by Mayo (1945) in the research that led to human relations management theory can be used to vary working conditions. These include such techniques as better lighting, music, or coffee breaks in which refreshments are served, designed to bring people together for social contact.

One common technique for varying working conditions over the past decade has been the use of flextime. Hundreds of U.S. corporations as well as companies throughout the world have allowed workers to create their own schedules, adapting them to their personal and family needs. Although companies retain the expectation that employees will work at least forty hours per week and be available for certain designated meetings or conferences, the start and end times for each day are determined by the workers themselves. This allows families to address needs for child care or elderly parent care, as well as permitting people to work during what they find to be their peak hours of productivity and to avoid spending valuable time on the road during rush hours.

A variation of flextime is telecommuting, in which employees who can meet all the expectations of their jobs through the computer are allowed to work at home. Both of these approaches are built on the assumption that jobs are designed in a way that there are measurable performance indicators that can be used to determine productivity and as a basis for performance evaluation. High levels of performance, using these techniques of job design, cannot be equated solely with the number of hours on the job.

Varying Working Conditions Example

A team of three social workers was assigned to a school district that included seven elementary schools, three middle schools, and two high schools. The team was responsible for the development and delivery of preventive programs on violence, teen pregnancy, use of drugs and alcohol, and other risk behaviors. They also received referrals from teachers and administrators when problem situations came up that required counseling with students and/or their families. All three social workers worked regular school hours from 7:30 A.M. to 3:00 P.M. Many problem situations were going unresolved because parents were generally not available during these hours. After studying the situation, the team members agreed that they would vary their work schedules in order to accommodate the availability of parents. Two workers would continue on the regular school schedule and would handle all the preventive programs and work with students when parent involvement was not necessary. The third would work out of her home, with official working hours from 12:00 noon to 8:00 P.M. She would take responsibility for all cases that involved parents. All agreed that if the new schedule imposed a hardship on anyone either in terms of workload or in terms of working hours, they would reevaluate the situation in six months and may consider job rotation at that time.

■ CONSIDERATIONS

For Varying Working Conditions

Basic Questions:	Is performance affected in a negative way by the existing work environment or work flow? Are aspects of the work tedious? Would some variation likely increase performance and productivity?
Time Frame:	Whenever it is recognized that working conditions may be a barrier to high levels of performance.
Process:	Interviews or focus groups with workers to understand their perspectives on barriers to high levels of performance. Ideas about how to improve working conditions should be solicited.
Analysis:	Causes of poor performance should be analyzed and objectives of change specified. There can be many causes, including inadequate knowledge and skill, burnout, or poor job design. There should be some assurance that varying working conditions will meet objectives of redesign.
Documentation:	New policy and procedures should be written. Job analyses and descriptions should be revised as needed.

Use of Technology

Use of technology refers to a planned attempt to reduce some of the tedious, repetitious, and redundant types of work and procedures by having equipment (usually, but not always, the computer) handle routine functions when possible. Rapp and Poertner (1992) describe the challenge that workers in human service agencies often face in relation to data collection:

> It is the [frontline workers] who shoulder most of the responsibility for inputting, updating, and correcting the data yet the systems have not produced many benefits for them. The paperwork demands have now reached crisis proportions. The needless collection of information diverts precious service time, lowers job satisfaction, reduces the likelihood of any information being used (information overload), reduces the accuracy of the information, and through it all, decreases performance. (p. 98)

Since the time these words were written, human service agencies have learned to make more efficient use of computer hardware and software, but there is much yet to be learned to optimize use of technology. Completing intake and screening forms and compiling all the necessary eligibility documentation can take weeks, including several appointments with each client. Some systems are still designed only to produce information for management purposes and are of little value to the workers who have the most responsibility for data input.

Over the past decade, taking advantage of computer technology, Hudson (1990) devised ways to streamline the intake and screening process by having clients sit at a terminal and enter data about themselves. By periodically identifying problems and levels of severity from their own perspectives, clients can develop a profile of problems and strengths that can be regularly updated, with client entries turned into graphs depicting progress in problem areas. This technology has the potential of relieving the worker of many hours of time devoted to intake and screening tasks. Instead, clients, at their own pace, can enter data and workers can take the time to study client profiles in preparation for more focused interviews.

Use of technology doesn't necessarily require use of computers. Something as simple as making a copy machine more readily available for direct use by staff can streamline the work flow. Use of cell phones and beepers can allow workers to be in places where they can get their work done while remaining available if they are needed.

Use of Technology Example

In a child residential treatment center it was discovered that children behaved differently in different programs at the center. One set of behaviors was seen in the recreation program, another in the classroom, and still another in group therapy. As a result, each program worked on different behaviors, sometimes at cross-purposes. When this was discovered, it was decided at a staff meeting to experiment with selecting target behaviors, scaling levels of performance, and having each program enter behavioral data into a network of linked computers, with printouts of progress to be made available to each program on a weekly basis. Staff from each discipline agreed to provide daily scores on each target behavior, and staff on the midnight to 8 A.M. shift agreed to do the necessary data entry. Through the use of technology the center was able to achieve much improved coordination on case planning.

■ C O N S I D E R A T I O N S

For Use of Technology

Basic Questions:	Are staff performing functions that can be performed better through the use of specialized equipment?
Time Frame:	Whenever it is discovered that the percentage of face-to-face time with clients or collateral contacts is decreasing or staff are spending inordinate amounts of time on tedious, routine functions.
Process:	Supervisors monitor how time is spent. Interview or use focus groups with staff to gather information on barriers to optimum performance.
Analysis:	Examine carefully all areas on which time is spent other than face-to-face contact with clients, families, or other collateral contacts. Determine whether any of these areas can be dealt with more efficiently through the use of equipment. Conduct at least a simple cost-benefit analysis. State objectives of new technology.
Report:	A summary report to the director and business manager should be compiled stating the problem, objectives of the change, proposed solution, and costs. Necessary policy and procedure changes should be drafted. Changes should be made to job analyses and descriptions as needed.

■ Toward a "Jobless" Work Environment

Dessler (1997) reports that organizations in the 1990s and beyond are grappling with a number of revolutionary forces including "accelerating product and technological change, globalized competition, deregulation, political instability, demographic changes, and trends toward a service society and the information age" (p. 109). As a result, he says, companies are becoming "de-jobbed"—a condition in which the traditional meaning of the term *job* has been blurred and responsibilities are often assigned in process rather than determined at the time of hiring. Several strategies—including (1) flatter organizations, (2) work teams, (3) the boundaryless organization, and (4) reengineering—have contributed to a trend toward less precision in defining jobs.

A "flat" organization refers to the way in which the organization is structured. Instead of a "tall" organization with many layers in its hierarchy, a flat organization has few layers and a wider span of control. The organizational chart appears flat when compared to the tall chart with many layers of management. When there is a wide span of control, workers assume greater responsibility for a wider range of tasks and often take on projects as workloads permit rather than as defined within a job description.

Work teams, as previously discussed, often have responsibilities assigned to the team rather than to the individual. Under this design, team members perform needed tasks according to their schedules, time available, expertise, and interests. These factors may not fit well with the concept of a specific job description. The boundaryless organization refers to widespread use of project teams that operate relatively independently. Team objectives (and, therefore, jobs) are defined and redefined on a regular basis, always with a focus on how the team can best contribute to the overall goals, objectives, and strategic directions of the organization and its programs. Workers adjust to fit the need rather than to respond to a job description.

Reengineering is a term used by Hammer and Champy (1993) and is defined as "the fundamental rethinking and radical redesign of business processes to achieve dramatic improvements in critical, contemporary measures of performance, such as cost, quality, service, and speed" (p. 32). They recommend that, instead of highly specialized division of labor, firms should emphasize combining tasks into integrated, unspecialized processes that are then carried out by committed employees.

Although the problems and needs of human service organizations cannot be directly compared to those of national and international business and industrial corporations, there are some similarities. Human service organizations often function in a highly turbulent environment. Political and economic changes can affect community, state, or national priorities. Community, family, and individual problems are changing. Given the uncertain nature of the human services environment, it would be shortsighted to insist on traditional organizational structure and job design and to assume a "business as usual" mentality. Incorporating concepts of excellence into job design will require ongoing environmental scanning, projecting future scenarios, and maintaining a flexible structure while ensuring that productivity and performance are maximized in the present as well.

SUMMARY

1. **What Is Job and Work Design?** Changing or reorganizing the tasks and responsibilities assigned to employees.
   - *When Can Job Design and Redesign Be Effective?* Many factors can affect productivity. Job redesign cannot solve all problems.
   - *What Can Work Design and Redesign Accomplish?* Work redesign can create a number of opportunities for change.
2. **Analyzing Job Responsibilities.** Job design can be analyzed using three models.
3. **Job- and Work-Design Techniques.** There are a number of alternatives that can be considered. Six are identified here.
   - *Job Enlargement.* Making the job more complex and challenging.
   - *Job Enrichment.* Assuming more responsibility for one's work.
   - *Job Rotation.* A planned exchange of job responsibilities.
   - *Creating Teams.* Reallocating collective responsibility from individuals to a group.
   - *Varying Working Conditions.* Increasing flexibility in the ways in which jobs are fulfilled.
   - *Use of Technology.* Reducing tedious, repetitive work through use of electronic or machine technology.
4. **Toward a "Jobless" Work Environment.** Flatter organizations, work teams, the boundaryless organization, and reengineering are contributing to less formal definitions of jobs and to more focus on accomplishing the work of the organization.

EXERCISES

Please complete the following sections of your manual based on the content covered in Chapter 5.

Section 5: Job and Work Design

5.1 Philosophy on job design. Establish the organization's philosophy on job design. Draw on the three models presented by Miles: traditional, human relations, and human resources.

5.2 Job design strategies. Establish job design strategies that are available to employees in the organization.

5.3 Staff eligibility. Establish criteria that must be met by staff to be eligible for job redesign and the conditions under which employees may apply for the job design options presented in Section 5.2.

REFERENCES

Burns, T., & Stalker, G. (1961). *The management of innovation.* London: Tavistock.

Davis, L. (1976). Developments in job design. In P. Warr (Ed.), *Personal goals and work design* (pp. 67–80). London: John Wiley & sons.

Dessler, G. (1997). *Human resource management* (7th ed.). Upper Saddle River, NJ: Prentice-Hall.

Hackman, J. (1977). Work design. In J. R. Hackman & J. L. Suttle (Eds.), *Improving life at work: Behavioral science approaches to organizational change* (pp. 96–162). Santa Monica, CA: Goodyear.

Hammer, M., & Champy, J. (1993). *Reengineering the corporation: A manifesto for business revolution.* New York: HarperCollins.

Hudson, W. (1990). *Multi-problem screening inventory.* Tempe, AZ: Walmyr.

Kossen, S. (1978). *The human side of organizations* (2nd ed.). New York: Harper & Row.

Mayo, E. (1945). *The social problems of an industrial civilization.* Boston: Division of Research, Harvard Graduate School of Business Administration.

Miles, R. (1975). *Theories of management: Implications for organizational behavior and development.* New York: McGraw-Hill.

Ouchi, W. (1981). *Theory Z: How American business can meet the Japanese challenge.* Reading, MA: Addison-Wesley.

Rapp, C., & Poertner, J. (1992). *Social administration: A client-centered approach.* New York: Longman.

Promoting Excellence through Well-Designed Motivation and Reward Systems

CHAPTER OUTLINE

- Understanding Employee Motivation
- Theories of Motivation
- Designing Effective Reward Systems
- Incorporating Intrinsic Rewards into the Reward System
- Allocating Extrinsic Rewards and Employee Benefits
- Compensation and Financial Incentives
- Paid Time Off
- Insurance and Retirement Benefits
- Employee Service Benefits
- Alternative Work Arrangements
- Job Security and Internal Mobility
- Recognition
- The Cafeteria Plan
- Motivation, Rewards, and Internal Consistency

CHAPTER OBJECTIVES

Upon completion of this chapter, the reader will be able to:

- Identify and summarize five different theoretical perspectives on motivation.
- Itemize and explain the basic criteria for a well-designed reward system.
- Define and explain the differences between intrinsic factors and extrinsic factors and how they affect motivation.
- Summarize eight different components of a complete reward system.

Assumptions

- That employees are most productive when they are highly motivated.
- That different people are motivated in different ways, and it is the responsibility of managers to find ways to motivate staff.
- That high levels of productivity should be rewarded; if not, motivation and morale are affected.
- That many intrinsic and extrinsic factors can be incorporated into a well-designed reward system.

Understanding Employee Motivation

Designing a well-integrated motivation and reward system is arguably one of the most important functions of management in its quest to achieve excellence in organizational performance. The basic functions of a human service agency in meeting the expectations of its mission have to do with serving clients. These core functions are carried out by line staff—not by managers or administrators. So the question becomes how do managers get line staff to work hard and to be as productive as they can possibly be in providing high-quality, effective services to clients?

Many newly appointed supervisors and managers take worker motivation for granted. There often seems to be the assumption that because workers are being paid a salary, it is reasonable to expect them to work to the limits of their abilities. It is not uncommon for managers, when confronted with the problem of an unproductive employee, to take a punitive approach; to issue a warning or put a memo into the employee's personnel record.

Taking employee motivation for granted or using a punitive approach as a first resort usually proves to be shortsighted. A more positive and potentially more successful approach is to design a motivation and reward system that is self-perpetuating and synergistic to keep staff performing at high levels. There are many theories about what motivates people to work hard, some of these theories are reviewed in the following sections. Equally important when examining the issue of motivation is an analysis of the fit of rewards to performance.

There are many organizations that reveal glaring inconsistencies when the concepts of motivation and rewards are examined and analyzed together in relation to each other. Some of the most counterproductive and destructive acts of management can come in relation to the giving of rewards. Unfairness can take a variety of forms. For example, an agency's mission may proclaim its commitment to improving the quality of life for the client population it serves. Some workers take the mission seriously and demonstrate their dedication by performing in a way that goes far beyond minimum expectations in the interest of helping their clients. Some coworkers, however, decide instead to spend much of their time currying favor with influential people in the organization and, in general, "playing politics." When the time comes to distribute rewards—whether they come in the form of salary increases, bonuses, days off, or employee of the month awards—if those who demonstrate success in working with clients are not rewarded over those who befriend and show loyalty to management, the organization is sending a powerful message. Lofty statements about commitment to mission and values made by managers who choose to reward their friends instead of rewarding performance tend to ring hollow. This is why an attempt to focus solely on motivation without also dealing with the design of the reward system is likely to achieve limited success.

Theories of Motivation

The concept of motivation has been explored from a variety of perspectives. Montana and Charnov (1993), drawing on the work of previous studies, identified twenty-five factors that motivate employees (see Figure 6.1). They then examined a number of studies to determine perceptions about motivation and how these perceptions compared to the twenty-five factors.

FIGURE 6.1

Questionnaire Used in Surveys on Motivation

Please indicate by placing an "X" next to the six items from the list below which you believe are the most important in motivating you to do your best work.

1. _____ Steady employment

2. _____ Respect for me as a person

3. _____ Good pay

4. _____ Good physical working conditions

5. _____ Adequate rest periods or coffee breaks

6. _____ Chance to turn out quality work

7. _____ Getting along well with others on the job

8. _____ Having a local employee paper

9. _____ Chance for a promotion

10. _____ Opportunity to do interesting work

11. _____ Pensions and other security benefits

12. _____ Not having to work too hard

13. _____ Knowing what is going on in the organization

14. _____ Feeling my job is important

15. _____ Having an employee council

16. _____ Having a written job description

17. _____ Being told by my boss when I do a good job

18. _____ Getting a performance rating

19. _____ Attending staff meetings

20. _____ Agreement with organization's objectives

21. _____ Opportunity for self-development and improvement

22. _____ Fair vacation arrangements

23. _____ Knowing I will be disciplined if I do a bad job

24. _____ Working under close supervision

25. _____ Large amount of freedom on the job (Chance to work not under direct or close supervision)

Source: Montana, P., & Charnov, B. (1993). *Management.* Hauppauge, NY: Barron's Educational Series, Inc., p. 200. Reproduced with permission from Barron's Educational Series, Inc.

The interesting finding among the four groups that completed the questionnaire was that out of the twenty-five factors only nine factors were selected by respondents in the four studies that were reviewed. Some differences emerged that seemed to reflect the point at which the respondents were in their careers. The following nine factors indicate the top preferences for each of the four studies:

1. Respect for me as a person
2. Good pay
3. Chance to turn out quality work
4. Chance for promotion
5. Opportunity to do interesting work
6. Feeling my job is important
7. Being told by my boss when I do a good job
8. Opportunity for self-development and improvement
9. Large amount of freedom on the job

There is a remarkable degree of consistency among these four groups of respondents in terms of what motivates them to work hard on the job. Over all it is clear that motivation emerges from only a few selected factors.

A number of different theoretical perspectives have been developed and research studies undertaken in an attempt to understand the phenomenon of motivation. In the following sections motivation is explored as understood from the perspectives of (1) meeting personal needs, (2) being challenged by the quality of the job, (3) pursuing achievement, (4) reinforcing performance with rewards, and (5) achieving a feeling that fairness and equity exist in the organization.

Motivating by Meeting Personal Needs

The classic work on understanding needs was developed by Maslow (1962). He identified five levels of need, which he described as (1) physiological, (2) safety and security, (3) social/affiliation, (4) esteem/recognition, and (5) self-actualization. For many years Maslow's framework has defined the way in which we look at and understand need. Physiological needs such as food, clothing, and shelter are basic to life, and until these needs are met it is difficult to focus on any other level of need, simply because the drive to satisfy these needs will consume almost all the energy and resources available. Safety and security needs have to do with freedom from fear of physical danger and deprivation, with some sense of predictability that one will be safe and secure for the foreseeable future. Social or affiliation needs are represented by the need to belong and to be accepted by various groups so that one's basic humanity can be expressed and reinforced in interpersonal interactions. Esteem or recognition needs refer to the need to have recognition and respect from others in the interest of developing a sense of uniqueness, self-confidence, and prestige. Self-actualization needs are those needs that have to do with the desire to become what one is capable of becoming, to perform at the highest levels in one's chosen areas of pursuit. Figure 6.2 illustrates Maslow's hierarchy of needs.

To understand and make use of Maslow's framework for management purposes, one must understand that a satisfied need is not a motivator. For example, if employees are fearful that

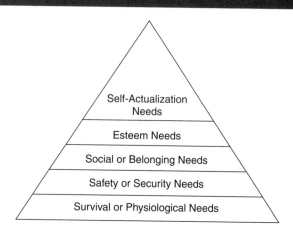

FIGURE 6.2

Maslow's Hierarchy of Needs

they may not be able to feed their children or pay the rent, then meeting physiological needs will motivate them to work. However, if they are highly skilled and in demand in the job market, and if they have a home, two incomes, two cars, and their basic needs are met, then simply meeting physiological, as well as safety and security needs, will not serve as a motivator. For these individuals social, esteem, or self-actualization needs must be addressed. In short, as each level is satisfied, that level will no longer motivate. One must look to the next higher level. The argument might be made that full self-actualization is never really achieved, so there are always challenges at this level when all other levels of need are satisfied. In addition, the ways in which needs are fulfilled can change over time, so that it is possible that one could move down the hierarchy as well as up.

One should be cautious about using Maslow's hierarchy too rigidly. He intended that it be seen as an overall framework, useful in tracking general patterns of need and fulfillment, not one that applies to every individual. A number of experts in the fields of culture and gender have pointed out that the drive for individualization, personal recognition, and uniqueness does not necessarily apply across all cultural and ethnic groups (Green, 1995; Locke, 1992). Ethnicity and gender are important factors to consider when attempting to understand employee motivation. When Maslow's concepts are used, the meanings of such concepts as esteem and self-actualization must be understood within cultural and gender contexts rather than attempt to apply a universal set of definitions across all work situations. However interpreted, Maslow does make an important contribution to the understanding of this complex concept of motivation in the workplace.

Motivating by Enhancing the Quality of Work Assignments

The idea that employees can be motivated by the nature of the job itself was first raised by McGregor (1960) in his discussion of Theory Y (for a review of McGregor's ideas, see Chapter 2). He believed that the opportunity to make use of talent and creativity on the job can meet some important needs for employees, and that every individual has the potential to be mature and self-motivated. Given these assumptions, the job of the manager becomes one of removing the barriers to high performance within the organization. This will enable the worker to maximize his or her potential. The way to squelch motivation, he believed, was to break responsibilities down into simple tasks and to closely supervise and control people in their efforts to complete their assignments, hence, the notion that motivation comes from the amount of freedom, flexibility, and creativity that can be exercised in carrying out the job.

An important study in support of the idea that motivation comes from the substance and structure of the job itself was published by Herzberg (1966) and is referred to as the two-factor theory of satisfaction and motivation. Herzberg and his colleagues divided work into two factors that they called motivating factors and hygiene factors. Motivating factors included items such as personal growth in competence, achievement, responsibility, and recognition. These factors are intrinsic to the work that is done and are called motivators because employees were motivated to obtain these factors and were willing to improve their work performance to do so.

Factors extrinsic to or outside of the work itself, such as wages, hours, working conditions, company policies, and supervisory practices, are called hygiene factors. Hygiene factors have the potential to raise or lower dissatisfaction but do not motivate employees to increase productivity or performance. This theory specifies that the tasks and responsibilities assigned to a job will enhance motivation only to the degree that motivators are designed into the work itself. Good pay and working conditions will keep down the level of dissatisfaction but will, in the long run, not inspire employees to perform at high levels. Intrinsic and extrinsic factors are depicted in Table 6.1.

Looking at the studies cited by Montana and Charnov (1993) referred to earlier in this chapter, it is evident that factors such as the opportunity to do quality work, the opportunity for self-development and improvement, the opportunity to do interesting work, and a large amount of freedom on the job are motivating factors today just as they were in the 1960s when Herzberg's studies were being conducted. When combining the two-factor theory with Maslow's framework, we can see that motivating or intrinsic factors would be defined in terms of esteem or self-actualization needs, whereas hygiene or extrinsic factors would fit with physiological, safety, and security needs. Social needs might fit into either category,

TABLE 6.1
Motivating and Hygiene Factors as Defined by Herzberg

Motivating Factors/Intrinsic to the Job (Motivate people to work hard)	Hygiene Factors/Extrinsic to the Job (Keep down the level of dissatisfaction)
Achievement	Organizational policy and administration
Recognition	Supervision
Work itself	Working conditions
Responsibility	Interpersonal relations with superiors, subordinates, and peers
Advancement	Salary
Growth	Status
	Job security
	Personal life

depending on the extent to which they related to the work to be performed as compared to interpersonal relationships in a social context.

Motivating employees by focusing on the quality of work assignments offers the manager some interesting insights as well as some useful tools for increasing and enhancing productivity and performance.

Motivating by Providing Access to Achievement

Over the years, behavioral scientists have observed that certain people have an intense need to achieve whereas others may be mildly motivated and still others not at all. McClelland (1961) studied the achievement motive for many years and found that people who are highly motivated to achieve need to set moderately difficult but potentially achievable goals. They tend to take a middle ground relative to risk. They are not gamblers who will choose the big risk in hope of a significant gain, but if they fail, their failure cannot necessarily be attributed to personal responsibility. Neither are they conservative individuals who choose small risks in which the gain is small but secure, and there is little danger of anything going wrong that might reflect on their abilities. Rather, achievement-oriented people tend to prefer a moderate degree of risk because they want to feel that their efforts and abilities had something to do with the outcome.

Achievement-motivated people are not necessarily motivated by the rewards of success. Motivation is directed more toward accomplishments. They are very much interested in their performance on the job and seek concrete feedback about what they can do to improve. They are less interested in feedback on personal qualities than on job performance. They tend to work well in positions that allow for autonomy and entrepreneurial behavior. They can make many positive contributions to organizations because they are constantly looking for ways to solve problems and make the organization better. However, some experts question whether achievement-motivated people make good managers. Because they are highly task oriented and work to their capacity, they tend to expect these behaviors from others. Accomplishing work through others presents a set of tasks and skills that does not always fit for those with high achievement motivation (Montana and Charnov, 1993).

Motivating by Reinforcing Performance with Rewards

A theoretical framework commonly referred to as expectancy theory, developed by Vroom (1964) attempts to expand on earlier findings that behavior is influenced by an individual's needs. Vroom discovered that productive behavior in a work setting is enhanced if the employee sees a positive relationship between effort, performance, rewards, and valued outcomes. In essence the theory proposes that motivated behavior is increased if extended efforts on the part of the employee produce higher levels of performance, if enhanced performance produces rewards, and if the rewards and outcomes of performance are valued by the organization. Montana and Charnov (1993) express expectancy theory as follows:

Motivation = the expectancy $\rightarrow$ the expectancy $\rightarrow$ preference of
that increased   that increased   the individual
effort will lead   performance will   for the rewards
to increased   lead to rewards
performance

For example, a manager may decide that in order to reduce the size of a waiting list for a counseling program, caseloads will be increased by 10 percent. In order to ensure that there is not a drop-off in quality of services, the manager asks first-line supervisors to track caseworker progress and success with clients and to record findings in quarterly performance reviews. Bonuses and compensatory time are promised in return for high levels of performance.

If the foregoing formula is correct, then it will mean that increased effort on the part of caseworkers will lead to greater progress and success with clients, and that progress and success with clients will lead to increased salaries and compensatory time off. However, if working longer hours and investing greater effort to keep up with the increased workload does not produce a higher level of performance, or if quality of counseling deteriorates with the increase in caseloads, motivation will suffer. Likewise, if promised rewards are not forthcoming or not considered to be worth the increased effort, motivation and performance will deteriorate.

Closely related to this is the work of B. F. Skinner (1969) on reinforcement. His research demonstrated that reinforced behavior will be repeated, and behavior that is not reinforced will be extinguished. Skinner's ideas about behavior modification were found to be relevant to the field of management when applied to reinforcing employee behavior. Reinforcers applied selectively tend to reproduce the desired behavior and performance. Positive reinforcers include rewards or positive feedback. Negative reinforcers include the withdrawal of an unpleasant experience or consequence, which has the effect of encouraging the desired behavior. Punishments are negative consequences designed to extinguish a behavior. Skinner's concepts can be useful in constructing a motivation and reward system.

The work of Vroom and Skinner on motivation and rewards might seem on the surface to contradict the work of Herzberg (1966). Herzberg found that factors extrinsic to the job itself, such as wages, hours, and working conditions, did not motivate higher levels of performance but rather served to reduce dissatisfaction with the job and the work environment. The important difference, however, is that Vroom and Skinner both focused on making a conscious and positive connection between a behavior and a reward. This approach is different from simply increasing salaries or modifying working conditions for workers across the board.

Both expectancy theory and reinforcement theory support the concept that a positive interrelationship between performance and rewards is critical to achieving high levels of motivation. A manager who attempts to motivate simply by meeting needs, enhancing the quality of the work assignment, or providing access to achievement will find that the effects dissipate quickly if they are not part of a systematic effort to reward positive behavior and extinguish unproductive behavior.

Motivating through Fairness and Equity

One of the most difficult challenges for managers is ensuring that fairness and equity exist in the distribution of pay and other rewards. The perception by employees that there is unfairness in the system has proved to be a powerful disincentive to optimum performance. According to Montana and Charnov (1993), perceptions of fairness and equity are affected by two factors:

1. Comparison of the compensation received to such factors as effort, job performance, education, experience, skill, and seniority.
2. Comparison of the perceived equity of pay and rewards received to those received by other people.

The first issue raises the question: Am I being paid a fair wage for what I do for this organization? The second raises the question: Am I being paid equitably in relation to coworkers? Because of the difficulty in measuring such factors as job effort and performance, few organizations can claim perfect balance in terms of fairness and equity. As a result, when individuals receive less than they believe they should, they are dissatisfied; when they receive more than they should, they are uncomfortable with the perceived overpayment and attempt to justify it in a variety of ways, but it does not serve as a motivator (Adams, 1965).

Motivation and rewards are very much intertwined. When certain conditions exist, reward systems have been demonstrated to motivate performance (Lawler, 1971; Vroom, 1964). The conditions are that rewards that are perceived to be important to employees are tied to effective performance in a timely manner. All of the variables mentioned—rewards, perception, importance, performance, and timeliness—come into play in using rewards to motivate employees. What is given to employees must be seen as a reward, and it must be important to employees in general and the recipient in particular. Rewards must be tied to performance, and it must be done in a manner that will ensure that employees perceive the relationship. All of this must be done within a time frame that ensures that employees will make the connection between the performance and the reward. Finally, for this system to have a positive, motivating impact on employees, they have to have a sense of trust that the system has integrity and will remain trustworthy in the future (Lawler, 1977).

■ Designing Effective Reward Systems

Lawler (1977) identifies a number of features that contribute to an effective reward system. In terms of overall considerations, he points out, reward systems must contribute to both organizational effectiveness and the quality of work life. If a system serves only to support the organization, for example, by rewarding only for extremely high workloads, but fails to improve the quality of work life, the system will not accomplish its objectives. Likewise, if it serves only to make employees happy and improve morale but fails to contribute to organizational effectiveness, the system again will be flawed and fail to achieve its objectives. For an organization to have an effective reward system its managers must understand how effectiveness is to be achieved and what its employees consider to be the important factors in determining quality of work life.

Building on these two principles, Lawler (1977, p. 167) identifies four necessary reward system properties:

1. *Basic Needs Satisfied.* A reward system cannot be expected to meet its objectives in a system in which the overall salary structure does not allow employees to meet their basic needs, or a system in which employees are frequently being terminated. Some degree of satisfaction with salary and job security must exist. On top of these factors, salary increases or other rewards must be sufficient enough that they can be spread among a majority of employees and still be perceived as meaningful in terms of satisfying basic needs.
2. *Competitive Benefits.* The reward levels in the organization must compare favorably with those in other organizations. If an organization is not competitive with salaries and benefits in other comparable organizations, employee turnover will increase, and the reward system will fail to meet its objectives.

3. *Equitable Distribution.* The rewards that are available must be distributed in a way that is seen as equitable by the people in the organization. The factors that determine how rewards are distributed should be as objective and as quantified as possible, and there should be an openness about the system so that all employees are aware of the criteria for performance and the rules for distribution of rewards. A system that allows for modification based on employee input is more likely to be seen as fair and equitable by employees.

4. *Employees as Individuals.* The reward system must deal with organization members as individuals. This principle relates to the discussion of Maslow's work at the beginning of this chapter. Not every employee has the same needs. Some will place a high value on salary increases whereas others may prefer a flexible schedule or the opportunity to work out of the home.

One of the ways in which individualization is accomplished is referred to as the Need-Path-Goal Model (Miles, 1975; Porter and Lawler, 1968). Following this model, a manager would attempt to (1) identify an employee's needs, (2) determine the employee's goals, and (3) establish a path designed to meet the needs and achieve the goal. The path is defined in terms of work performance and achieving organizational and program objectives. Working from this simple concept, Miles developed an expanded Need-Path-Goal Model based on Maslow's framework. This expanded model is illustrated in Figure 6.3.

FIGURE 6.3

A Framework for Analyzing Motivation

Needs	Paths	Goals
Self-realization (actualization)	Outstanding performance (high commitment, effort, and regular improvement in skill and capability)	Challenging work (job with opportunity for growth, creativity, responsibility)
Esteem (ego)		Promotions, recognition from superiors, titles and other marks of status, pay
Social (belonging)	Group norms determine (may emphasize high or low effort-performance)	Recognition from peers Esteem of coworkers Acceptance by group
Safety (security) Physiological (food, clothing, shelter, etc.)	Minimally acceptable performance (meeting at least lower limits of standards—no major violations of rules and regulations)	Job tenure, seniority, pension plans, etc., avoidance of censure from superiors Regular pay and benefits, working conditions

Source: Miles, R. (1975). *Theories of management.* New York: McGraw-Hill, p. 137. Reproduced with the permission of The McGraw-Hill Companies.

Incorporating Intrinsic Rewards into the Reward System

In exploring the elements of a sound reward system, it is useful to return briefly to the work of Herzberg (1966) and his concepts of intrinsic or motivating factors versus extrinsic or hygiene factors.

Designing a reward system so that intrinsic factors are incorporated into the system involves changes primarily in the areas of organizational structure and job design (topics covered in the previous two chapters). Well-designed work assignments will ensure meaningful work, achievement, and other such intrinsic rewards. Well-designed structure will ensure responsibility, will support recognition, and will provide opportunity for advancement. Organizational structure and job design should be systematically addressed as a part of the motivation and reward system. The relationships between motivation, performance, and rewards should be clear. Both intrinsic and extrinsic rewards are necessary components of a complete reward system.

Allocating Extrinsic Rewards and Employee Benefits

Many of the issues to be addressed in defining an effective reward system come under the heading of extrinsic rewards. Most organizations make available a number of options within their reward systems. In a competitive market within a strong economy, employers are increasingly discovering that creativity and flexibility in designing rewards pay off in terms of satisfied employees and reduced turnover. Several decades ago when the issues surrounding rewards were first raised for discussion, options were limited to such considerations as salary increases, a few basic fringe benefits, promotions, and special awards or recognition. As we move into the twenty-first century, CEOs of major corporations are recognizing that the creative use of benefits not only reduces turnover and increases employee loyalty but also affects the bottom line. Here a number of factors that go into a complete reward system are examined, including (1) compensation and financial incentives, (2) paid time off, (3) insurance benefits, (4) employee service benefits, (5) alternative work arrangements, (6) job security and internal mobility, and (7) recognition.

Compensation and Financial Incentives
Determining the Basic Salary Structure

Designing fair compensation systems is a challenge to any manager but is especially difficult for those who manage nonprofits in which resources are typically scarce and the workload demanding. Designing a fair and equitable compensation system requires an analysis of the worth and value of each position to the organization. Among the many factors to be considered are (1) the complexity of the job, (2) the importance to overall organizational effectiveness, (3) the responsibilities carried, including supervision of subordinates, (4) the level of knowledge and skill required to perform the job, (5) the number and level of other employees, and (6) the current and future financial stability of the agency.

Jensen (1997) points out that attempting to deal with these issues as they emerge and failing to design a systematic salary policy are major impediments to productivity. Designing such a policy, he says, should include the following principles:

- *Put your basic compensation policies in writing before making decisions about anyone's pay.* This increases clarity and allows for the development and refinement of an official agency position on compensation. He states that the following factors must be prioritized: (1) attraction and retention of employees, (2) employee confidence in and acceptance of the pay plan, (3) client or funding source confidence in and acceptance of the pay plan, (4) control of costs, and (5) facilitation of equitable salary adjustments.

- *Decide how salaries will be increased.* The two basic options are by merit or by automatic progression. Some organizations opt for automatic progression that advances individuals on a predetermined schedule, regardless of work quantity or quality. This can be demoralizing to staff. Rewarding merit is ideal but difficult to define and quantify in a way that makes the rewards fair and equitable.

- *Determine the value of each job in your agency.* A job analysis should be conducted for each position. The job analyses, collectively, should be analyzed in relation to each other in order to develop a hierarchy of jobs in the agency, from the highest levels of responsibility for organizational success to the lowest. Jobs within the job hierarchy are then clustered in terms of similar levels of responsibility, and grade levels are assigned, with Grade 1 being the lowest salary category on up through the highest grade.

- *Devise a permanent structure for your pay system, including dollar values for each job.* Dollar values for each job are determined through a salary survey, which is used to establish the market value of key jobs in each salary grade. Once a market value is established for each grade, that salary figure is used as the midpoint for the salary structure. Jensen suggests that a salary range from –15 percent to +15 percent of the midpoint be established for each grade, but percentages can be tailored to the needs and resources of the agency. Within this structure, individual salary levels are then set.

- *Anticipate the problems you will have in everyday administration of salaries.* Jensen suggests that these problems will include the following: How often should salaries be reviewed? How large and how frequent should raises be? Who should make decisions about pay? How confidential should salary matters be? What laws must be considered in administering salaries? How can funds be generated for regular salary increases?

Merit Increases

If they are truly to reflect merit, increases must be tied in some way to performance. This means that the performance appraisal system must be integrated into the overall motivation and reward system. Performance appraisal will be discussed in detail in Chapter 13. At this point we need to look only at how employee performance relates to the reward system. For example, some organizations devise a system in which performance appraisal instruments are tailored to positions, and after all items have been evaluated and scored, an overall score is determined and placed into categories similar to the following:

1 = *Unsatisfactory.* This employee completed less than 80 percent of activities and/or achieved less than 80 percent of the objectives established in the performance contract at the beginning of the performance year. Requires a major commitment of supervisory time.

2 = *Below expectations.* This employee was able to complete at least 80 percent of activities and achieve at least 80 percent of the major objectives but requires considerable direction and guidance.

3 = *Meets expectations.* This employee's performance demonstrates completion of at least 90 percent of the activities, and meets at least 90 percent of the objectives established in the performance contract at the beginning of the performance year.

4 = *Above expectations.* The results of this employee's performance surpass expectations established in the performance contract at the beginning of the performance year, and he or she is able to perform with minimal direction and guidance.

5 = *Clearly superior.* The results of this employee's performance clearly surpass expectations established in the performance contract at the beginning of the performance year. The employee performs independently, and the effects of this employee's work can be seen in program results.

Within this type of a framework, pay increases may be divided into five levels, with a percentage of increase tied to each level. Employees who achieve the highest rating within each job classification receive the highest percentage of merit increase. Employees who receive a rating of three or below would get a cost-of-living adjustment but no merit increase. This scheme is depicted in Table 6.2.

TABLE 6.2

A Plan for Tying Merit Increases to Performance Appraisal Scores

	Performance Appraisal Overall Score				
	1	2	3	4	5
Level of Staff	**Unsatisfactory**	**Below Expectations**	**Meets Expectations**	**Above Expectations**	**Clearly Superior**
Management/ Administration	No merit increase	No merit increase	No merit increase	Up to 4% merit	Up to 6% merit
Supervisory Staff	No merit increase	No merit increase	No merit increase	Up to 4% merit	Up to 6% merit
Direct Service Staff	No merit increase	No merit increase	No merit increase	Up to 5% merit	Up to 7% merit
Paraprofessional Staff	No merit increase	No merit increase	No merit increase	Up to 6% merit	Up to 8% merit
Support Staff	No merit increase	No merit increase	No merit increase	Up to 6% merit	Up to 8% merit

The value of this approach is that it brings together a number of important principles of salary increases. First, it establishes the principle that employees will be rewarded when performance is exemplary. This can serve to reinforce what has been stated in mission, vision, and philosophy statements. Second, it ties performance to the size of the increase.

If the framework for the system is made available to all employees, they will know in advance what is required to maximize their merit increases and will see that those who perform get rewarded. Finally, it enforces the principle that people who perform below expectations or who need a great deal of supervision will likely remain at low salary levels until performance changes.

■ CONSIDERATIONS

For Planning Merit Increases

Basic Questions:	What types of behaviors and performances does the organization want to reward? How can performance be evaluated in a way that is fair and equitable to all? How can the organization provide meaningful rewards and yet keep within cost-containment guidelines?
Time Frame:	Criteria for rewards should be reevaluated on an annual basis.
Process:	Supervisory and management personnel should review performance and reward data after each round of annual performance evaluations and merit increases.
Analysis:	Performance scores and merit increases should be rank ordered and correlated to determine if there is consistency within the system. The rank ordering of employees by performance scores should be evaluated against some other criteria as a check of validity.
Policy Changes:	If any criteria or scoring systems are changed as a result of the analysis, the policy statement on merit increases should be revised to reflect the changes.

COLA, Lump-Sum Salary Increases, and Bonuses

Cost-of-living allowances (COLA) are typically tied in some formal or informal way to the consumer price index (CPI), which establishes an inflation rate for each year. COLA increases are given with the assumption that failure to enable employees to keep up with inflation results in a net decrease in disposable income. COLA is awarded across the board to all employees, usually in terms of a percentage of salary. COLA may be at, above, or below the CPI, depending on the resources available to an agency in any given year.

Both COLA and merit increases generally come in the form of a percentage increase in salary. Some employers are concerned that percentage increases can lead to significant salary discrepancies over time. For example, an employee who is making $75,000 is making $50,000 more than a person with a $25,000 salary. If a 5 percent salary increase is awarded, the higher-paid person is now making $78,750 and the lower person is making $26,250. The discrepancy is now $52,500, and it grows every year that a percentage increase is awarded.

	Current salary	Increase of 5%	New Salary
Manager	75,000	3,750	78,750
Caseworker	25,000	1,250	26,250
Difference	50,000	2,500	52,500

To counteract this growing discrepancy, some organizations design a salary structure that will permit a fixed-dollar amount across the board instead of a percentage. This plan runs the risk of discouraging higher-salaried employees, but this effect may be softened if they are included in the planning and implementation of the system, helped to recognize its benefits to lower-salaried employees, and perhaps compensated in some other ways not affecting salary.

Another option that some organizations have found useful is to award bonuses for achieving individual or program objectives. Merit and COLA increases are typically added to base salary. This means that a salary increase awarded for good performance in one year is paid for in every subsequent year as well, regardless of performance. In addition, employee-related expenses such as taxes, insurance premiums, and retirement contributions are figured on an ever-increasing salary base.

For example, if an employee makes a salary of $40,000 and employee-related expenses (fringe benefits) are 20 percent of base salary, then the total package of salary and benefits comes to $48,000 ($40,000 base plus $8,000 fringe benefits). A salary increase to $45,000 means that costs to the organization will escalate by $6,000, from a total package of $48,000 to $54,000, $5,000 for the salary and $1,000 for employee-related expenses.

Base salary	=	$40,000
Fringe benefits at 20%	=	$8,000
Total salary and benefits	=	$48,000
Salary increase at 12.5%	=	$45,000
Fringe benefits at 20%	=	$9,000
New salary and benefits	=	$54,000
Total increased cost to agency	=	$6,000

Each year as COLA and merit increases are added to base salary, the total benefit package escalates. Employees and unions support this trend as a way of allowing workers to increase their base salaries beyond the inflation factor reflected in COLA. Some employers, however, believe that a year of exemplary performance ought to be rewarded in that year but not added to base salary. In these systems, salaries may be increased by a cost-of-living factor for all employees and then one-time bonuses awarded in relation to performance and the organization's ability to pay.

■ C O N D E R A T I O N S

For Assessing COLA, Lump-Sum Increases, and Bonuses

Basic Questions: Can the agency afford to commit itself to an annual cost-of-living adjustment so that employee salaries will keep up with inflation? Can the agency afford additional salary increases tied to performance? If so, should these increases come in terms of a percentage of salary, a fixed-dollar amount, or a bonus?

Time Frame: Salary issues should be reconsidered on at least an annual basis.

Process: The management team should include this discussion as a regular agenda item for consideration at the beginning of the fiscal year. Input should be solicited from employees at all levels.

Analysis: Budget figures should be used to determine the pool of dollars available. The impact of COLA, fixed-dollar increases, or bonuses should be calculated and the findings compared.

Policy Changes: Existing policies on salary increases should be modified to reflect any changes.

■ Paid Time Off

One of the most expensive benefits awarded to employees is the pay received for time not worked. This pay comes as a result of such benefits as vacation, sick leave, unemployment insurance, pregnancy or parental leave, holidays, sabbaticals, and other such arrangements. In a survey published in 1995, payments for time not worked amounted to 10.4 percent of total payroll costs (Bureau of National Affairs, 1995). The only item that was larger than payment for time not worked was medical and related benefits, which amounted to 11 percent of total payroll costs.

Vacation and holidays are typically part of an employer's benefit package. The number of days varies considerably from one employer to another and is usually tied in some way to time in service to the organization. A typical plan might offer two weeks of vacation for one to five years of service, three weeks for six to ten years, and four or more weeks for eleven or more years of service. Most organizations offer about ten paid holidays per year, days on which the agency is closed and services to clients are not available. These holidays usually include all the major federal government-declared holidays, often with a mix of state-observed holidays and special holidays offered by the agency such as the day after Thanksgiving.

Sick leave, like vacation, is earned through time on the job. Typically, one-half to one day per month is earned. Days may be accumulated and taken as needed, and most sick leave policies grant full pay when sick days are used. Some organizations also offer what is referred to as personal days where employees are allowed to take time off to handle personal business or perhaps to celebrate a birthday.

Over the years, paid time off has become a complex benefit to administer because it requires extensive tracking to ensure that employees take off only the time that they have earned in each category of paid time off. In addition, the paid time off benefit raises the question of whether policies and practices are structured in a way that provides an incentive to employees to take off the maximum number of days to which they are entitled, thereby reducing overall organizational productivity. To counteract this incentive, some organizations will pay employees for vacation and sick days accumulated but not used. This provides an incentive to minimize time off the job.

Because of the many complexities in monitoring the various types of paid time off, some organizations have created a simple plan that lumps all types—vacation, holidays, sick time, personal time—into one category and have developed a formula for the total number of days off per year to which each employee is entitled. Employees are not asked to categorize or justify paid time off. They are required simply to plan with their immediate supervisor to ensure that there is coverage within the unit and that the time taken off is properly recorded.

Unemployment insurance should also be calculated into the total picture of paid time off, although the costs are not the same to the agency because they are covered by government-sponsored insurance programs. All states have unemployment compensation laws that follow federal guidelines and provide for continuing income in the event that a person is unable to work. The benefits are paid for by a tax on employers. If employees suffer an injury or disability that keeps them off the job, there will be costs to the agency if additional help must be employed to cover the workload of the injured or disabled employee.

Given the high cost of paid time off, the complexity of administering and monitoring employees' use of time off, the complex needs of working families, and the high value placed on paid time off by employees, it is important that a plan is designed that takes into consideration employee needs for flexibility as well as agency needs for cost containment and ease of administration.

■ CONSIDERATIONS

For Assessing Policies for Paid Time Off

Basic Questions:	What is the financial and workload impact on the agency of one day of paid time off for one employee? How much paid time off can the agency afford? How much paid time off do the agency's competitors offer? What form of paid time off is most efficient for the agency—categories such as sick and vacation time, or simply a total number of hours off per year?
Time Frame:	The impact of paid time off on the budget and on worker performance, together with employee satisfaction with current practices, should be evaluated toward the end of each fiscal year.
Process:	Supervisory and management staff should review the budget and assess the impact of paid time off on workload. Workers should be surveyed for their satisfaction with current practices.
Analysis:	The impact of current paid time off policies on the budget and on worker performance should be assessed. Worker input should be analyzed. Budget projections for the coming year, together with employee feedback, should be used to propose modifications.
Policy Changes:	Policies on paid time off should be revised as needed.

■ Insurance and Retirement Benefits

Insurance and retirement benefits are generally considered part of the total system of compensation rather than part of the reward system. In the early days of creating benefit packages, the most common type of insurance provided was health insurance. According to a 1991 survey of employers, about 92 percent of medium and large firms and 69 percent of small firms make some type of health insurance available to their employees (Bureau of National Affairs, 1991). A survey published in 1995 indicated that medical and related benefits accounted for, on average, just over 11 percent of total payroll costs (Bureau of National Affairs, 1995). The percentage of premium paid by employer and employee varies, but in most organizations the employer pays the major share while the employee pays the remainder.

Over the years various types of insurance programs have been introduced into benefit packages. A survey of 1,020 companies nationwide indicates that in 1998 40 percent of the respondents offered some assistance with elder care. Of those employers offering elder care programs, 81 percent offer resource and referral services; 35 percent offer long-term care insurance, and 14 percent offer counseling (Langdon, 1999). Long-term care insurance is offered to employees who expect to have responsibility for caring for their aging parents. The national average cost for long-term care was about $38,000 per year in 1995, but in New York State costs were $75,000 to $80,000 per year (Spragins, 1995). By some estimates, cost for full-time nursing care will soon reach $100,000 per year. For this reason, a number of insurance plans are offered that will underwrite some of the costs of long-term care when it is needed. Some organizations work in a collaborative way with insurance companies to make these types of policies available to their employees. The agency may pay some of the cost of premiums or the employee may be expected to pay the full cost.

Some organizations also offer group life insurance. The share of the premium paid by the employer varies with the type of organization and available resources. In some cases, group life insurance premiums are paid entirely by the employer. In others, the employer will negotiate the best benefits possible and will then make the opportunity available to the employee with the expectation that the employee will pay the entire premium.

Retirement plans are also an important part of a complete benefit package. They are generally designed in a way that encourages loyalty and longtime employment with the organization. A defined-benefit-pension plan is one that includes a formula for determining retirement benefits. Any employee can calculate ahead of time how much income may be expected at the point of retirement (Dessler, 1997). These plans typically incorporate the number of years of employment and average salary for the last few years prior to retirement. This type of plan is designed to reward long-term employment and also to protect the organization from having any dramatic increase in salary in the last year of employment carry over to many years of retirement. Averaging the last few (usually three to five) years tends to produce a more realistic salary base from which a defined-benefit plan may be calculated, as illustrated below.

Policy: Pension equals 2% of the average salary for the last five years prior
to retirement times the number of years of employment, as follows:

Average salary for the last five years	=	$57,500
2% of $57,500	=	$1,150
Number of years of employment	=	32
Total annual pension amount	=	$36,800

Another alternative is a defined-contribution plan, which allows the employee to set up a retirement account and specifies what contribution an employer will make (Dessler, 1997). In this type of plan, no commitment is made to the eventual benefit amount, only to the contribution. One popular type of defined contribution plan is the 401(k) plan, based on Section 401(k) of the Internal Revenue Code. Employees may have a portion of their salary deducted before it is taxed and invested in an approved retirement plan. Retirement or pension plans are offered at the discretion of the employer, and the size and attractiveness of the benefits often depend on the supply of and demand for workers as well as the nature of benefit packages that competitors are offering.

Social Security should also be considered when calculating the benefit package. However, financial planners warn that it should never be considered as a main source of retirement income—only as one leg of a three-legged stool that includes a retirement plan, personal savings and investments, and Social Security. Like company retirement plans, Social Security includes contributions from both employer and employee. An important difference is that Social Security is mandated by the federal government and is an entitlement to those who qualify. Regular annual benefit statements are sent to participants in the Social Security program.

Organizations use insurance and retirement benefits primarily to attract and hold good employees. They are not expected to serve as motivational factors or to influence day-to-day performance. In addition to providing insurance and retirement benefits that are competitive with other similar organizations, it is also recognized that for employees to achieve maximum productivity, they need to be relieved of stress as much as possible. Worrying about health, about caring for elderly parents, or about providing for survivors in the event of an untimely and unexpected death can cause unnecessary stress for employees that experience these events. Viewed from this perspective, insurance and retirement benefits become a way of protecting employees from situations of financial disaster and supporting a continuation of quality of life, thereby allowing employees to focus on the work at hand.

For many employees, the connection between insurance and retirement benefits and day-to-day performance is fairly remote. Workers seldom make the connection in the same way that they do with salary, merit increases, or bonuses. Some organizations prepare an annual statement of benefits designed to remind employees that there is more to their compensation package than salary alone.

If benefits are intended to be valued by employees and seen as a reward for performance, they must be designed in a way that employees have input into what particular benefits are meaningful to them. A flexible design that seems to accomplish this objective, referred to as the *cafeteria plan* will be discussed toward the end of this chapter.

■ C O N S I D E R A T I O N S

For Assessing Insurance and Retirement Benefits

Basic Questions: How much of the budget can be allocated to insurance and retirement benefits? What formula will provide the most generous retirement benefits possible while keeping within budgeted amounts? What types of insurance are most in demand by employees?

Time Frame:	Insurance and retirement benefits should be reevaluated when it appears that either more or fewer resources will be available for these plans, or when an opportunity (such as an investment) is presented that promises to increase benefits.
Process:	The business manager should draw on outside expertise to get the best information available. Employee input and satisfaction should be solicited. Any proposed changes will eventually go to the agency director and the board.
Analysis:	Each alternative should be presented in a spreadsheet format that compares strengths and weaknesses of alternative plans.
Policy Changes:	Policy changes on insurance and retirement benefits should be reflected in the policy manual.

■ Employee Service Benefits

One area of benefits that has increased dramatically in the last decade is that of personal support services. This covers a wide range of resources that are made available to employees to help meet family needs (such as child care or counseling for substance abuse problems), educational and career needs, health and wellness needs, or financial planning needs. These services are in response to a recognition that keeping up with the demands of raising a family, maintaining good health, achieving career goals, and remaining financially stable can be overwhelming, especially in a family in which both parents are working. Many employers attempt to relieve some of the burden by providing easy access to various resources that are designed to support employees in meeting some of these areas of need.

One of the most popular of these employee service benefits is the provision of child care or a child care subsidy. The percentage of U.S. women with children under age 6 in the workforce has increased dramatically over the past few decades. Finding good-quality child care is an extremely high priority for families with children in which both parents work. Some of the larger corporate employers, in recognition of this concern, have developed child care programs that are provided within the employer's facility. Others pay all or part of child care expenses at approved child care facilities. In a 1998 survey of employers, 97 percent of employers surveyed offered dependent care spending accounts to help employees cover child care costs. Eleven percent offered on-site child care, 15 percent sick or emergency child care programs, and 48 percent resource and referral services (Langdon, 1999).

When financial planning services or prepaid legal services are offered as a benefit, the arrangement usually involves professional consultation made available to agency employees with a financial planner or attorney who negotiates a special rate with the agency in exchange for the opportunity to expand his or her clientele. Shared payment arrangements between agency and the employee vary depending on agency resources available and the importance of this benefit to employees as compared to other options.

Another benefit that has been popular in the field of human services is the educational subsidy to allow employees to continue their education. This can include reimbursement for tuition, subsidy for expenses such as books and other equipment, or it could involve a flat scholarship amount per year. Many of these types of subsidies are dependent on successful completion of course work, and demonstrated progress toward the employee's stated educational objective. Some employers pay only for courses directly related to the job, but others will also reimburse for courses that are not directly related but may contribute to employee growth or the completion of a degree. Periodically the federal government will make subsidies available for education in an area such as child welfare in which there is a high demand for trained personnel. The contract usually calls for one year of obligation to the agency for each year of subsidized education.

Over the years, many employers have discovered that it is a good investment to provide counseling services to employees to help them overcome problems with such issues as indebtedness, family discord, abuse of drugs or alcohol or other personal problems. This service has evolved into what has become known as the employee assistance program (EAP). There are four basic models of EAP in use today: (1) the in-house model in which the services are offered by a company-employed counselor, (2) the out-of-house model in which the company contracts with an individual or with a social service agency that specializes in this type of counseling, (3) the consortium model in which several organizations pool resources for the purpose of establishing EAP services, and (4) the affiliate model in which a vendor already under contract to an employer subcontracts with a professional counselor to provide counseling to employees (Dessler, 1997).

These examples barely scratch the surface of employee service benefit options. Essentially employers are limited only by their own creativity and the resources available for these types of benefits. Employers have learned that such benefits as wellness programs, sometimes including health club memberships, smoking cessation clinics, weight reduction programs, and others can improve health and increase energy levels as well as raise company morale. Overall trends show an increasing investment in these types of benefits as employees seek to improve their quality of life in their professional as well as their personal lives.

■ CONSIDERATIONS

For Assessing Employee Service Benefits

Basic Questions:	What budget resources are available to underwrite the cost of employee service benefits? What benefits are important to employees?
Time Frame:	Whenever resources become available, employees express an interest, or an opportunity is presented to the organization.
Process:	Business manager explores opportunities, solicits input from staff, presents alternative plans to the management team.
Analysis:	Explore costs and benefits to other organizations that have provided similar employee service benefits.
Policy Changes:	Write or refine the policy on employee service benefits if there are changes.

■ Alternative Work Arrangements

As the number of families with two adults working has increased, so has the demand for more flexible work schedules. Managing a household often requires that someone be available during the working day, and employers have discovered that employees can be more productive when they are relieved of worries about household management. This concern for employee quality of life both on and off the job has led to a variety of alternative work arrangements including (1) flexible working hours, (2) job sharing, and (3) telecommuting.

The idea of giving employees flexible working hours was first introduced by a German aerospace firm in 1967 (Kossen, 1978). Thousands of U.S. corporations and government entities have subsequently adopted the practice. Often referred to as flextime, the concept enables workers to adapt their work schedules to blend with the demands of their personal lives. Workers are still expected to work the full number of hours, but they are able to choose their start and completion times, within the limitations established by the employer. This permits a parent, for example, to take a child to school or day care in the morning, and to pick the child up in the afternoon at times that coincide with the child's needs and schedule rather than being dictated by the parent's work schedule. In a 1998 survey of employers, 79 percent of the companies surveyed offered flextime; 66 percent offered part-time employment, and 40 percent offered job sharing (Langdon, 1999).

Another approach to alternative work arrangements is job sharing. This practice requires that two workers share a single job, including all work responsibilities as well as salary and fringe benefits. The advantages include many of those cited earlier for flextime. In addition, employers have found that part-time employees tend to approach their work with greater energy and often put in more than a half-day's work for a half-day's pay (Kossen, 1978). A disadvantage is that job sharing can be more expensive for the employer in terms of the cost of benefits as well as the increased need for training and staff development.

Telecommuting is the practice of allowing employees to work at home with the understanding that a home computer will be connected to the employer's electronic network and the employee will stay in touch through the use of e-mail, fax, voice mail, or other forms of telecommunication. This arrangement works only for those positions in which the majority of responsibilities can be fulfilled through the use of the computer. The primary advantages are that telecommuting allows employees to work out of their homes, thus meeting both home and work responsibilities, and also allows them to use time for work that would otherwise be spent in travel. The disadvantages are that it requires precise definitions of work expectations and performance measures and often reduces or eliminates the kind of face-to-face dialogue that is needed for problem solving. Interpersonal interaction in human service organizations can be important in such functions as client staffings or staff meetings in which policy and procedural issues may be addressed. This can be remedied by requiring that the telecommuting employee be present on site at certain specified times for these regularly scheduled functions or be available for a conference call.

■ CONSIDERATIONS

For Assessing Alternative Work Arrangements

Basic Questions: What impact will alternative work arrangements have on the budget, on collaborative work with staff, on supervision, on performance evaluation, and on intra-agency communication?

Time Frame: Whenever it appears to the management team that efficiency, effectiveness, quality, or productivity could be increased and/or morale improved through alternative work arrangements without unreasonable costs to the agency.

Process: Business manager, together with management team, conducts a cost-benefit analysis. Staff input is solicited. A report is submitted to the executive for approval.

Analysis: Impact of alternative work arrangements on services, work flow, communication, and workload management should be assessed. A pilot project may be undertaken during which a time and motion study may provide useful information.

Policy Changes: Detailed policies should spell out who is eligible for alternative work arrangements, under what conditions, subject to what expectations, and guidelines for participation in all human resource functions including staff development, training, performance appraisal, and others.

■ Job Security and Internal Mobility

Job security is one factor that influences career decisions (Schein, 1978). Some employees are willing to make sacrifices (including limiting their career options) in exchange for maintaining a stable, secure career in familiar surroundings. Insecurity about employment status can produce a high level of stress on the job and can limit productivity and performance. Some organizations deal with this factor by awarding some type of permanent status. Within educational institutions this status is referred to as tenure. In government employment it is referred to as permanent civil service status. A probationary period is usually required during which the employer has flexibility relative to termination, based on established performance criteria.

Few employers in the field of human services have the stability of resources to guarantee lifetime employment. Employment arrangements need the flexibility to allow for termination subject to certain fiscal or performance conditions. However, this doesn't prevent an employer from conveying to staff a philosophy that supports permanency of employment to the extent that workload and resources permit.

Recruiting, selecting, orienting, and training staff are expensive. Losing experienced employees can affect the capacity to meet program and organizational expectations. Written policies for reductions-in-force can be designed to convey to employees that long-term loyalty and high performance are valued and will be rewarded with job security to the greatest extent possible within the resources available.

Internal mobility can include lateral mobility, allowing workers to move to other positions at the same level or vertical mobility, rewarding workers with a promotion. Policies can be designed to ensure that when a vacancy occurs, an internal search will be conducted first, before anyone outside the organization will be considered. This type of open-posting system allows employees to self-nominate for open positions or for promotions. It is also possible for management to identify employees who appear to have potential for making significant contributions to the organization and to plan with them for career development. This plan may include a systematic rotation through selected jobs within the agency, or it may include special assignments. These approaches can be helpful in communicating to an employee that he or she is valued, and that the organization will make every attempt possible to provide stability of employment.

■ CONSIDERATIONS

For Assessing Practices of Job Security and Mobility

Basic Questions: What types of job security and mobility benefits can the agency offer? What benefits are meaningful to staff? What are the legal and financial implications?

Time Frame: When the management team is convinced that the issues of job security or mobility, if not addressed, may cause the agency to lose good staff members.

Process: Business manager explores the implications of job security and mobility practices on the budget, including data collected from other agencies. Management team participates in deliberation. Staff input is solicited. Proposals go to the agency director and board for final approval.

Analysis: Cost-benefit analysis should be prepared. Legal advice on implications for employee rights and agency commitments.

Policy Changes: Policies on job security and mobility should specify who is eligible and under what conditions. Rights and responsibilities of agency and employee should be stated.

■ Recognition

Lawler (1977) identifies five characteristics that rewards should have, including (1) importance, (2) flexibility, (3) frequency of award, (4) visibility, and (5) low cost. A reward should be seen as important by staff and especially by recipients if it is to be valued and pursued. Second, there should be enough flexibility to allow the reward to be tailored to meet the needs of the employee. Third, an award should be given frequently enough that it is identified with performance but not so frequently that it loses its meaning. Fourth, other employees in the organization should know about the reward. This meets the esteem needs of the recipient while, at the same time, communicating to workers that they, too, can achieve the reward through high levels of performance. Finally, the lower the cost the easier it is for the organization to provide the reward consistently over time.

Using these criteria, one reward that has many positive characteristics is some type of recognition through a special award, certificate, plaque, or designation as employee of the month. Lawler (1977) points out that these types of recognitions rate high on flexibility, high on visibility, low in cost, and frequency is discretionary. The major disadvantage is that they may be seen as low in importance. If the status of recognition can be enhanced through staff and management participation, or by adding a modest benefit such as a gift certificate, this technique can be valued as at least a small part of the overall reward system.

■ CONSIDERATIONS

For Assessing Recognition as Part of Reward System

Basic Questions: What kinds of awards will have meaning to staff? Can some gift or monetary value be attached to the award? How often should awards be given? How can visibility and prestige be maximized?

Time Frame: Policy and practices on awards should be reevaluated on an annual basis, based on the experience the previous year.

Process: The human resources director may be the appropriate person to take the lead in consultation with the management team. Input from staff should be solicited. Changes should be presented to the management team for approval.

Analysis: Review staff input. How meaningful are the awards to staff? Are timing and frequency appropriate?

Policy Changes: Revise policies on recognition as needed. Notify staff of changes.

■ The Cafeteria Plan

Many benefits and extrinsic rewards within organizations tend to be offered to all employees across the board. Employers typically allocate a percentage of salary to be available for what is referred to as employee-related expenses (ERE), including the employer's share of taxes, insurance, retirement, and other benefits offered. Over the years employers have discovered that such factors as age, marital status, number of children, and other factors affect how employees perceive their benefit package. For example, young families tend to prefer more flexible hours whereas older workers may appreciate the opportunity to purchase long-term care insurance for aging parents. When a fringe benefit program is structured rigidly with exactly the same benefits to all, the program may fail to match up with the needs of some workers. The result is that benefits are valued less than they might be if employees could tailor their benefit package to their needs.

In the interest of being responsive to individual preferences while remaining within the resources allocated to employee benefits, some organizations opt for what is called the cafeteria-benefit plan. This plan involves setting aside a dollar figure or percentage of salary for each employee and allowing employees to spend the resources to buy the fringe benefits they want and need at this point in their lives. Often retirement benefits are exempted from the cafeteria options in the interest of ensuring that some type of pension will be guaranteed to each employee at the point of retirement and will not have been exhausted in earlier years. A typical cafeteria plan might offer some of the following options:

- *Policy:* Total employee-related expenses may not exceed 26 percent of base salary; 5 percent will be allocated to a retirement plan. Employer's share of Social Security, Medicare, worker's compensation, unemployment compensation, and other applicable taxes will be set aside. The remaining dollars may be allocated among the following options:
  - Health insurance
  - Dental insurance
  - Life insurance
  - Long-term care insurance
  - Short- or long-term disability insurance
  - Child care subsidy

■ Motivation, Rewards, and Internal Consistency

Given the extensive theory and research developed around how to motivate workers, it is clear that employee motivation is a complex phenomenon and cannot be addressed in a simplistic or unidimensional manner. The research seems to indicate that employees will work hard and aspire to be productive if they:

- feel challenged by their work.
- have the resources and the flexibility necessary to achieve performance expectations.
- find that performing at a high level brings them a sense of competence.
- believe that their performance is valued, as measured by the ways in which rewards are allocated.

Dealing with all of these issues requires both a balance and an integration of what Herzberg (1966) refers to as intrinsic and extrinsic rewards.

The intrinsic dimension must be addressed by ensuring that there is a sense of job satisfaction and accomplishment for each employee. Attention to the overall organizational structure and to how each individual job is designed is an important step in creating a motivation and reward system. In addition, each employee needs to feel that he or she has a positive, supportive relationship with immediate supervisor and upper management. This relationship, however, exists within a context in which the primary focus is on meeting organizational and program goals and objectives. An employee's personal and professional goals are established within the organizational context. As we have seen, extrinsic rewards vary widely and offer a range of creative options including various approaches to pay, to individually tailored benefits, and to incentives.

A critical issue in evaluating an organization's motivation and reward system is whether rewards are consistent with (1) the agency's mission, (2) management's theories and philosophies about motivation, and (3) employee uniqueness and individuality. As with all components of organizations, the first standard of measurement for internal consistency is the mission statement. If the mission, for example, is "to ensure a safe, healthy, and nurturing environment for all children served by the agency," then policies and procedures for the allocation of rewards must ensure that those who support the mission in some tangible way are rewarded for their performance. Establishing measurable criteria and monitoring performance are complex undertakings and will be addressed in later chapters on job analysis and performance appraisal.

A second criterion used to determine consistency is management's position on motivation. This is an elusive criterion because seldom is there a consensus position coming from a management team on the subject of employee motivation. In fact, it may be the rare management team that even discusses motivation from a theoretical or philosophical perspective. In this chapter five different perspectives on employee motivation have been identified: (1) motivating by meeting personal needs, (2) motivating by enhancing the quality of the work assignment, (3) motivating by providing access to achievement, (4) motivating by reinforcing performance with rewards, and (5) motivating through fairness and equity.

These perspectives provide frameworks for creating a motivation and reward system, beginning with an attempt to achieve consensus on a consistent philosophy. Does the organization support the notion that employee personal needs ought to be taken into consideration in making workload assignments? Does the organization believe that the role of management is, at least in part, to address the quality of work life, including the quality of jobs as they have been defined for staff? Does the organization agree that access to achievement is an important motivator? Are managers and administrators convinced that rewards directly tied to performance can motivate high levels of performance? Should fairness and equity be considerations in assessing motivation? Achieving consensus on these types of perspectives will help management develop a consistent philosophy around which a reward system can be constructed.

Finally, system integrity will be affected by the extent to which management recognizes employee uniqueness and individuality. Each employee will have his or her own interests, commitments, and talents. Ideally each should be encouraged to apply them in a way that maximizes benefits to the organization, its programs, and its clients. If employees can be rewarded in a way that is meaningful to them, the rewards will have a greater chance of contributing to the quality of work life and organizational effectiveness.

SUMMARY

1. **Understanding Employee Motivation.** Employees are motivated by a variety of factors. Managers need to understand how each of these factors affects their employees.

2. **Theories of Motivation.** There are some motivating factors that are common to all employees and some factors that are unique to certain individuals.
   - *Motivating by Meeting Personal Needs.* Maslow identified a hierarchy of needs that is useful in understanding employee motivation.
   - *Motivating by Enhancing the Quality of Work Assignments.* For some, motivation comes from use of their creative abilities.
   - *Motivating by Providing Access to Achievement.* Achievement-motivated people are motivated by personal accomplishments.
   - *Motivating by Reinforcing Performance with Rewards.* Some are motivated by a positive relationship between effort, performance, rewards, and outcomes.
   - *Motivating through Fairness and Equity.* Some are motivated by the perception that the distribution of rewards is based on rational criteria.

3. **Designing Effective Reward Systems.** Lawler says reward systems should satisfy basic needs, offer competitive benefits, distribute them equitably, and treat employees as individuals.

4. **Incorporating Intrinsic Rewards into the Reward System.** Job-design factors can become part of a reward system.

5. **Allocating Extrinsic Rewards and Employee Benefits.** Benefits go to all employees; rewards are for merit.

6. **Compensation and Financial Incentives.** The following three factors should be considered in constructing a compensation and incentive package:
   - *Determining the Basic Salary Structure.*
   - *Merit Increases.*
   - *COLA, Lump Sum Salary Increases, and Bonuses.*

7. **Paid Time Off.** These benefits include vacation, holidays, sick leave, and other days off.

8. **Insurance and Retirement Benefits.** A wide variety of insurance and retirement benefits are offered by employers.

9. **Employee Service Benefits.** Services to meet family needs are increasingly being offered by employers.

10. **Alternative Work Arrangements.** Flexible working hours, job sharing, and telecommuting offer additional employee benefits and rewards.

11. **Job Security and Internal Mobility.** Not all organizations can guarantee permanent employment, but longevity can be encouraged and rewarded.

12. **Recognition.** Recognizing high-performing employees is inexpensive and can be made meaningful.

13. **The Cafeteria Plan.** Employees choose a mix of benefits that is meaningful to them.

14. **Motivation, Rewards, and Internal Consistency.** Rewards given must be consistent with overall agency philosophy and mission.

EXERCISES

Please complete the following sections of your manual based on the content covered in Chapter 6.

Section 6: Motivation and Rewards

6.1 Philosophy on motivation. State the organization's philosophy or assumptions about motivation and its relationship to performance and productivity.

6.2 Benefits. List all the benefits to be made available to employees and explain how each is calculated.

> Example: **6.2.1 Compensation.** Compensation for each position shall be determined by using the salary structure document attached as Document 6.2.1a.
>
> **6.2.2 Paid time off.**

6.3 Rewards earned by meritorious performance. List the rewards that are available to staff, and explain how each can be earned through performance on the job.

REFERENCES

Adams, J. (1965). Inequity in social exchange. In L. Berkowitz (Ed.), *Advances in experimental social psychology* (Vol. 2, pp. 267–297). New York: Academic Press.

Bureau of National Affairs. (1991). Employee benefits in small firms. *Bureau of National Affairs Bulletin to Management,* June 27, 196–197.

Bureau of National Affairs. (1995). BNA Datagraph. *BNA Bulletin to Management,* January 5, 4.

Dessler, G. (1997). *Human resources management* (7th ed.). Upper Saddle River, NJ: Prentice-Hall.

Green, J. (1995). *Cultural awareness in the human services: A multi-ethnic approach* (2nd ed.). Boston: Allyn & Bacon.

Herzberg, F. (1966). *Work and the nature of man.* Cleveland: World.

Jensen, J. (1997). Salary management for nonprofits. *The Grantsmanship Center Magazine,* Fall, 4–14.

Kossen, S. (1978). *The human side of organizations* (2nd ed.). San Francisco: Canfield.

Langdon, J. (1999, July 27). Employers sweeten benefit pots, poll says. *The Arizona Republic,* p. E9.

Lawler, E. (1971). *Pay and organizational effectiveness: A psychological view.* New York: McGraw-Hill.

Lawler, E. (1977). Reward systems. In J. Hackman & J. Suttle (Eds.), *Improving life at work: Behavioral science approaches to organizational change* (pp. 165–226). Santa Monica, CA: Goodyear.

Locke, D. (1992). *Increasing multicultural understanding: A comprehensive model.* Newbury Park, CA: Sage Publications.

Maslow, A. (1962). *Toward a psychology of being.* Princeton, NJ: Van Nostrand.

McClelland, D. (1961). *The achieving society.* Princeton, NJ: Van Nostrand.

McGregor, D. (1960). *The human side of enterprise.* New York: McGraw-Hill.

Miles, R. (1975). *Theories of management: Implications for organizational behavior and development.* New York: McGraw-Hill.

Montana, P., & Charnov, B. (1993). *Management.* Hauppauge, NY: Barron's Educational Series.

Porter, L., & Lawler, E. (1968). *Managerial attitudes and performance.* Homewood, IL: Irwin-Dorsey.

Schein, E. (1978). *Career dynamics: Matching individual and organizational needs.* Reading, MA: Addison-Wesley.

Skinner, B. F. (1969). *Contingencies of reinforcement: A theoretical analysis.* New York: Appleton-Century-Crofts.

Spragins, E. (1995). Elder care. Beyond retirement. *Newsweek, 126*(21), 67–69.

Vroom, V. (1964). *Work and motivation.* New York: Wiley.

CHAPTER 7

Using Data and Information to Achieve Excellence

CHAPTER OBJECTIVES

Upon completion of this chapter, the reader should be able to:

- Identify the types of data and information needed by constituents outside the organization.
- Explain how data and information are used within the organization for planning, operations, human resources, technical resources, and financial planning purposes.
- Discuss the steps to developing an integrated management information system.
- Give examples of how data and information can be used for program and organizational improvement.

Assumptions

- That well-run organizations base their planning, decision making, and actions on data and information to the greatest extent possible.
- That an agency's management information system should focus on its own information needs, especially its performance guidance system's needs, and that the requirements of external sources should be incorporated into the system after the agency's needs have been addressed.
- That data and information are essential to continuous quality improvement in programs and services.

■ The Importance of Information

We are constantly reminded by various media sources that we live in what observers refer to as the information age. With widespread use of computers, even very small organizations can build and maintain a database that will serve a variety of purposes. Data and information that have for years been available only to highly specialized technical personnel are now readily available to anyone with access to an agency's database, a local area network, or the Internet.

For over a century people who worked for and managed human service agencies have focused their data collection efforts on the helping process rather than client outcomes, simply because no data or information were available on the results of the helping process. Now, thanks to advances in technology, professionals in the human services find themselves in an era in which it is possible to identify expected outcomes for cases assigned to workers, to track effort and resources invested in each case, and to determine whether expected outcomes were achieved. By aggregating data available across many cases, it is possible to develop working hypotheses about the most efficient and effective ways to help people in need.

Over time, when enough data and information have been compiled so that intervention techniques can be refined and streamlined, this new knowledge will revolutionize the ways in which helping professionals are educated and the ways in which they practice. In the meantime, it is incumbent upon managers and administrators to ensure that information systems are designed in a way that will yield useful information.

■ The Quality of Information

In approaching the task of designing a management information system for an organization, managers and administrators find that there are many challenges and risks. The greatest risk is that information produced will not be useful for either knowledge building or for decision making. Computers are capable of producing a tremendous volume of data, but stacks of printouts that collect dust are testimony to the fact that not all data are useful. Early experiences with computers often revealed that funding sources were more concerned with tracking dollars than they were with tracking the quality or effectiveness of service.

Kettner and Martin (1998) point out that the introduction of purchase of service contracting (POSC) brought with it some practices that had a powerful influence on how data collection systems were designed. The era of widespread contracting for social services began in the late 1960s. The emphasis in data collection requirements established by the federal government has changed over the years, as follows:

- In the earliest years of POSC (1968–1979) the focus was on fiscal accountability. An American Public Welfare Association study attributed this financial orientation to reporting demands established by the federal government (Slack, 1979). The study pointed out that "concentration at the highest federal levels on financial management and efficiency [have resulted in] . . . a relatively weaker focus on quality, adequacy and effects of services" (p. 30).
- From 1980 to 1990 state public social service agencies began to assert their authority and attempted to get control of the statewide human services system. The majority of

services delivered during this period were contracted out to private nonprofit or for-profit agencies. Data collection increasingly focused on service provision data. This included tracking service type, units of service provided, and other resources expended in the helping process. The emphasis on accountability for programs and services influenced social service agency managers to redesign their data collection systems to track details associated with service provision.

■ Since the early 1990s, as a result of a number of congressional and executive initiatives at the federal level, the emphasis in accountability has been on organizational and program performance. For social service agencies, this means finding ways to track client outcomes and to report on such dimensions as efficiency, effectiveness, quality, and productivity.

This three-decade progression in terms of data collection and reporting can provide some important lessons to those responsible for designing management information systems in the early decades of the twenty-first century. Probably the most important lesson is that the local agency must determine its own information needs. Systems should not be designed solely to meet the needs of the funding source. Multiple funding sources are very common in contemporary practice—the rule rather than the exception. An agency may have as many as ten or even twenty different funding sources. Some have attempted to design a mini-information system to fit the needs of each funding source. Needless to say, this is highly inefficient and rarely yields information useful to the agency itself. A more efficient and effective system can be created if the designer will incorporate the needs of both external stakeholders as well as internal units into a single system. In the following sections we will explore ways that this undertaking can be accomplished.

■ Types of Data and Information Needed in Organizations

Chapter 3 looked at the organization as a system and attempted to explain why it is so important to organizational integrity that decisions be made and work be done not in isolation but with consideration of the impact on the entire system and each of its subsystems. Decisions to expand or reduce services, to hire or lay off staff, to seek out new revenue sources or reduce sources of funding all impact many parts of the organization. The time may come when some of these actions must be taken, even though they may have an adverse impact on one or more units within the organization. Management should ensure, however, that the best data and information are available for decision making so that the impact of changes can be anticipated to the greatest extent possible.

External Data and Information Considerations

In exploring the external environment or task environment in Chapter 3, external factors were examined in terms of (1) economic, (2) sociological, (3) political, and (4) technological environments. Each of these domains should be reconsidered when exploring the need for information. The economic domain is made up of funding sources, contributors, referral sources, consumers, and competitors. What questions must the organization be able to answer to maximize its effectiveness in relation to each of these entities? The sociological domain includes consideration relative to the community and larger political subdivisions within which the agency functions. Developing a profile of people, problems, needs, strengths, and opportunities will require regular data collection, aggregation, and reporting. The political domain includes regulatory and accrediting bodies, including the agency's board of directors. What concerns will be raised by these bodies in the future? What information will be needed to address these concerns? Finally, the technological domain encompasses all the areas of professional and technical advancement that must be monitored to ensure that the agency remains on the cutting edge as new developments and innovations emerge. Each of these four domains must be tracked in some way and questions anticipated so that the agency will have the necessary data and information when they are needed and expected.

■ CONSIDERATIONS

For External Data and Information Needs

Economic: What information is needed and expected from funding sources, contributors, referral sources, and consumers? What does the agency need to know about its competitors?

Sociological: What types of people live in the community in terms of basic demographics such as age, ethnic group, gender, socioeconomic status, and other factors? What types of problems, needs, strengths, and opportunities exist in the community?

Political: What are the data and information expectations from regulatory bodies, accrediting organizations, or the board of directors?

Technological: What technological and professional advancements should the agency track and how can innovations be incorporated into the service delivery system?

Internal Data and Information Considerations

For uses internal to the organization, data and information will be generated for administrators and managers, supervisors and workers. Chapter 3 identified the important internal components as (1) organizational purpose, mission, and philosophy, (2) organizational planning, (3) organizational operations, (4) human resources, (5) technological resources, and (6) financial resources. These organizational components also provide a useful framework for identifying and organizing data and information considerations. Revisiting organizational mission, purpose, and philosophy serves as a reminder that there is a long-range vision around which the organization has been structured, and it is important to develop indicators that will help decision makers understand how the agency and its programs are progressing toward that vision. The organizational planning framework is of vital importance to the design of the management information system. Review of plans will reveal strategic, long-term, and program-planning goals, objectives, and activities. If these plans are well designed, they should contribute to moving the agency toward its mission and purpose, and they should also suggest the types of data and information that will be needed to determine if these plans are on track. A review of organizational operations will be useful in understanding where the departments, divisions, or units are in relation to established expectations. Indicators that measure efforts and accomplishments should be incorporated into the information system. Questions about the optimum utilization of human resources will suggest a number of data needs about such factors as qualifications of staff, employment, performance evaluation, and training information. A systematic review of technological resources will suggest the types of information needed to stay current in areas of vital importance to agency functioning. Financial data and information will be tracked with the budget, to be covered in Chapter 8.

■ CONSIDERATIONS

For Internal Data and Information Needs

Organizational Purpose:

What factors or variables need to be tracked in order to monitor the agency's progress toward achievement of organizational purpose? Does the mission identify the populations and expected outcomes that require data collection?

Organizational Planning:

Strategic, long-range, and program plans specify goals and objectives that will require the use of measurement criteria to determine whether they have been achieved. What criteria are specified, and what data elements are specified or implied?

Organizational Operations:

What performance expectations have been established for each of the departments, programs, or units within the organization? What data will be needed in order to monitor and evaluate performance against these expectations?

Human Resources:

What reports will require data on staff qualifications, demographic characteristics, licensing, certification, staff development and training, or other staff characteristics? What data elements must be tracked in order to complete these reports?

Technological Resources:

How can the agency remain current in the identification of developing technologies, including computer hardware and software, communications equipment, and new developments in practice models?

Financial Resources:

How can revenues and expenditures be tracked in a way that will keep management informed about cash flow and will provide an early warning if there are any indications of financial problems during the remainder of the fiscal year?

■ Developing Integrated Information Systems

One of the major challenges in designing information systems is capturing enough data to answer important questions without attempting to capture so much that the result is information overload. The goal is to design a system that includes all appropriate and necessary data elements yet has the flexibility to meet the reporting needs of all constituents.

In most instances this goal can best be accomplished by constructing the management information system around a framework that includes several subsystems. The centerpiece of the system will focus on organizational operations, including data about programs and services. This system will include data about all clients served, the program(s) within which they are served, volume and type(s) of service(s) provided, and other service- and client-outcome variables. Data and information produced from this system will establish performance indicators and will answer questions about progress toward the achievement of goals and objectives. Rapp and Poertner (1992) refer to this as the performance guidance system.

Secondary systems will focus on other units within the organization that do not provide direct services. One subsystem will focus on human resources information and will contain a complete personnel file on each employee including demographics, date of employment, performance evaluation data, training and staff development data, career development data, and other relevant information. Another will focus on financial information including tracking all funding received and ensuring that specifications are followed and tracked. An accounting and bookkeeping system may be designed to track expenditures and issue payroll checks. Designing the financial resources information system will be the subject of the next chapter.

There may be other reasons to set up specialized information systems. Perhaps the agency is undertaking a major capital campaign to fund new facilities, and it is important to track donors and the funds to which their donations have been allocated. Some agencies may have such a large volunteer workforce that it warrants its own volunteer information system for training, workload assignment, or scheduling purposes. Rapp and Poertner (1992) refer to these as housekeeping systems. They exist primarily for the purpose of relieving staff of paperwork transactions and increasing the efficiency of these subunits.

Although all these ancillary or housekeeping systems are important for their own purposes, the centerpiece remains the overall organizational performance guidance system. This is the system that will aid in determining whether the organization is performing in a way that is consistent with its reason for existence (its mission). It is important that data and information on organizational performance be produced within an integrated system that is capable of yielding comparative data and information across all programs. Separate "mini-information systems" for each program, service, or funding source run the risk of fragmenting the monitoring and evaluation efforts and undermining the concept of shared vision.

Each part of the system, regardless of its ultimate purpose, must go through a series of steps designed to ensure that necessary data elements are included while, at the same time, the system remains as lean and streamlined as possible.

■ Steps to Developing an Integrated Management Information System

Many planners and administrators, in designing information systems, submit to the temptation to follow what appears to be a logical course of action and design or redesign their systems chronologically. What that means is that they begin at the point of asking the question "What data do we need to collect as a part of our information system?" They next move to designing or redesigning data collection forms and complete the remaining steps that follow chronologically to the final step of generating reports. This can prove to be a somewhat haphazard method for constructing a system.

> For example, in a brainstorming session about data collection in a residential treatment center, staff members offered their suggestions. One person pointed out that it was important to have a complete history on both parents. Another suggested that, because so many of the children had multiple sets of parents, a history should be taken on each parent determined to be significant to the child. A third person had read a research report that concluded that the age at which a child is removed from natural parents is highly significant. Another wanted to know the ordinal position of the child in the natural family. In an attempt to accommodate a wide range of interests, the consultant designing the information system developed forms that incorporated all suggestions. The form was twelve pages long, with many items that could not be completed because there were no adults in the child's life who could answer questions about natural parents or early childhood experiences. Furthermore, there was no consensus on how the data were to be used, other than to satisfy the curiosities of staff.

For these reasons, it makes more sense to begin at the end or output side of the information system rather than at the beginning or input side. The first steps should concentrate on determining how data will be used in final reports that will be prepared at the end of the program year. If the person or committee responsible for designing or redesigning the system can get administrators, managers, supervisors, and staff to think through the questions that need to be answered, then the rest of the process can follow logically from that framework. Kettner, Moroney, and Martin (1999) identify seven steps to be followed in designing a management information system for a single program. Although this chapter is not intended to cover the subject at the same level of technical detail, it will explore how some of the same steps and concepts can be applied to an agency-wide performance guidance system as described by Rapp and Poertner (1992). The following seven steps can be used to develop an agency-wide system:

Step 1.   Identify input, throughput, output, and outcome elements for each department or program.

Step 2.   Identify the questions to be answered by the management information system.

Step 3.   Identify the data elements needed to answer the questions.

Step 4. Develop the tables, charts, and graphs that will display data needed for reports.

Step 5. Design data collection procedures and instruments.

Step 6. Design the data entry, processing, and reporting system.

Step 7. Run the system, compile sample data, and debug the system.

Step 1: Identifying Input, Throughput, Output, and Outcome Elements

Understanding the systems framework in which all components of the service system are captured under the headings of inputs, throughput, outputs, and outcomes is essential to setting up a management information system. This framework will be described briefly at this point, but the reader is directed to more comprehensive coverage of the topic in the reference section at the end of this chapter. The systems framework is depicted in Figure 7.1.

Identifying Inputs The systems model roughly depicts a chronological flow of production of products or services in an organization and is used to understand how all the elements of the operation work together. Inputs represent a summary of all the raw materials and resources available to the organization at its point of origin. The point of origin, for purposes of systems analysis, is usually considered to be the beginning of the fiscal year. For most human service organizations this means July 1. For some it is October 1, in order to fit with the federal fiscal year. For some it coincides with the calendar year.

In creating an information system it can be helpful to think through the raw materials and resources that are necessary to achieve organizational and program objectives and that are available to the agency. The raw materials of human service agencies are the clients/consumers who come for service. The resources include staff, facilities, equipment, and material resources. A listing of both client data and staff data potentially useful in the system and an inventory of facilities, equipment, and material resources, such as food, clothing, or cash awards made to clients, will help in understanding the nature of the input data

FIGURE 7.1

The Systems Framework Applied to Data Collection

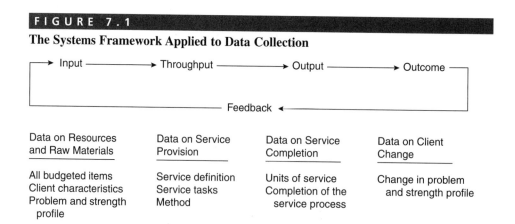

elements to be included in the information system. The following list summarizes input elements for programs, human resources, and finance:

Program Input Elements: Client demographic and descriptive characteristics; client social history data; client problem and strength profile; facilities, equipment, and material resources used by clients.

Human Resources Input Elements: Staff demographic and descriptive characteristics.

Financial Resources Input Elements: Line item amounts for each program.

Identifying Throughputs   In any system, raw materials must be converted into finished products through some type of conversion process. We perhaps recognize this process more readily with the production of everyday products such as tools, equipment, or food products. Raw materials such as steel, aluminum, or rubber are fed into the front end of the production line, are melted down and poured into precast forms, cooled down, polished and refined, and come out the other end as a hammer, a chisel, or a screwdriver.

With human beings, the process is a bit less obvious, yet in systems terms the same definitions apply. Raw materials in the form of people with problems or needs enter the system at the intake and screening end of the helping process. Through the provision of a mix of supportive services and participation in the helping process, the person with problems is converted into a person whose needs are met or who is capable of coping with his or her problems. This conversion process, in systems terms, is referred to as throughput.

In human services, throughput includes all the direct services provided such as counseling, case management, therapy, job training, and others, together with supportive services such as child care, transportation, food, clothing, housing, or financial assistance needed in order to achieve program and case objectives. Data associated with throughput will be necessary to reflect the types of services provided. Throughput elements for programs, human resources, and finance are summarized in the following list.

Program Throughput Elements: Services provided, broken down into specific tasks performed by workers; method of intervention, such as individual, group, or family treatment.

Human Resources Throughput Elements: Staff development and training activities completed during the year; performance appraisal data.

Financial Resources Throughput Elements: Identification of daily expenditures for each line item, by program.

Identifying Outputs   As raw materials are converted, the focus shifts to the creation of finished products or completed services. Outputs in a tool manufacturing plant would be identified as the number of each product completed (usually referred to as units). Combining the number of products produced with resources expended to produce the products enables the manufacturer to know the cost of production of each unit, as illustrated here:

Number of widgets produced =   1,000
Cost of production   = $5,000
Cost per unit   = $5

In human services, the output focus shifts to measurement of service provision and completion. Two types of outputs are tracked. The first type is called intermediate outputs and refers to the volume of services (units of service) provided. The second is called final outputs and refers to the completion by the client or consumer of all prescribed services (Kettner et al., 1999).

Volume of service (the intermediate output) is measured in terms of the number of units of service provided to clients. Units are defined in terms of time, episode, or material. A time unit is either the actual time spent face-to-face with a client (e.g., one hour), or a general definition that captures a range of time frames such as a child care day. A child care day may refer to a time frame such as any period of child care of six hours or more between the hours of 6 A.M. and 6 P.M. Monday through Friday.

An episode unit refers to one contact between worker and client, regardless of time frame. Group therapy sessions, for example, may cover a range of time frames from a half-hour to two and a half hours, depending on the topic and the makeup of the group. Rather than attempt to identify the number of minutes or hours a particular client attended group therapy during the course of treatment, a unit of service would simply be defined as one client attending one group session.

A material unit is a direct exchange of a tangible item such as a food basket, an article of clothing, or a direct cash donation. Material units, like time and episode units, are tracked to determine their contribution, if any, to client success in achieving program and case objectives. Examples of units of service are provided here:

Time Units:	One hour of counseling; one day of residential treatment
Episode Units:	One group session; one referral
Material Units:	One food basket; one cash voucher; one article of clothing

In addition to tracking the volume of services provided, service completion or final outputs are also defined and recorded for each client. Capturing data about service completion for each client presumes that the service provider has established a definition for service completion. For example, in family counseling, in order to achieve program objectives it may be necessary that couples commit themselves to completing twelve sessions. In order to provide a bit of flexibility, the definition of *service completion* may be stated as follows: "A service completion is defined as both participants attending at least ten of the twelve sessions, including the first and last session." If a couple did not complete the required sessions, they would be considered dropouts for record-keeping purposes. Intermediate and final outputs for programs, human resources, and financial resources are summarized here:

Program Output Elements

Intermediate	*Final*
Tracking the daily provision of units of service for each client in each program	Tracking the number of clients who complete the program as specified in the definition of completion

Human Resources Output Elements

Intermediate	*Final*
Tracking of volume of staff development and training attended	Tracking the number of staff members who complete courses or achieve certificates or licenses
Tracking of effort toward achievement of performance goals and objectives	Tracking completion of performance goals and objectives

Financial Resources Output Elements

Intermediate	*Final*
Tracking of daily expenditures for each line item, by program	Periodically summarizing expenditures in relation to budgeted items

Identifying Client Outcomes   The reason for existence of all human service programs is to enable clients or consumers to resolve problems and improve their quality of life. The basic design of programs and services presumes that clients or consumers are being helped to achieve some tangible results such as improving relationships and communication between spouses, overcoming an addiction, or improving parenting skills. However, it is impossible to know whether these results have been achieved unless expected results are defined in measurable terms, tracked, and recorded. When this is done, the individual client record reflects success with each case, whereas aggregated data reflect overall program success. Client outcomes can be measured in terms of (1) numeric counts, (2) use of standardized scales, (3) use of level of functioning scales, and (4) client satisfaction. Numeric counts refers to a statistic that represents the number or percentage of specified outcomes that are achieved. For example, in a program designed to help juveniles who leave the correctional system to readjust to life in the community, one measure of success would be the number of juveniles served by the program who have no subsequent arrests. This is a very general measure and fails to identify many other factors that may indicate success such as improved school attendance or a successful employment experience. Nevertheless, many funding sources specify this type of single indicator as the criterion for success.

Standardized scales are objective instruments that have been designed to measure a particular dimension of a problem, a need, a strength, a behavior, or other factor. They have been tested and are expected to yield reliable and valid results. Standardized scales have been designed to measure such factors as self-esteem, depression, knowledge, aptitude, and many other factors. Level of functioning scales are similar to standardized scales, with the exception that they are designed by staff or other experts to fit a particular program and population. These scales are used to rate clients on various dimensions that the program is designed to address. For example, a program to serve the homeless may develop a level of functioning scale that measures housing, employment skills, health and nutrition, and other such dimensions. Assessing these factors at intake and exit provides data on how much each client improved during the course of treatment.

Client satisfaction is measured by preparing a series of questions and asking respondents to indicate their reactions to each question in terms of whether they are very satisfied, somewhat satisfied, somewhat dissatisfied, or very dissatisfied (or some similar wording).

For some types of services, such as transportation, this measure may actually be more reliable than the others mentioned (Martin, 1988). For others, such as programs to reduce child abuse or prevent teen pregnancy, client satisfaction is not as meaningful as tracking indicators of client and program success. Client outcomes are summarized in the following list for program outcome elements only. Data and information collected for such organizational components as human resources or financial resources do not typically define or use outcome indicators.

Program Outcome Elements

Numeric counts are nominal measures of client achievements (e.g., 87 percent of those in a pregnancy prevention program graduated from high school without becoming pregnant).

Standardized scales are objective measures developed by experts and are applicable to a specific client population, problem, or other factor (e.g., Minnesota Multiphasic Personality Inventory).

Level of functioning scales are objective measures developed for a specific program or service and are not necessarily validated for use outside the program (e.g., job skills, transportation, housing).

Client satisfaction instruments are used to determine client perceptions of various dimensions of services provided (e.g., how satisfied a client is with promptness of service, worker's ability to understand the client's needs, and the relevance of referrals).

Step 2: Identifying the Questions to Be Answered by the Management Information System

In framing the questions to be answered, a systematic approach can be achieved by exploring the information needs of both external and internal constituencies discussed earlier in this chapter.

Identifying the Information Needs of External Constituencies
Economic Considerations

■ *Funding Sources.* Present and future funding is an important consideration in constructing a management information system. It is important to develop a reputation with funders for being able to produce relevant and responsive information in a timely way. Learning the information needs of funders is typically a straightforward undertaking. From each funding source a contractor can expect to receive a set of instructions specifying data, information, and reporting expectations. Types of questions from funding sources typically include the following:

Input Questions: What is the demographic profile of the client population? How many unduplicated clients are being served? What types of problems and needs are clients bringing, and how many are in each category? What resources are devoted to each program and service?

Throughput Questions: What services are provided? How are these services defined? What methods are used?

Output Questions: What volume of services is provided to each client? How many clients complete all of the services they need to be successful in achieving outcomes? How many drop out of the program?

Outcome Questions: How is success defined in each program? How many clients have achieved success by this definition? How many have not achieved success?

Some funding sources will not ask for this much information. Some will ask for more. This sampling is intended to provide a brief overview of the types of issues that may be raised by funding sources that have implications for the design of an information system.

- *Contributors.* Identifying information needs for contributors is usually less complex than for funding sources. Contributors like to have assurances that their charitable donations were used efficiently and effectively and achieved their stated purposes. Although a special report may be prepared to keep contributors informed of agency activities, it is more typical that communication will be through such media as newsletters and annual reports. Types of questions may include the following:

Input Questions: What is the demographic profile of people served? How much of the resources went into direct service versus administration?

Throughput Questions: What services were provided, and in what volume?

Outcome Questions: What percentage of people served achieved successful outcomes?

Clearly the types of questions raised by contributors will vary depending on the size of the contribution and the ongoing relationship with the agency. If the contribution is a one-time donation, there may be no expectation of feedback. If a corporation sponsors an agency on a regular basis, the expectations for feedback on its return on investment will likely be greater. In any case, it is always wise to provide as much information as possible to past and potential donors for the purpose of keeping up their interest in and support for the work of the agency.

- *Referral Sources.* The types of information needed for referral sources may differ a bit from funders and contributors. Referral sources are likely to be much more interested in the details of the service process, including types of direct and supportive services provided, methods or techniques used, qualifications of staff, or service availability. This is not to say that they are uninterested in the agency's success rates, merely that they need to know that if they refer a client, he or she will be served in a timely fashion with services that are relevant to the problem or need. Types of questions may include the following:

Input Questions: For what types of problems and needs do you provide services? What is the demographic profile of people served? What types of special needs can be accommodated? What are the costs for each type of service?

Throughput Questions: What direct and supportive services do you provide? What is the level of intensity and volume provided, and how are decisions made about volume, intensity, type, and duration of treatment?

Output Questions: How long does it take for a client to complete the program? What constitutes completion? Is there follow-up after completion?

Outcome Questions: What are your success rates in each of your programs?

Referral sources are concerned about the best interests of their clients. In addition, in some instances referral sources will be paying for the service provided and will be held accountable by their own funding sources for the ultimate success of services received by their clients. Agencies that expect to maintain an ongoing relationship with referral sources should be prepared to provide feedback that will assure efficient, effective, and high-quality services at the lowest possible cost.

- *Consumers.* The information needs of consumers will vary greatly, depending on the nature of a program and the relationship of the consumer to the agency. Service options in some communities may be competitive, and the consumer may want information before making a decision. Employee assistance programs sponsored by major employers are frequently designed to help employees deal with substance abuse, mental health problems, or marital discord. Some employees may be encouraged to shop around to find the services most suited to their needs. In other instances there may be only one provider. An abusing parent, for example, may be court ordered to participate in parent effectiveness training with a specifically designated provider. In any case, when consumers seek information about the agency and its programs, it is likely to be very similar to that sought by referral sources identified previously. The perspective is the same—a concern for receiving the highest-quality service in a timely manner with the best possible chance for achieving positive results at the lowest possible cost.

- *Competitors.* In considering competitors, the issue is not what information competitors would like to have, but rather what data and information an agency should generate in order to measure its own performance against that of competitors. Competition is a relatively new phenomenon in the field of human services. Prior to widespread use of purchase of service contracting in the late 1960s, private, nonprofit agencies were funded primarily by charitable donations and served as many people as resources would allow. In the current social services environment, the majority of funding comes through competitive bidding for contracts, not unlike construction companies that bid for government contracts on roads, bridges, or buildings. So competition is a factor in agency survival in the contemporary practice environment.

It is in the interest of human service agencies to observe and study their competition in order to understand those areas in which they might have a competitive advantage. If certain competitors consistently win major government contracts, why are they so successful? Do they provide better-quality services? Are their unit costs lower than others? Are their staff more qualified? Do they market their services better? Data collection about one's own efforts in these areas may reveal organizational weakness that can be addressed in a way that improves the agency's competitive advantage.

Sociological Considerations   Examining the sociological domain in terms of information needs guides the agency toward a focus on the surrounding community and larger political subdivisions (city, county) in terms of its people, problems, needs, strengths, and opportunities. Successful organizations do not simply continue business as usual indefinitely. Intelligent strategic planning requires a data- and information-gathering capacity designed to produce ongoing profiles of various community characteristics. One source of information, for example, is the U.S. Census. Regular reports are published that provide data on many demographic characteristics of all counties and cities with populations of more than 50,000. These characteristics include total population, income, ethnicity, gender, education, housing, unemployment, and many other factors useful in understanding the local community (U.S. Bureau of the Census, 1994). Community surveys conducted by state and local government entities or data provided by such organizations as the local chamber of commerce can also be used to help develop a community profile.

Identifying key variables and tracking them over a period of years can help an agency to understand how populations, problems, and needs change over time. This information can be incorporated into strategic planning efforts to ensure that agency services remain relevant to changing needs.

Political Considerations   A number of external constituencies are required to make decisions about organizational operations and, therefore, need a regular flow of data and information. These entities include regulatory agencies, accrediting organizations, and governing boards. Each of these entities is held accountable in some way for the performance of the agency. It is not impossible, for example, that an unhappy consumer could include any or all of these entities in a court action. Therefore, it is important that the agency understand the information needs of these decision-making bodies and include them in the data collection and information system. Their focus will be on factors related to efficiency, effectiveness, productivity, and quality. For this reason, information needs will be similar to those identified previously for the funding source. However, regulations, standards, guidelines, and policies should be examined carefully to ensure that reports to these bodies will contain the necessary information in the format requested.

Technological Considerations   Finally, some systematic method for tracking technological developments will help keep the agency current on changes in the field. Efforts should be directed toward learning about successful new models of practice as well as new developments in the computer and communications industries. Systematic and formal data collection may not be necessary to compile this information. Managers, supervisors, and other staff may discover, for example, through attendance at professional conferences or review of the literature, the availability of specialized professional knowledge and skill or new software. Information about new developments should be compiled and disseminated on a regular basis. This may be accomplished through direct dissemination in memo or newsletter form, or some method may be designed to enter data and produce periodic reports on innovations.

Identifying the Information Needs of Internal Constituencies

Organizational Purpose, Mission, and Philosophy.

Basic Questions: What data and information are needed to inform the agency whether its performance is on track with its stated purpose, mission, and philosophy?

Do input data reflect resources that allow successful performance?

Are people served consistent with the mission statement?

Do throughput data indicate adequate and relevant attention to the needs of the populations served?

Do output data indicate a rate of completion that is consistent with the purpose?

Do outcome data indicate a rate of success that internal and external constituents feel is consistent with the mission and vision expectations?

Organizational Planning.

Basic Questions:
Are there written objectives in a strategic plan, a long-range plan, or program plans?

What data elements will be needed to determine whether or not objectives have been achieved?

Organizational Operations.

Basic Questions:
Have input, throughput, output, and outcome data elements been defined for each program?

Are they being recorded and entered into the system in a reliable manner?

Is the system capable of producing the necessary monitoring and evaluation reports that will allow for measurement and comparison of program performance?

Human Resources.

Basic Questions:
Have data elements been defined that will permit a demographic profile of the staff?

Are elements included that will satisfy information needed by regulatory or accrediting bodies?

Is information collected that may be useful in understanding what staff characteristics seem to contribute to successful experiences with clients (e.g., ethnicity, gender, education, experience)?

Technological Resources.

Basic Questions:
Do staff have regular access to new and developing technology, including research findings about specialized methodologies?

Is there some systematic method for staff to express their interest in or need for new knowledge, information, or equipment?

Financial Resources.

Basic Questions:
Are financial resources and expenditures tracked in a manner that is useful in determining costs of services?

Will data and information produced be useful for comparison purposes, both internally with other programs and externally with the programs of other providers?

Separating and Prioritizing Information Needs   From the foregoing examination of the information needs of external and internal constituencies, it is clear that careful design of a management information system can be a complex and time-consuming process. The sheer volume of questions and considerations raised in this chapter, however, may be deceiving for a couple of reasons. First, not all questions raised have implications for data collection and processing. Although all questions should be considered from the information system perspective, efficiency will require that some information needs be dealt with in other ways, such as newsletters or special reports.

Second, when considering the major information system that is central to organizational operations—the performance guidance system—a review of the information needed reveals many redundancies across all external and internal constituencies. For example, in examining input needs, many stakeholders, both internal and external, will need the same demographic information. Service efforts and accomplishments can be formatted in a way that satisfies a range of information needs. These issues will be addressed as the text moves to a discussion of identifying data elements. Each of the remaining steps necessary to building an information system will be explored in the following sections, using a job preparation and placement agency as an example.

Job Finders, Inc. Example
The agency used as an example is called Job Finders, Inc. It is an organization that came into existence shortly after welfare reform, when the Temporary Assistance to Needy Families (TANF) program replaced the Aid to Families with Dependent Children (AFDC) program. Under the new program eligibility for benefits expires after two consecutive years, and recipients are expected to be in some way engaged in education, training, or employment. Job Finders, Inc. agreed to accept TANF recipients under contract to the state public social services agency and to provide a range of employment-related services. These services include (1) intake, screening, and assessment, (2) prejob preparation, (3) case management for support services, (4) job skills training, (5) job placement, and (6) ongoing mentoring and follow-up. Clients were expected to move through the system as depicted in the flowchart in Figure 7.2.

Step 3: Identifying Data Elements Needed to Answer Questions

The input-throughput-output-outcome framework establishes the basic logic for the identification and selection of data elements. Once the logic of this framework is understood and the questions to be answered have been posed in Step 2, the next step is to identify and select specific data elements that will be used to generate the information needed to answer the questions. The Job Finders, Inc. example will be used to illustrate the types of data elements needed to guide decision making for programs and services. In the interest of limiting the focus of the remaining sections to basic concepts and issues, discussion and examples will emphasize primarily the data elements relating to programs and the performance guidance system will be covered. Data and information needs at the organizational level and at the community level will also be discussed briefly.

The following sections illustrate the types of variables that would be selected from the Job Finders, Inc. programs in order to provide data and information about program efficiency, effectiveness, quality, and productivity.

FIGURE 7.2

Flowchart of Job Finders, Inc. Service Process

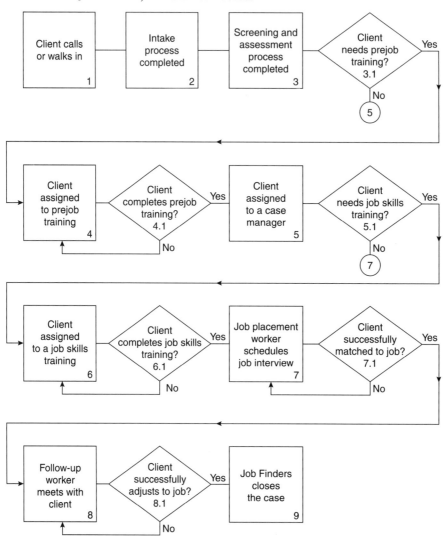

Elements Used in Monitoring, Evaluating, and Reporting on Clients and Programs

Input Elements   In order to ensure that all necessary information can be produced on clients served, the following client-related variables would be included in the system:

1. *Eligibility*   Resident of Middletown

Currently receiving Temporary Assistance to Needy Families

Referred by state public social service agency

2. *Demographic or descriptive factors*	Age, gender, ethnicity, marital status, number of dependent children, education, disability status
3. *Social history factors*	Employment history; work-related skills; substance abuse history, if any; availability of family or other support
4. *Client problem and strength profile*	Scaling of problems and strengths on a five-point scale in which problems are indicated at levels 1 and 2, and strengths are indicated at levels 4 and 5 in the following categories: food and nutrition, housing, health, employment, education, income and budget, transportation, social and emotional health, family relations, and youth education and development

Throughput Elements   In order to ensure that all required information can be produced on services provided, it is necessary to define what is meant by each of the services provided and also to select a unit of service for each. The following service definitions and units are examples of what might be used in the Job Finders, Inc. programs and services:

Phase of Service Process	*Definition*
Intake, Screening, and Assessment	Collection of all necessary data, information, and documentation
	Determination of eligibility and appropriateness for services
	Administration of assessment instruments
Definition of Unit of Service	One hour of face-to-face contact between client and intake worker = one unit (time unit)
Prejob Preparation	Training in the types of skills that are necessary for finding and keeping a job, including completion of applications, interviewing, grooming, and other such considerations
Definition of Unit of Service	One session of prejob training provided by subcontractor = one unit (episode unit)
Case Management	A case manager works directly with a client and with collateral contacts in order to assist client in achieving the client's goals and objectives designed to solve problems and meet needs
Definition of Unit of Service	One hour of effort by case manager devoted exclusively to a case, either face-to-face, collateral contact, or case recording = one unit (time unit)
	One item of in-kind assistance such as food, clothing, or cash assistance given to a client = one unit (material unit)

(continued)

Phase of Service Process	*Definition*
Job Skills Training	Classroom or on-the-job training focused on the development of job-related skills
Definition of Unit of Service	One hour of training provided either by a subcontractor or by an employer = one unit (time unit)
Job Placement	Identification of job openings; contact by case manager with employer; interviews arranged; process continued until a job is secured
Definition of Unit of Service	One hour of effort by job placement worker devoted exclusively to a case, either face-to-face, collateral contact, or case recording = one unit (time unit)
Ongoing Mentoring and Follow-Up	Periodic meetings with a mentor who has been trained and is matched to a client; focus of meetings is on work survival skills
Definition of Unit of Service	One contact between mentor and client = one unit (episode unit)

Output Elements   In order to ensure that all necessary data and information can be compiled on units of service provided and service completions, the following definitions might be used in the Job Finders, Inc. management information system:

Service	*Definition of Service Completion*
Intake, Screening, and Assessment	Completion of all forms, submission of all required documentation, and completion of all assessment tools
Prejob Preparation	Attendance at a minimum of eight hours of prejob training provided by a subcontractor
Case Management	Keeping at least 80 percent of all appointments with the case manager and fulfilling at least 80 percent of follow-up tasks
Job Skills Training	Attendance at a minimum of 90 percent of all scheduled training sessions
Job Placement	Completion of all interviews as scheduled until successfully employed
Ongoing Mentoring and Follow-Up	Participation in at least 90 percent of scheduled meetings with an assigned mentor and fulfilling at least 90 percent of follow-up tasks

Outcome Elements   In order to ensure that the necessary data and information can be compiled on client outcomes, the following definitions of outcomes might be used in each of the Job Finders, Inc. programs:

Outcomes	*Definitions*
Intermediate Outcomes	Client shall demonstrate mastery of at least ten defined prejob preparation skills as measured by pretest/posttest.
	Client shall demonstrate mastery of at least 80 percent of the content covered in job skills training as measured by posttest.
	Client shall secure employment in a position that pays above minimum wage and includes health and retirement benefits.
Final Outcome	Client shall maintain employment in the same or higher-level job and receive positive performance appraisals for at least one year following completion of services.

Elements Used in Monitoring, Evaluating, and Reporting on Organizational Performance

In addition to the data and information needed to monitor, evaluate, and report on program performance, additional reports will need to be generated that deal with the entire organization as a unit. Some of the factors to be addressed in constructing the information system should include:

Staff Characteristics	The human resources department will be expected to produce profiles of staff for a number of audiences, including funding sources, equal employment opportunity inquiries, and others. Demographic and descriptive variables are needed that will meet the information needs of both internal and external sources.
Strategic Objectives	Data and information are needed that reflect demographic, income, and employment trends over the next ten years at the city, county, and state levels.
Long-Range Objectives	Data and information are needed that assess the projected need for prejob training, job skills training, and job placement over a five-year period and direct efforts toward employment markets expected within the next five years.

Elements Used in Understanding the Problems, Needs, and Strengths of the Community

Information available on community conditions varies widely, depending on a community's interest in and capacity for surveying its population. Resources in the government documents section of a library can provide a rich source of information about a community.

Population Profile	Data and information are needed that reveal population trends over a twenty-year period, dating from ten years in the past through ten years into the future, focusing on basic demographic variables used in the programs.
Problem Analysis/ Needs Assessment	Data and information are needed on community perceptions of problems and needs, collected through an annual survey from a random sample of the population.

Step 4: Developing the Tables, Charts, and Graphs That Will Display Data Needed for Reports

Identifying appropriate and useful data and collecting these data in an efficient manner is an important step in the process of constructing an information system. However, data alone will not be useful unless elements are displayed in a manner that contributes to meaningful analysis. Single, discrete data items are relatively useless. For example, suppose the Job Finders, Inc. program reports that 166 clients were placed in jobs in the first year of operation. Does this number reflect a strong performance, a weak performance, failure, or success? With this single, discrete statistic we do not know. We must have more information.

Meaningful information is presented in the form of tables, charts, and graphs. Tables are structured in terms of columns and rows, with cells providing the data indicated by column and row headings. Tables are the simplest and most straightforward way of presenting data but not always the most easily understood by the consumer. Charts and graphs, including pie charts, bar graphs, and line graphs, present a picture that can be absorbed more quickly. They also have more visual appeal.

In developing a strategy for presentation of data and information in reports, it may be helpful to first develop tables with appropriate columns and rows. Once the data are available in this format, decisions can be made about translating information into more appealing graphic formats. But first it is critical that data be analyzed in a way that brings meaning out of otherwise unrelated elements.

In order to take on meaning, data must be presented in a way that they can be compared to other data. The comparisons can be from across a number of variables within the same program or organization, from a different period of time in the same program or organization, or from a comparable program or organization. These types of comparisons are referred to as (1) cross-sectional analysis, (2) time series analysis, and (3) comparison to other data units (Kettner, Daley, & Nichols, 1985). Comparisons can be depicted by use of tables, line graphs, bar graphs, pie charts, or combinations of graphic techniques.

Cross-sectional analysis refers to data used to depict a profile of a unit or organization using selected variables that all reflect the same time frame. For example, selected variables might be used within a particular program to depict client demographics (e.g., age, gender, ethnicity) or the types of problems and needs clients bring to the agency (e.g., marital disputes, depression, domestic violence). These types of presentations allow for comparisons across groups (e.g., comparing the number of clients ages 20 to 29 to the number of clients ages 50 to 59). Cross-sectional analysis can be useful for a number of program or organizational monitoring efforts or in producing periodic reports. It may be important to know whether the profile of people served within a program matches projections or expectations. The board will expect to be informed about whether programs and services are meeting objectives, and whether program costs and unit costs remain within budgeted allocations. Table 7.1 illustrates a cross-sectional analysis of client demographic variables within a job preparation program.

Time series analysis is a technique that is used with the same population and problem over time to reveal trends. A range of time increments can be used, depending on what is most useful, relevant, and available to the agency. If data available within the agency are used, then almost any time frame is possible, including weekly, monthly, or longer. If exter-

TABLE 7.1

Cross-Sectional Analysis of Selected Clients in the Job Finders, Inc. Program

Type of Family	Current Income	Access to Health Care	Shelter	Food and Nutrition	Transportation	Child Care
		Percentage of Clients Assessed as Being in Crisis				
Single female, no children	51%	60%	21%	18%	22%	—
Single male, no children	48	55	18	12	24	—
Single female, 1 or more children	67	78%	44	28	33	62
Single male, 1 or more children	47	56	38	32	30	68

nal data are used, the analysis will be limited by data availability. Census data, for example, are available in ten-year increments with interim reports provided on selected variables.

Creative use of time series analysis can be very helpful in anticipating future demand for programs and services. For example, an organization might wish to monitor the number of requests for services within each of its programs on a monthly basis over a period of several years to help in long-range planning efforts. Tracking demand for service by location or by funding source can provide useful planning information. Another use might be a comparison of demand trends with client satisfaction trends. A sample graph is illustrated in Figure 7.3.

Comparison with other data units allows the analyst to select data displays that are important to the understanding of agency or program performance and to compare them to other similar agencies or programs. This comparison allows an agency to bring meaning

FIGURE 7.3

Time Series Analysis of Applications to the Job Finders, Inc. Program

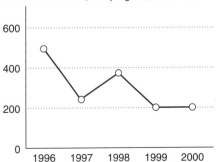

Number of applicants to the Job Finders, Inc. program, 1996–2000

TABLE 7.2			
Comparison of Job Finders, Inc. to Other Data Units			
Program	Percentage of Applicants Successfully Completing a Job Training Program and Remaining on a Job for One Year		
	1997	1998	1999
Job Finders, Inc.	35%	47%	53%
Community Employment, Inc.	22	28	34
Job Training & Preparation, Inc.	49	44	42
Employment Solutions, Inc.	62	61	60

to data and information about its own performance by examining its indicators in relation to other agencies' performances. Factors such as number of clients served, unit costs, and percentage of clients achieving success in other agencies can serve as useful benchmarks, but only if the data are comparable. For example, comparing the incidence of crime in Los Angeles to that in Great Falls, Montana, will not be particularly revealing because of the tremendous discrepancies in size and complexity between the cities. When cities or other units are similar in terms of total population and demographic breakdown, comparisons are more meaningful. One way to control for size is to report incidence per 100,000 (or other constant number) population. Likewise, when agencies or programs are compared, populations and variables should be examined to ensure comparability.

It is likely in the future that comparison with other data units will be used to compare the performance of programs across the board by funding sources. For example, if a state government is spending $20 million per year on job preparation and placement, the state may find it necessary to compare all contracting agencies to determine which ones merit renewal of their contracts and which ones should be discontinued. Comparison with other data units is depicted in Table 7.2.

In all comparisons, whether they are cross-sectional, time series, or with other data units, it is important that the comparisons be carefully examined to ensure comparability. Cross-sectional comparisons are useful only if they reflect the same type of client population during approximately the same time frame. Time series must reflect the same data unit and same data elements over different, subsequent time frames. In comparing other data units there should be some assurance that the units have the same characteristics. As funding sources increasingly require performance measures, agencies will be expected to develop indicators that reflect the status of such factors as resources, service volume provided, client outcomes, or ratios of client outcomes to full-time equivalent staff (Government Accounting Standards Board, 1993).

Format for Reporting Data and Information to Outside Sources   Once data elements have been selected and a complete set of data displays has been prepared, a format for reporting should be designed. Rapp and Poertner (1992) suggest five principles that managers should consider:

- Every report needs a standard. There should always be comparison data.
- Too much information reduces the ability to perform. Reports should be designed to be used. Clutter and information overload detract from use. Attend to simplicity of appearance.
- Aesthetics are important. Graphs and charts should be clear and easy to understand.
- Labels should be in English. Plain language and commonly understood terms should be used.
- Level of aggregation should be appropriate to the user. If a report is to be used at the worker level, the worker should be able to recognize his or her own performance in relation to that of others. (pp. 128–133)

When the types of data to be collected and the format in which data will be reported have been established, the next step in building an information system is to design data collection forms.

Step 5: Designing Data Collection Procedures and Instruments

Earlier in this chapter, client, program, organizational, and community variables were presented and discussed. In order to build useful, informational profiles in each of these areas, data must be collected following the formats developed in earlier steps. The more traditional approach to data collection is to develop data collection forms that require paper and pencil completion. Subsequent procedures are then established for data entry and aggregation. A more efficient approach is to have workers enter data electronically directly into the system. This approach requires the development of computer screens and menus that present questions and then provide a list of options, one of which may be selected with a simple click of the mouse.

Client and program variables are used to track program and service performance on an ongoing basis. Organizational data will be used for the purpose of periodic reporting on staff demographics or on progress toward strategic or long-range objectives. Community data will be used for the purpose of environmental scanning and future strategic, long-range, or program-planning efforts.

Collecting Program Data   Program data collection forms or screens are the most detailed and extensive part of an agency's information system. Developing information about programs requires that input, throughput, output, and outcome data be collected on each client. Efficient data collection requires careful planning. Information about clients is usually needed in some sort of chronological order. For example, the first set of questions should focus on determining eligibility for services. If a client is not eligible, it is not efficient to complete the rest of the identifying and screening information. Once eligibility is established, background social history, job history, and other factors can be compiled.

One approach to establishing a chronological order for data collection is to begin with a flowchart of the process a client goes through from entry through exit from the system (see Figure 7.2). Each of the processes in the flowchart represents a phase of client service and usually also represents one or more face-to-face contacts between worker and client. Working from this type of flowchart, those responsible for designing an information system can organize the data elements listed in the previous section of this chapter so that each element is collected at the time it is needed. For example, the following variables are those identified earlier. For each, the data collection form is indicated, and an illustration is provided.

Client-Related Variables	*Data Collection Form or Computer Screen*
• Eligibility factors (e.g., residence)	Intake Form/Face Sheet
• Demographic or descriptive factors (e.g., age)	Intake Form/Face Sheet
• Social history factors (e.g., work history)	Screening Form
• Client problem and strength profile	Assessment Form

A sample intake form or face sheet is depicted in Figure 7.4.

Service-Related Variables	*Data Collection Form or Computer Screen*
1. Type of service received	Service Provision Form
2. Volume of service received	Service Provision Form
3. Material resources received	Service Provision Form
4. Referrals to other services	Service Provision Form

FIGURE 7.4

Example of Part of an intake Form or Face Sheet

Application for Services

Client Identification Number_____ Date of Application _____ Worker ID Number_____

Applicant's Name _____ Telephone _____
                (last, first, middle initial)

Applicant's Residence _____
                (number, street, apt.#, city, state, zip)

Gender	**Ethnicity**	**Family Type**	**Education**
___ Female	___ African American	___ Single parent/female	___ 00 to 08
___ Male	___ Asian American	___ Single parent/male	___ 09 to 12
	___ Caucasian	___ Two-parent	___ High school grad
	___ Hispanic/Latino	___ Single person	___ Some college
	___ Native American	___ Two adults, no child	___ College grad
	___ Other	___ Other	

FIGURE 7.5

Example of Part of a Service Provision Data Collection Form

Job Finders, Inc. Case Management and Service Provision Data Collection From

Worker ID _____   Week of _____

Client ID	Case Management		Services Received		Referrals to Other Agencies	
Number	Milestone	Units	Type(s)	Units	Agency Code	Units Received
⎣_⎢_⎢_⎢_⎦	⎣_⎢_⎢_⎦	⎣_⎢_⎢_⎦	⎣_⎢_⎢_⎦	⎣_⎢_⎢_⎦	⎣_⎢_⎢_⎦	⎣_⎢_⎢_⎦
⎣_⎢_⎢_⎢_⎦	⎣_⎢_⎢_⎦	⎣_⎢_⎢_⎦	⎣_⎢_⎢_⎦	⎣_⎢_⎢_⎦	⎣_⎢_⎢_⎦	⎣_⎢_⎢_⎦
⎣_⎢_⎢_⎢_⎦	⎣_⎢_⎢_⎦	⎣_⎢_⎢_⎦	⎣_⎢_⎢_⎦	⎣_⎢_⎢_⎦	⎣_⎢_⎢_⎦	⎣_⎢_⎢_⎦
⎣_⎢_⎢_⎢_⎦	⎣_⎢_⎢_⎦	⎣_⎢_⎢_⎦	⎣_⎢_⎢_⎦	⎣_⎢_⎢_⎦	⎣_⎢_⎢_⎦	⎣_⎢_⎢_⎦

A sample service provision form is depicted in Figure 7.5. This form would be completed daily after each client contact has been completed. Code numbers, drawn from a code book, would be inserted into the appropriate spaces. These numbers would then be entered into the computer by a data entry person.

Output and Outcome Variables	Data Collection Form or Computer Screen
1. Completion of services	Service Provision Form
2. Achievement of outcomes at the point of termination	Service Provision Form
3. Achievement of outcomes at the point of follow-up	Service Provision Form

In a computerized system, recording output and outcome variables requires only the entering of precoded outputs and outcomes onto a form or directly into the computer. These data can either be recorded on a special form designed for the purpose of tracking outputs and outcomes, or a column on the service provision form may be used. In the example in Figure 7.5, case management milestones would correspond to phases of the helping process depicted in the flowchart (see Figure 7.2). Successful achievement of milestones could be used to track outputs, including units of service provided and completion of the full complement of prescribed services.

Collecting Organizational Data   As discussed in Step 2, organizational data are used to address concerns related to strategic and long-range planning, to operations, human resources, technological resources, and financial resources. For example, if the strategic plan calls for development of branch offices, identification of client population by census tract or zip code may help an agency to understand some of the problems clients face in terms of access to agency resources. Identification of a growing population of Spanish-speaking only clients could lead to planning for more bilingual workers.

Organization-wide data and information may also be used for human resources purposes. The human resources director (or business manager) may develop a database on staff for monitoring and reporting staff demographics, credentials, or other factors. Funding, regulating, and accrediting organizations may require reports on staff profiles to ensure compliance with affirmative action and equal employment opportunity laws. Some of the demographic variables that may be required include age, sex, ethnicity, education, or licenses/certificates required for technical positions. Any or all of these variables may need to be aggregated by level of staff to permit examination of demographic profiles by position.

An additional use of data might be to track the performance appraisal system. Supervisors and managers may want to find ways to correlate performance appraisal scores with staff productivity as a way of validating the scoring system. A question that should always be on the minds of supervisors and managers is the following: Are those workers who are most committed to the mission and most productive ranked among the highest, and are those known to be low or nonproductive workers ranked among the lowest in the performance appraisal system?

Some suggested items that might be used to compile an organizational report follow:

Strategic Planning:	Collection of data using indicators tied to strategic goals and objectives.
Example:	Tracking of hiring patterns to determine whether the goal of increasing the number of professionally trained staff is being achieved.
Operations:	Collection of data on performance measures for each program.
Example:	Mean number of units of service provided per client; number and percentage of clients completing each program; and percentage of successful outcomes.
Human Resources:	Collection of data to track staff credentials for accreditation purposes.
Example:	The number of counseling staff who have successfully passed the state licensing examination.

Collecting Community Data   Community data and information are useful to an organization primarily in terms of monitoring changes and trends and ensuring that populations served and services provided are consistent with community demographic profiles and needs assessments. In most instances agencies will use data and information compiled by other sources, because it is very expensive and time consuming to conduct original studies. Many federal, state, and local government studies are available, and most can be found in the government documents section of a library. State public social service agencies and

United Way offices often collect data that can be made available in report form to local agencies. The following selected variables illustrate the types of data and information that might be collected and aggregated, using a time series analysis, in compiling community data for planning purposes.

Community Demographic Profile, 1980–2000
Community Needs, 1980 through 2000

Age	*Gender*	*Race/Ethnicity*	*Community Priorities*
00 to 05	Female	African American	Employment
06 to 09	Male	Asian American	Education
10 to 19		Caucasian	Housing
20 to 29		Hispanic/Latino	Transportation
30 to 39		Native American	Health
Etc.		Other	Food and Nutrition

Step 6: Designing the Data Entry, Processing, and Reporting System

Developing a data-processing system in the 2000s should not be addressed without considering the state of the art of computerization. As Weinbach (1998) points out, "Computerization is no longer a choice. As human service organizations become more and more competitive, managers who resist information technology advances are likely to be left behind" (p. 295). Systems used in the 1980s and 1990s typically required data entry on paper by the worker with subsequent transfer to a data entry person who would then enter the data into the computer. These now obsolete systems have given way to direct entry by workers. Data and information about each case can be typed directly into the record. Drop-down menus can present options on each variable and require only a click to complete each item in the demographic section. Figure 7.6 illustrates the type of format that may be used for direct data entry. Simplified procedures also allow for easy aggregation of data. Having access to a computer consultant, either paid or volunteer, has become as essential to effective management as having a business manager.

FIGURE 7.6

Illustration of a Format That May Be Used for Direct Data Entry into a Computer

Client ID Number ☐☐☐ Date of Birth ☐☐-☐☐-☐☐☐☐ State of Residence ☐☐

Gender ☐ Ethnicity ☐☐ Education ☐☐ Years of previous employment ☐☐

Type of employment ☐☐ Highest salary ☐☐☐☐☐ Career interest ☐☐☐

Step 7: Run the System, Compile Sample Data, and Debug the System

The seventh and final step cannot be completed until appropriate software has been selected to accept data and produce the necessary reports and until data have been entered into the system. Even though data will be very limited in the early phases after the system is activated, it is advisable to run sample reports. The focus of this step is to ensure that workers are entering data in an accurate and timely manner and that the software is capable of aggregating data in the ways needed for reporting purposes. Tables, charts, and graphs produced should be shared with workers and their review and comments solicited. Workers should be viewed as full partners in the creation and implementation of this system in order to encourage maximum participation and use of available data and information. Early debugging of the system will help to build assurances that when information is needed for monitoring, evaluating, or reporting purposes it will be accurate and available in the format expected.

■ Using Data and Information to Ensure Organizational Consistency and Integrity

The true value of a management information system will be measured not by the volume of the data processed but by the extent to which it provides information that enables an agency to achieve and maintain excellence. The organizational planning system is designed to maintain a clear sense of vision and focus. Beginning with the mission statement, planning becomes increasingly precise by stating goals, objectives, and activities, with objectives and activities being stated at a high level of specificity. If planning at the strategic, long-range, and program levels is integrated and flows from the mission statement, these plans can be useful in establishing guidelines for the design of the management information system. With performance measurement focused on programs and services as the centerpiece, organizational-level information can be utilized to ensure that structure and functions are in harmony with and supportive of optimal performance.

Community-level information is used to ensure that the organization and its programs remain relevant to the changing environment. If the design of the management information system is guided by these priorities, it should also be able to answer questions or provide information required by its stakeholders, including funding sources. When additional questions need to be answered, the information should be produced within the framework described previously.

SUMMARY

1. **The Importance of Information.** Data and information are increasingly required for funding and decision making for human service organizations.

2. **The Quality of Information.** The demands for data and information have changed over the years. Primary consideration should be given to agency needs. External needs should be incorporated into the agency's management information system (MIS).

3. **Types of Data and Information Needed in Organizations.** Data systems should help organizations understand the implications of decisions.
   - *External Data and Information Considerations.* In constructing an MIS, planners should consider economic, sociological, political, and technical factors.
   - *Internal Data and Information Considerations.* For internal use, MIS planners should consider organizational purpose, planning, operations, human resources, technical resources, and financial resources.

4. **Developing Integrated Information Systems.** There are many subsystems that should feed into the overall agency MIS.

5. **Steps to Developing an Integrated Management Information System.** Planning an MIS should follow a rational strategy to avoid information overload.
   - *Step 1: Identifying Input, Throughput, Output, and Outcome Elements.* Each of these elements must be identified and defined.
     Identifying Inputs
     Identifying Throughputs
     Identifying Outputs
     Identifying Client Outcomes
   - *Step 2: Identifying the Questions to Be Answered by the Management Information System.*
     Identifying the Information Needs of External Constituencies
     - *Economic Considerations.* These considerations include funders, contributors, referral sources, consumers and competitors.
     - *Sociological Considerations.* These considerations include profiles of people, problems, needs, strengths, and opportunities.
     - *Political Considerations.* These considerations include regulatory agencies, accrediting organizations, and governing board.
     - *Technological Considerations.* These considerations include new developments in technology and professional practice.

     Identifying the Information Needs of Internal Constituencies
     - *Organizational Purpose, Mission, and Philosophy.* These factors should guide decision making about data collection.
     - *Organizational Planning.* Data and information are needed to monitor implementation of plans.
     - *Organizational Operations.* Monitoring and evaluation efforts require data and information.
     - *Human Resources.* Reports and monitoring of compliance with plans require data and information.
     - *Technological Resources.* Currency of technological resources should be tracked.
     - *Financial Resources.* Tracking of financial resources is critical to monitoring organizational performance.

       Separating and Prioritizing Information Needs. The performance guidance system is central to all data collection. Many other data and information needs can be incorporated into this system.

■ *Step 3: Identifying Data Elements Needed to Answer Questions.* Questions are answered by generating data that, when aggregated, become information.

Elements Used in Monitoring, Evaluating, and Reporting on Clients and Programs. Each element is selected based on its contribution to generating needed information.
- *Input Elements.*
- *Throughput Elements.*
- *Ouput Elements.*

Elements Used in Monitoring, Evaluating, and Reporting on Organizational Performance. Staff characteristics are compiled for human resources purposes. Data and information regarding strategic and long-range planning are compiled.

Elements Used in Understanding the Problems, Needs, and Strengths of the Community. Population and social-problem trends help in understanding community needs.

■ *Step 4: Developing the Tables, Charts, and Graphs That Will Display Data Needed for Reports.* Data displays include cross-sectional analysis, time series analysis, and comparison with other data units.

Format for Reporting Data and Information to Outside Sources. Reports should be designed in a way that they are easy to understand.

■ *Step 5: Designing Data Collection Procedures and Instruments.* Systems need to be designed to collect data. Manual completion of forms and direct electronic data entry are options.

Collecting Program Data. Data collection needs follow the flowchart of client services.

Collecting Organizational Data. Data are collected for either human resources, budgeting, or planning purposes.

Collecting Community Data. Community demographics and needs assessment data are collected and compiled.

■ *Step 6: Designing the Data Entry, Processing, and Reporting System.* Data are either collected on forms and entered into the system by a data entry person or are entered directly into the system by the staff who collect them.

■ *Step 7: Run the System, Compile Sample Data, and Debug the System.* Sample reports, reviewed by staff, should be helpful in making necessary changes to the MIS design.

6. **Using Data and Information to Ensure Organizational Consistency and Integrity.** Data and information should be used for program and organizational improvement.

EXERCISES

Please complete the following sections of your manual based on the content covered in Chapter 7.

Section 7: Collecting Data and Information

7.1 Philosophy. Establish agency philosophy about data and information. Why data and information need to be collected; how they will be used, and so on.

7.2 **Reports.** Identify the major reports that must be produced by the agency's management information system each year. Include a brief statement of content to be included in each report.

Example: **7.2.1 Reports to funding sources.**

7.2.2 Reports to regulatory bodies.

7.2.3 Report to the board.

7.2.4 Annual program summaries.

7.2.5 Annual human resources report.

REFERENCES

Governmental Accounting Standards Board (GASB). (1993). *Proposed statement of the Governmental Accounting Standards Board on concepts related to service efforts and accomplishments reporting.* Norwalk, CT: Author.

Kettner, P., Daley, J., & Nichols, A. (1985). *Initiating change in organizations and communities: A macro practice model.* Monterey, CA: Brooks-Cole.

Kettner, P., & Martin, L. (1998). Accountability in purchase-of-service contracting. In M. Gibelman & H. Demone (Eds.), *The privatization of human services: Policy and practice issues* (Vol. 1, pp. 183–204). New York: Springer.

Kettner, P., Moroney, R., & Martin, L. (1999). *Designing and managing programs: An effectiveness-based approach* (2nd ed.). Thousand Oaks, CA: Sage.

Martin, L. (1988, November). *Consumer satisfaction surveys: Are they valid measures of program performance?* Paper presented at the Eleventh National Conference on Specialized Transportation, Sarasota, FL.

Rapp, C., & Poertner, J. (1992). *Social administration: A client-centered approach.* New York: Longman.

Slack, I. (1979). *Title XX at the crossroads.* Washington, DC: American Public Welfare Association.

U.S. Bureau of the Census. (1994). *The County and City Data Book.* Washington, DC: Author.

Weinbach, R. (1998). *The social worker as manager: A practical guide to success* (3rd ed.). Boston: Allyn & Bacon.

Managing Resources
to Support Excellence

CHAPTER OBJECTIVES

Upon completion of this chapter, the reader will be able to:

- Explain the purpose and meaning of a budget for a human services organization.
- Identify and discuss the concepts and issues associated with five revenue sources.
- Explain the differences between line-item, functional, and program budgeting.
- Create a line-item, functional, and program budget.
- Apply budgeting concepts to an agency budget and produce a budget report.

Assumptions

- That in order to generate the kind of data and information expected from a human service organization today, it is necessary to integrate budget and services data.
- That functional and program budgeting concepts can produce the kind of information needed for accountability to all reporting and funding sources.
- That managers in human service organizations need to be familiar with the concepts but are not expected to handle the details of budgeting and financial management.

■ Budgeting Issues in Human Services

Dealing with finances in a nonprofit industry was, for many years, something like playing a baseball game without keeping score. Lohmann (1980) expresses well the critical difference between nonprofit financing and commercial enterprises:

> In business and commercial settings, technical financial concerns and substantive goal-oriented concerns, along with certain standard assumptions about managerial and employee motivations, converge around the question of profits. At that point, the whole thing makes sense. However, the recognition that most human service organizations, by definition, are generally indifferent to questions of "profit" and "gain" except in the loosest and most metaphoric sense has never been successfully followed up by identification of a criterion that might serve a comparable purpose in the non-profit sector. (p. 2)

For example, when Peters and Waterman (1982) undertook their study of excellence in U.S. corporations, their study design called for an in-depth examination of excellent companies to determine what factors seemed to contribute to excellence. To select their sample, they chose and imposed six measures of long-term superiority:

1. Compound asset growth
2. Compound equity growth
3. The average ratio of market value to book value
4. Average return on total capital
5. Average return on equity
6. Average return on sales (pp. 22–23)

None of these criteria could be used to select the top one hundred nonprofit organizations in the country. The concepts of growth, return on investment, equity, and sales as measured in dollar amounts do not reflect the reason for the existence for nonprofit organizations. Concepts such as profit and loss measured in dollars simply do not work as measures of success in the nonprofit world. Yet dollar figures are important to nonprofits and are used in a variety of ways as indicators of organizational productivity, efficiency, effectiveness, and quality. Nonprofit goals and objectives are increasingly monitored and evaluated by the use of financial measures. Service-provision data are used in conjunction with financial data as a basis for calculating program performance measures. Performance measurement is increasingly being used by funding sources and will be discussed in more detail later in this chapter.

Perspectives on the Meaning of a Budget

Views of various authors differ about the meaning of all the activities and efforts that culminate in the document that is referred to as the budget. Gates (1980) says, "In the budget can be embodied a plan, a statement of program, an ordering of priorities, a means of ensuring accountability to a wide variety of interests, a method of control, as well as an instrument for improving organizational efficiency and effectiveness" (p. 190). Lohmann (1980) frames the process this way, "Financial management is not necessarily concerned with a separate set of ends and management processes. It is, rather, a unique language for talking about and analyzing the relationship between ends and means, and for determining the best means of goal attainment, once the ends of service have been established" (p. 6). Wildavsky (1964) points out that the budget process is, ultimately, one that translates financial resources into human purposes.

If an entrepreneur intends to begin a new for-profit venture, he or she will begin with a business plan that will examine the short- and long-range market for the new product or service, strategies for production and distribution, an analysis of the competition, perhaps identification of a unique niche in the market, and other considerations. Start-up funds are a consideration, and a bank loan is a typical source of funding. However, it is not expected that the business owner will come back each year for new funding indefinitely into the future. If the business plan is sound, the expectation is that profits generated in year 1 will be used to underwrite the costs of year 2, and so on.

Conversely, if an individual or group starts up and runs a nonprofit organization, the expectation is that he or she will go back to funding sources on an annual basis and ask for more money. There are no profits left at the end of year 1 to run the agency in year 2. If the agency expects to continue, there must be an ongoing effort focused on fund-raising from one of the revenue sources available.

■ Revenue Sources

McMurtry, Netting, and Kettner (1991) conducted a study of about four hundred agencies to determine sources of funding and patterns of adaptation to declining resources. The study revealed the following funding sources:

1. Government contracts
2. Charitable contributions
3. Client fees
4. Public grants
5. Private grants
6. Other sources

Lohmann (1980) identifies five categories of funding sources:

1. Government funding from tax-based sources
2. Fees
3. Grants
4. Organized fund drives
5. Charitable contributions

Other authors add for-profit subsidiaries and various restructuring options (such as merging or franchising) as ways of increasing resources. It is incumbent upon the chief executive officer and board of directors of a nonprofit agency to ensure that there is in place a fund-raising plan, and that there is a reasonably steady and predictable flow of funding to support programs and services on an ongoing basis. In the following sections we will explore some of the important considerations from a manager's or administrator's per-spective on (1) government funding, (2) grants and contracts, (3) client fees, (4) charitable giving, and (5) other strategies to increase resources.

Government-Funded Programs

By far the major source of funding for social service programs is federal and state gov-ernments. Selected problems are addressed by cities, counties, or regional associations, but often even programs sponsored by local governments draw heavily on federal and state funding sources. Government funding tends to be organized around population groups and problem areas. Funding streams tend to begin within a framework of services by age group. One group includes children (sometimes defined as children and families). A second group focuses on various types of problems and needs experienced by adults, including employment, mental health, or substance abuse. A third focuses on the needs of the elderly. Other funds are earmarked for the physically or developmentally disabled and other special populations. A substantial portion of funds targeting population groups comes in the form of entitlements and, as such, bypasses the traditional congressional budgetary process (Gates, 1980).

For funds that are governed by the budgetary process, it is important to recognize that the process is both financial and political. Although the mainstream programs at both fed-eral and state levels tend to receive continuation funding, prominent social issues, high-visibility media coverage, and effective lobbying efforts can influence the budgeting process as well. A first step in developing a fund-raising strategy targeting government funds is to identify the domain(s) within which the agency fits and can provide needed services.

Within the field of child welfare, for example, Liederman (1995) points out policy and practice tend to follow social and economic swings and to adapt to changing conditions. From a strict child protection approach in the early 1980s, service delivery has shifted to a child-centered, family-focused approach. This philosophy becomes the impetus for a range of programs and services including family preservation, family foster care, kinship care, independent-living services, adolescent pregnancy and parenting services, and oth-ers. At the other end of the age spectrum, the Administration on Aging sponsors a national network of public and private agencies responsible for providing services at the local level to meet the needs of the elderly. As Bellos and Ruffolo (1995) point out, this network "is composed of 10 regional A of A offices, 57 state units on aging, 670 local area agencies on aging, almost 200 Native American tribal organizations, 1500 nutrition sites and 2700 local service provider agencies" (p. 167). Services include homemaker, chores, home health, transportation, home-delivered meals, adult day care, and many others.

Local agency directors who expect to receive funding for services that fall within the child welfare or aging networks can improve their chances for participation if they keep track of proposed programs, legislation, and funding streams initiated at the federal and state levels. By participating in the political process, an agency director, board member, or selected staff members can become integral parts of the decision-making processes and will understand the rationale and the politics of government funding. This knowledge puts an agency director and other participants in a position of strength when the time comes to submit grant or contract proposals to fund agency programs.

Grants and Contracts

Prior to the implementation of Title XX of the Social Security Act in the late 1970s, the use of tax dollars by private, nonprofit agencies was limited. When public funding was used by private agencies, the mechanism under which the transfer of resources was made tended to be an assistance-type relationship in which government funding was used to assist an agency in carrying out its services. State agencies recognized that it was in the best interest of the stability of the community-service network that certain types of agencies remain solvent and able to provide necessary services. This type of relationship involved little control from the government-funding source and minimal accountability from the local agency. Title XX changed all that. Reisch (1995) reports that one of the factors that shaped the Title XX legislation was "the purchase of service requirements pioneered in the late 1960s, which led to government departments contracting out for the delivery of mandated services with existing nonprofit or private-sector institutions or agencies" (p. 1986). Title XX dramatically increased the resources available for purchase of service contracting and led to a revolution in the way states and private, nonprofit agencies related to each other around the payment for and provision of services.

For a period of time following passage of this amendment, many state human service agencies made no distinction between grants and contracts and used both to fund the same services interchangeably. This led to a number of disputes over the rights and prerogatives of state agencies in their relationships with private, nonprofit agencies because the rights and responsibilities of parties are different under a contractual relationship from those of a grant. Some laws apply only to contracts, others only to grants. Federal legislation was eventually passed to resolve these issues. The Federal Commission on Government Procurement developed criteria for differentiating between the appropriate uses of grants and contracts. The commission's recommendations were translated into law in the form of the Federal Grant and Cooperative Agreement Act of 1977.

The Federal Grant and Cooperative Agreement Act established the principle that contracts were to be used for procurement relationships. Grants were to be used for assistance relationships. In practice what this means is that if a government agency expends funds to carry out activities for which the government is responsible, then a procurement relationship exists and a contract is required. If the government expends funds to assist an agency in carrying out the agency's programs and services, then an assistance relationship is established and a grant is awarded (Kettner & Martin, 1987).

For example, when children are removed from a home by a government agency for the purpose of protecting the children, the government is obligated to care for those children until a final decision is made about return or permanent placement. Many government agencies, in this instance, will procure or purchase foster-care services from a private, nonprofit agency. The client (in this case, the child) remains the responsibility of the government agency even while he or she is under the care of a foster home served by the nonprofit agency.

There may also be an instance in which there is a shortage of foster homes in a community. The government agency may grant funds to a family-service agency to strengthen its foster care recruitment, training, and licensing program. In this case, the government agency would be awarding the agency a grant to carry out its own programs because these programs benefit the community, and the agency does not have the necessary resources to increase or strengthen the program on its own (Kettner & Martin, 1987).

Contracts generally carry more obligations and establish higher expectations for accountability than do grants. The definition of a contract is "[a] promise or set of promises for breach of which the law gives a remedy or the performance of which the law in some way recognizes a duty" (Office of Federal Procurement Policy, 1979). Contracts in human services are subject to competitive bidding, with awards made not necessarily to the lowest bidder but rather to the agency that demonstrates the highest capability of providing the best-quality programs and services requested at the lowest cost. In short, considerations such as capability and quality, demonstrated by a strong record of services provided in the past, enter into the decision.

Types of Contracts   There are different approaches to contracting, each with its own unique requirements and methods of payment. The four most commonly used approaches are (1) cost reimbursement, (2) unit cost, (3) fixed fee, and (4) incentive (Kettner & Martin, 1987).

A cost-reimbursement contract is distinguished by the inclusion of a budget. The budget becomes part of the contract and is used as a basis for paying the contractor for performance of services. The concept of reimbursement is key because only those costs actually incurred are reimbursed under this type of contract. This means that the total amount listed in the budget may not be the same as that paid on the contract because the budget represents an estimate of expected costs and reimbursement is paid only for services actually provided. Under a cost-reimbursement contract, a special arrangement may have to be made to underwrite a cash flow sufficient to provide services up front, prior to reimbursement. For example, the local Catholic Social Services agency may provide services to help immigrants adjust to their communities under a $240,000 cost-reimbursement contract. For its start-up year the funding source may advance the agency $20,000 prior to any provision of service. Subsequent payments would be based on actual costs incurred.

A unit-cost contract is one in which the contractor is paid by the unit, usually defined in terms of time (e.g., one hour of service) or episode (e.g., one session). A definition of a unit is established in the contract (e.g., one hour of counseling) as well as the cost for that unit (e.g., $75 per unit). Services are then provided. The number of units is recorded and the government-contracting agency is billed, usually on a monthly basis. For example, a contractor providing home-delivered meals might be paid $3 per meal delivered. If the contractor provided 1,000 meals per month, the contractor would bill the government-contracting agency for $3,000 at the end of the month. This method differs from cost-reimbursement contracting in the sense that it is not a reimbursement for costs actually incurred. The contractor is paid $3 per meal regardless of the actual cost of the meal. If the contractor is able to reduce the cost of providing meals (or services), the savings can be put back into the agency budget as profit. A nonprofit agency is allowed to make a profit as long as the profit goes back into programs and is not distributed to those who have control over the organization such as its director, officers, or members.

A fixed-fee contract is one in which a total price is established and is paid on completion of the service. This type of contract requires a service that can be conceptualized and delivered within a specified time frame so that there is a clear beginning and ending point. Services such as the provision of a workshop, psychiatric consultation, and program evaluation are often contracted for a fixed fee. The service is provided within a specified time frame and paid for on completion of the service and often the submission of a final report.

An incentive contract is a cost-reimbursement, unit-cost, or fixed-fee contract with special incentives included. In an incentive contract, all or part of the contractor's compensation is tied to performance. An incentive contract might be used, for example, in a program designed to move participants from welfare to work by teaching them word processing and other computer skills. The basic contractual relationship would be a unit-cost contract that would pay the education and training costs for each participant who remains in the program to the point of completing the training course.

This means that the service provider would not be compensated for those participants who drop out of the program. If the target population is considered to be a group at risk of dropping out, so much funding may be lost because of those who drop out of the program that potential providers may be discouraged from submitting proposals. One solution is an incentive contract in which the provider is paid the full cost of providing service to all participants who remain in the program to completion, and an additional 15 percent or 20 percent for those who are placed in a job and remain there for six months. This type of contractual arrangement provides a double incentive: first, an incentive to put effort into keeping participants in the program, and second, an incentive to place program graduates into good-quality jobs.

Martin (2001) discusses performance contracts and the ways in which they affect a contractor's compensation. A performance contract is defined as "one that focuses on the outputs and outcomes of service provision and ties either contract payments, contract extensions and renewals, or both to their achievement" (p. 170). This type of contracting has important implications for performance expectations of those that will implement the contract. If, for example, a contract requires that a specified number of clients must complete an alcohol rehabilitation program and must remain alcohol-free for six months following treatment, the contracts may need to be managed on a daily or weekly basis in order to meet the specifications for reimbursement. Clinical staff may need to produce a certain amount of service daily, weekly, monthly, and quarterly in order to achieve full contractual compensation. Contract renewal or extension may depend on the number or percentages of cases that have been evaluated as successful in accordance with a specified definition. All these management responsibilities must receive careful consideration and planning prior to entering into a contractual relationship to provide services or achieve results.

Agencies that contract with government funding sources often subcontract selected services to other providers. It is important that agency managers and administrators understand the full range of contracting options both for acquiring funding to support programs as well as for subcontracting with other agencies and programs to provide specialized services.

Grants   Findings from a study of funding patterns (McMurtry et al., 1991) revealed that about 35 percent of responding agencies used funds drawn from public-grant sources and 31 percent from private-grant sources. Grants from all sources accounted for a mean share of about 15 percent of the budget of agencies using this funding source. Public grants are drawn from a variety of federal, state, and local government sources. Private grants are awarded from foundations and corporations. Rapp and Poertner (1992) list four types of foundations:

- *Independent or family foundations.* Funds are drawn from a family or group of individuals who combine resources to support special interests such as education, the arts, health, or mental health.

- *Corporate foundations.* Funds are drawn from profits of the corporation and awarded by a board of directors.
- *Operating foundations.* These foundations are created within a parent organization and are used to fund projects of the parent organization. Many universities have foundations and solicit direct contributions as well as resources bequeathed in wills and trusts.
- *Community foundations.* Funds are held in trust for other foundations. Grant awards are made in accordance with donor guidelines and interests. There may be special boards or committees for each fund. A larger board represents the community foundation and deals with overall policy issues. Some nonprofit agencies may keep their charitable funds on deposit with a community foundation. The advantage is that smaller funds get the benefits of larger returns resulting from the pooling of funds.

Most grant funds have a specialized focus and support innovative projects. As such they do not represent a dependable source for funding the ongoing operating costs of an agency but rather provide a source for expansion, experimentation, and sometimes research.

Requests for Proposals

Opportunities to bid for grants and contracts come in the form of requests for proposals (RFPs) that must in some way be made available within the public domain so that all potential bidders have an equal opportunity to submit a proposal. At the federal level, publications such as *The Federal Register* list all federal appropriations. Many special-interest groups sift through the information in *The Federal Register* and publish information about their areas of interest and make them available to state and local agencies on their mailing lists. These interest groups focus on such areas as child welfare, health, mental health, drugs and alcohol, aging, and many other common social problems and populations. Local agencies that hope to stay abreast of funding trends should make certain that they get onto all the appropriate mailing lists, including e-mail, and are systematic about the ways in which they track funding opportunities and follow up with competitive proposals.

Writing proposals requires both knowledge and skill and can require a significant investment of staff time. It is in the agency's interest to develop proposal-writing skills in as many staff as possible. Excellent literature is available on the subject of proposal writing (Kiritz, 1980; Lauffer, 1982). Universities offer courses and workshops are offered around the country designed to teach staff the necessary skills.

Client Fees

Within the field of human services, fees for service have always been approached with a certain amount of ambivalence. In a for-profit business, an owner expects to offer a product or a service in exchange for a fee. The fee is published, it is the same for every customer, and it is the customer's decision as to whether or not the product or service is worth the money spent. Human service programs have a different kind of mission and motive. They are not in business to serve customers and make money. Rather, they exist to help individuals, families, and communities deal with a range of complex social, interpersonal, or individual problems. People who most need help may decide that services are not a priority if they must compete with food, clothing, or shelter within a very limited budget.

For example, a single mother may be receiving public assistance and may want to become self-sufficient. A local human service agency has a program of prejob training, job-skills training, and job placement. The actual cost of the program is about $10,000 per person. Charging her a fee would eliminate any possibility that she could use these services and become self-supporting. Furthermore, eliminating clients such as this single mother would defeat the purpose for which the program was created. The same principle can be applied to programs designed to help people overcome addictions, strengthen marriages, or learn better parenting skills. So some argue for full government funding and free public services to the greatest extent possible, following the model of public schools.

There are, however, people who need services who can afford to pay some or all of the cost, either out of pocket or through their health insurance plans. Personal and family problems are by no means limited to the poor. Family breakdown, divorce, addiction, family violence, and many other problems cut across all socioeconomic levels. So the question is then raised about whether the government should fund the cost of services to those who can afford to pay or are covered by an insurance plan.

A 1991 study (McMurtry et al.) explored the trends in demand for services from three different groups of clients: (1) high-pay clients (who personally or through insurance pay the agency more than the break-even cost of services), (2) contract-eligible clients (whose service costs are paid under purchase-of-service contracts with public agencies), and (3) low-pay clients (who pay less than the break-even cost of services or nothing at all). Although most agencies reported increased demand from all three client types over the previous three years, 85 percent reported increased demand from contract-eligible clients and 84 percent reported increased demand from low-pay clients, whereas only 46 percent reported increased demand from high-pay clients.

However, when exploring trends in revenues, the source of greatest revenue increases was from high-pay clients and the lowest revenue increases from contract-eligible clients. This framework is helpful in understanding the complex differences between a for-profit business and a nonprofit agency. In business, a high level of demand is invariably a good thing because it means increased revenues. In a nonprofit agency, high demand increases revenues only when it comes from those who pay more than the break-even cost of services. Because government contracts typically pay less than the break-even cost of services, demand from either contract-eligible or low-pay/no-pay clients has a negative impact on the budget (Kettner & Martin, 1996). In some instances this situation represents a Catch-22, in which funding sources (including federal and state governments) may require that services be provided to those who cannot pay but then pay less than the break-even costs to the contractor. Contractors must then make up the deficits caused by providing these services from other sources. This financial arrangement would never happen when the government contracts for building roads or bridges, for example, but it is very common in human services. These different perspectives on supply and demand are not intended to discourage an agency from serving contract-eligible or low-pay/no-pay clients. Rather, the intent is to encourage the manager or administrator to try to understand the phenomenon of demand and how it affects the nonprofit human service organization.

Types of Client Fees   In order to address some of the problems presented by assessing client fees, agencies have developed creative practices over the years designed to accomplish a variety of objectives. Lohmann (1980) identifies five types of fees: (1) participation fees, (2) flat-rate fees, (3) sliding-scale fees, (4) fair-share-of-cost fees, and (5) fees paid by a third party.

Participation fees are nominal charges (such as $1 or $2 per appointment) that are intended to represent a good-faith pledge on the part of the client to participate in the service process. Their purpose is not to generate funds but rather to establish a symbol of a contractual relationship between agency and client that each will faithfully keep its commitments.

Flat-rate fees or fixed fees are those in which a rate per hour or rate per appointment is established and applied equally to all clients. These fees may be established as hourly (e.g., $75 per hour) or per visit (e.g., $40 per group session). This chapter will explore later how such unit costs are calculated. Flat-rate fees are intended to generate income and are generally set above the break-even cost so that profit can be generated that can be used for other purposes within the agency, including subsidizing the provision of services to those who cannot afford the flat-rate fees.

Sliding-scale fees are fees that are in some way tied to a client's ability to pay. Their purpose is to offset the cost of providing services to the greatest extent possible while not excluding from service those who cannot afford to pay the full cost of services. Fees on the highest end of the scale usually are set above the break-even cost. Criteria used to determine fees take into consideration such factors as family income and size of family. Administration of this type of fee system sometimes raises problems for both workers and clients. Workers typically prefer to keep the helping relationship and the financial relationship separate, whereas the agency may find it necessary to involve the worker in determining a client's ability to pay.

Fair-share-of-cost fees are calculated by taking the total cost of a program or service and dividing by the number served. If, for example, the salary and overhead costs of providing group treatment were $72 an hour and there were six group participants, each would be assessed $12 per session. The purpose is to cover the cost of providing services. This formula is usually applied to services for which costs can be easily calculated and for services that could not be provided without the cost-sharing method. Specialized courses and workshops often use this method as do agencies that provide recreational trips for seniors and other types of groups. The method is most effective when there is agreement ahead of time that all participants can afford to and are willing to pay their fair share.

The final type of client fee is the third-party fee. Increasingly health plans are covering costs of mental health treatment. Many of the major corporations and even some small businesses sponsor employee assistance programs in which the cost of treatment for personal problems is paid for by the employer. Others include mental health treatment in their basic health insurance coverage. These services are paid for based on the increasing recognition of the impact of such problems as addiction, family disruption, or depression on job performance. For those who are not employed, the cost of services may be covered by a government contract as discussed in the previous section. The type of contract may affect the form and amount of payment.

There are clearly some areas of overlap among the revenue sources discussed. Financial managers should avoid double-counting or in any way overestimating anticipated revenues. Over the years detailed records of fees should be maintained so that reasonably accurate estimates of revenue can be made as each annual budget is prepared.

Charitable Giving

Donations come from a variety of sources. The largest collaborative effort designed to raise funds for charitable organizations is the United Way. It is a nationally organized effort with many local branches throughout the country. Both national and local publicity campaigns are sponsored by the United Way. The annual fund-raising effort is coordinated within a specified time frame throughout the country. The business community strongly supports this effort, and their employees pledge gifts to the United Way. Annual allocation plans are made to disburse funding to member agencies. Agencies become members through an application process, and decisions about membership are made by a board of directors at the local level. Member agencies are expected to follow United Way policies in terms of campaign participation, reports, audits, and evaluations. There are also restrictions on agency fund-raising activities, because a basic principle of the United Way is to coordinate appeals for contributions and reduce the number of appeals to corporations and individuals (Rapp & Poertner, 1992, pp. 212–213).

Another charitable giving strategy is direct solicitation from individuals or business enterprises. Direct solicitation may come in the form of a telephone campaign, direct mail, or a special event. The use of telephone or direct mail requires developing lists of prospects and extensive use of volunteers. For telephone solicitations, a script must be developed and volunteers trained. For direct mail, a campaign theme is selected and publicity materials prepared. Some agencies use professional consultants for these purposes. If these strategies are to be used, it is important to weigh carefully the costs of consultation and fund-raising against the amount of the charitable donations that will eventually be available for agency expenditures. Agencies that receive funding from United Way must be certain that they are operating within its guidelines for independent fund-raising.

Special events, when planned and carried out effectively, can raise substantial amounts of money. Agencies have used a wide variety of events. Some of these include thousand-dollar-a-plate dinners, auctions of items donated, celebrity sporting events, and many other creative games, contests, or tournaments. With special events detailed planning is critical. They require a substantial number of dedicated volunteers who are willing to make significant time commitments. Resources, including both a dollar allocation as well as in-kind resources, will be necessary to achieve a successful special event.

Fund-raising done by an agency, regardless of which strategy is used, must be approached with the same intensity and attention to detail that are used in the provision of services. Activities cannot be run successfully with only part-time attention from a few staff. They must receive diligent advanced attention—up to six months or a year before the event or campaign. Every aspect, from the design of the fund-raising effort to marketing to planning for the comfort and enjoyment of the participants, must be committed to paper and incorporated into a plan. The plan should be submitted to the agency's board of directors for discussion and approval so that there is no question about the board's total support for and commitment to the project. Volunteers and participants should be thanked in every way possible and affordable to be sure that they are aware that their contributions are recognized and appreciated. Administered properly, charitable fund-raising can become a significant part of an agency's annual revenue.

Other Strategies to Increase Resources

Sometimes it is possible for an agency to exhaust all of the foregoing options and still not have adequate resources to support even a stripped-down budget. Or it may be that an agency is able to provide services and meet a need, but because of economies of scale the agency could be much more efficient and effective if resources were combined with those of other providers. Or perhaps a for-profit, money-making opportunity presents itself that would allow the agency to become, to a significant extent, self-supporting. When these situations occur, the strategy of choice is restructuring. Restructuring options include (1) merging, (2) franchising, and (3) establishing a for-profit subsidiary (Netting & Kettner, 1987).

A merger implies the "complete absorption of one organization by another or the joining of two or more organizations into a new common identity" (Aldrich, 1979, p. 303). Mergers can be horizontal, vertical, or conglomerate. Horizontal mergers involve the coming together of two or more organizations that deliver the same services, such as two child care centers merging to take advantage of economies of scale. Vertical mergers involve the acquisition of a provider of services that are different from those typically provided by the parent organization, such as a family-service agency and a senior center merging into one administrative unit in order to provide intergenerational services. Conglomerate mergers involve changing the scope of service by providing a greater volume of the same services, by extending the agency's geographical boundaries, or by acquiring organizations that provide totally unrelated services. Merging has been a common practice in the child care industry and the long-term care industry over the last decade, and a number of national chains have developed with child care centers or nursing homes in many communities across the country.

Franchising is a practice that has been around in the business world for many years. The process begins with a parent organization that provides a product or service. The organization discovers methods for maximizing efficiency and effectiveness and builds a reputation for quality service at a reasonable cost. The organization is expanded by teaching others how to follow the parent organization's successful model. In the for-profit world, the franchisee pays an initial and/or an ongoing fee to the franchiser and is expected to adhere to policies and procedures, including quality-control methods, established by the franchiser.

A for-profit subsidiary is established when a nonprofit organization sets up a subunit within the organization that may be run as a business and may legally make a profit. The subsidiary charges for its products or services and may use profits to support the nonprofit agency's budget. As Hansmann (1981) points out, "The defining characteristic [of a nonprofit] is that it is barred from distributing profits, or net earnings, to individuals who exercise control over it, such as its director, officers, and members. This does not mean that a nonprofit organization is prohibited from earning a profit. Rather, it is the distribution of profits that is prohibited" (p. 501).

National organizations such as the Salvation Army and Goodwill have long established for-profit subsidiaries that accept donations of used clothing, furniture, and appliances and resell them through their secondhand stores. Nursing homes often establish for-profit pharmacies and laundries. Gift shops and T-shirt sales are other examples of how nonprofit agencies may legally generate profits. Developing a for-profit subsidiary requires the creation of a legal entity that operates independently of the agency and that is subject to all the laws and regulations of any other business.

As the competitive environment for human services increases, and as pressures increase for efficiency, effectiveness, productivity, and quality, it is likely that restructuring strategies will find their way into more strategic plans of human service organizations.

■ The Budget Cycle

Planning and implementing a budget involves a series of activities that begins well before the beginning of the actual budget or fiscal year. It is not unusual that, once a fiscal year begins, planning is immediately initiated for the next fiscal year. In addition, some follow-up activities are required after the fiscal year is over, thus causing overlap of work associated with up to three different fiscal years. For example, an agency could be in the planning year for one budget, the implementation (or fiscal) year for a second budget, and the evaluation year for a third budget. Vinter and Kish (1984) have identified the following activities that are associated with the various phases of the budget cycle:

> *Program and budget planning*
> Needs assessment and feasibility study
> Program planning
> Cost estimating
> Budget development
>
> *Funds procurement*
> Budget request submission
> Negotiation with funder
> Re-budgeting and resubmission
> Award and acceptance
>
> *Fiscal management*
> Designation of cost and responsibility centers
> Internal funds allocation and re-budgeting
> Establishment of restricted accounts
> Financial transactions, recording, and accounting
> Operations monitoring and reporting
> Cost control and containment
>
> *Performance assessment, financial reports, audits*
> End-of-year financial statements
> Financial audit
> Performance audit
> Cost analysis
>
> *Recycle*
> Program re-planning
> Continuation budgeting
> Cost-finding and rate-seeking (pp. 26–27)

Because the issue of organizational integrity is so important to achieving and maintaining excellence in an organization, it is vital that those who oversee the management of the organization see all of these phases as parts of the overall budget cycle and not as unrelated events or processes. Each phase is related in some way to all the others, and each activity should be understood and carried out as a part of the cycle. When this is the case, the likelihood is that accountability expectations will be met, and each budget cycle will represent a learning experience upon which the agency can build to strengthen and improve future performance.

Fiscal Years

In order to have an orderly, predictable calendar around which to plan, it is necessary for an agency to select a fiscal year that will be used for budget purposes. Fiscal years vary for different funding sources.

- The federal government uses October 1 to September 30 as its fiscal year.
- Many states use July 1 to June 30 as the fiscal year.
- Some foundations use the calendar year, January 1 through December 31.

These overlapping time frames can complicate budgeting, monitoring, and evaluating responsibilities, because funding sources usually expect an end-of-the-year report that coincides with their fiscal year. Agencies accommodate overlapping calendars by establishing their own fiscal year and by reporting revenues and expenditures as they fall within their own budgeting cycle. For example, if an agency follows a July 1 through June 30 fiscal year and receives funding from a foundation that follows a calendar year, one-half of the funding would be accounted for in part of one fiscal year (January 1 through June 30), and one-half in part of another (July 1 through December 31). Table 8.1 depicts overlapping fiscal years.

When the time comes for end-of-the-year reporting, two options are available. If acceptable to the funding source, reports are based on the agency's fiscal year. When a funding source's fiscal year does not coincide, the proportion of funds expended during the agency's fiscal year is reported. When this method is not acceptable to a funding source, a separate budget is established and monitored. In instances in which agencies receive federal funding that is passed through a department or division of state government, the state may be willing to take responsibility for coordinating budget cycles and develop a statewide report for

TABLE 8.1

Illustration of Overlapping Fiscal Years, by Quarters

	Overlapping Fiscal Years			
	January 1 to March 31	**April 1 to June 30**	**July 1 to September 30**	**October 1 to December 31**
Calendar Year	1st Quarter	2nd Quarter	3rd Quarter	4th Quarter
July 1 to June 30 Fiscal Year	3rd Quarter	4th Quarter	1st Quarter	2nd Quarter
October 1 to September 30 Fiscal Year	2nd Quarter	3rd Quarter	4th Quarter	1st Quarter

the federal government on how program funding has been allocated and spent. In short, there are many different ways to handle overlapping budget cycles, and agency administrators and managers need to know state, federal, and other funding source requirements in order to compile a plan that will meet the budgeting and reporting needs at all levels.

■ Resource Allocation

Experts in the field of budgeting and accounting have provided a range of different budgeting options over the years. Some of the descriptive terms applied to budgeting include:

- *Line-item budgeting*
- *Program budgeting*
- *Performance budgeting*
- *Program planning and budgeting (PPBS)*
- *Zero-base budgeting (ZBB)*
- *Outcome budgeting* (Lynch, 1995; Martin, 1997)

Definitions of these terms vary with different authors, and some terms are used interchangeably. In order to limit this discussion to budgeting approaches that are useful for human service agencies, the text will focus on three types of budgets: (1) line-item budgeting, (2) functional budgeting, and (3) program budgeting. Line-item budgeting simply lists the categories and dollar amounts that are used to illustrate planned expenditures for the entire agency for the coming year. Functional budgeting systems provide information about the costs of providing program products and services. Program budgeting systems are used to calculate the costs of achieving program results or outcomes. The following example illustrates the types of information that can be provided by each budgeting system. Each system will be described in more detail in the following sections.

Line-Item Budget	*Functional Budget*	*Program Budget*
The cost of salaries and wages for fiscal year 20XX is $185,000.	The cost of providing one congregate meal to one person is $8.75.	The cost of raising the nutrition level for one person to minimum standards is $3,160.

Line-Item Budgeting

A line-item budgeting system is the simplest and most basic of the three options. Developing a line-item budget requires four steps:

Step 1. Designing a standardized line-item budget format
Step 2. Developing common budget definitions and terms
Step 3. Identifying all revenues and expenses
Step 4. Balancing the budget (Kettner, Moroney, & Martin, 1999, p. 177)

Some funding sources over the years have required that certain line items be used to track expenditures. Table 8.2 illustrates line items that have been used by four different funding sources.

TABLE 8.2

Resource Categories Use by Various Funding Sources

Federal (Department of Education)	Grantsmanship Center	United Way	Campaign for Human Development
Personnel	Personnel	Salaries	Personnel
Fringe benefits	Salaries and wages	Employee benefits	Salaries
Travel	Fringe benefits	Payroll taxes, etc.	Fringe benefits
Equipment	Consultants and	Professional fees	
Supplies	contract services	Supplies	Office expenses
Contractual		Telephone	Consumable
Construction	Nonpersonnel	Postage and shipping	supplies
Other	Space costs	Occupancy	Equipment
Indirect charges	Rental, lease,	Rental and maintenance	purchased
	or purchase	of equipment	Equipment rental
	of equipment	Printing and publications	Equipment maintenance
	Consumable	Travel	and repairs
	supplies	Conferences, conventions,	Reproduction and
	Travel	and meetings	printing
	Telephone	Specific assistance	Postage and freight
	Other costs	to individuals	Telephone and
		Membership dues	telegraph
		Awards and grants	
		Miscellaneous	Travel expenses
		Depreciation of building	Staff
		and equipment	Consultant
		Payment to affiliated	Board or committee
		organizations	
		Capital expenditures	Occupancy expenses
		Current restricted fund	Utilities
		Land, building,	Rent or lease
		and equipment	Repairs and
		fund depreciation	maintenance
		Other	
			Program expenses
			Materials
			Stipends
			Insurance
			Outside services
			Consultants
			Contractors
			Other

Source: Kettner, P. M., Daley, J. M., & Nichols, A. W. (1985). *Initiating change in organizations and communities: A macro practice model.* Monterey, CA: Brooks Cole. Reprinted with permission of Wadsworth, a division of Thomson Learning. Fax 800-730-2215.

The line-item format is really quite simple and straightforward. Line items are mutually exclusive. Each line item is clearly defined. All revenues and expenditures must be accounted for in a line-item budget. Totals of all expected revenues must equal totals of all expenditures.

The line-item budget allows spending to be monitored in relation to amounts allocated but does not provide information that can be used to determine efficiency, effectiveness, productivity, or quality. A business manager, accountant, or bookkeeper typically has responsibility for monitoring a line-item budget. As funds are spent they are accounted for within the established categories. At the end of each month the budget manager calculates the ratio of budget allocated to budget spent in each category to see how it compares to the percentage of the fiscal year that has elapsed. When spending patterns in any one category are out of line with where they should be at that point in the fiscal year, a warning should be sent to the responsible managers and administrators. The Pinetree County Senior Center's annual budget shown in the following section is an example of a line-item budget.

Funding sources frequently require that a budget-justification sheet be attached to the budget. A budget-justification sheet is used to explain how each line item is calculated. A sample budget-justification sheet is illustrated in Table 8.3.

Functional Budgeting

Moving to the next level of complexity, functional budgeting requires combining program and service data with budget data. With functional budgeting, no longer are simple budget categories the focus of the system. Rather, total program-cost figures are calculated and used as a basis for determining the cost per unit of service for each program. As discussed in the previous chapter, units can be defined in terms of time, episode, or material goods provided directly to clients. For example, a child care center might use a functional budgeting system to determine the cost of one hour or one day of child care. A congregate-meal program might use these same concepts to calculate the cost per meal. A family-counseling agency might use functional budgeting to determine the cost of one couple completing the full complement of prescribed counseling sessions.

According to Kettner et al. (1999), creating a functional budgeting system requires seven steps:

Step 1. Developing a line-item budget

Step 2. Determining the agency's program structure

Step 3. Creating a cost-allocation plan format

Step 4. Identifying direct and indirect costs

Step 5. Assigning direct costs to programs

Step 6. Allocating indirect costs to programs

Step 7. Determining total program costs (p. 181)

TABLE 8.3

Sample Budget-Justification Sheet for the Pinetree County Senior Center

Pinetree County Senior Center
Budget Justification

1. **Personnel**

Executive director	$60,000	Recreation director	$24,000
Supervisor	35,000	Cook	20,000
Case manager	28,000	Secretary/receptionist	18,000

These salaries have been determined by salary survey to be competitive with comparable salaries in other organizations and have been formally approved by the board.

2. **Operating Expenses**

Rent:	$8 per square foot; office space = 1,500 sq. ft.; cafeteria/socialization and recreation area = 1,000 sq. ft.; 2,500 sq. ft. @ $8 = $20,000 per year
Utilities:	The center's share of utilities is $166 per month = $1,992
Telephone:	$35 per phone line per month for 6 employees = $2,520
Postage and shipping:	$20 per month per employee = $1,440
Printing and publication:	$20 per month per employee = $1,440
Supplies:	Food @ $1.50 per person per day (50 people, 5 days per week, 52 weeks per year) = $19,500
Supplies, office:	$30 per month per employee = $2,160
Equipment purchase/rent:	$500 per month for 2 copy machines, 1 fax, 2 cell phones = $6,000
Equipment maintenance:	Average costs have been $100 per month = $1,200
Professional fees:	$400 per month for Soc and Rec for speakers, entertainment, consultation = $4,800
Miscellaneous:	$100 per month for unanticipated expenses = $1,200

3. **Travel**

In-state travel @ $50 per month for 4 employees = $2,400

Out-of-state travel @ $500 per year for 4 employees = $2,000

Conferences and meetings @ $200 per year for 4 employees = $800

Step 1 is accomplished as described previously in the section on line-item budgeting. Budget categories are selected and dollar amounts are allocated to each category. Total expenditures must equal total revenues. The following budget will be used as an example to explain how a functional budgeting system evolves, step by step, beginning with a line-item budget.

Pinetree County Senior Center—Annual Budget

Personnel	
Executive director	$60,000
Supervisor	35,000
Case manager	28,000
Recreation director	24,000
Cook	20,000
Secretary/receptionist	18,000
Total Salaries and Wages	$185,000
Employee-Related Expenses @ 25%	$46,250
Operating Expenses	
Rent	$20,000
Utilities	2,000
Telephone	2,520
Postage and shipping	1,440
Printing and publication	1,440
Supplies—food	19,500
Supplies—office	2,160
Equipment purchase/rental	6,000
Equipment maintenance	1,200
Professional fees	4,800
Miscellaneous	1,200
Total Operating	$62,260
Travel	
In state	$2,400
Out of state	2,000
Conferences and meetings	800
Total Travel	$5,200
Total Agency Budget	**$298,710**

FIGURE 8.1

**Organizational Chart for the Pinetree County
Senior Center**

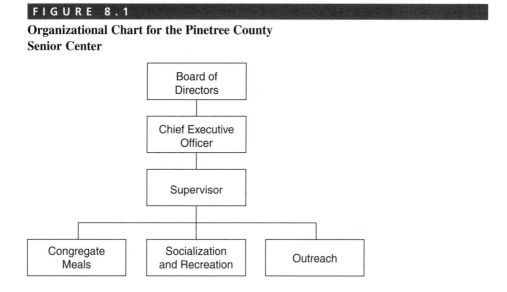

Step 2, determining the agency's program structure, is accomplished by identifying and defining the programs offered by the agency. The term *program* has been defined as "an aggregate of actions directed toward accomplishing a single goal" (Rapp & Poertner, 1992, p. 29) or "a range of services within a specifically defined category . . . usually continuing over a number of years and . . . designed to meet a . . . defined set of objectives" (Kettner, Daley, & Nichols, 1985, p. 38). In short, programs are organized activities designed to meet needs and achieve objectives. For budgeting purposes, the programs defined as making up the agency's program structure should be mutually exclusive (no overlap in services or activities) and exhaustive (should account for all services provided by the agency). Figure 8.1 illustrates the program structure for the Pinetree County Senior Center.

Step 3, creating a cost-allocation-plan format, is accomplished by creating a format that can be used to translate a line-item budget into a functional or program budget. The same categories or line items used in the line-item budget are used in the cost-allocation-plan format. The amount budgeted for each line item, instead of remaining a single figure, is spread out over the agency's programs. Developing a functional budget, therefore, requires that one column of the budget page be dedicated to each program. In addition to dedicating a column to each program, a column is also dedicated to indirect costs. Thus, if an agency has three programs, the budget will be spread out across four columns, one for each program and one for indirect costs. When a cost cannot be allocated exclusively to one program, it is placed in the indirect-cost column. The purpose of creating a cost-allocation-plan format is so that a total program cost can be calculated for each program in a way that takes both direct and indirect costs into consideration. A cost-allocation-plan format follows.

Pinetree County Senior Center—Cost-Allocation-Plan Format

	(1) Congregate Meals	(2) Socialization and Recreation	(3) Outreach	(4) Indirect Cost Pool
Personnel				
Executive director				
Supervisor				
Case manager				
Recreation director				
Cook				
Secretary/receptionist				
Total Salaries and Wages				
Employee-Related Expenses @ 25%				
Operating Expenses				
Rent				
Utilities				
Telephone				
Postage and shipping				
Printing and publication				
Supplies—food				
Supplies—office				
Equipment purchase/ rental				
Equipment maintenance				
Professional fees				
Miscellaneous				
Total Operating Expenses				
Travel				
In state				
Out of state				
Conferences and meetings				
Total Travel Expenses				
Total Direct Program Costs				

Step 4, identifying direct and indirect costs, results in the allocation of each line item to either a program column or to the indirect-cost-pool column. Direct costs are defined as "those items of expense that are to be incurred by a social service agency for the benefit of only one program" (Kettner et al., 1999, p. 183). Examples are salary and wages for staff who work exclusively in one program or rent for facilities that are used for only one program. Indirect costs are "those items of expense that are to be incurred for the benefit of two or more programs" (Kettner et al., 1999, p. 183). Such items as the salary of the executive director, rent for office space if used by two or more programs, or office supplies are generally considered to be indirect costs.

Step 5, assigning direct costs to programs, requires the use of the cost-allocation-plan format created in step 3. In allocating costs to programs, a decision must be made about each line item in terms of selecting the program (and column) to which the item will be assigned. Using the definition of direct costs as referring to those items that benefit only one program, items are examined for their appropriate allocation. Item 1, the salary of the executive director, for example, clearly benefits more than one program, so this salary is not treated as a direct cost. In the Pinetree County Senior Center example, the cook, recreation director, and case manager function exclusively within the congregate meals, socialization and recreation, and outreach programs, respectively. Study each of the following line items to see if they comply with the definitions of direct and indirect costs.

Pinetree County Senior Center—Cost Allocation Plan Format

	(1) Congregate Meals	(2) Socialization and Recreation	(3) Outreach	(4) Indirect Cost Pool
Personnel				
Executive director				$60,000
Supervisor				35,000
Case manager			$28,000	
Recreation director		$24,000		
Cook	$20,000			
Secretary/receptionist				18,000
Total Salaries and Wages	$20,000	$24,000	$28,000	$113,000
Employee-Related Expenses @ 25%	$5,000	$6,000	$7,000	$28,250
Operating Expenses				
Rent				$20,000
Utilities				2,000
Telephone				2,520
Postage and shipping				1,440
Printing and publication				1,440
Supplies—food	$19,500			
Supplies—office				2,160
Equipment purchase/rental				6,000
Equipment maintenance				1,200
Professional fees		$4,800		
Miscellaneous				1,200
Total Operating Expenses	$19,500	$4,800	0	$37,960
Travel				
In state		600	600	1,200
Out of state		500	500	1,000
Conferences and meetings		200	200	200
Total Travel Expenses	$0	$1,300	$1,300	$2,400
Total Direct Program Costs	$44,500	$36,100	$36,300	$181,810

Step 6, allocating indirect costs to programs, involves a return to the line items within the budget that have not been assigned to programs. Using the definition that an indirect cost is one that benefits two or more programs, all items that fit this definition should be assigned to the indirect-cost column. This column represents what agencies often refer to as overhead expenses. The concept of indirect costs or overhead is an important one for managers and administrators to understand. These are costs that are associated with providing services. Programs could not run and services could not be provided without them. Rent, utilities, and supplies, for example, are essential to enabling people in need to deal with their problems. The important issue with indirect costs is that a formula must be found that will allow for a fair, equitable, and accurate allocation of indirect costs back into programs so that the real cost of providing services can be determined. A number of such formulas are available and are discussed in the following sections.

Allocating Indirect Costs to Programs   Indirect-cost-pool dollars must be factored back into programs in a fair, equitable, and accurate way. It is important to remember here that the agency's business is running programs and providing services to people in need. Overhead costs are part of the cost of providing services. To determine accurate costs of providing services we must know how much of the overhead expenses should be allocated to each program. The cost-allocation formulas most commonly used by social service agencies are (1) total direct costs, (2) direct labor costs, (3) direct labor hours, and (4) direct costing (Hay & Wilson, 1995; Horngren, Foster, & Datar, 1997).

The total-direct-costs formula uses direct program costs as the basis for calculating how much of the indirect-cost pool should be allocated to each program. The steps to calculating the amount of indirect costs that is allocated to each program are as follows:

- The direct program costs of each of the three programs are added up.

- The sum is the total direct cost of programs.

- Each program's direct-cost figure is then divided by the total direct cost of all programs in order to calculate a percentage share for each program.

- Each of these percentages is then applied to the total of the indirect cost pool column.

- This process yields a different dollar figure for each program, which represents the program's share of the indirect-cost pool.

The total direct and indirect program cost is a very important figure for functional and program-budgeting purposes. The following illustration uses the total program-cost figures from the Pinetree County Senior Center's cost-allocation plan to depict the calculations used to arrive at total program-cost figures.

Pinetree County Senior Center—Cost-Allocation-Plan Format

	Congregate Meals	Socialization and Recreation	Outreach
Column totals	$44,500	$36,100	$36,300
Total Direct Program Costs	44,500	+ 36,100	+ 36,300 = 116,900
Program share	44,500/116,900 = 38.1%	36,100/116,900 = 30.9%	36,300/116,900 = 31.0%
Allocate indirect costs	38.1% × 181,810* = $69,270	30.9% × 181,810 = $56,179	31.1% × 181,810 = $56,361
Total Direct Program Costs	$44,500	$36,100	$36.300
Indirect costs	+ 69,270	+ 56,179	+ 56,361
Total Direct and Indirect Program Costs	$113,770	$92,279	$92,661

Total Indirect-Cost Pool = $181,810

Note that there are several points at which the total direct-cost formula can be checked for accuracy. In calculating each program's share of indirect cost:

- The percentages for all programs must add up to 100 percent, as they do in this example.

- The indirect costs for all programs must add up to the total of the indirect-cost pool. In this example, the total of the indirect-cost pool is $181,810, and the amounts allocated to each of the three programs add up to $181,810.

- The total direct and indirect program costs for all programs must add up to the same amount as the total agency budget using the line-item format. In this case, the total program costs for the three programs is $298,710, which is the same as the total agency budget.

Formulas using direct labor costs and direct labor hours provide for flexibility in situations in which total direct costs do not accurately reflect demands on agency resources. Human services is considered to be a labor-intensive industry. A quick review of the Pinetree County Senior Center budget, for example, shows that salaries plus employee-related expenses account for 77.4 percent of the total agency budget. It can be argued that a fairer, more equitable and accurate way of determining how the indirect cost pool should be allocated would be to use figures derived from personnel costs rather than total direct program costs. Using direct labor costs and direct labor hours formulas, operating and travel expenses are ignored.

Direct labor costs are determined in the same way as total direct costs, with the exception that only personnel-related costs are used, as follows:

- Total personnel costs for each program are added up.
- The personnel costs for each program are divided by the sum of personnel costs for all programs.
- The resulting percentages are applied to the total of the indirect-cost-pool column.
- The resulting dollar figures become the allocated indirect costs for each program.

The following illustration uses direct labor costs.

Pinetree County Senior Center—Cost-Allocation-Plan Format

	Congregate Meals	Socialization and Recreation	Outreach
Total salaries and wages	$20,000	$24,000	$28,000
Employee-related expenses @ 25%	5,000	6,000	7,000
Direct Labor Costs	25,000	+ 30,000	+ 35,000 = 90,000
Program share	25,000/90,000 = 27.8%	30,000/90,000 = 33.3%	35,000/90,000 = 38.9%
Allocate Indirect Costs	27.8% × 181,810 = 50,543	33.3% × 181,810 = 60,543	38.9% × 181,810 = 70,724
Total Direct and Indirect Program Costs	$44,500 + 50,543 $95,043	$36,100 + 60,543 + $96,643	$36,300 + 70,724 + $107,024 = $298,710

Note once again that there are a number of opportunities to check for accuracy:

- Program shares add up to 100 percent.
- Indirect costs add up to $181,810.
- Total program costs for the three programs add up to the same figure as the total agency budget using the line-item format, $298,710.

Note the differences in total program costs using the two different formulas (total direct costs versus direct labor costs). Using direct labor costs, congregate meals is allocated

$18,727 less from the indirect-cost pool; socialization and recreation is allocated $4,364 more; outreach is allocated $14,363 more. The differences can be accounted for by the relatively large item ($19,500) for food supplies, which is included in the total direct-cost formula but not in the direct labor-cost formula. This example illustrates the need for alternative formulas. When one formula yields a result that appears to skew the total program costs and unit costs because of one or two particularly large line items, a different formula can be adopted in the interest of providing more accurate total program-cost figures.

In some instances there may be a concern that the direct labor-costs method is unfair and presents an inaccurate picture of the division of labor across programs. Imbalances may occur when employees in one program are professional and are paid higher salaries than those in the other programs. The argument can be made that employees in the other programs, though lower salaried, work just as long and hard as the higher-salaried employees and create just as much a demand for a share of indirect costs. When this imbalance in salaries inflates one program's share of indirect costs, the direct labor hours method can be used to ensure equity between the programs.

The formula used is number of hours worked per year per worker (40 hours per week × 52 weeks per year). This formula ignores salary and uses working hours as a basis for calculating a program's share of indirect costs. Using direct labor hours at the Pinetree County Senior Center, we find that the cook, the socialization and recreation director, and the outreach case manager each contribute 2,080 hours per year. Each program, then, is entitled to an equal one-third share of the indirect-cost pool ($181,810 divided by 3 = $60,603.33 per program). This figure would be added to direct program costs to determine total direct and indirect program costs.

Finally, direct costing is a method that can be used when none of the foregoing formulas produce a fair, equitable, or accurate way of dividing up the indirect-cost pool. A unique measure or formula is developed for each line item. For example, rent may be allocated by calculating the number of square feet used by each program as well as by those who serve more than one program. The percentage of total square feet used by each program then becomes the basis for allocating the indirect costs for rent. In the same manner, a unique formula would be developed to allocate costs for telephones, office supplies, and other indirect cost items, and percentages would be used to determine each program's share of that line item.

Table 8.4 illustrates some commonly accepted bases for converting indirect costs to direct costs.

Step 7, determining total program costs, is accomplished by adding each program's share of the indirect-cost pool to the program's direct costs. As illustrated in the previous examples, the following steps lead to a calculation of total program costs:

- Each of the four columns is totaled.
- The indirect-cost pool is divided among the programs.
- Each program column is totaled.

These calculations result in a dollar figure for each program that can be used to establish a variety of costs including the cost of providing one unit of service to one client, the cost of one client completing all prescribed services, and the cost of one client achieving a successful outcome for each program.

TABLE 8.4

Some Suggested Options for Direct Charging of Indirect Costs

Indirect Cost Item	Allocation Base
Accounting	Number of transactions processed for each program
Auditing	Hours worked on each program
Budgeting	Hours worked on each program
Data processing	Hours of computer system use by each program
Employees[a]	Hours worked on each program
Insurance	Square feet of office space occupied by each program
Janitorial	Square feet of office space occupied by each program
Legal	Hours worked for each program
Telephone	Number of telephones
Mail	Number of documents processed
Printing and reproduction	Number of jobs/number of pages
Utilities	Square feet of office space occupied by each program

[a]Employees who work for more than one program—such as an agency executive director.

Source: Kettner, P. M., Moroney, R. M., & Martin, L. L. (1999). *Designing and managing programs: An effectiveness-based approach* (2nd ed.). Thousand Oaks, CA: Sage. Reproduced with the permission of Sage Publications.

The Value of Functional Budgeting It should be clear at this point that functional budgeting is significantly more complex than line-item budgeting. At the same time, functional budgeting provides many tools that are more valuable than the simple line-item budget. The purpose for going through all the steps of functional budgeting is to get to the bottom line, which, in this case, is called total direct and indirect program costs, or for the sake of a shorter title, total program costs. Once total program costs have been calculated in a way that is fair, equitable, and accurate, these totals can be used in many important ways. In functional budgeting, the objective is to determine the cost of functions or processes. In monitoring and measuring human service efforts, these functions are referred to as units of service.

As presented in the previous chapter, units of service can be defined in terms of (1) a time unit, (2) an episode unit, or (3) a material unit. Units are selected and defined for each program according to their utility, appropriateness, potential for accuracy, feasibility, and ease of use. For example, in a center that provides food baskets to needy families, it may be more accurate to count every can of soup, every block of cheese, and every box of cereal given out, but is it feasible or appropriate? When monitoring units of service takes up so much time in attention to detail that other functions and activities suffer, the unit as defined is in some way inappropriate. That is why food programs use the concept of one food basket as one unit of service. Child care programs could use a time clock and charge by the hour or even by fifteen-minute segments. Many day care centers, however, find that it is easier to use one-half-day time units. If a child is present only in the morning or only in the afternoon, the parent is charged for one-half day. If the child is there for both morning and afternoon, the parent is charged for a full day. This eliminates tracking exact times of drop-off and pick-up. In the Pinetree County Senior Center, units of service have been defined as follows.

Pinetree County Senior Center

Congregate Meals	Socialization and Recreation	Outreach
1 meal = 1 unit	1 person participating in one activity = 1 unit	1 face-to-face contact with a client in his or her own home = 1 unit

The challenge, then, becomes to calculate the total number of units that can be provided in one year. That number divided into total program cost figures will produce a unit cost.

- In the congregate meals program, fifty meals are provided each day, five days a week, fifty-two weeks a year, for a total of 13,000 meals per year.
- The socialization and recreation program has six different stations where games and activities are regularly offered. Each station can accommodate four participants. Activities are offered from 9 to 11 A.M. and 1 to 3 P.M. five days a week, fifty-two weeks per year, so there are twenty-four "seats" for participants in the morning and twenty-four in the afternoon. Total capacity to provide socialization and recreation units, then, equals forty-eight per day, times five days per week, times fifty-two weeks per year, or 12,480 socialization and recreation units per year.
- The outreach worker makes twenty face-to-face contacts per week with seniors who are living in their own homes and are socially isolated. Total outreach units then equal twenty contacts times fifty-two weeks per year or 1,040 outreach units per year.

Some programs may choose to use a standard other than fifty-two weeks per year in order to allow for holidays and vacations. The important issue is that if and when program productivity and unit costs are compared with other agencies (possibly competitors for the same dollars), it is important that the same standard be used, otherwise the results will not be comparable.

Using these unit definitions, unit costs are calculated as follows (using the first cost-allocation plan, the total direct-cost method):

Pinetree County Senior Center

	Congregate Meals	Socialization and Recreation	Outreach
Total program costs	$113,770	$92,279	$92,661
Divided by units per year	13,000	12,480	1,040
Cost per unit of service	$8.75	$7.39	$89.10

These types of cost comparisons provide invaluable tools to the manager and administrator for understanding the cost of various functions within the agency. In this example, outreach is substantially more expensive than either meals or socialization and recreation. The personalized, one-to-one attention from a professionally trained person drives up the cost when compared to group activities that require little staff participation.

In addition to calculating the cost of providing one unit of service for one person, functional budgeting also provides the tools needed to calculate the cost of one client completing the full complement of prescribed services. The concept of service completion (or outputs) was discussed briefly in the previous chapter, with examples drawn from a job training and placement program. In tracking service provision, it is important to know how many individual units have been provided but also to know how many clients complete (or drop out from) the program. In defining a service completion, there is an implicit assumption that program goals and objectives have been established, and that the program is designed so that if a client completes the service process there is a high probability that he or she will be successful in resolving problems and that program objectives will be achieved. For example, if two days (sixteen hours) of prejob training have been planned as a part of a job training and placement program, then it is important to know how many trainees participated in the full sixteen hours and how many received less than that amount.

Let's assume that at the Pinetree County Senior Center, the meal program was designed to improve nutrition, but in order to achieve that objective a person had to eat at least four meals per week for at least twenty-six consecutive weeks in order for there to be a difference in nutritional level. If, out of the fifty regular participants, forty-two people met that attendance criterion, then in order to calculate the cost of one client completing the program, total program cost of $113,770 would be divided by forty-two, for a cost per client of $2,709. Cost per final output figures are summarized as follows.

Pinetree County Senior Center

	Congregate Meals	Socialization and Recreation	Outreach
Total program costs	$113,770	$92,279	$92,661
Divided by number of clients who complete the fully prescribed service process	42	34	180
Cost per service completion	$2,709	$2,714	$515

Interestingly, when the number of service completions are tracked and recorded, the outreach program suddenly looks like a better buy. Twenty contacts per week times fifty-two weeks per year leads to 1,040 contacts at a cost of $89.10 per contact for the outreach program. But if, during the course of the year, the outreach worker serves about 240 unduplicated clients, and if 180 of these complete all prescribed services, then the cost per completion is substantially less than it is for the other two programs. These are some of the interesting ways that the tools of functional budgeting can be used to compare and contrast the cost of various functions within and across programs.

Program Budgeting

All of the steps necessary for functional budgeting are also necessary for program budgeting. Again, the critical dollar figure needed for program budgeting is the total program cost figure, calculated in a way that is as fair, equitable, and accurate as possible. In the same way that program outputs were defined and used to calculate cost per unit or cost per completion for functional budgeting, program outcomes are specified and used to calculate costs per outcome for program budgeting.

The rationale for using program outcomes as a basis for defining program budgeting is that enabling clients to achieve success in a way that improves their quality of life is the reason for existence of programs. Functions contribute to the provision of services, but client outcomes are the critical measures of program success. So if we want to know something about the success of a program, by definition we want to know about client outcomes. And if we want to know something about the cost of achieving program success, we use program budgeting techniques to determine cost per successful outcome.

Program budgeting has its roots in the early stages of program planning, when program goals, objectives, and activities are established. A program's outcome objectives specify criteria that will be used to measure program success. For example, using the Pinetree County Senior Center, an outcome objective for the congregate meals program might be stated as follows:

> By the completion of the program at least fifty seniors will achieve acceptable levels of nutrition for people sixty-five and over, as measured by established nutritional standards.

In the process of completing the functional budget, it was discovered that forty-two seniors met the participation standards for successful completion of the nutrition program. When nutrition levels were measured on the forty-two people who completed the program, thirty-six of them demonstrated positive improvements in nutrition levels to the extent that they met minimum specified standards. The following summary illustrates a method for calculating successful outcomes.

The Congregate Meal Program	
Number of participants	= 50
Number who met the criteria for successful program completion	= 42
Of those who completed the program, the number who demonstrated improved nutrition levels	= 36

In the same way, outcomes would be stated for the socialization and recreation program in terms of reducing social isolation and developing a social network. Outcomes for the isolated elderly served in the outreach program would be defined in terms of satisfactorily resolving immediate problems and developing a network of resources on which they could call in times of difficulty. Simulated outcome findings and cost per outcome are illustrated as follows.

Pinetree County Senior Center

	Congregate Meals	Socialization and Recreation	Outreach
Total program costs	$113,770	$92,279	$92,661
Divided by number of clients who successfully achieve specified outcomes	36	28	120
Cost per intermediate outcome	$3,160	$3,296	$772

We note that cost per outcome is higher than cost per completion of service because not all seniors who completed services achieved successful outcomes. The outcomes achieved at the point of completion of all prescribed services are referred to as intermediate outcomes.

Some programs follow clients for a period of time after they leave the program in order to learn something about the persistence and tenacity of change. It's an important issue. Do people change only during the time that they are under the close guidance of program personnel? To what extent do changes last after they leave the program? Certainly it is the intent of program funders that positive changes be permanent, but it is impossible to know with certainty without systematic follow-up. When there is a follow-up study, the outcomes recorded at the point of follow-up are called final outcomes and represent yet another measure of program budgeting.

A strict follow-up design with the Pinetree County Senior Center would require that only those who achieved success at the point of completion of the program would be contacted to determine if their successful achievements persisted over time. It should be expected, once again, that the number of successful outcomes at the point of follow-up will be fewer than the number recorded at the completion of services. For this reason, the cost per successful final outcome will be higher than the cost per successful intermediate outcome.

It may be that selected programs and agencies are interested in tracking program dropouts as well as completers or in tracking program failures as well as successes. All of these factors have the potential to provide valuable information, and if an agency has the resources to track all of its clients, undoubtedly much can be learned.

In a sense, this approach goes back to Taylor (1947) and the field of scientific management. The more that is measured on the job, the more we can learn. The more we learn, the more we can apply to the helping processes. The more knowledge we apply to the helping processes, the more efficient and effective these processes will become, and the better the results achieved with clients.

■ Managing Resources to Support Excellence

It is possible to run a human service agency for many years and to survive on a bare minimum of information, including budget information. In some cases funding sources, boards of directors, and other stakeholders are either satisfied with very general information or they are not aware that more precise measures are possible. However, it is very difficult to improve organizational and program performance without precise, accurate, and relevant reports. Continuing with the example of the Pinetree County Senior Center, in one version, there could be an annual report that looks like the following:

Pinetree County Senior Center—Annual Budget

	This Year	Last Year
Total salaries and wages	$185,000	$174,900
Employee-related expenses @ 25%	46,250	43,725
Operating expenses	62,260	58,500
Travel	5,200	5,200
Total agency budget	$298,710	$282,325

What can you say about the agency's performance other than that there was about a 5.5 percent overall increase in the budget? Are programs being run more efficiently (lower cost for the same or better services)? Are services more effective (better results than the previous year)? None of these questions can be answered with this format, and yet it is the type of information provided year after year by many agency directors to their boards and funding sources. Consider the following alternative format.

Pinetree County Senior Center

	Congregate Meals	Socialization and Recreation	Outreach
Inputs			
Total program costs	$113,770	$92,279	$92,661
Outputs			
Units of service provided	13,000 meals	12,480 activities	1,040 home visits
Service completions	42 participants	34 participants	180 clients
Outcomes			
Intermediate outcomes	36 participants	28 participants	120 clients
Successful final outcomes	32 participants	27 participants	100 clients
Cost-Efficiency Ratios			
Cost per unit of service	$8.75 per meal	$7.39 per activity	$89.10 per home visit
Cost per service completion	$2,709 per participant	$2,714 per participant	$515 per client
Cost-Effectiveness Ratios			
Cost per successful intermediate outcome	$3,160 per success	$3,296 per success	$772 per success
Cost per successful final outcome	$3,555 per success	$3,418 per success	$927 per success

Using the latter format, informed decisions can be made about the relative returns on investment in each program, and resources can be directed in ways that will increase the likelihood of success in the future. In addition, comparing previous years' performances to this year's provides an opportunity to determine direction and trends for each program in terms of efficiency and effectiveness. Even if we go no further than these examples, it should be clear that tools such as functional and program budgeting are essential to the achievement of excellence. They are essential not because someone in a position of authority requires their use but because agency managers and administrators truly believe they cannot achieve excellence without them. Making use of the types of data and information that they provide ultimately separates status quo, mediocre agencies from progressive, excellent ones.

SUMMARY

1. **Budgeting Issues in Human Services.** Historically budgets have not had the same meaning to human service organizations as they have to business and industrial organizations.
   - *Perspectives on the Meaning of a Budget.* Much information is contained in a budget beyond dollar figures. It is a statement of priorities and has many other purposes.

2. **Revenue Sources.** These include government funding, grants, contracts, client fees, charitable giving, and other funding strategies.
   - *Government-Funded Programs.* Government initiatives tend to be organized around populations, problems, and needs.
   - *Grants and Contracts.* Grants are used to assist in the provision of services or problem resolution. Contracts are used to procure needed services.
       Types of Contracts. These include cost reimbursement, unit cost, fixed fee, and incentive.
       Grants. Public grants come from government sources. Private grants come from foundations, including independent/family, corporate, operating, or community foundations.
   - *Requests for Proposals.* Opportunities to bid for grants or contracts come through requests for proposals (RFPs) disseminated by the funding authority.
   - *Client Fees.* There are many approaches to assessing fees, depending on client eligibility and ability to pay.
       Types of Client Fees. These include participation, flat rate, sliding scale, fair share of cost, and third party.
   - *Charitable Giving.* Many agencies receive United Way funding. Some also do their own solicitation and other fund-raising activities.
   - *Other Strategies to Increase Resources.* These include merging, franchising, and developing a for-profit subsidiary.

3. **The Budget Cycle.** Includes the stages of program and budget planning, funds procurement, fiscal management, performance assessment, financial reports and audits, and a recycling for the next fiscal year.
   - *Fiscal Years.* Most common are July 1 through June 30 or October 1 through September 30. Some use the calendar year.

4. **Resource Allocation.** A variety of budgeting systems can be used. Three are described here.

- *Line-Item Budgeting.* Requires defining line items and making allocations for the whole organization for a year.
- *Functional Budgeting.* Requires defining line items, making allocations to programs for the year, and incorporating indirect costs into programs.

    Allocating Indirect Costs to Programs. There are several formulas that can be used to allocate indirect costs to programs.

    The Value of Functional Budgeting. Much more detailed information is available from functional budgeting than there is from line-item budgeting. Can be used to determine the costs of functions or processes.

- *Program Budgeting.* This approach is used to calculate the cost of program success, defined in terms of client outcomes.

5. **Managing Resources to Support Excellence.** Good budget and program data can help agencies in their efforts toward achieving excellence.

EXERCISES

Please complete the following sections of your manual based on the content covered in Chapter 8.

Section 8: Budget.

8.1 Line-Item Budgeting. Establish a format for line-item budgeting. Attach a copy of a sample line-item budget as Document 8.1a and a sample budget justification sheet as Document 8.1b.

8.2 Functional and Program Budgeting. Establish a format for functional and program budgeting. Attach a copy of a sample format as Document 8.2a.

8.3 Reports. Create a format for annual reporting of service efforts and accomplishments. Attach a copy of a sample report as Document 8.3a.

REFERENCES

Aldrich, H. (1979). *Organizations and environments.* Englewood Cliffs, NJ: Prentice-Hall.

Bellos, N., & Ruffolo, M. (1995). Aging: Services. In *Encyclopedia of social work* (19th ed., pp. 165–173). Washington, DC: National Association of Social Workers.

Gates, B. (1980). *Social program administration: The implementation of social policy.* Englewood Cliffs, NJ: Prentice-Hall.

Hansmann, H. (1981). Reforming nonprofit corporation law. *University of Pennsylvania Law Review, 129* (January), 497–623.

Hay, L., & Wilson, E. (1995). *Accounting for governmental and nonprofit entities.* Chicago: Irwin.

Horngren, C., Foster, G., & Datar, S. (1997). *Cost accounting: A managerial emphasis.* Englewood Cliffs, NJ: Prentice-Hall.

Kettner, P., Daley, J., & Nichols, A. (1985). *Initiating change in organizations and communities: A macro practice model.* Monterey, CA: Brooks Cole.

Kettner, P., & Martin, L. (1987). *Purchase of service contracting.* Newbury Park, CA: Sage.

Kettner, P., & Martin, L. (1996). The impact of declining resources and purchase of service contracting on private, nonprofit agencies. *Administration in Social Work, 20*(3), 21–38.

Kettner, P., Moroney, R., & Martin, L. (1999). *Designing and managing programs: An effectiveness-based approach* (2nd ed.). Thousand Oaks, CA: Sage.

Kiritz, N. (1980). *Program planning and proposal writing.* Los Angeles: The Grantsmanship Center.

Lauffer, A. (1982). *Getting the resources you need.* Beverly Hills: Sage.

Liederman, D. (1995). Child welfare overview. In *Encyclopedia of social work* (19th ed., pp. 424–433). Washington, DC: National Association of Social Workers.

Lohmann, R. (1980). *Breaking even: Financial management in human service organizations.* Philadelphia: Temple University Press.

Lynch, T. (1995). *Public budgeting in America.* Englewood Cliffs, NJ: Prentice-Hall.

Martin, L. (1997). Outcome budgeting: A new entrepreneurial approach to budgeting. *Journal of Public Budgeting, Accounting and Financial Management, 9,* 108–126.

Martin, L. (2001). *Financial management for human service administrators.* Boston: Allyn and Bacon.

McMurtry, S., Netting, F., & Kettner, P. (1991). How nonprofits adapt to a stringent environment. *Nonprofit Management & Leadership, 1*(3, Spring), 235–253.

Netting, F., & Kettner, P. (1987). Franchising, merging, and profit-making ventures: Implications for health and human services. *Journal of Voluntary Action Research, 16* (4), 15–21.

Office of Federal Procurement Policy (1979). *Principles of government contract law.* Washington, DC: Government Printing Office.

Peters, T., & Waterman, R. (1982). *In search of excellence: Lessons from America's best-run companies.* New York: Harper & Row.

Rapp, C., & Poertner, J. (1992). *Social administration: A client-centered approach.* New York: Longman.

Reisch, M. (1995). Public social services. In *Encyclopedia of social work* (19th ed., pp. 1982–1992). Washington, DC: National Association of Social Workers.

Taylor, F. (1947). *Scientific management.* New York: Harper & Row.

Vinter, R., & Kish, R. (1984). *Budgeting for not-for-profit organizations.* New York: Free Press.

Wildavsky, A. (1964). *The politics of the budgetary process.* Boston: Little, Brown.

CHAPTER

9

Maximizing Organizational Performance through Human Resources Planning

CHAPTER OBJECTIVES

Upon completion of this chapter, the reader will be able to:

- Identify the major protected classes covered by human resources law and cite the laws, executive orders, and regulations that prohibit discrimination.
- Create a framework for human resources planning for a human service organization.
- Explain how four different strategies can be used to change an organization's personnel profile.
- Prepare a plan for initiating changes in the human resources system.

Assumptions

- That every organization should analyze its staff needs and attempt to produce what it considers to be an optimal personnel profile.
- That diversity in areas of expertise and in demographics can contribute to creativity, high energy, and high levels of productivity.
- That an organizational culture that attempts to make full use of the talents and abilities of its staff will contribute to optimum performance.
- That human resources planning can contribute to achieving an organization's optimal personnel profile.

■ Selecting, Hiring, and Retaining the Optimum Mix of Staff

The foregoing chapters have examined some of the elements that play a part in contributing to organizational excellence. This chapter will examine what may well be the most important component of organizational life—the staff. It will explore ways to maximize organizational performance by selecting, building, and retaining the right mix of staff. When coaches or managers recruit and build athletic teams, their first priority is talent. But successful teams also value an ingredient that they refer to as "chemistry." In fact, it is not unusual for teams with good chemistry to be more successful than teams that have better talent but lack good chemistry. Unfortunately, no one ever seems to define the term. It has something to do with positive relationships between and among members of a team or group and includes such factors as mutual support, leadership, and mentoring. One would be hard-pressed to duplicate the phenomenon without more specific guidelines.

In many ways organizations are more successful or less successful based on the extent to which they function as a team. Even some very large organizations have been successful in promoting a team spirit, with an attitude of mutual caring and support between and among employees at all levels in the organization but especially between management and staff. Southwest Airlines, for example, during the 1990s was consistently cited as one of the best places to work, based on surveys of employees in major corporations. Their high level of motivation and morale begins at the top and is reinforced throughout the organization. Many similar examples exist throughout management literature.

Achieving such harmony and balance is no accident. It is the result of careful planning and of a clear understanding of what types of people work best together to achieve high levels of productivity while demonstrating a firm commitment to the organization's mission. This type of planning does not begin at the point at which there is a vacancy and it is time to hire a replacement. It begins long before that point, early in the life of the organization when a human resources plan is compiled with a clear sense of direction and vision focusing on the qualities and characteristics that are needed to achieve the organization's mission, goals, and objectives. In many instances, however, a newly appointed manager may discover that such planning has never taken place. Fortunately, it is never too late to begin human resources planning. With staff turnover and newly funded positions, opportunities to hire more staff will present themselves, and these occasions should be recognized as critical milestones in the process of achieving excellence.

A core or hub around which human resources planning revolves is made up of three elements: human resources law, a profile of staff needs, and a job analysis for each position. With these elements at the core, a plan is developed that involves (1) recruitment, (2) selection, (3) orientation, (4) supervision, (5) training and development, (6) performance appraisal, (7) promotion and career development, and, if necessary, (8) termination. These components are depicted in Figure 9.1.

Note that each segment of the planning process as depicted in the diagram goes through job analysis and profile of staff needs, all the way to the core in human resources law. The diagram is designed in this way to indicate that each segment must take all these core issues into consideration and must ensure internal consistency and integrity throughout the entire human resources plan. For example, in planning for recruitment and screening of applicants for an open position, a search committee must consider not only how to

F I G U R E   9 . 1

Human Resource Functions Anchored in Job Analysis, Staff Needs, and Human Resources Law

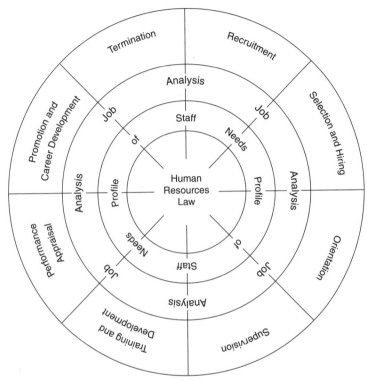

Source: Schmidt, M., Riggar, R., Crimando, W., & Bordieri, J. (1992). *Staffing for success.* Newbury Park, CA: Sage, p. 4. Adapted with the permission of Sage Publications.

attract applicants but also must be familiar with the job analysis for the position, the profile of staff needs, and human resources law.

Human Resources Law

The recent history of corporate life in the United States is filled with examples of lawsuits filed in court and complaints filed with the Equal Employment Opportunity Commission (EEOC) over such issues as race, sex and age discrimination, sexual harassment, and failure to accommodate for an employee's disability. Although the U.S. Constitution and its amendments have guaranteed equal treatment for well over one hundred years, as a practical matter Congress and presidents took little action to support and defend individual rights until the early 1960s (Dessler, 1997). Following landmark legislation contained in the Civil Rights Act of 1964, a series of federal and state laws has been passed and executive orders issued focused on safeguarding the rights of various protected classes. Early acts were focused generally on prohibiting discrimination based on race, color, or national origin. Later acts focused on more specific groups defined by age, disability, veteran status, or other factors. Some of the highlights of these acts and orders are covered in the following sections. The intent is to provide a brief overview. For comprehensive coverage, copies of the original acts, amendments, and executive orders or more complete reference works should be consulted.

Race, Color, or National Origin

Titles VI and VII of the Civil Rights Act of 1964 (as amended)   Title VI prohibits discrimination based on race, color, or national origin in programs or activities that receive federal financial assistance. It is enforced by the Department of Education, Office for Civil Rights in which complaints are filed by persons who believe they are victims of discrimination. Organizations found guilty of discrimination may lose their federal financial assistance.

Title VII prohibits discrimination in employment, stating that it shall be unlawful for an employer:

1. To fail or refuse to hire or to discharge an individual or otherwise to discriminate against any individual with respect to his/her compensation, terms, conditions, or privileges of employment, because of such individual's race, color, religion, sex, or national origin.

2. To limit, segregate, or classify his/her employees or applicants for employment in any way that would deprive or tend to deprive any individual of employment opportunities or otherwise adversely affect his/her status as an employee, because of such individual's race, color, religion, sex, or national origin. (Dessler, 1997, p. 35)

Title VII created the Equal Employment Opportunity Commission (EEOC), which has the power to investigate employment-related discrimination in response to complaints filed by persons who feel that they have been victims of discrimination. Remedies may include back pay, attorneys' fees, injunctions, or compensatory and punitive damages.

Affirmative Action

Executive Orders   Following the passage of the Civil Rights Act of 1964, during the Johnson administration, it was recognized that the mere absence of verifiable discrimination was not enough to change the patterns of employment and increase the numbers of ethnic minorities and women in the workforce. Executive Orders 11246 and 11375 created the concept of affirmative action. Under these executive orders, employers with fifty or more employees and a federal contract of $50,000 annually are required to have a written plan with specified goals and timetables illustrating how they will bring an increased number of women and minorities into the workforce. Discrimination based on age or physical handicap is also prohibited. The Office of Federal Contract Compliance Programs (OFCCP) was established and made responsible for enforcement of laws relating to affirmative action.

Sex/Gender

Equal Pay Act of 1963   This act, amended in 1972, prohibited discrimination in rates of pay when jobs involve equal work performed under the same or similar conditions. Equal work is defined as including equivalent skills, effort, and responsibility. The act applies to all educational institutions and other employers that are covered by the Fair Labor Standards Act. It is enforced by the EEOC, and remedies include back pay and salary increases.

Title IX of Education Amendments of 1972   This title prohibits discrimination on the basis of sex in education programs or activities. All recipients of federal financial assistance must comply, and violators can lose federal funding. Enforcement is through the Department of Education, Office for Civil Rights. Applications have been primarily but not exclusively focused on gender equality in educational and athletic programs.

Sexual Harassment   EEOC guidelines define sexual harassment as

> unwelcome sexual advances, requests for sexual favors, and other verbal or physical conduct of a sexual nature that takes place under any of the following conditions:
>
> - Submission to such conduct is made either explicitly or implicitly a term or condition of an individual's employment.
> - Submission to or rejection of such conduct by an individual is used as the basis for employment decisions affecting such individual.
> - Such conduct has the purpose or effect of unreasonably interfering with an individual's work performance or creating an intimidating, hostile, or offensive work environment. (Rowe, 1981, p. 44)

Employers have a duty to maintain a work environment that is free of intimidation and can be held responsible if they fail to take corrective action. Many precedents for dealing with sexual harassment have been established through court cases.

Veterans' Status

Vietnam Era Veterans' Readjustment Assistance Act of 1974   Under this act, employers with federal contracts of $10,000 or more must demonstrate affirmative efforts to employ qualified special disabled veterans and veterans of the Vietnam era. The act is administered by the Department of Labor, OFCCP, and Veterans' Employment Service. Remedies include termination or cancellation of contracts or exclusion from future contracts.

Age

Age Discrimination in Employment Act of 1967 (amended 1978)   This act applies to federal, state, and local government agencies and private employers of twenty or more persons. The act makes it unlawful to discriminate against either applicants or employees between the ages of forty and sixty-five. The 1978 amendments extended the upper age limit to seventy, with no upper limit for federal government employees. The act is enforced by EEOC in response to complaints filed by persons who believe they have been victims of discrimination in employment. Remedies include back pay, reinstatement, or promotion, where appropriate, and attorneys' fees.

Disabilities

Vocational Rehabilitation Act of 1973   This act extends the concept of affirmative action to the employment of qualified persons with physical disabilities or limitations. The act also requires organizations to make reasonable accommodations to buildings or to the physical environment so that people with physical limitations can function independently. Much attention in individual cases has been focused over the years on what constitutes "reasonable accommodation." OFCCP has enforcement authority for the rehabilitation act, and remedies include withholding of federal funds and termination or cancellation of contracts.

Americans with Disabilities Act of 1990   This is a major, comprehensive act that prohibits discrimination on the basis of disability in private sector employment, in services provided by state and local governments, in places that accommodate the public, in transportation, and in telecommunications relay services. Title I applies to employment, Title II to public services and public transportation, Title III to public accommodations and private transportation, and Title IV to telecommunications. Each title has a different enforcing agency with different sanctions or remedies applied.

To be in compliance with the ADA, employers must meet the following specifications:

a. An employer must not deny a job to a disabled individual if the person is qualified and able to perform the essential functions of a job. Reasonable accommodation must be made to enable a qualified person to perform an essential function, unless making the accommodation would cause an undue hardship.

b. Employers are not required to lower performance standards to accommodate a job candidate, as long as all standards and tests are job related and apply to all employees and candidates for the job.

c. Employers may not make preemployment inquiries about a person's disability. Questions must be focused on the candidate's ability to perform job functions.

d. Employers may not ask job applicants questions about health, disabilities, medical histories or previous worker's compensation claims.

e. Employers should have clear job descriptions which specify essential functions. This is not specifically required by ADA, but becomes an important issue if a legal question arises. (Dessler, 1997, p. 50)

Civil Rights Act of 1991   This act provides for damages and jury trials in cases of intentional sex, religious, and disability bias. These rights were previously available only to racial and ethnic minorities. Signed by President Bush, the act overturned a number of Supreme Court decisions that were unfavorable to victims of employment discrimination.

■ The Letter of the Law versus the Spirit of the Law

Human resources law is an area of specialization within the legal profession, and it is not realistic to expect that agency managers and administrators will be familiar with every act or executive order. New laws are continually being proposed at the federal and state levels. Precedents are being established through court decisions. All of these developments make it imperative that agency directors have available to them a consulting attorney with expertise in human resources law. The dynamic nature of this field requires a fresh look at recent changes in the law each time a situation with legal implications emerges. When a human resources problem is handled without the benefit of legal expertise, the agency administrator runs the risk of relying on outdated information, and the penalties can be severe.

The responsibility of the human service agency administrator or manager, especially one committed to excellence, is to understand the spirit of laws that protect potentially vulnerable people and to incorporate this spirit into the agency's human resource plan. The field of human services is in some ways qualitatively different from business and industry in this regard. Although a business may focus on having a diverse workforce in response to the letter of the law, a human service agency must recognize that its business is to serve a diverse community. In order to be effective in helping people use their strengths to deal with their problems and needs, there must be a recognition that strengths, problems, and needs may be understood differently within cultural and gender contexts. Effective use of staff goes far beyond merely hiring a diverse workforce in order to satisfy the letter of the law.

Valuing, Respecting, and Maximizing the Benefits of Diversity

A brief review of Thomas's (1991) concepts of affirmative action, valuing differences, and managing diversity may be useful in understanding the unique responsibilities of human service agencies as they determine the makeup of their workforces.

Level 1, affirmative action, Thomas reminds us, is an approach that acknowledges that women and persons from various ethnic groups have historically been excluded from many employment opportunities. In some instances this exclusion has been the result of discrimination, in that the woman or ethnic applicant presented qualifications that were superior to those of the person hired. Because employing organizations were not taking the initiative to remedy these types of discrimination, it became necessary to coerce them to change their hiring practices. Although the practice of affirmative action has produced results in terms of increased numbers of women and people of color being hired, the practice has failed to bring about fundamental changes in the ways that organizations view and define their jobs. Qualities that women and persons from ethnic groups bring to the workplace are not necessarily valued when the approach to diversity is limited simply to affirmative action.

Level 2, valuing differences, represents a higher level of appreciation of diversity and is designed to encourage mutual understanding and respect within the workplace. In this type of organization, training and sensitivity sessions are focused on understanding the dynamics of individual differences. Employees, especially managers and administrators, are encouraged to explore how differences might be used in constructive ways to improve the quality of work life and increase productivity. As staff members gain an appreciation for the meaning of culture and gender to an individual's identity, there is a hope and an expectation that staff members will become less inclined to perceive their own cultural identities as superior and more inclined to treat other cultural identities as different but not inferior. Although greater levels of understanding are achieved in this type of organization, says Thomas, valuing differences has little impact on empowering the workforce or drawing on the strengths that each unique individual has to contribute to the organization.

Level 3, managing diversity, goes beyond hiring based on gender and racial preferences and beyond enhancing mutual understanding. Managing diversity focuses on initiating fundamental changes in the organizational culture. Its objective is the full utilization of employees' potential, both as individuals and as members of a team. Within this system there is a recognition that people bring with them to the workplace more than just their educational achievements and their experience. Lifetime experiences as a member of an ethnic group, as a woman, as a disabled person, as a gay or lesbian, or for that matter as a white male nurture a perspective that can be valuable to an organization. The more diverse the perspectives the greater (potentially) the strength of decision making, when diversity is addressed in a positive way. Organizations that manage diversity look for that unique niche that employees can fill to keep the organization productive, competitive, and on the cutting edge of change and innovation.

Encouraging Full Participation

Daley and Angulo (1994), in their study of the makeup of boards of directors of nonprofit agencies, introduced the concepts of demographic and functional diversity. Demographic diversity refers to factors such as age, gender, ethnicity, or other characteristics that, because of the different life experiences they foster, may cause individuals to view issues from different perspectives. Functional diversity refers to the extent to which representatives of diverse groups have a voice in and participate in the life of a group or organization. Although efforts may be made to include representatives of previously excluded demographic groups, it often happens that their voices continue to be excluded from the functional life of the group or organization by ignoring input or continuing business as usual by valuing input only from dominant group members. When this happens, the organization achieves only demographic diversity without the full participation envisioned by functional diversity and fails to enjoy the full benefits that new voices and new perspectives can provide.

Conscientious Attention to Issues Surrounding Sexual Harassment

Employees do not function well in an environment that they believe is hostile and threatening. The Equal Employment Opportunity Commission has issued guidelines that state that an employer is expected to be proactive in ensuring that the workplace is free of sexual harassment and intimidation. Employers should be aware of three major factors that can be used to prove sexual harassment and should raise the following questions to ensure that these situations are not present within the organization:

- *Quid Pro Quo.* Are there any instances within the organization where an employee who rejects a supervisor's advancements could be negatively impacted through denial of tangible benefits like raises, promotions, training, or travel opportunities?

- *Hostile Environment Created by Supervisors.* Are there units within the organization where a supervisor's advancements may have such a profound psychological or emotional effect on one or more employees' ability to function that they cannot perform under existing conditions?
- *Hostile Environment Created by Coworkers or Nonemployees.* Are there units within the organization where people in the workplace whose presence is sanctioned by the employer create an environment that an employee might consider hostile, and that inhibits optimum performance? (Dessler, 1997, p. 39)

Employers are increasingly being held responsible for preventing and eliminating sexually harassing and intimidating environments, and precedents for court judgments are rapidly accumulating. Perhaps as important, however, is the spirit of the directives on sexual harassment. The employer who aspires to excellence in organizational performance wants a workplace environment in which employees feel comfortable and confident and are able to perform at the highest levels. This is more likely to happen when employees recognize the benefits of diversity and project a sense of mutual respect.

When an organization develops a culture in which diversity is incorporated into the philosophy of management, in which widely varying perspectives are welcomed, and in which the work environment is free of intimidation, it is moving toward the spirit of human resources law and is probably, at the same time, less likely to find itself in violation of the letter of the law.

■ Human Resources Planning

Earlier in this chapter we identified three elements that formed the foundation of an organization's human resources plan: (1) human resources law, (2) a profile of staff needs, and (3) a job analysis for each position. This section will discuss the second element, the profile of staff needs. Development of such a profile is based on the working hypothesis that there is an optimal mix of staff in terms of abilities, demographics, and personal characteristics, and that the more closely the organization approximates the ideal profile, the greater is the likelihood that it will be successful. Success is typically measured in terms of achievement of strategic and program goals and objectives in a way that is consistent with the mission of the organization.

Strategic plans ask the question, "Where do we hope to be in the next four to five years?" The attempt is to anticipate changing community needs, demographics, economics, location of population centers, and other such variables, and to project new and redesigned programs and services, branch offices, technology, and other solutions. The human resources plan attempts to anticipate the types of personnel that will be needed to take on the new challenges presented within the strategic plan. As Cascio (1987) defines it, human resources planning is "an effort to anticipate future business and environmental demands on an organization and to meet the personnel requirements dictated by these conditions" (p. 214). The process, he says, involves an analysis of current conditions, a forecast of the future, the development of a plan of action, and an evaluation of efforts.

■ CONSIDERATIONS

For Human Resources Planning

Basic Questions: What types of resources do we need now in terms of knowledge, skills, personal characteristics, diverse backgrounds, education, and experience? What types of resources will we need in the future? What types of discrepancies are there between present and future needs? How will we achieve the mix of staff that we need in a timely way so that we are optimally prepared for coming changes?

Time Frame: Preparation of an initial plan will take a substantial investment of time and resources. After the initial plan has been developed, management and board, with staff input, should review and update it annually.

Process: The lead person in human resources produces a profile of current staff. Total staff brainstorm about future personnel needs in relation to the strategic plan, based on both internal and external data and information available. A retreat setting is preferable.

Analysis: Review types of knowledge, skills, personal qualities, diverse backgrounds, education, and other variables represented by those currently employed as compared to those needed. Examine supply of and demand for persons with needed qualifications, both internally and externally.

Report: A plan with goals, objectives, activities, and timetables for carrying out the full spectrum of the human resources processes. Any or all of the following policies and procedures may be included: recruitment, selection, hiring, staff development and training, performance evaluation, retention, promotion, and termination.

■ Achieving Excellence through Human Resources Planning

A variety of methods and strategies has been proposed for optimizing the mix of staff in response to the expectations of the strategic plan. Schmidt, Riggar, Crimando, and Bordieri (1992) define the human resources planning process in terms of four interrelated subprocesses: (1) conduct a current human resources audit, (2) forecast human resource supply and demand, (3) develop and implement an action plan, and (4) control and evaluate these procedures. The following section will make some slight modifications but will basically follow this same logic. The steps recommended include:

1. Project personnel needs in accordance with strategic goals and objectives.
2. Develop a plan for achieving the desired personnel profile.
3. Implement the changes necessary to achieve the plan's goals and objectives.
4. Monitor and evaluate the effects of changes as they are implemented.

These steps will be covered in the following sections.

Step 1: Project Personnel Needs

Estimating or forecasting personnel needs requires a number of subprocesses. A useful framework for projecting personnel needs is a matrix that presents a profile of job expectations and qualifications. Within the matrix, each position from top administrator through entry-level support staff is included. Each position must then be examined first in terms of job expectations. What are the minimum qualifications? What are the educational and experience requirements? Are there any special personal characteristics, such as "ability to work as a member of a team," that are required? All this information is contained in the job analysis (which will be covered in the next chapter). In projecting personnel needs, the attempt is to identify these factors in a brief, summary format so that those developing the human resources plan will understand the expectations of the position. A format for summarizing job expectations and qualifications is illustrated in Figure 9.2.

When a profile of job expectations and qualifications has been compiled, it is helpful to know how well the existing staff profile fits with the ideal. One approach to gathering information about existing personnel is what Schmidt et al. (1992) describe as a personnel and skill inventory. The personnel and skill inventory is an instrument used to gather employee information. Specific information depends on organizational needs, but suggestions include "name, age, length of employment with the organization, education, experience, present position, performance level and past company achievements, and an assessment of future potential of each employee" (p. 14). Compiling information about existing staff using the personnel and skill inventory can provide a valuable profile that will be useful in identifying current strengths as well as areas that need to be addressed in human resources planning.

A third tool useful for projecting personnel needs is a matrix that depicts agency demographics. In this matrix, each position within the agency is again used as part of the framework, with selected demographics such as age, gender, ethnicity, education, and other

FIGURE 9.2

Profile of Job Expectations and Qualifications

	Top Administrative	Middle Management	First-Line Supervision	Direct Service	Paraprofessional	Support Staff
Minimum qualifications						
Education required						
Experience required						
Major duties						
Skills required						
Special qualities						

Summary of Agency Demographics

	Top Administrative	Middle Management	First-Line Supervision	Direct Service	Paraprofessional	Support Staff
Ethnicity/ Race African American Asian American Caucasian Hispanic/Latino Native American Other						
Gender Female Male						
Age Under 20 20–29 30–39 40–49 50–59 60 and over						
Disabilities						
Veteran Status						

important variables identified for each position. It may be useful at this point to review human resources law to ensure that each of the protected classes has been included in this matrix. Incorporating protected classes into the matrix gives this tool, in a sense, a dual purpose: (1) it permits an overview in terms of demographic diversity, and (2) it provides a reminder that there are employees (e.g., pregnant employees, Vietnam-era veterans) who are covered by various state and federal laws and executive orders. Once the demographic matrix has been developed, the lead human resources person for the agency fills in the cells, based on information drawn from personnel records. Because this matrix may contain confidential information, care must be taken to ensure that it is not shared with anyone who is not authorized to receive personnel information and to ensure that affected staff have agreed to release the information. A format for summarizing demographic factors is illustrated in Figure 9.3.

Working from these basic documents, which identify job qualifications, staff skills, and other characteristics, and a demographic profile of current staff, human resource planners develop the optimum personnel profile. Goals and objectives contained in the strategic plan form the basis for projecting need. The following example illustrates how an agency might use the strategic plan to develop a human resources plan.

An agency that provides services to children and families is located in a community whose demographic profile is changing with the influx of immigrants from Southeast Asia. The agency has developed goals relating to initiating culturally centered programs, more emphasis on extended family, the need for bilingual, bicultural staff, and perhaps a new branch office. From these goals an ideal or optimal staff profile is generated, again examining job expectations, current staff qualifications, and demographic diversity. The profile is then used to ensure that the appropriate job qualifications and demographic considerations are incorporated into the human resources plan.

A final activity to be undertaken in step 1 is to attempt to forecast the number of vacancies that should be anticipated for each position within the agency. A review of voluntary and involuntary terminations over the past three to five years should provide some useful information. The total number of budgeted positions at each level provides a baseline for analyzing turnover. The number of employees who left a particular position divided by the number of positions budgeted in a given year will yield a percentage of turnover. For example, if an agency budgets for sixteen Caseworker I positions in budget year 2001–2002, and if four Caseworker I staff resign or retire during that year, the turnover rate for that year is 25 percent. By adding together the numbers over two, three, or more years, turnover rates can be calculated for extended periods of time. Some residential treatment centers and child care agencies have found that the position of Child Care Worker has a turnover rate of over 100 percent. What that means is that more staff quit their jobs during a given year than there are positions (some positions turn over more than once during the year). Turnover should be analyzed not only in terms of percentages but also for the purpose of understanding why staff leave the agency. Recruitment, hiring, and training are expensive, and loss of staff should not be taken lightly. Furthermore, it can take anywhere from several weeks to several months to replace and train an employee, depending on the complexity of responsibilities and the available job pool. During that time, services not provided can result in significant lost revenue. Surveys and exit interviews can be helpful in understanding reasons for turnover. Figure 9.4 illustrates an approach to turnover analysis.

FIGURE 9.4

Format for Calculating Turnover Rates

	Top Administrative	Middle Management	First-Line Supervision	Direct Service	Paraprofessional	Support Staff
Budgeted positions this fiscal year						
Voluntary terminations this fiscal year						
Involuntary terminations this fiscal year						
Total terminations this fiscal year						
Turnover rate (total terminations divided by budgeted positions)						

Step 2: Plan for Achieving the Desired Personnel Profile

When an optimum profile has been developed, the next question is: "How will the mix of employees needed in the future become a reality over time?" The first resort is often to think only in terms of turnover within the agency and recruitment and hiring from outside. This, however, is only one of many options. More immediate and, in many cases, less costly options exist within the current system. This section will explore (1) internal options made possible by organizational change, (2) internal strategies focused on the human resources system, and (3) external strategies.

Internal Strategies to Change the Personnel Profile   Chapters 4, 5, and 6 looked at ways to change the organization to achieve greater efficiency, effectiveness, quality, and productivity. Approaches included reviewing (1) organizational structure, (2) job design, and (3) the motivation and reward system. These techniques may also be used to promote the desired personnel profile.

Changing the Organizational Structure   In Chapter 4, options for both formal and informal organizational structure were explored. Formal structure includes departmentalization by program, function, process, market, consumer/client, or geographical area. Changing from one type of departmentalization to another can present opportunities for reassignment of personnel. The following example illustrates how organizational restructuring can create opportunities to change the personnel profile.

> A family-service agency is structured by program with three program managers, one each for foster care, adoptions, and family counseling. In response to a need for closer cooperation between the foster care and adoptions staff, it was determined that these two programs could be combined into one program under the heading of child welfare, with branch offices established to serve target communities. New positions were then created to manage the combined programs and to oversee each branch office. Because these positions require different skills, an internal search was opened and selection made from existing staff. The family counseling program was then subdivided into marital and family, adolescent, and individual counseling programs in response to a changing profile of problems and needs. Once again, this restructuring effort makes available new positions that can be filled internally based on newly established selection criteria.

Figure 9.5 illustrates an approach to restructuring of programs.

Informal structures include the linking pin, project team, collegial, and mixed-matrix models, as described in Chapter 4. The foster care and adoptions staff described in the forgoing example could be brought into a closer working relationship through the use of the linking-pin model.

> Instead of restructuring by bringing the adoption and foster care programs together under one program manager, the two programs could be linked through specialized positions. Certain casework positions would be designated as

FIGURE 9.5

Changing the Personnel Profile by Changing the Organizational Structure

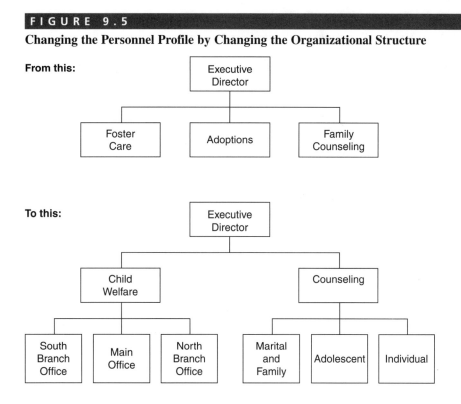

linking-pin positions between foster care and adoptions units. Others would be designated as the linking pin between management and staff. Once again, this structure provides opportunities to redesign jobs and appoint personnel from within to newly created positions. In a redesigned family counseling program, a modified collegial model could be used to provide greater flexibility in working with client families. Each worker would operate relatively independently and would turn to team members for consultation. One team member would be designated as liaison to management for communication and reporting purposes. This would have the effect of eliminating the supervisory positions and opening up new specialist positions within the team.

Linking-pin and collegial models are illustrated in Figure 9.6. Project team and mixed-matrix models described in Chapter 4 can be used in similar ways to create new positions.

Changing the Job Design   Chapter 5 explored six approaches to job design and redesign that included (1) job enlargement, (2) job enrichment, (3) job rotation, (4) creating teams, (5) varying working conditions, and (6) using technology. Job enlargement refers to adding responsibilities and making the job more complex and challenging. Job enrichment refers to having workers assume more responsibility for their own work, thus decreasing the need for supervision and requiring new and different approaches to monitoring, evaluation, and accountability. Both job enlargement and job enrichment can be

FIGURE 9.6

Changing the Personnel Profile by Creating New Organizational Structures

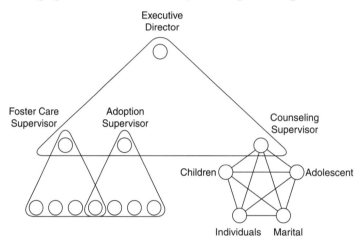

used to change a job description, thus requiring new and different skills and necessitating a selection process, as illustrated in the following example.

A social service agency contracts to provide counseling services through its employee assistance program to employees of corporations in the metropolitan area. Referrals are accepted from affiliated corporations, and employees are counseled around drug, alcohol, or family problems. As clients come in for service, they are assigned on a rotating basis to available caseworkers. The agency's assistant director notices that the work has become very routine and that referrals from affiliated corporations have declined slightly over the last two years. No new contracts have been developed over the past eighteen months, even though new businesses in the community increased by 9 percent during that same period.

Job enlargement could be used in this instance to create positions in which corporations within the community are assigned to specific workers. Instead of simply waiting for referrals, the worker would be expected to market the program to corporation executives and negotiate new contracts. Workers would be paid on an incentive basis, with those who bring in new contracts realizing substantial financial rewards for their efforts. Monthly reports would be designed to monitor marketing efforts and progress toward goals. Redesigned in this way, the job calls for new skills, a job advertisement, and a selection process.

In the same way, jobs can be redesigned by creating teams, varying working conditions, or introducing technology. Redesigned jobs can then be opened to a competitive selection process.

Using the Human Resources System to Make Personnel Changes   The human resources system (formerly referred to as the personnel system) includes everything from initial recruitment for the job through termination. Each of the components of the human resources system will be covered in detail in the following chapters, but this section will briefly address (1) performance appraisal, (2) staff training and development, (3) career development, and (4) termination.

The performance appraisal system, when conscientiously integrated with the organization's mission, strategic plan, structure, job design, and motivation and reward system, can serve as a valuable tool to change the personnel profile in a positive way. Performance appraisal for every employee is typically an annual event, sometimes with quarterly or semiannual progress reports. Some organizations treat appraisal in a routine, perfunctory manner designed merely to meet the letter of personnel policies. Although a simplified, routine approach to evaluation may require less time and effort on the part of the evaluator, it provides minimal useful information for changing the personnel profile. A well-integrated performance appraisal system is tied to the work performed, accurately indicates, through a scoring system, each employee's level of performance, and provides a reliable indicator of an employee's strengths and weaknesses. By charting and comparing performance appraisal data for all employees, managers and administrators can identify employee skill and productivity profiles and can work with supervisors and employees to get the highest performers into key positions.

Another set of options for moving employees into key positions includes staff training and development and career development. Training can include on-the-job training, in-service training provided by the agency, or out-service training workshops and institutes provided by professional organizations and other groups. Career development requires careful planning between supervisor and employee focused on the employee's short- and long-range career goals. Through mentoring and on-the-job training, an employee can be groomed for higher-level responsibilities. Staff development and training options can be integrated into the career plan by selecting courses and workshops that will provide a foundation of knowledge and skill for the responsibilities to be assumed.

A technique referred to as replacement charting may be useful in grooming employees for higher-level responsibilities (Schmidt et al., 1992). Replacement charts are "visual representations of who will replace whom in the event of a job opening" (Werther & Davis, 1989, p. 103). A replacement summary accompanies the chart and indicates potential candidates' strengths and weaknesses. The purpose of replacement charting is to encourage managers and administrators to focus on the future and to think in terms of making optimal use of the talent available within the organization. Charts, however, should be used as planning tools and not as foregone conclusions about personnel decisions.

A final option for changing the personnel profile, to be used in extreme circumstances, is termination. Terminating an employee against his or her will is a difficult and time-consuming process and can be very costly to the agency if not handled conscientiously and carefully. Because termination is so emotionally charged, requires a substantial paper trail, and consumes so much of a supervisor's time, many organizations fail to exercise this option and choose to keep a nonproductive or even a destructive employee on the payroll. However, it should be recognized that termination is a two-edged sword. Although making the difficult decision to terminate may be traumatic to the organization, taking the passive approach and ignoring poor performance can have an even more insidious effect and can erode morale for many staff members. Once staff recognize that management lacks the will to terminate an employee who clearly is not performing up to job expectations, a new minimum standard is established for performance. Employees know they will not be terminated as long as they do not fall below this new minimum standard. In some ways, a termination that is warranted—once carried out—can reinvigorate remaining staff and can provide a new sense of respect for the organization.

Using Internal Options with Integrity   None of the foregoing approaches discussed in this section should be interpreted to mean that managers and administrators should be intentionally manipulative in planning to achieve a desired personnel profile. If the organization is to be restructured in any way, the restructuring should be designed to provide more effective, better-quality services in a more efficient manner. If jobs are redesigned, the effort should be undertaken to make better use of knowledge and skill, to eliminate or reduce inefficient functions, to get better results, or to achieve other objectives related to service provision and outcomes. If performance appraisal, training, career development, and termination are used as part of a strategy to change the personnel profile, the strategy should be open and above board. All employees should know about opportunities and about the standards that will be used to make personnel decisions.

When any of the foregoing strategies is used in a manipulative way simply to move one employee aside and move another into a key position, the action taken is very likely to be recognized by employees for what it is, and they are unlikely to support either the action or the promoted employee. Anything less than an open and honest approach to personnel-related decisions will invariably lead to grievances, lawsuits, or at the very least, employee competition, jealousies, and low employee morale. Handled with integrity, however, these changes can be useful in moving the organization toward optimal use of its personnel and toward excellence in overall organizational performance.

External Strategies to Change the Personnel Profile   Important focal points for changing a personnel profile are the recruitment and selection processes established by the agency. It is not unusual to find that these processes are undertaken in a routine manner with the assumption that a superior candidate will somehow emerge from the pool of applicants. Marsden (1996) notes that informal recruitment practices have a number of drawbacks. "Current employees and others who distribute information about openings through interpersonal channels will tend to pass it along to socially similar persons" (p. 135). Informal recruitment through current staff limits the organization's ability to reach heterogeneous applicant pools, causes employers to miss opportunities to attract qualified personnel, and inhibits efforts to comply with equal employment opportunity regulations.

Successful organizations today need diversity. Search committees, in fact, should be looking for someone who is in some way different from those who are already employed by the organization. Finding someone who fulfills a particular demographic and skills profile is not likely to happen if the recruitment and selection processes are handled in a perfunctory manner. To maximize the recruitment opportunity, those in charge of the recruitment, selection, and hiring processes, with extensive staff input, should work to develop a profile of desirable qualities for the position. These qualities should include knowledge, skills, personal characteristics, and demographics that can clearly be tied to the job and will move the organization toward achievement of its desired personnel profile.

Schmidt et al. (1992) suggest that human resources planning should reflect the organization's affirmative action goals. Some of the activities they propose include:

1. Special recruitment efforts toward underrepresented groups.
2. Training to eliminate bias toward underrepresented groups.
3. Removal of barriers to employment that work to the disadvantage of underrepresented groups.
4. Preferential hiring of qualified members of underrepresented groups. (p. 20)

Demographics that warrant special consideration include ethnicity, gender, disability, age, and other factors covered by human resources law. Sexual orientation, although not covered by the law in terms of special employment consideration, is a characteristic that also contributes to diversity and adds a voice and a perspective from an oppressed and under-represented group. Again it should be emphasized that first consideration is always given to qualifications, and no attempt should be made to circumvent qualifications itemized in the job announcement. The focus of effort in recruitment must be on attracting as large and diverse a pool of applicants as possible, thereby offering a wide range of choices at the point of selection and hiring. More will be said about recruitment and selection in Chapter 11.

Step 3: Implement Changes Necessary to Achieve the Plan's Goals and Objectives

Once all of the options proposed in step 2 have been examined and considered, a specific set of strategies and tactics is selected and translated into goals, objectives, and activities. Human resources goals typically focus on future employment of people with the characteristics that will help to achieve demographic and skill diversity and will contribute toward the achievement of strategic and long-range goals and objectives. The following examples illustrate the types of goals, outcome objectives, process objectives, and activities that might be included in a human resources plan.

Goal: To recruit, select, and hire people who demonstrate exemplary qualifications and provide a wide range of diverse characteristics consistent with the agency's mission and strategic plan

Outcome Objective 1: By December 31, 2005, at least 75 percent of agency hires for Caseworker I, II, and III positions will rank among the top 10 percent of candidates for vacant positions and will fit within the desired personnel profile.

Process Objective 1.1: By June 30, 2002, the job analysis for Caseworker I, II, and III positions will be revised to reflect culture and gender competencies, final draft to be approved by management team.

Activities:
1. Appoint a task force to revise job analysis for each position.
2. Complete review of existing job analysis for each position.
3. Identify culture and gender competencies.
4. Draft revision of job analysis for each position.
5. Circulate first draft to relevant staff members.
6. Incorporate feedback from staff.
7. Circulate second draft to relevant staff members.
8. Forward final draft to management team.

Process Objective 1.2: By September 30, 2002, the job description and announcement for Caseworker I, II, and III positions will reflect the revised job analysis for each position, final wording to be approved by the management team.

Activities: Repeat preceding activities.

Additional outcome and process objectives (and their activities) would focus on any other strategies needed to move the organization toward the achievement and the retention of its desired personnel profile. These additional objectives may propose changes in organizational structure, job design, and motivation and reward systems, or any of the components of the human resources system. In translating desired outcomes into goals, objectives, and activities, human resource planners should carefully consider the appropriate target of change. Options may include such factors as organizational culture and philosophy, agency policy, or procedures and practices.

Organizational philosophy and culture are probably the most elusive targets and, consequently, the most difficult to change. Philosophy and culture encompass the underlying values, beliefs, and traditions supported over time by staff but rarely found in any written form. Changing values, beliefs, and traditions requires a substantial investment in terms of time and energy devoted to articulating current philosophy, identifying needed changes, proposing specific changes, and following up to reinforce the value and importance of the proposed changes. The following example illustrates the need for a change in organizational culture and philosophy.

A large social service agency provides services to families referred by the Child Protective Services division of the state department of Child Welfare. Over the years the number of Spanish-speaking-only clients has increased, and a position of translator has been created to address the language barrier. Managers and supervisors recognize that some qualities very important to the worker-client relationship were lost by using the translator as a go-between and are attempting to create new positions for bilingual/bicultural workers. Existing workers, for a variety of reasons, oppose this change, expressing the belief that caseloads should not be segregated by ethnic group and strongly defending the quality of their relationships with their Spanish-speaking-only clients. Management recognizes that if they force the change without the support of existing staff, a permanent rift might be established between old and new staff, and it could conceivably be along racial and ethnic lines. A series of workshops is proposed, focused on culture and the casework relationship, designed to coopt existing staff into understanding the problem and becoming part of the solution. Although there is a recognition that this approach will be time-consuming, it is felt that in the long run the effort will be worthwhile if it contributes to a permanent change in philosophy toward building positive relationships between existing staff, new staff, and Spanish-speaking-only clients.

Changes that have the greatest formalized support are those that are translated into policy. Flynn (1985) defines policy as "those principles which give expression to valued ends and provide direction to social welfare action" (p. 6). He makes the point that a great deal of social welfare action takes place at the agency level, and agency employees need to be aware of the implications of social agency policies.

Agency policy is created in written form, approved by a board of directors, and published in some form for use by staff. Some agencies issue a complete policy manual to each new staff member. There is an expectation that new staff members will become familiar with the policy manual over time, and that all staff members will carry out their responsibilities in a way that is consistent with agency policy. Changes or additions to agency policy must be written out in a format that is consistent with the rest of the manual and submitted through the chain of command to the agency director and ultimately to the board of directors for a decision. A paragraph or two explaining the rationale for the new or revised policy usually accompanies the policy statement. Once formally approved by the board, it is expected that all employees will follow new or revised policies, and it is for this reason that policy changes are most likely to achieve the desired result. A proposed policy change is illustrated below.

Section 9: Employee Recruitment

Old policy: 9.1 A strategy for recruitment shall be established by employees who are appointed to the recruitment and selection committee.

New policy: 9.1 The recruitment and selection committee shall complete all of the following steps in planning for the recruitment of new employees:
1. Review the job analysis for the position to be filled.
2. Review the agency's summary on applicable human resources laws.
3. Review the agency's human resources plan.
4. Identify recruitment sources designed to attract applicants who have the necessary qualifications and who will contribute to demographic and skill diversity.
5. Develop and implement a plan for communicating job availability information to recruitment sources.

If a less formal approach to change is preferred by human resource planners, they may wish to target procedures or practices. Procedures typically follow policies and specify in greater detail how policy is to be implemented. They may be written out and inserted into a policy manual, or they may be placed in a separate document. Different units within an organization may have their own procedural manuals. In some cases, procedures may take on the form of protocols or step-by-step processes designed to ensure uniformity in the way certain types of cases are processed. Because child abuse and neglect and family violence cases have important legal implications, it is not unusual to find that highly specific procedures are required. Procedures do not require approval by a governing board. In some instances they may be approved within the unit affected. In changing or proposing new procedures, the level of decision making depends to a great extent on the scope of programs and staff affected.

An even less formal approach can be taken when changing or initiating new practices. The term *practices* refers to the ways in which staff members perform certain aspects of their jobs. Practices are not formalized in writing, so changes must be agreed to by consensus. Little can be done to enforce new or changed practices if staff do not agree to support the change. If practices cannot be successfully changed through informal agreement, a more formal change, in writing, of policies or procedures may be necessary. The following example illustrates how staff members might agree on a change in practice.

An agency provides treatment programs for drug and alcohol abusers. A series of scales is administered by the worker, designed to produce a profile of problem severity in a number of areas. Administration of these scales requires about one-and-one-half to two hours of time. Workers agreed informally to experiment with having clients self-administer the scales without direct face-to-face involvement from the worker. Some workers were concerned that important information would be lost and were reluctant to support the change, although all agreed that a significant amount of time would be saved if clients completed the scales on their own. Because uniformity in the way the scales are administered is an important consideration, either workers must unanimously agree to the change practice, or a written policy or procedure must be approved through the proper channels.

In writing and implementing goals, objectives, and activities for the human resources plan, those responsible should carefully consider the appropriate target for each desired change and explore the options of philosophy and culture, policy, procedures, and practices.

Step 4: Monitor and Evaluate the Effects of Changes

A complete human resources plan will include a number of sets of goals, outcome objectives, process objectives, and activities. Contained within a well-written objective will always be some criteria for monitoring and/or measurement. For example, in the outcome objective used earlier in this chapter, the expected outcome is that 75 percent of agency hires for Caseworker I, II, and III positions will rank among the top 10 percent of candidates for vacant positions and will fit within the desired personnel profile. These outcomes can be measured in two ways. First, the selection process must be reviewed for all hires for Caseworker I, II, and III positions to determine their overall ranking in relation to other applicants for the vacant positions. This approach to measurement presumes that there is a valid and reliable scoring system for applicants and that records have been kept on all applicants for the designated positions. Examining the ranking of each person hired will enable human service managers to determine whether, by December 31, 2005, at least 75 percent of new hires for Caseworker I, II, and III positions actually ranked among the top 10 percent of applicants.

A second approach to measuring the achievement of Outcome Objective 1 is to examine the desired personnel profile for Caseworker I, II, and III positions for the agency. This document should reflect the balance of demographics, including age, gender, ethnicity, and other factors that the agency is attempting to achieve. By comparing the desired profile to the existing profile, a determination can be made of which characteristics are needed to achieve the desired profile. Comparing demographics of new hires to those needed will help to determine how successful the agency has been in recruiting and hiring to meet diversity needs. In the same way, knowledge, skill, and personal characteristics profiles can be used to help the agency move toward the achievement of an optimum mix of staff who bring the highest professional qualifications as well as a rich and diverse blend of demographic and personal characteristics.

The approach to human resources planning proposed here is not without risks. Whenever human characteristics are translated into numbers, there is always the risk that the numbers become reality for planners and evaluators. Numbers that suggest success may foster convictions that the system is the solution. If recruitment and selection goals and objectives are met, the organization may feel no need to continue to examine the system for its validity and reliability.

However, it should be recognized that hiring is really the beginning, not the end, of implementing the human resources plan. There are many ongoing components to human resources planning. Proposed changes may relate to changes in organizational structure, in job design, in the motivation and reward system, or in recruitment, selection, or any part of the human resources system. Those who monitor and evaluate the plan must continually determine, first, if the recommended change was made. Second, if the change was made, they must evaluate the results. For example, Process Objective 1.1 earlier in this chapter proposed that job analysis documents for Caseworker I, II, and III positions be revised. Revision of a job analysis is not for its own sake but rather so that the knowledge, skills, and personal characteristics identified become more in line with the realities of the job. Changes are then incorporated into the job description and, at the time of a vacancy, into the job announcement. All this activity is undertaken so that persons hired will bring the knowledge, skills, and personal characteristics needed to do the job as envisioned in strategic, long-range, and program plans.

Viewed in this way, monitoring and evaluating the human resources plan are cyclical activities in which one review leads to another, eventually encompassing a comprehensive review and evaluation of the entire service system, and the extent to which it is supported by the human resources plan.

SUMMARY

1. **Selecting, Hiring, and Retaining the Optimum Mix of Staff.** Internal harmony and teamwork among staff are important for optimum organizational functioning. Planning increases the likelihood that staff will work well together.

2. **Human Resources Law.** Many protections are built into laws, regulations, and executive orders. Managers cannot be expected to know all the details but should be familiar with the general parameters of human resources law.
   - *Race, Color, or National Origin.*
     Titles VI and VII of the Civil Rights Act of 1964 *(as amended).* Prohibit discrimination based on race, color, and national origin.
   - *Affirmative Action.*
     Executive Orders. Executive Orders 11246 and 11375 created the concept of affirmative action. Employers with fifty or more employees and a federal contract of $50,000 or more are required to have a written plan to increase the numbers of minorities and women in the workforce.
   - *Sex/Gender.*
     Equal Pay Act of 1963. Prohibits discrimination in rates of pay when jobs involve equal work under equal conditions.
     Title IX of Education Amendments of 1972. Prohibits discrimination on the basis of sex in education programs and activities.
     Sexual Harassment. Court cases have established the employer's responsibility to maintain a work environment that is free of unwelcome sexual verbal or physical contact.
   - *Veterans' Status.*
     Vietnam Era Veterans' Readjustment Assistance Act of 1974. Employers with federal contracts of $10,000 or more must demonstrate affirmative efforts to employ disabled and Vietnam vets.

- *Age.*

  Age Discrimination in Employment Act of 1967 *(amended 1978).* Employers may not discriminate against applicants or employees between the ages of forty and sixty-five because of their age.

- *Disabilities.*

  Vocational Rehabilitation Act of 1973. Extends the concept of affirmative action to the employment of qualified persons with physical disabilities or limitations. Americans with Disabilities Act of 1990. Prohibits discrimination based on disability. Civil Rights Act of 1991. Provides for damages and jury trials in cases of discrimination.

3. **The Letter of the Law versus the Spirit of the Law.** Human service agency managers should be acquainted with the laws but use consultants for decision making. Encouraging diversity will support compliance with the spirit of the law.

   - *Valuing, Respecting, and Maximizing the Benefits of Diversity.*
   - *Encouraging Full Participation.*
   - *Conscientious Attention to Issues Surrounding Sexual Harassment.*

4. **Human Resources Planning.** A profile of staff needs should be developed that reflects an optimal mix of staff in terms of demographic characteristics, abilities, and personal qualities.

5. **Achieving Excellence through Human Resources Planning.** A strategy should be developed designed to achieve the optimum mix of staff.

   - *Step 1: Project Personnel Needs.* A matrix should be designed to present a profile of job expectations and qualifications for each position. A personal and skill inventory will reflect a profile of actual employee skills and qualifications. A matrix of current staff demographics and a forecast of vacancies are basic tools used for human resources planning.

   - *Step 2: Plan for Achieving the Desired Personnel Profile.* Achieving the optimum profile is not something that will just happen. It must be planned, changes initiated, and effects monitored and evaluated.
     Internal Strategies to Change the Personnel Profile. Some actions can be taken internally to work toward achieving the optimum mix of staff.
     - *Changing the Organizational Structure.* Restructuring may create new positions and allows for moving people around within the organization.
     - *Changing the Job Design.* Changing a job can open it up to an internal selection process.
     - *Using the Human Resources System to Make Personnel Changes.* Performance appraisals, career planning, and termination can initiate changes in jobs that may lead to new openings.
     - *Using Internal Options with Integrity.* Changes should genuinely be needed and not be manipulated just for the sake of making the change.
     External Strategies to Change the Personnel Profile. Recruitment and selection processes, if used effectively, can help achieve the optimum personnel profile.

■ *Step 3: Implement Changes Necessary to Achieve the Plan's Goals and Objectives.* Human resources goals, objectives, and activities should be written out in detail as the basis for human resources planning.

■ *Step 4: Monitor and Evaluate the Effects of Changes.* Data and information should be collected and used to monitor and evaluate the effects of change.

EXERCISES

Please complete the following sections of your manual based on the content covered in Chapter 9.

Section 9: Human Resources Planning

9.1 Compliance with Affirmative Action/Equal Employment Opportunity Requirements. Write a policy statement that makes clear your agency's position on compliance with all federal and state requirements for affirmative action and equal employment opportunity. Include an attachment that summarizes the major laws or cite references.

9.2 Job Expectations and Qualifications. Identify the variables to be used to establish job expectations and qualifications. Attach, as Document 9.2a, a format that can be used to display overall job expectations and qualifications for the organization.

9.3 Staff Demographics. Identify the variables to be used to establish a demographic profile for the organization. Attach, as Document 9.3a, a format that can be used to display an overall organizational demographic profile.

REFERENCES

Cascio, W. (1987). *Applied psychology in personnel management* (3rd ed.). Englewood Cliffs, NJ: Prentice-Hall.

Daley, J., & Angulo, J. (1994). Understanding the dynamics of diversity within nonprofit boards. *Journal of the Community Development Society, 25*(2), 172–188.

Dessler, G. (1997). *Human resource management* (7th ed.). Upper Saddle River, NJ: Prentice-Hall.

Flynn, J. (1985). *Social agency policy: Analysis and presentation for community practice.* Chicago: Nelson-Hall.

Marsden, P. (1996).The staffing process: Recruitment and selection methods. In A. Kalleberg, D. Knoke, P. Marsden, & J. Spaeth (Eds.), *Organizations in America: Analyzing their structures and human resource practices* (pp. 133–156). Thousand Oaks, CA: Sage.

Rowe, M. (1981). Dealing with sexual harassment. *Harvard Business Review, 61* (May–June), 42–46.

Schmidt, M., Riggar, T., Crimando, W., & Bordieri, J. (1992). *Staffing for success: A guide for health and human service professionals.* Newbury Park, CA: Sage.

Thomas, R. (1991). *Beyond race and gender: Unleashing the power of your total work force by managing diversity.* New York: AMACOM.

Werther, B., Jr., & Davis, K. (1989). *Human resources and personnel management* (3rd ed.). New York: McGraw-Hill.

CHAPTER 10

Using Job Analysis as a Basis for Ensuring Consistency within the Human Resources System

CHAPTER OUTLINE

- What Is Job Analysis?
- Conducting a Job Analysis
- Methods of Collecting Job Analysis Information
- Job Analysis as Central to the Human Resources System
- The Job Description
- Job Specifications
- The Job Announcement
- Investing Time in Job Analysis

CHAPTER OBJECTIVES

Upon completion of this chapter, the reader will be able to:

- Explain the differences among job analysis, job description, job specifications, and job announcement.
- Develop a complete job analysis and job description on a designated position within a human service organization.
- Identify and discuss four methods of collecting job information.
- Explain the role of job analysis in influencing the direction of human resource functions.

Assumptions

- That a job analysis for every position in the organization is critical to a comprehensive understanding of the position and its role in the organization.
- That all human resources functions—recruitment, selection, hiring, orientation, training, development, performance appraisal, and termination—should be consistent with the job as presented in the job analysis.
- That job descriptions and job announcements should be written carefully with full knowledge of the job analysis and human resources law.

■ What Is Job Analysis?

Most people in the workplace are familiar with the term *job description*. Far fewer know what goes into a thorough job analysis, yet it could be argued that job analysis is significantly more important in terms of the many purposes it fulfills. Dessler (1997) defines job analysis as follows:

> Organizations consist of positions that have to be staffed. *Job analysis* is the procedure through which you determine the duties of these positions and the characteristics of the people who should be hired for them. The analysis produces information on job requirements, which is then used for developing *job descriptions* (what the job entails) and *job specifications* (what kind of people to hire for the job). (p. 83)

Job analysis, says Dessler, is useful in collecting information on the following: (1) work activities, (2) human behaviors, (3) machines, tools, equipment, and work aids used, (4) performance standards, (5) job context, and (6) human requirements.

A similar definition is proposed by the College and University Personnel Association (1998). Job analysis is described as the first stage of defining a job. The employer identifies key elements of the job by undertaking a study of the tasks, duties, responsibilities, and organizational relationships of the job. The second stage of the job definition process is writing the job description, which summarizes the job analysis. The final stage of job definition is "the preparation of job specifications, which identify the knowledge, skills, and abilities that prospective applicants should possess to perform a job adequately" (p. 3). In summary:

Job Analysis	A thorough study of a job in which tasks, duties, and other job characteristics are examined for their consistency and fit with each other and used to establish job expectations.
Job Description	A summary of job tasks, duties, reporting relationships, and other job-related functions used to explain job expectations.
Job Specifications	The knowledge, skills, and abilities that prospective applicants should possess to perform the job adequately.

Brody (1993) describes job analysis a process of interaction between supervisors and staff focused on data collection about the major aspects of the job. Ultimately the organization clusters its inventory of tasks under major activities and scales them down to a manageable number. The resulting job specifications include skills, knowledge, training, and experience required to perform each job.

Schmidt, Riggar, Crimando, and Bordieri (1992) draw on the definition of the U.S. Department of Labor (1982), which defines job analysis as a process that describes the following:

1. What the worker does in terms of actions or functions.
2. How the work is done—the methods, techniques, or processes involved.
3. The results of the work—the goods produced or services rendered.
4. The necessary worker characteristics—the knowledge, skills, abilities, and other characteristics needed to accomplish the job.
5. The context of the work in terms of environmental and organizational factors and the nature of the work itself. (p. 33)

Fine and Wiley (1971) summarize task analysis (a subcomponent of job analysis) into a sentence that includes the following components: (1) who, (2) performs what action, (3) to whom, (4) upon what cue, (5) using what tools, work aids, or skills, and (6) to produce what performance goal?

Job Analysis as Both a Process and a Product

In much of the literature, job analysis is described as a process that results in documents called job descriptions and job specifications (College and University Personnel Association, 1998; Dessler, 1997; Schmidt et al., 1992). Although a dynamic and interactive process is critical to successful job analysis, the focus should not be exclusively on process. It is also advisable that a product or document be produced and kept on file for each position within the organization. There are several reasons for capturing the analytical work in the form of a document.

First, job analysis when done properly is a substantial undertaking. Significant resources are invested in the process, including time from staff who occupy the position, from supervisors of the position, from program managers, and possibly from outside consultants. When completed, it is the most comprehensive study of a job ever done within the organization. Second, it is likely, in a world of changing organizational structure and job design, that a job analysis will be repeated on any given position at some time in the future. Having on file the previous job analysis as a baseline document upon which new activities and tasks are built and others deleted can save a significant amount of time and resources for the agency. Third, the literature on human resources is consistent in recommending that job analysis be central to all components of the human resources system, including recruitment, selection, hiring, orientation, training, performance appraisal, and termination. It is more likely that the job analysis will be used to guide human resources processes if it exists as a document and is available for reference purposes than if it is merely a process that results in a number of documents used for other purposes. For these reasons, the following section will explore the elements to be included in a job analysis that will make it most useful to human service organizations.

■ Conducting a Job Analysis

What Is a Job?

In exploring the procedures for conducting a job analysis, it is perhaps appropriate to first examine the question of what we mean by the term *job*. Schmidt et al. (1992) suggest the use of the following definitions in exploring work activities:

Element: The smallest unit into which work can be divided.
Task: Several elements carried out for a specific purpose.
Duty: Several related tasks.
Position: A combination of duties performed by an individual.
Job: A group of positions with similar duties.
Job family: A group of jobs calling for similar worker characteristics.

For example, in examining the work of a counselor or therapist in a child guidance agency the following examples might fit with each of the preceding terms:

Element	Collecting social history data and information.
Task	An interview, in which several elements are combined.
Duty	The intake and screening process. In some organizations the duty might be defined as the full set of responsibilities assumed with a particular client.
Position	All of the duties performed by a counselor or therapist, including direct face-to-face contact, collateral contacts, data collection, case recording, and more.
Job	The job may be entitled Child Psychologist, Child Psychiatrist, or Child Counselor. The job analysis, job description, and job specifications are all focused on this level of work activity but may incorporate some of the other elements described such as duties and tasks.
Job family	The job family may be entitled something such as Child Behavioral Health Specialist to distinguish the family from a category such as Adult Behavioral Health Specialist.

The Elements of Job Analysis

Dessler (1997) identifies the following items as factors to be identified and defined in a job analysis:

- Work activities—actual work performed.
- Human behaviors—the ability to perform certain types of tasks.
- Machines, tools, equipment, and work aids used—the knowledge and skill needed to use necessary equipment.
- Performance standards—expectations for quantity, quality, and speed for each duty.
- Job context—physical work environment, work schedule, and other factors.
- Human requirements—job-related knowledge, skills, training, personal attributes. (p. 83)

The College and University Personnel Association (1998) states that the job analysis is intended to produce a job description and job specifications that include these items:

- Essential functions—functions the person holding the job must be able to perform unaided or with reasonable accommodation.
- Knowledge, skill, and abilities needed to perform a job adequately.
- Entry requirements in terms of education and experience, and equivalencies.

In distilling these many proposed elements of the job analysis process into a format for use in human service organizations, eight topic areas are proposed as components of a complete job analysis:

Part 1.   Duties and tasks
Part 2.   Methods
Part 3.   Results expected in relation to duties
Part 4.   Required knowledge and skills
Part 5.   Essential functions
Part 6.   Entry requirements in terms of education and experience
Part 7.   Worker characteristics
Part 8.   The context of the work

Not every element of the preceding list is essential for every job or organization. It is important to establish priorities and a rationale for what is to be included. The scope and detail included may hinge on available resources. Some types of organizations have generous resources available for this function and can hire outside consultants to manage and conduct the entire job analysis process. Most human service organizations, however, will have to rely on the abilities and willingness of existing staff to take on job analysis as an additional function beyond their already full-time jobs. With this in mind, the process should be made as efficient and streamlined as possible. The following sections will focus in more detail on each of the eight parts recommended for job analysis.

Part 1. Duties and Tasks   Basic to the job analysis is the identification of work activities. As suggested by a number of authors, work activities should be broken down into categories that identify the major duties for the position and then itemize the tasks that must be completed in the course of performing duties. For example, a job analysis for the position of Case Manager might include the categories of Intake and Screening, Assessment, Planning and Contracting, Implementation and Monitoring, and Evaluation and Termination. Each of these duties would be defined in more detail by listing the tasks associated with them. Under the duty of Intake and Screening, the following tasks might be listed.

Duties and Tasks
Duty 1: Intake and Screening

Task 1   Completion of intake form
Task 2   Determination of eligibility for services
Task 3   Identification of presenting problem(s) and need for services
Task 4   Explanation of the service provision process

In the foregoing example, case management duties are presented in a chronological order in which they are addressed with clients, beginning with the first contact with a client and following through to termination of the relationship. For this type of job, a chronological approach is logical and systematic. For jobs in which this approach is not possible, such as secretary or supervisor, duties should be listed in the order of importance or frequency of occurrence. In addition to direct responsibilities with clients, many direct service positions include some administrative-type duties such as participation in staff meetings, membership on committees or task forces, report writing, and other such responsibilities. These should also be included in the job analysis in the interest of making it as accurate a reflection of reality as possible.

Part 2. Methods   A comprehensive listing of all duties and tasks establishes a framework for some of the remaining elements of the job analysis. For each duty or for each task, whichever is relevant, methods and techniques utilized to carry out the duty or task should be identified. This step helps to make explicit the ways in which duties and tasks are fulfilled and helps to clarify the knowledge and skill needed to meet job expectations. For example, completing an intake form is typically accomplished through a face-to-face interview with a client. Determination of eligibility may require that the client provide certain documents and that the worker certify that they have been seen and that information provided by the client has been verified. Methods and techniques can include one-to-one interviewing, group activities, classroom presentations, data collection, data entry, or any number of other approaches to the completion of duties and tasks. The following example illustrates:

Duties and Tasks		Methods
Duty 1:	Intake and Screening	At least one face-to-face interview in office or client's home. Collection of necessary data and documents from client. Orientation session on service processes with client.
Task 1	Completion of intake form	
Task 2	Determination of eligibility for services	
Task 3	Identification of presenting problem(s) and need for services	
Task 4	Explanation of the service provision process	

Part 3. Results   For each duty or task there is an expectation that some result or some form of completion or closure will be achieved. When the duty of intake and screening has been completed, a number of results are anticipated. It is expected that the process will result in the collection of information that is recorded in the case record. Certain forms must be completed. Decisions must be made as to whether the client is eligible, is appropriate for service, and wishes to continue with the process. These factors become indicators of whether or not the intake and screening process has been completed.

Specification of results serves two purposes. First, duties and tasks, especially those related to providing services to clients, are not undertaken merely for the sake of completion and closure. They are performed so that clients will improve and programs will be successful in meeting their objectives. In this context it is worthwhile to think through the details of each job and to establish an understanding of expected results for each set of duties and tasks so that the focus is consistently on client progress. The cumulative achievement of results in connection with duties and tasks ideally should result in successful client outcomes. A second purpose of establishing results is that they provide milestones that can be useful in tracking progress with cases as well as serving other purposes such as conducting performance appraisals for staff. Chapter 13 will discuss the importance of creating a performance appraisal document that is consistent and compatible with the job analysis.

Duties and Tasks	Methods	Results
Duty 1: Intake and Screening	At least one face-to-face interview in the office. Collection of necessary data and documents. Orientation session on service processes with client.	Upon completion of Intake and Screening, case manager and client will achieve a mutual understanding and agreement about:
Task 1 Completion of intake form		
Task 2 Determination of eligibility for services		1. Client eligibility
Task 3 Identification of presenting problem(s) and need for services		2. Use of information 3. Nature of presenting problems and needs
Task 4 Explanation of the service provision process		4. The service provision process

Part 4. Required Knowledge and Skill Once methods have been established, the knowledge and skills required to carry out duties and tasks should be defined. Uninformed practice is characterized by random, unpredictable acts that lack a consistent rationale. Informed practice is based on the systematic use of knowledge. Knowledge includes theoretical and conceptual knowledge about the field represented by the job as well as knowledge about agency programs, policy, and procedures related to the job. For example, using the four tasks cited earlier, it is clear that a person performing in the position of Case Manager would have to understand the intake process, would have to know agency policies on eligibility for service, would have to know something about human behavior within the context of the social environment, and would have to understand the agency's service provision process.

Skill is something that "is directly observable in the act" (Lewis, 1976). Although knowledge cannot be assessed without the possessor sharing it in some form, skill is evident to the trained eye by observing actions. Some positions require psychomotor skills such as typing, driving a vehicle, or using a particular piece of software. Professional positions typically require more complex skills that are incorporated into the helping process. Necessary skills for a case manager may include such qualities as the ability to form positive and trusting relationships, the ability to understand etiology, or the ability to develop a working intervention hypothesis. Lewis (1976) argues that, for the professional practitioner, knowledge and skill cannot be separated. "When reference is made to 'knowledge and skill,' or 'knowledge, values, and skill,' . . . support is given to the misleading notion that skill itself does not encompass knowledge and values" (p. 3). Careful attention should be given to the identification of the knowledge and skill required for a job because this determination in turn influences other factors, including minimum job qualifications for hiring.

Cultural and Gender Competencies

There is a growing recognition of the importance of culture, ethnicity, and gender to effective practice in human service organizations. However, although human service professionals are increasingly being encouraged to incorporate knowledge of culture and gender into their analytical frameworks, it is rare to find requirements for cultural or gender competencies incorporated into documents such as a job analysis, a job description, or a statement of job qualifications.

A case can be made that attention should be devoted to the knowledge and skills needed to practice competently across cultural and gender boundaries. These areas of knowledge and skill will not necessarily be vital to every position within the organization. It is not uncommon, however, to find that workers, the majority of whose caseloads are made up of people from other cultures, have no job expectation that they will demonstrate understanding of those cultures. Throughout the agency wherever there is client contact, it may be wise to give careful consideration to the competencies needed for effective practice with the major ethnic groups served by the agency and to identify gender issues for special consideration, if warranted.

Many authors have long argued that there are important cross-cultural differences, and that they matter in situations in which help is offered across cultural lines (Green, 1995; Locke, 1992; Sue & Sue, 1990). Given the long and not so positive history between ethnic groups and the helping professions such as psychology, counseling, and social work, the quality and effectiveness of cross-cultural practice cannot be taken for granted or left to chance.

Cultural competence is defined as "a set of congruent behaviors, attitudes, and policies that come together in a system, agency, or profession and enables that system, agency, or profession to work effectively in cross-cultural situations" (Chung, 1992). Culture is defined as including thoughts, communications, actions, customs, beliefs, values, and institutions of racial, ethnic, religious, or social group. In a culturally competent system of care, the importance of culture is acknowledged at all levels of the system, and the system is committed to the expansion of cultural knowledge and the adaptation of services to ensure cultural relevance.

Cultural competence is defined as a continuum with six levels: (1) cultural destructiveness, (2) cultural incapacity, (3) cultural blindness, (4) cultural precompetence, (5) cultural competence, and (6) cultural proficiency. Cultural competence and proficiency involve the incorporation of a body of knowledge and a range of skills related to effective understanding of and practice with various ethnic groups (Cross, Bazron, Dennis, & Isaacs, 1989).

Theory development and research on gender have also produced findings that encourage increasing development of knowledge and skill in cross-gender practice. Gilligan (1982) has developed a theoretical explanation of role and behavior differences. Tannen (1990) has conducted extensive research among boys and girls in kindergarten and school settings as well as men and women in the workplace and has concluded that there are behavioral differences that can be attributed to gender. The issue is not whether one agrees with specific theoretical perspectives or conceptual frameworks regarding ethnicity or gender. Rather, the point is that perhaps the time has come to move beyond general discussions of the importance of culture and gender and to begin to tie knowledge and skill expectations to jobs where relevant. It is very likely that as these dimensions are explored, many expected competencies will emerge in the field of human services.

The job analysis process, adding knowledge and skills, is depicted in the following illustration.

Duties and Tasks	Methods	Results	Knowledge and Skill
Duty 1: Intake and Screening	At least one face-to-face interview in the office.	Upon completion of Intake and Screening, case manager and client will achieve mutual understanding and agreement about:	Knowledge of human behavior in terms of bio-physical, cognitive psychosocial, cultural, and gender factors as related to the age group services. Excellent interpersonal skills, interviewing skills, data collection skills. Data entry using agency software.
Task 1 Completion of intake form			
Task 2 Determination of eligibility for services	Collection of necessary data and documents.	1. Client eligibility	
Task 3 Identification of presenting problem(s) and need for services	Orientation session on serice processes with client.	2. Use of information 3. Nature of the presenting problems and needs	
Task 4 Explanation of the service provision process		4. The service provision process	

Part 5. Essential Functions   Because of the risk of discrimination in hiring, identifying essential functions has become an important part of the job analysis and job description. The College and University Personnel Association (1998) recommends that essential functions actually be made a part of every job description. Essential functions are defined as follows:

> Whether a particular function is "essential" is a factual determination that the EEOC says must be made on a case-by-case basis. Essential functions are those functions that the individual who holds the position must be able to perform unaided or with the assistance of reasonable accommodation. The EEOC says that any inquiry into whether a particular function is essential initially focuses on whether the employer actually requires current or prior employees in the position to perform those functions. For example, any employer may state that typing is an essential function of a position. If, in fact, the employer has never required any employee in that particular position to type, this will be evidence that typing is not actually an essential function of that position. (Duston, Russell, & Kerr, 1992, p. 3)

A university handbook on recruitment states that essential functions must be listed on the announcement of vacancy. The handbook defines essential functions as follows:

> The essential functions are those core or required duties of a position as opposed to marginal responsibilities of a position. The following factors should be used in determining essential functions:

- The reason the job exists is to perform that function.
- There are limited numbers of employees available among whom the performance of that job function can be distributed.
- The function may be highly specialized so that the person is hired for his/her expertise or ability to perform the particular function.
- The employer's judgment as to which functions are essential.
- The amount of time spent on the job performing the specific function.
- The consequences of not requiring the incumbent to perform the function.
- The work experience of past incumbents in the job.
- The current work experience of incumbents in similar jobs. (Arizona State University Office of Equal Employment Opportunity/Affirmative Action, 1995)

In identifying essential functions the job analyst reviews the duties and tasks section and the methods section for the purpose of selecting those items that, if not performed satisfactorily, would prevent the jobholder from meeting job expectations. For example, it may be essential to successful performance of the case management job to perform the duties associated with the helping process such as intake and screening, assessment, contracting with client, and others. There may, however, be options for the ways in which data collection and entry are accomplished. A blind worker may be able to use specialized equipment to transcribe notes and monitor client progress. In this instance, following standard data collection and entry procedures would not be an essential function. A listing of those functions considered to be essential, with a brief explanation if needed, should suffice for this part of the job analysis.

Part 6. Entry Requirements in Terms of Education and Experience   When the job has been clearly conceptualized in terms of what the jobholder is expected to know and to do, consideration should be given to entry requirements. Minimum qualifications should be established in terms of education and experience. Qualifications must pass the test of job-relatedness. Only those items required for adequate performance and, therefore, representative of minimally acceptable standards for selection, and later, for performance should be included (Cascio, 1987).

Rigid and exclusive requirements, though not intended, may have the effect of discriminating against protected groups that have not had equal access to opportunities for education and experience. Many legal questions have been raised about whether minimum qualifications are job related. In a review of job qualifications, the EEOC found that more than 65 percent of jobs specifying the need for a college degree could easily be performed by high school graduates (Driessnack, 1979). As a result, the concept of equivalency has been established. This permits a combination of education and experience to substitute for rigid educational requirements. Entry requirements may be expressed as follows:

Qualifications
- Master of social work (MSW) degree from a program accredited by the Council on Social Work Education (CSWE) or master's degree in a related field with equivalent requirements for internship.
- At least two years of successful experience in a social service agency providing direct services to children and families.

Part 7. Worker Characteristics   Some jobs require special individual traits or characteristics that cannot really be described as skills or abilities. Schmidt et al. (1992) define these as "physical, sensory, and mobility traits; tolerances for certain working conditions" (p. 34). Dessler (1997) refers to them as personal attributes such as aptitudes, physical characteristics, personality, or interests. For example, in human service organizations it may be the case that workers are expected to work together in teams or perhaps to share cases in some instances. A worker characteristic, then, might be the ability to work closely and compatibly with colleagues and to share responsibility and authority. A person who was interested only in working independently and making his or her own decisions would not be well suited to this position. Or a position may require a great deal of patience in working with certain types of clients.

Worker characteristics are another element of the job analysis that should be handled with great care. The same precautions that apply to minimum qualifications should be applied to worker characteristics. Those characteristics that are identified as desirable should be screened for potential bias toward protected groups. For example, a candidate for a position that requires teamwork and shared decision making may come across as less comfortable in an interview situation if he or she represents an ethnic group, gender, or sexual orientation not represented on the interview panel. Candidates who share demographic characteristics with the interviewers may have a subtle advantage in terms of being perceived as more compatible or collegial. In the limited time allowed to make a hiring decision, some worker characteristics can be difficult to assess. Worker characteristics may be expressed as follows.

Worker Characteristics
- Comfortable in working closely with coworkers and reaching mutually agreeable decisions.
- Able to express differences.
- Able to engage in problem-solving processes to resolve differences.
- Demonstrated commitment to children's issues.

Part 8. The Context of the Work   This final section of the job analysis is one that can be used as a catch-all for anything else one needs to know about the position that has not been covered in the previous six sections. In developing a job analysis, it is helpful to identify factors that might be of use in comparing a position in an organization to a similar position in another organization. These factors would include location on the organizational chart, identification of immediate superior and his or her position in the organization, identification of number of staff supervised and their positions in the organization, description of workload, support services needed to perform the job, and other such contextual or environmental considerations.

Most of these factors are straightforward and require little analysis. Attaching a copy of the organizational chart together with a brief narrative will help to understand the location of the position within the organization, the level of the immediate supervisor, and the responsibility for supervision, if any. Workloads in human service organizations are typically defined in terms of caseloads, numbers of workers supervised, or numbers of programs managed. Brody (1993) points out that organizations are beginning to determine caseloads based on the number of problems presented, their intensity, and the nature of the intervention that will be required. The job analysis can be helpful in determining what types of cases should be assigned to what level of worker, and how many cases of each type can be handled. Other relevant factors such as contact with the public, types of decision making expected, or support services needed may be included in this section as well. The context of work may be described as in the following example.

Additional Job-Related Information

Position in the Organization:	Within the Child and Family Services Program, entry level
Supervised by:	Unit supervisor within the Child and Family Services Program
Number of employees supervised:	None
Workload expectations:	Standard caseload twenty cases
Support services available:	Child care and transportation

Figure 10.1 illustrates a format that could be used to compile a complete job analysis document.

■ Methods of Collecting Job Analysis Information

A variety of methods or strategies can be used to complete the job analysis. Among the more common are (1) the interview, (2) the questionnaire, (3) direct observation, and (4) participant diaries or logs.

FIGURE 10.1
Proposed Format for Job Analysis

Format for Job Analysis

Job Title_____ Date of Completion_____

Duties and Tasks	Methods	Results of Duties	Knowledge and Skills
Duty 1......................	1.....................	1.....................	1.....................
Task 1........................	2.....................	2.....................	2.....................
Task 2........................	3.....................	3.....................	3.....................
Task 3........................	4.....................	4.....................	4.....................
Etc.......................	Etc.	Etc.	Etc. ....

Essential Functions	Qualifications	Worker Characteristics	Context of Work
1.....................	1.....................	1.....................	1.....................
2.....................	2.....................	2.....................	2.....................
3.....................	3.....................	3.....................	3.....................
Etc.	Etc......................	Etc......................	Etc......................

Job Analysis Interviewing

Data and information about the job can be gathered directly from employees who are knowledgeable about the job using structured interviews. Staff involved in the process may include employees who currently hold the position to be studied, supervisors of those employees, and a human resources specialist. Each representative brings a different perspective to the job analysis. Those who hold the position understand the job from the perspective of one who is responsible for fulfilling job responsibilities on a day-to-day basis. These employees should be able to provide detailed information about duties and tasks and the methods that are most commonly used. They may also have ideas about the knowledge, skills, and worker characteristics needed, but supervisors should be able to pro-vide a helpful perspective on these factors as well. If job expectations for cultural and gen-der competence are to be established, these content areas should be developed by people with some knowledge of the literature, a good understanding of what is meant by the term *cultural competence,* and an ability to recognize those duties and tasks that may call for this special area of expertise. A human resource specialist brings knowledge about how the job analysis is used and can help to ensure that it is written in terms that are specific enough to make it useful in other human resource functions as well.

Interviewing for the purpose of job analysis involves planning and preparation. Questions should be organized in a way that all the information needed about a particular part of the job is gathered through a series of related questions. When interviews move about randomly with no apparent logic or pattern to the questions, the interview becomes inefficient and interviewees often lose interest. For example, some level of agreement should be reached among all the participants on the major duties, that is, the major categories of job responsibilities associated with the position. For a case manager, these duties may involve such responsibilities as Intake and Screening, Assessment, Planning and Contracting, Implementing and Monitoring, and Evaluation and Termination. Once consensus has been achieved by the participants, one way to approach interviewing in a systematic way is to take the first duty—Intake and Screening—and to identify (1) tasks, (2) methods, (3) knowledge and skill, and (4) results. Each duty can then be systematically addressed to determine how the interviewee perceives the job as it relates to each of these categories. This is not the only way to approach the job analysis systematically. The point is that the interviewer should not jump from duties to questions about where the job is located on the organizational chart and then back to questions about knowledge and skill. Questions should be simple, not compound. The interviewer should be certain that answers are understood and recorded before moving on to the next section of the interview schedule.

Another option, still using an interviewing strategy, is to meet with a group of employees who currently hold the position being studied. If there is a large number of employees who hold the position, it may be useful to select a diverse group, including new and long-time employees, younger and older employees, men and women, different ethnic groups, and so on in the interest of drawing on a wide range of perspectives. Focus group techniques can be used to ensure that an agenda is followed and that perspectives are sought from all participants. Free-flowing discussion is generally not encouraged in group interviews. Whether interviews are individual or group, the interviewer will be expected to take notes during the course of the discussion and to compile them in an orderly fashion that ultimately results in a draft of the job analysis. Once the document has been drafted it should be circulated for review and comment to all participants. Relevant feedback should be incorporated into a second and subsequent drafts until a substantial majority of the participants agree on the way the job analysis is framed and worded.

Job Analysis Questionnaires

Constructing and disseminating questionnaires to employees who currently hold the position being studied (and their supervisors) can be either an alternative or a supplement to interviewing. The decision about whether to use questionnaires will depend to some extent on the number of staff employed in the position being studied and the type of information needed. Having staff members answer questions in writing on their own time is less time-consuming than face-to-face interviewing. Where quantitative data and information are required, they can be more easily gathered through the use of questionnaires than through discussion. For example, if the job analyst needs to know size of caseload or average number of client contacts per month, these data can be compiled by questionnaire. If, however, the severity and complexity of problems brought by clients to the agency are important variables, it may be that consensus can be achieved more directly through discussion of levels of severity than by having workers attempt to describe what they mean by severity and complexity.

For these reasons, job analysts sometimes find that a combination of interview and questionnaire can be useful in producing the type and quality of information needed. Questionnaires completed prior to a group discussion tend to serve as a warm-up exercise and get employees thinking in advance about the kinds of questions that need to be answered, thus making discussion time more efficient. A sample job analysis questionnaire that might be used in a human service agency for the position of Case Manager is illustrated in Figure 10.2.

A number of structured job analysis questionnaires prepared by professional job analysis organizations are available. The Position Analysis Questionnaire (PAQ) is based on many years of research and covers more than 100,000 jobs (McCormick & Jeanneret, 1988). The PAQ contains 194 items, each of which represents a basic element that may be a part of the job. Each item receives a rating. The resulting profile rates the job on five basic traits: (1) having decision-making/communication/social responsibilities, (2) performing

FIGURE 10.2

Job Analysis Questionnaire for a Case Manager

Job Analysis Questionnaire

Name _____   Job Title _____

Highest Degree _____   Total Years of Experience in the Field_____

Job Title of Supervisor _____   Years of Experience in This Position_____

1. **Duties:** Of the following major duties associated with your job, please indicate order of importance or priority from your perspective and estimate the percentage of time you spend on each duty.

                                   Order of Importance   Percentage of Time

    Intake and Screening
    Assessment
    Planning and Contracting
    Implementation and Monitoring
    Evaluation and Termination
    Case Conferences
    Case Recording
    Staff and Administrative Meetings
    Other

2. **Methods:** Please list the methods you use in carrying out the duties of your job (e.g., interviewing, casework, group work, testifying in court, etc.).

3. **Results:** What results are expected for each of the duties listed in Item 1?

4. **Knowledge and Skills:** Please list the major areas of knowledge and skill you believe are necessary to carry out the duties of your job.

5. **Special Qualification:** Please identify any special qualification you believe a person should have if he or she is to excel in this position.

    Also Frequency of Supervision, Size of Workload, Etc.

skilled activities, (3) being physically active, (4) operating vehicles/equipment, and (5) processing information (Dessler, 1997, p. 93). These types of profiles make it possible to compare jobs along these five dimensions.

The Management Position Description Questionnaire (MPDQ) is designed to analyze management and professional positions (Page, 1988). Using a format similar to the PAQ, the MDPQ identifies the extent to which managers are involved in a range of activities and produces scores and a profile that permit comparisons. The advantage of structured job analysis questionnaires is that they are used across many different types of businesses and industries, and comparative data are available. The disadvantage is that they may not produce the kind of information that is needed specifically for job analysis purposes in human service organizations.

Observation

Like all of the other techniques used in job analysis, observation requires planning. A framework for duties and tasks must be established so that observers have some idea of what they are observing. If there are multiple observers, the framework should be designed in a format that ensures that data will be collected in approximately the same manner from one observation to the next. Observers should be trained in techniques of observing, recording, and compiling findings. Observation is best suited to jobs that involve a significant amount of repetition in activities that can be observed (Schmidt et al., 1992). It is less practical for more complex jobs of managers, supervisors, administrators, or professionals in which a significant amount of time may be spent on such tasks as reading, discussion, or analysis, and it is difficult for an observer to know, without interrupting the person being observed, what duties and tasks are being performed. If the position being studied is one in which there is contact with clients, an issue of confidentiality is raised. A worker-client interaction cannot be observed by a third party without permission from both worker and client.

Observation may be used in combination with an interview. An employee is observed for a specific period of time and extensive notes are compiled. Following this observation, the employee is interviewed and asked to interpret any of the duties and tasks not fully understood by the observer. Observation is time-consuming and not as efficient as some of the other approaches to job analysis. It is best reserved for analysis of duties and tasks that are repetitious, involve some physical activity, and whose purpose can be understood by the observer. An observation schedule for an intake interview might look like the following illustration.

Date: 5/5/03   *Time:* 10:15–11:30   *Employee Observed:* R. Jenkins

Duties and Tasks Observed	*Time Spent*	*Topics Covered*	*Problems*
Duty 1: Intake and Screening			
Task 1. Completion of intake form			
Task 2. Determination of eligibility			
Task 3. Identification of presenting problem(s)			
Task 4. Explanation of services			

Diaries and Logs

Very early in the development of the field of management, Frederick Taylor, father of scientific management, developed a technique that came to be known as a time and motion study (Taylor, 1947). This type of study involved recording the activities and motions performed by a worker and the amount of time required for each. Taylor's interest was to find the "one best way" to perform each function by reducing the number of motions and the time it took for each motion to an absolute minimum (Kanigel, 1997).

Essentially the same principle is used in job analysis when workers are asked to keep diaries or logs. Workers are asked to record in a log duties and tasks as they are performing them, and also to record the amount of time required to complete them. For example, a caseworker in a homeless shelter may be asked to stop what he is doing every fifteen minutes and record what he did during that period of time. Or, as an alternative, he may be asked to complete an activity and then to write out a brief description of the activity and indicate how long it took. In either case, the focus is on determining what types of duties and tasks are being performed by personnel who hold a particular position and how long it takes to perform each task. Follow-up interviews or discussion groups can be used to help supplement information gathered through the use of diaries and logs. The following format is one that might be used for a diary or log.

Date   Beginning Time   Ending Time   Description of Activity

Any of the foregoing techniques may be used in combination with each other in the interest of getting complete information in the most efficient manner possible. Job analysts must always be mindful of the fact that the work goes on, and employees continue to carry full workloads even while the job analysis is being conducted.

■ Job Analysis as Central to the Human Resources System

When a job analysis has been completed, it should form the basis of decision making about the job. The job analysis becomes the document that provides the internal consistency and integrity for everything that happens in shaping or modifying the nature of the job. Traditionally, the first activities to follow completion of the job analysis are the preparation of the job description and job specifications. These will be discussed in the following sections. However, beyond these documents, a series of human resource activities emerges from the job analysis as well. These activities include recruitment, selection, hiring, orientation and training, career planning and development, performance appraisal, promotion, and termination. These must not be seen as independent activities but rather as a series of interconnected processes, all of which draw on the job analysis for their focus.

For example, in designing recruitment materials, the job analysis helps to define not only the parameters of the position but also the types of personnel to be recruited. Selection criteria must be consistent with the job analysis. Orientation should be not only to the organization but also to the job as defined and described in the job analysis. Performance appraisal should be consistent with all materials used in recruitment, selection, orientation, and training. The job analysis provides the basis for this consistency.

When each of these processes is approached independently of the others, there is a risk that they may lose those common threads that tie them together. In the absence of a job analysis, selection criteria may be defined by a search committee. When orientation to the job is not part of an overall plan, it may be provided by a disgruntled worker. Without job analysis as its core reference document, performance appraisal may be based on factors influenced by loyalty and personal relationships rather than on job-related performance criteria. This type of failure to maintain a consistent focus on the essential elements of the job can ultimately lead only to poor performance on the part of employees and mediocrity in terms of overall agency effectiveness.

In addition to human resources functions, the job analysis can be used for other purposes as well. Schmidt et al. (1992) propose its use for efficiency and safety improvements (Levine, Thomas, & Sistrunk, 1988), affirmative action program planning (Berwitz, 1988), and development of job aids (Inaba, 1988). Dessler (1997) suggests that job analysis may be used for classification of positions and decisions about compensation, as well as a number of job design considerations.

In summary, it is suggested here that job analysis be considered both a process and a product. As a product or document, there will be core components that will be useful for reference purposes in creating additional documents or in providing a focus for certain activities. As a process, job analysis is really never finished. Sections of the document may need to be updated. Depending on the purpose for which it is to be used, it is possible that a document may not provide all the necessary information, and a process may be needed to supplement information available. For example, if the purpose of conducting a job analysis has to do with reevaluating levels of compensation, additional information may be required on independent decision making and the amount of supervision needed. If the purpose has to do with increasing diversity, the focus may be on cultural competence. Thus, although job analysis data and information may be contained in a formal document, it should always also be understood as a dynamic process designed to yield new and current information.

■ The Job Description

Two important documents that should result from the job analysis are the job description and job specifications. Each of these documents serves specific purposes.

The job description has been defined as ". . . an organized presentation of facts about a job that distinguishes it from other jobs including its purpose, tasks, responsibilities, and worker characteristics" (U.S. Department of Labor, 1982, p. 37). Dessler (1997) proposes the following sections as parts of a complete job description:

- Job identification
- Job summary
- Relationships, responsibilities, and duties
- Authority of incumbent
- Standards of performance

- Working conditions
- Job specifications

Schmidt et al. (1992) use the following categories in their example of a job description:

- Job summary
- Job duties
- General duties
- Relationships
- Qualifications

The job description is designed to fulfill a number of purposes. It represents a summary of the job analysis in terms of defining duties and tasks, working relationships, and qualifications. It is also a document that can have legal status in terms of expressing the organization's position on job expectations to those who hold the job. It's not uncommon for workers, for example, to question certain assigned activities if they do not fall within duties described in the job description. When used in conjunction with recruitment activities, the job description represents to all applicants a statement of what kinds of responsibilities the organization expects the successful candidate to assume and what criteria the applicant must meet in order to qualify for the position.

Parts of the Job Description

In order to meet the many different expectations of job descriptions in human service organizations while keeping the document as concise as possible, it is proposed that they include at least the following headings: (1) job title and summary information, (2) duties, responsibilities, and essential functions, (3) reporting, supervision, and collaborative relationships, and (4) job specifications.

Job Title and Summary Information   The job title and summary information section should list the title and a brief summary statement of the kinds of duties and responsibilities involved. For example, the job of transportation specialist for a child welfare agency might be summarized in the following way:

> Using an agency vehicle, transports clients and sometimes other family members to casework, medical, court, or other appointments and other destinations consistent with the case plan, as requested by caseworkers.

These summary statements are designed as a quick reference to help the reader understand the overall scope of the job without going into too much detail.

Duties, Responsibilities, and Essential Functions   The duties and responsibilities and the essential functions sections are probably the most important parts of the job description in terms of their legal implications and should receive careful review from a number of perspectives including incumbent workers, supervisors, and human resources specialists. Duties can be taken directly from the job analysis. The kind of detail included in a listing of tasks is not necessary in the job description.

For example, in a child welfare agency, a foster care worker position may include the following duties:

1. Participates in the intake process with children in need of foster care and their families.
2. Coordinates foster care placement plans with all relevant parties.
3. Manages assigned cases.
4. Provides direct counseling to children and their families of origin and foster families when indicated.
5. Consults with other professionals involved with the families of origin and foster families.
6. Maintains written case records and prepares necessary reports.
7. Participates in the agency's foster home recruitment efforts.
8. Participates in the agency's foster parent training programs.

Although all of these duties are considered to be important enough to be included in the job analysis and perhaps even in the job description, when it comes to selecting essential functions, duties should be more carefully scrutinized using criteria and definitions proposed earlier in this chapter.

For example, an applicant may be in every other way qualified to perform all the duties relating to the casework process but may be unable to conduct a foster parent training session because of a disability that prevents him or her from standing for long periods as required in conducting classroom training. Is there a place for such an employee within the agency? Can he or she perform the job of foster care social worker if he or she is unable to conduct foster parent training sessions?

This type of scrutiny and analysis of duties and tasks is what is required in determining essential functions. It is an important part of the job description and job announcement. Identifying duties and tasks for a job analysis is approached from the perspective of preparing a comprehensive listing of duties, not from a perspective of limiting duties and tasks. The recruitment, selection, and hiring processes, however, are filled with legal considerations, and identifying and reaching consensus on essential functions is an exercise that will sharpen the agency's understanding of expectations while possibly preventing legal problems at the point of hiring.

Reporting, Supervision, and Collaborative Relationships   A clear description of reporting/supervising/collaborating relationships is essential for the purpose of clarifying the role of the position within the agency. The person to whom a position reports and the person who supervises that position are usually the same, but in special circumstances these responsibilities may be separated. On a traditional organizational chart a box above the position will represent the immediate supervisor. This depiction typically implies that this is the person who gives work assignments, who provides guidance and instruction when needed, who conducts the performance appraisal, and who makes recommendations on salary increases, promotions, or other personnel matters. A simple statement, such as "This position reports to the Program Supervisor of the Foster Care Program," is sufficient to describe reporting and supervising relationships.

In the unusual instance in which there is some type of matrix management relationships, it is possible that the reporting relationship is through the traditional chain of command, whereas day-to-day supervision or consultation is provided by a person with special expertise. For example, if a position of cross-cultural specialist exists within the foster care program, it is possible that the program supervisor would represent the reporting relationship whereas a specially designated senior person with cross-cultural expertise would provide the supervision or consultation on matters of professional knowledge and skill related to the dynamics of ethnicity and culture.

Collaborative relationships can also be described in a sentence or two. For example, the following statement might be used to explain that the person who fills the position of foster care worker is expected to establish and maintain professional relationships both inside and outside the agency:

> This position maintains close working relationships with the children, foster families, and program staff. Carrying out a comprehensive case planning approach requires the position to maintain a high degree of outside contact with contracted service providers, community resources, tutors, professional consultants, physicians, dentists, school personnel, psychotherapists, juvenile courts, and natural parents.

■ Job Specifications

A well-thought-out and clearly written job analysis provides a sound basis for determining job specifications. Job specifications "identify the knowledge, skills, and abilities that prospective applicants should possess to perform a job adequately" (College and University Personnel Association, 1998, p. 3). Education, training, experience, physical capabilities, job knowledge, dexterity, and personal interests and characteristics may be included in job specifications (U.S. Department of Labor, 1982). Job specifications are typically expressed as minimum acceptable qualifications. However, they must meet the job-relatedness test in order to withstand legal challenges. For this reason, the use of equivalencies has evolved in which experience and demonstrated ability to do the job may substitute for rigid educational qualifications, for example.

Job specifications should contain at least two major sections: (1) knowledge and skill, and (2) qualifications. The position taken earlier in this chapter is that the job analysis should include these sections to ensure consistency among all the components of a job. If the issues of knowledge, skill, and qualifications have been addressed in the job analysis, there may be no need for a separate document on job specifications. If agency policy or practice requires a separate document on job specifications for each job, the content may be taken directly from the job analysis, or it may be developed in a more elaborate and detailed manner in the job specifications document. Job specifications should also be included as part of the job description.

Knowledge and Skill

A section on knowledge and skill is an important part of job specifications because it helps to establish expectations for what the incumbent or applicant brings to the position.

Expected knowledge and skill must reflect a clear relationship to duties and tasks. For example, the foster care worker may be required to demonstrate knowledge and skill in the following areas:

- Knowledge of theories of human behavior and stages of human development
- Skill in assessing child, adolescent, and family problems and needs
- Skill in providing psychotherapeutic treatment through individual, family, and/or group work
- Knowledge of the history and traditions of the major ethnic groups served by the agency
- Skill in building and maintaining effective cross-cultural relationships
- Knowledge of state and federal laws and policies governing foster care
- Knowledge of major child welfare issues
- Skill in advocating for major child welfare policy changes at the state level

An alternative to listing specific knowledge and skill requirements is the knowledge, skills, and ability (KSA) statement. Instead of specifying minimum levels of education and experience, the KSA statement provides a narrative statement that describes the knowledge, skills, and abilities required to perform the job (College and University Personnel Association, 1998). For example, instead of itemizing knowledge and skill needed for the foster care worker position, a general statement of qualifications might read as follows:

> Requires a thorough knowledge of foster care practices, with the ability to apply established counseling methods to practice situations. Requires work with families, foster children, and other parties relevant to the stability and maintenance of foster care placements.

This type of statement, because it is more general, is less likely to be challenged as not being job related.

Qualifications

The second and final section of job specifications, qualifications, covers expectations for education, experience, and worker characteristics as identified in the job analysis. Educational requirements are commonly established for positions but must be carefully considered to ensure that they do not pose a discriminatory barrier. For example, the U.S. Supreme Court found an employer's requirement of a high school education discriminatory in locations where statistics showed that the requirement disqualified African Americans at a much higher rate than whites and for which there was no evidence that the requirement related to successful job performance in any significant way (College and University Personnel Association, 1998).

It is incumbent on the employer to determine whether a person who has not achieved a specified level of education can perform the duties of a position. When in doubt about qualifications in either education or experience, it may be better to refine criteria in duties and tasks, and/or knowledge and skill so that the focus is more clearly on the applicant's ability to do the job and less on his or her past history.

Language proficiency is another qualification that can be used as long as it can be demonstrated that it is job related. If the policy has an adverse effect on a particular ethnic group, federal law requires that the hiring organization be able to demonstrate that the policy is related to job performance (College and University Personnel Association, 1998).

These foregoing factors represent suggested sections for a job description. There is not unanimous agreement in the literature on all of the parts, and it is always advisable to maintain flexibility and adaptability to agency needs in determining a format for job descriptions. Because of the potential legal ramifications, and for the purpose of guiding those who write these documents, it is useful to establish, in agency policy, what sections are to be included in the basic job description document. A sample job description is illustrated in Table 10.1.

TABLE 10.1

Job Description

Job Description	
Job Title:	Foster Care Worker
Job Summary:	The person filling this position develops and implements treatment plans to address each child's current needs while designing long-term goals to help the child achieve optimum physical, emotional, and social growth and development.
Job Duties:	1. Participates in intake and screening process with families who are accepted for service. 2. Completes social history and psychosocial assessment on family. 3. Coordinates work with all relevant parties to develop and implement placement plans. 4. Manages assigned cases, maintains regular contact with children and foster parents. 5. Develops and coordinates therapeutic, health, educational, legal, cross-cultural, and other resources. 6. Complies with all legal and court-related requirements affecting the case. 7. Maintains case records and prepares necessary reports. 8. Participates in foster home recruitment and training efforts.
Essential Functions:	1. Participation in all functions related to direct contact with foster children, their foster families, and their natural families. 2. Coordination of all agency and community resources necessary to the well-being of children and their foster and natural families. 3. Compliance with legal requirements.
Relationships:	The person filling this position reports directly to the program manager for the foster care program. May report to the director of training for responsibilities related to recruitment and training of foster parents.
Qualifications:	Master of social work (MSW) degree from a school of social work accredited by the Council on Social Work Education. At least four years of clinical experience in a child welfare, foster care, or other child and family setting. Ability to relate well to youth and families from many different cultural and ethnic groups.

■ The Job Announcement

When a vacancy occurs, the job description and job specifications are valuable resources for developing the job announcement. This document is written with potential applicants as the target audience, so they should be provided with as much information as possible about the critical elements of the job and the application process. Included in the job announcement should be the following items:

1. Title of the position.
2. Duties, responsibilities, and essential functions.
3. Reporting, supervisory, and collaborative relationships.
4. Qualifications.
5. Application materials required.
6. Application deadline.
7. Name and address of the contact person.
8. A statement that the agency is an equal opportunity/affirmative action employer, if applicable. This statement is a federal, affirmative action requirement.
9. Optional, but useful, is a brief description of the agency and the types of services it provides.

An alternative is to develop a shorter version of the job announcement and to include in the job application packet a copy of the job description and other relevant documents. Job announcements, in a sense, represent a part of a contracting process. Once positions are advertised, employers are limited to evaluating applicants on the basis of the advertised criteria. Job announcements should also be seen as one small part of the recruitment process. Both the position and the agency should be described in the types of positive terms that would encourage an applicant to want to apply for the job.

■ Investing Time in Job Analysis

Developing and maintaining the types of documents recommended in this chapter is a major, time-consuming undertaking. Compiling a job analysis for each position within the organization involves almost all levels of staff and can require a considerable amount of research. Once the job analysis is completed, the job description, job specifications, and job announcement should flow in a fairly direct and straightforward way from the core document and not require a great deal of additional analysis or research. The question is inevitably raised: Is it worth the time and effort involved? The answer is that the job analysis forms the foundation or core of all of the remaining human resources processes. Is it important to have consistency and integrity in the human resources system? For those organizations that aspire to excellence, there is little question that the time and energy spent on building a solid foundation for the human resources system clearly represent a sound investment.

SUMMARY

1. **What Is Job Analysis?** Job analysis is the procedure through which an employer determines the duties of a position and the characteristics of an individual who should be hired for it.
   - *Job Analysis as Both a Process and a Product.* Job analysis is typically defined as a process that produces job descriptions and job specifications. There may also be some value in human service organizations in producing a job analysis document and keeping it on file for future reference.

2. **Conducting a Job Analysis**
   - *What Is a Job?* The concept of a job fits into a taxonomy that provides classifications for the smallest components, called elements, through the highest and most complex classification, called the job family.
   - *The Elements of Job Analysis.* Proposed elements include the following eight parts:
     Part 1. Duties and Tasks. Duties are the major categories; tasks are the more detailed activities in each category.
     Part 2. Methods. The ways in which duties and tasks are carried out.
     Part 3. Results. The accomplishments that are expected when duties and tasks are completed.
     Part 4. Required Knowledge and Skill. What does the person who holds this position need to know and be able to do to carry out duties and tasks?
         Cultural and gender competencies. What cultural or gender competencies are expected in fulfilling job expectations?
     Part 5. Essential Functions. Those functions that the person who holds this position must be able to perform.
     Part 6. Entry Requirements in Terms of Education and Experience. What levels of education and experience are required of the person who holds this position?
     Part 7. Worker Characteristics. What individual traits or characteristics are required of the person who holds this position?
     Part 8. The Context of the Work. This category includes such factors as location on the organizational chart, supervision, workload expectations, and other factors not covered in parts 1 through 7.

3. **Methods of Collecting Job Analysis Information.** A framework for analysis should be established, along with a plan for collecting data and information.
   - *Job Analysis Interviewing.* One-to-one interviewing requires an interview schedule. It can be time-consuming if several staff are interviewed for each job to be analyzed, but it is a good opportunity to get detailed information.
   - *Job Analysis Questionnaires.* Questionnaires or surveys are much easier to deal with than individual interviewing. More staff can be surveyed. Questions must be carefully designed and the instrument easy to complete.
   - *Observation.* Planning with someone familiar with the job is important so that the observer knows what to look for.
   - *Diaries and Logs.* These represent a form of time and motion study. Data can be useful for understanding the duties and tasks, their priorities, and how much time staff spend on each.

4. **Job Analysis as Central to the Human Resources System.** All human resources functions from recruitment through termination should be based on the job analysis.

5. **The Job Description.** An organized presentation of facts about a job.
   - *Parts of the Job Description.* Parts should include job title and summary information; duties, responsibilities, and essential functions; and reporting, supervisory, and collaborative relationships.

   Job Title and Summary Information. This section includes a brief, one- or two-sentence summary of the job.

   Duties, Responsibilities, and Essential Functions. Major duties are listed in this section. Essential functions are defined.

   Reporting, Supervision, and Collaborative Relationships. This section defines who provides supervision or consultation, specifies the person or position to whom this position reports, and identifies other working relationships.

6. **Job Specifications.** The information for job specifications is drawn from the job analysis. If a job analysis document is kept on file, a separate job specifications document may be redundant. The data and information compiled are very important for many purposes.
   - *Knowledge and Skill.* This section defines what the person who fills this position needs to know and be able to do in order to fulfill the requirements of the position.
   - *Qualifications.* This section defines what education, experience, or other worker qualifications are expected of the person who fills this position.

7. **The Job Announcement.** This document includes selected items from the job description and job specifications, with additions that provide information about the application process.

8. **Investing Time in Job Analysis.** The process of job analysis is time-consuming, but it can produce an understanding of a job that is potentially very valuable. Data and information gathered during the job analysis process are useful in many ways.

EXERCISES

Please complete the following sections of your manual based on the content covered in Chapter 10.

Section 10: Job Analysis

10.1 Policy Statement on Job Analysis. Write a policy statement that makes clear your agency's requirement that a job analysis will be written for each position within the organization, and state what your job analysis must include. Attach a sample job analysis of one position in the organization, identified as Document 10.1a.

10.2 Policy Statement on Job Descriptions. Write a policy statement that makes clear your agency's requirement that a job description will be written for each position within the organization, and state what your job description must include. Attach a sample job description for one position in the organization, identified as Document 10.2a.

REFERENCES

Arizona State University Office of Equal Employment Opportunity/Affirmative Action. (1995). *Nondiscrimination and affirmative action: Legal basis.* Unpublished monograph. Author.

Berwitz, C. (1988). The role of job analysis in achieving affirmative action. In S. Gael (Ed.), *The job analysis handbook for business, industry, and government* (Vol. 1, pp. 173–189). New York: John Wiley.

Brody, R. (1993). *Effectively managing human service organizations.* Newbury Park, CA: Sage.

Cascio, W. (1987). *Applied psychology in personnel management* (3rd ed.). Englewood Cliffs, NJ: Prentice-Hall.

Chung, D. (1992). Asian cultural commonalities. In S. Furuto, R. Biswa, D. Chung, K. Murase, & F. Ross-Sheriff (Eds.), *Social work practice with Asian Americans* (pp. 274–275). Newbury, CA: Sage.

College and University Personnel Association (CUPA). (1998). *Interview guide for supervisors* (5th ed.). Washington, DC: Author.

Cross, T., Bazron, B., Dennis, K., & Isaacs, M. (1989). *Towards a culturally competent system of care.* Washington, DC: Georgetown University Child Development Center, Technical Assistance Center.

Dessler, G. (1997). *Human resource management* (7th ed.). Upper Saddle River, NJ: Prentice-Hall.

Driessnack, C. (1979). Financial impact of effective human resource management. *Personnel Administrator,* 24 (December), 62–66.

Duston, R., Russell, K., & Kerr, L. (1992). *ADA compliance manual for higher education: A guide to Title I.* Washington, DC: College and University Personnel Association.

Fine, S., & Wiley, W. (1971). *An introduction to functional job analysis: A scaling of selected tasks from the social welfare field.* Kalamazoo, MI: Upjohn Institute for Employment Research.

Gilligan, C. (1982). *In a different voice.* Cambridge, MA: Harvard University Press.

Green, J. (1995). *Cultural awareness in the human services: A multi-ethnic approach* (2nd ed.). Boston: Allyn & Bacon.

Inaba, K. (1988). Job aid preparation. In S. Gael (Ed.), *The job analysis handbook for business, industry, and government* (Vol. 1, pp. 243–258). New York: John Wiley.

Kanigel, R. (1997). *The one best way: Frederick Winslow Taylor and the enigma of efficiency.* New York: Penguin.

Levine, E., Thomas, J., & Sistrunk, F. (1988). Selecting a job analysis approach. In S. Gael (Ed.), *The job analysis handbook for business, industry, and government* (Vol. 1, pp. 339–352). New York: John Wiley.

Lewis, H. (1976). The structure of professional skill. In B. Ross & S. Khinduka (Eds.), *Social work in practice* (p. 3). Washington, DC: National Association of Social Workers.

Locke, D. (1992). *Increasing multicultural understanding: A comprehensive model.* Newbury Park, CA: Sage.

McCormick, E., & Jeanneret, P. (1988). Position analysis questionnaire. In S. Gael (Ed.), *The job analysis handbook for business, industry, and government* (Vol. 2, pp. 825–842). New York: John Wiley.

Page, R. (1988). Management position description questionnaire. In S. Gael (Ed.), *The job analysis handbook for business, industry, and government* (Vol. 2, pp. 860–879). New York: John Wiley.

Schmidt, M., Riggar, T., Crimando, W., & Bordieri, J. (1992). *Staffing for success: A guide for health and human service professionals.* Newbury Park, CA: Sage.

Sue, D., & Sue, D. (1990). *Counseling the culturally different: Theory & practice* (2nd ed.). New York: John Wiley & Son.

Tannen, D. (1990). *You just don't understand: Women and men in conversation.* New York: Ballantine.

Taylor, F. (1947). *Scientific management.* New York: Harper & Row.

U.S. Department of Labor. (1982). *A guide to job analysis.* Menomonie, WI: Materials Development Center, Stout Vocational Rehabilitation Institute, University of Wisconsin-Stout.

Strengthening the Organization through Excellent Recruitment, Selection, and Hiring Practices

- The Importance of Sound Recruitment Practices
- Basic Recruitment Concepts and Issues
- The Preplanning, Recruitment, Selection, and Hiring Processes
- Recruitment
- Employee Selection
- Hiring

Upon completion of this chapter, the reader will be able to:

- Prepare a plan for recruitment, selection, and hiring for a designated position within a human service organization.
- Write a job announcement that is based on the job analysis and complies with human resources law.
- Design instruments for preliminary and secondary screening.
- Plan a structured interview that complies with human resources law.

Assumptions

- That job openings represent important opportunities to improve the organization that should not be wasted by failure to follow sound recruiting practices.
- That preliminary and secondary screenings are crucial to the selection process and require carefully crafted instruments and procedures to increase the likelihood of making the best selection.

■ The Importance of Sound Recruitment Practices

Bringing together the right mix of personalities and talents is vitally important to maximizing organizational effectiveness, and the opportunities to change the makeup of personnel are few and limited. That is why it is so important to take advantage of opportunities when they present themselves, and one that occurs fairly regularly in most human service agencies is the filling of a vacancy. Agencies that have planned ahead will be prepared to make the most of this opportunity and will generate a large and diverse pool of applicants from which to choose. Other agencies will take actions only as they are absolutely necessary and will often find that they are not able to improve the organization by bringing on a highly talented and enthusiastic new employee, as they hoped they would. The Lakeside Mental Health Clinic was such an agency.

> Lakeside provides services to individuals and families in need of help with drug, alcohol, and mental health problems. They employ fifteen clinical staff and attempt to promote teamwork among the three programs because it often happens that clients who come for services could logically be served by more than one program. Although most of the staff were committed to collaboration and teamwork, a small group, led by Frieda S., was very possessive about what the unit saw as its "turf" and attempted in every way to maintain exclusive control of the treatment plans for clients served by this unit. Frieda was a recovering alcoholic. She was able to persuade several of the staff in the alcohol program that clinical staff in the drug and mental health programs did not really understand alcohol addiction and would not be able to provide effective treatment to clients suffering from alcohol addiction. As a result, many clients with multiple problems were treated only for their alcoholism and frequently suffered relapses. Efforts by administrators to get Frieda to work more collaboratively resulted in lip service to the team concept, but behavior did not change.
>
> Frieda was a longtime employee and showed no signs of interest in changing jobs, so it was with a good deal of surprise that program managers, agency administrators, and clinical staff learned of her plans to move back to a small town to be closer to her family. Although outwardly expressing their appreciation for her many years of service, agency staff members were secretly celebrating and looking forward to getting a new person into the position. There was such a strong sense that a new hire would be an improvement that little effort was put into the recruitment process.
>
> Two days before Frieda left the agency her position was advertised in the local paper. Because of the heavy demand for services, the position had to be filled promptly. Instead of a rush of applicants there was merely a trickle. By the closing date four applications had been received. Two applicants did not qualify for the position. Follow-up telephone calls revealed that one of the two qualified applicants had accepted another job, leaving only one qualified applicant. When the interview process was completed, the interview team and

staff members in general were less than impressed but felt that at least the new employee would pick up the mounting caseload responsibilities left behind by Frieda and could probably do an adequate job, which she did. In a short time, however, the new employee made it clear that she preferred to work alone and was not really interested in collaboration and teamwork.

This is the type of missed opportunity that happens all the time in social service agencies. In the more forward-looking agency, where there is excitement about the mission and function of the agency, and where administrators and managers are looking for every opportunity to move a bit closer to excellence, there tends also to be a recognition that a vacancy is a very precious opportunity to make a positive change. In this type of agency, way before the first hint that an employee is about to leave the agency, much of the machinery is already in place to support active recruitment and conduct a thorough search.

◼ Basic Recruitment Concepts and Issues

Recruitment of staff has only one clear and singular purpose: to generate a maximum number of highly qualified and diverse applicants. A large pool, although more work for those who must process the applications, is a compliment to the agency, a reflection of the attractiveness of the position, and an affirmation of the quality of the recruitment process.

As established in Chapter 10, recruitment is rooted in equal employment opportunity/ affirmative action law, in human resources planning, and in the job analysis. Figure 11.1 depicts this relationship.

Establishing Employment Policies

Policies establish guidelines within which organizations function and serve as the reference documents for agency operations in each area of responsibility. An organization can save itself time and trouble by thinking through important issues before there is pressure to fill a vacancy. Employment policies ensure that decisions made during a recruitment and selection process will not be unique to the situation but rather will follow established pro-

---

FIGURE 11.1

Recruitment Planning Based on Job Analysis, Profile of Staff Needs, and Human Resources Law

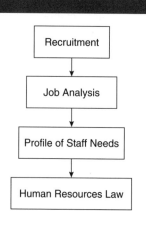

cedures using approved criteria. Jensen (1981) proposes eight sections that should be included in employment policies:

1. *Statement of nondiscrimination.* A statement that applicants will be considered regardless of sex, race, age, religion, veteran status or disability.
2. *Hiring authority.* Who will have the final authority to make an offer of employment? This often depends on the size of the organization. It may remain at the top or may be delegated.
3. *Starting salary approval.* This authority to set starting salaries also may remain at the top or be delegated. Supervisors sometimes recommend, while top management retains final approval.
4. *Promotion from within.* Policies should make clear the rights of employees to apply for open positions. Some organizations agree to consider internal candidates before the position is opened to outside applicants.
5. *Hiring of friends and relatives.* Guidelines should be established so that it is clear that friends and relatives do not get positions simply because of their relationships.
6. *Use of reference checks.* The point in the process when references are to be consulted should be established in policy so that it does not vary from one candidate to another or one search to another. Also the format—written or telephone.
7. *Use of tests.* What tests, if any, will be used? When will they be administered? How will they be scored? How will the scores be used? Answers to these questions will help keep testing practices within the law.
8. *Recruitment sources used.* Use of a range of recruitment sources and strategies can help to insure a diverse pool of applicants. (pp. 20–23)

Changes in Status

Recruitment, selection, and hiring are parts of a process that begins, hopefully, with a very large pool and ends with a single, final candidate. The status of the pool of potentially interested people changes as the process moves forward, as depicted in Figure 11.2.

At the beginning of the process, those who have a potential interest in the open position(s) are considered part of a target audience or potential recruits. This means that the

Changing Status of the Pool of People Who May Be Interested in a Job Opening

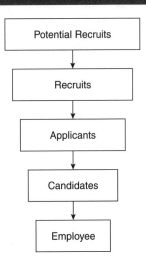

recruitment and selection committee has reviewed the human resources plan and has determined that people with certain characteristics will be targeted. Potential recruits fall into categories based on qualifications, demographics, and other considerations. When the recruitment budget has been examined and target audiences are reduced to those that will actually receive recruitment materials, the status of the pool changes to recruit. Ideally the pool of recruits continues to be very large and diverse in accordance with a well-thought-out recruitment plan. Once an application is submitted, the status changes to applicant. The applicant pool is an important group to the agency and should be treated with great attention to detail because anyone in this pool could soon become a coworker, and impressions made during the recruitment and selection process tend to be lasting.

When the date for applications has closed, the selection process begins. A common approach to narrowing down the pool is first to eliminate all those applicants who do not meet qualifications. Those applicants remaining are then organized, using a variety of techniques that will be discussed later in this chapter, into a priority listing from the most qualified and suitable to the least. When the list has been pared down to those applicants who will be invited for an interview, the status changes to candidate. The list of candidates is often referred to as the "short list." In small nonprofit agencies, when there is only a single position to be filled, it is common to invite up to three candidates for an interview. In larger agencies in which there are multiple positions to be filled, the number of candidates will be determined by the number of positions to be filled. A good rule of thumb is to have at least three qualified and suitable options available for each open position. Finally, when the interviews have been completed and an offer is made and accepted, the status changes to employee.

■ The Preplanning, Recruitment, Selection, and Hiring Processes

Preplanning, recruitment, selection, and hiring procedures include a number of steps to be completed between the time it is first known that there will be a vacancy and the point at which the new employee is hired. A planning tool, such as a Gantt chart (a project management chart named after its originator, Henry Gantt), can be very useful in laying out the process and projecting time frames for each phase or activity. Typical activities in each phase will include the following:

Preplanning
■ Review the job analysis, profile of staff needs, and human resources law.

Recruitment
■ Write the job announcement.
■ Identify target audiences and potential recruits. Disseminate recruitment and application materials. Process applications and respond to applicants.

Selection
■ Preliminary screening.
■ Secondary screening.
■ Interview candidates.

Hiring
■ Offer of employment.

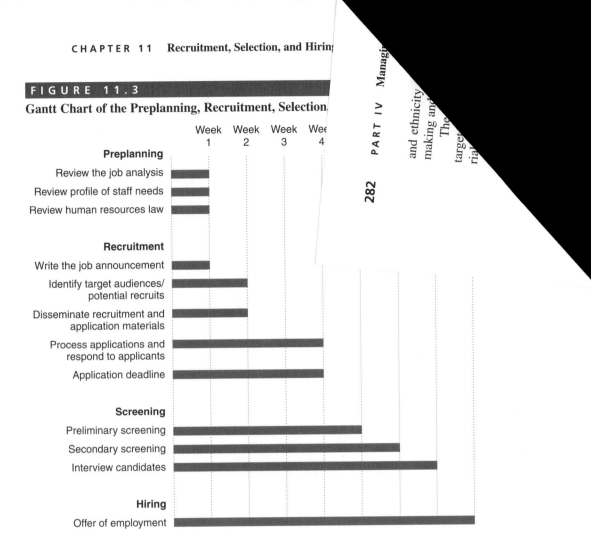

FIGURE 11.3

Gantt Chart of the Preplanning, Recruitment, Selection

Figure 11.3 depicts the steps of the recruitment, selection, and hiring processes in Gantt chart form. If a more compressed timeframe is necessary the Gantt chart can depict days instead of weeks.

■ Recruitment

The processes involved in bringing a new employee on board require knowledge, skill, experience, and input from a variety of perspectives. Organizations that leave these processes in the hands of one person are vulnerable to perceptions of bias. For these reasons, it is advisable that a recruitment and selection committee be appointed by the hiring authority. Weinbach advises, "The selection of a new staff member is not and should not be a unilateral decision by any one individual. Input can be gleaned from a number of sources, but difficult decisions must be made regarding the soliciting of available help and how much influence it should have in the final decision to hire or not to hire a potential employee" (Weinbach, 1998, p. 100). A recruitment and selection committee will ideally represent program staff, supervisory staff, management, and support staff. Diversity in terms of gender, age,

will help to ensure that important perspectives are represented in decision
recommendations.

recruitment process includes (1) writing the job announcement, (2) identifying the
audience and potential recruits, (3) disseminating recruitment and application mate-
s, and (4) processing applications and responding to applicants.

Preparing the Job Announcement

Once the advanced planning activities have been completed, the first order of business in
recruiting is to develop the job announcement. This is the document that will be disseminated to everyone who inquires about the position. Job announcements, like job descriptions, are usually straightforward, factual descriptions of the job, slightly modified to guide
the interested recruit toward application. Schmidt, Riggar, Crimando, and Bordieri (1992,
p. 52) suggest that the following items be included in a job announcement:

- Position or title
- Brief description of the job
- Description of agency
- Qualifications
- Location
- Starting date
- Time frame for applications
- Statement of what to submit (or how to apply)
- An equal opportunity/affirmative action employer

The College and University Personnel Association (1998) emphasizes the importance
of "essential functions" in advertising the position. The Equal Employment Opportunity
Commission regulations address three aspects of essential functions:

1. Whether performance of a function is the reason that a position exists,
2. The number of other employees available to perform the function, and
3. The degree of expertise or skill required to perform the function. (p. 18)

Concerns about essential functions reflect the fact that many job descriptions or job
announcements contain items that are considered part of the job but are seldom performed.
A written job announcement or job description that includes essential functions and is sent
to all applicants is more likely to withstand challenges than one developed after applicants
or candidates have been reviewed.

The job announcement (together with other materials sent to applicants) takes on the
form of a legal document. Screening and selection must be based on criteria that have been
disseminated to all applicants. Preparation of the job announcement should include a
review of the job analysis and the job description. A sample job announcement is included
as Table 11.1.

Identifying Target Audiences
and Potential Recruits

The next task faced by the recruitment and selection committee is to identify the groups to
be targeted for recruitment and the methods to be used. Review of the human resources plan

TABLE 11.1

Job Announcement

Job Announcement	
Position or Title:	Case Manager III
Brief description of the job:	The person filling this position develops and implements plans to address problems faced by clients who are homeless, unemployed, and who have few resources to become self-sufficient. The focus of planning with clients is on identifying and meeting individual needs in order to develop the stability necessary to begin to explore the employment and training markets.
Essential functions:	Intake and screening functions; assessment of client needs; planning with client for rehabilitation; collaboration with community agencies; evaluation of client progress.
Description of agency:	New Directions is a 72-bed residential facility for single, homeless men. It is located near the downtown area of a city of over 500,000. Many resources to serve this population are located within the immediate neighborhood. Funding is from federal and state programs.
Qualifications:	Master of social work (MSW) degree from a school of social work accredited by the Council on Social Work Education. At least two years of experience in providing direct services to clients who are homeless and/or unemployed. Ability to relate comfortably with the homeless and with other agencies that provide services to this population.
Starting date:	July 1, 20XX
Time frame for applications:	Applications will be accepted through May 25, 20XX.
Statement of what to submit (or how to apply):	All applicants must submit (1) a completed copy of the application form, and (2) a current résumé to: Carolyn Holmes, Chair Recruitment and Selection Committee New Directions 555 E. Main City, State, Zip
An equal opportunity/ affirmative action employer:	New Directions is an equal employment opportunity, affirmative action employer.

and the job analysis will help to develop a profile of the types of applicants the committee would like to see in the pool. The goal, as previously stated, is to generate a maximum number of highly qualified and diverse applicants. Job qualifications, including education, experience, and required knowledge and skill, will begin to set limits on potential recruits. For example, if the job requires a master of social work (MSW) degree, a large metropolitan area may have as many as five or six thousand people who have the necessary degree, but requirements for experience, knowledge, and skill may pare that list down to two or three thousand. Desired demographic characteristics may lead the recruitment effort in a direction of sending recruitment materials to specialized sources where they are more likely to be noticed by African American, Latino, Asian American, Native American, disabled people, or older workers who are potential recruits.

Business and industry turn to a number of sources for applicants, including advertising, employment agencies, temporary help agencies, executive recruiters, college recruiting, and computerized employee databases (Dessler, 1997). Jensen (1981) proposes that at least the following sources be used: (1) state employment agencies, (2) private employment agencies, (3) local high schools, (4) colleges and universities, (5) community organizations, (6) newspaper ads, (7) employee referrals, and (8) contacts with other organizations (p. 23).

For human service agencies, the usefulness of these sources will vary, depending on the type(s) of position(s) open. Clearly, advertising and job postings are basic and must be a part of every recruitment strategy. Local daily newspapers provide a source for advertising, as do professional journals and newsletters. It is important to ensure that advertising efforts include newspapers, journals, and newsletters that are targeted to highly specialized audiences, such as newspapers that serve ethnic communities. In this way it is more likely that a diverse pool of applicants will be generated. Figure 11.4 illustrates an advertisement for a position as a case manager in a homeless shelter.

Employment agencies and temporary help agencies may be a source of applicants for hourly positions such as secretaries, receptionists, child care workers, maintenance, bookkeepers, and others. These sources are unlikely to be of great value in recruiting professionals, managers, or executives. Some communities have specialized job banks or "hot lines" that provide information on job openings for selected professional or technical positions. These centers can serve as good resources if the information is updated at least every few days and if the telephone number or Web site is given wide publicity. A significant part of recruitment by some of the major corporations today is conducted over the Internet. Many organizations provide an opportunity for interested recruits to complete an application electronically, thus saving time for the applicant and generating a larger pool for the organization.

Executive recruiters (also known as headhunters) are "special employment agencies retained by employers to seek out top-management talent for their clients" (Dessler, 1997, p. 144). Their fees can reach $30,000 to $40,000, so it is unlikely that this source would be used by a small agency. However, the large nonprofit or the public agency that is willing to make the investment may find the payoff can be significant in terms of the pool of qualified and suitable applicants generated. Local agencies rarely have the resources to conduct the kind of search that an executive recruitment firm is able to carry out. For the local agency it can be discouraging when, using traditional methods of advertising, the majority of applicants prove to be people who have, for one reason or another, not worked out well in other positions and are looking for an opportunity to get away from a bad situation rather than for the challenge of leading an agency into a bright and dynamic future. For executive positions, a regional or national search by an executive recruiter may well be worth the investment.

College recruiting can be a productive source of talent for agencies that need to fill entry-level professional positions. Many universities have career days, often featuring specialized

FIGURE 11.4

Job Advertisement

Make an investment in Human Potential

NEW DIRECTIONS

Is a temporary shelter for homeless, unemployed single men. We employ highly skilled professionals who are committed to work in collaboration with other community-based agencies to contribute to the rehabilitation of men who lack skills needed for independent living.

Position: Case Manager III

The person filling this position develops and implements plans to address problems faced by clients who are homeless, unemployed and who have few resources to become self-sufficient. Duties will include intake and screening functions; assessment of client needs; planning with client for rehabilitation; collaboration with community agencies; evaluation of client progress.

Qualifications

Master of Social Work (MSW) degree from a school of social work accredited by the Council on Social work Education. At least two years of experience in providing direct services to clients who are homeless and/or unemployed.

Application Deadline:

May 25, 20XX
Starting date:
July 1, 20XX

All applicants must submit (1) a completed copy of the application form, and (2) a current résumé to:

Carolyn Holmes,
Chair Recruitment and
Selection Committee
New Directions
555 E. Main
City, State, Zip

An Equal Opportunity/Affirmative Action Employer

areas of employment such as teaching or human services. Schools of social work, psychology departments, or counseling departments also may set aside a day in which those near graduation may meet potential employers. In addition, many agencies find that providing internships for students presents an opportunity to observe the student's work habits, skills, and personal qualities over a period of time to determine whether the person might be compatible with agency staff.

Disseminating Recruitment and Application Materials

Packets should be prepared for dissemination to all those who inquire about the position. Again, budget constraints may influence the method. If the pool is small, mailings are usually affordable. Some organizations require that interested persons either pick up application packets or get the information over the Internet. Contents, at a minimum, should include the job announcement and an application form. Brochures and program materials are also helpful. Application forms generally require a number of types of information including (1) identifying information such as name, address, citizenship, and other items; (2) education, (3) employment history, (4) special honors and achievements, and (5) professional memberships and/or service activities. Some organizations ask simply for a résumé and references. It is important, at the point of preparing application materials, to remember that résumés follow no uniform, prescribed format, and information provided may not be adequate for screening purposes.

Dessler (1997) states that a completed application should allow a selection committee to make judgments in four areas:

1. On substantive matters such as meeting job qualifications,
2. On the applicant's previous progress and growth,
3. On the applicant's length of employment in previous positions, and
4. On the applicant's likelihood of success in the vacant position. (p. 154)

If the position requires specialized knowledge, skills, and/or personal qualities, the application materials should be designed to ensure that information needed for screening purposes is provided by applicants. It will be time well spent to take the agency's standardized application form, if one exists, and examine it side by side with the job announcement. The question to be answered is: What information will the recruitment and selection committee need to have in order to make informed decisions in screening applicants and selecting candidates? Job qualifications and specifications or essential functions identified in the job description may require that an addendum be attached to the application, soliciting information that is needed to complete the initial screening in a fair, impartial, and thorough manner. Dessler (1997) suggests that most organizations need several application forms to cover the range of needed information from entry-level or hourly personnel through top-management applicants. Figure 11.5 illustrates a standardized type of application form.

Figure 11.6 illustrates an addendum specific to a position of Case Manager III in an agency that provides temporary shelter to homeless, unemployed single men.

FIGURE 11.5

Job Application Form

Employment Application

Position Applying for _____ Date of Application _____

Schedule ( ) Full-time   ( ) Part-time

Personal Information

Name _____ Social Security Number _____ Authorized for Employment in U.S.? ____

Address _____ Home Telephone Number _____

Education

Name of Institution	City, State	Focus of Studies	Graduated, Degree
			Yes No
High School			
Community College			
College/University			
Graduate School			
Other			

Employment History

Name of Employer	Address	Dates of Employment		Position	Duties	Salary
		From	To			

Soliciting Reference Letters

Brief comments at this point are appropriate about the use of references in the application process. Most applicants (and most references, for that matter) would prefer that references not be required unless the applicant has reached the candidate status. Job announcements, depending on the attractiveness of the position, may generate anywhere from ten to more than a hundred applications. If three letters of reference are required for every applicant, a great deal of paperwork may be produced, much of which will prove to be of little value. Of greater concern, busy people have been asked to take the time to write letters that may not even be read. It is usually more efficient, both for the applicant and for the screening

FIGURE 11.6

Supplement or Addendum to Standardized Employment Application

Supplementary Employment Application for Case Manager III Position

Name _____ Social Security Number _____ Date of Application _____

Please describe briefly your responsibilities in your previous employment in dealing with homeless clients.

Please share your perspectives on the positives and negatives of working with this population.

Please describe briefly your experiences in collaborating with other community-based organizations.

Please share your perspectives on the positives and negatives of collaborating with community agencies.

Please explain briefly why you are interested in this position.

committee, to request that letters of reference be sent only when an applicant has at least made it through the first level of screening. It is also a common practice for the person making the final decision about hiring to telephone references as a follow-up to the reference letter. Jensen (1981) offers the following suggestion about references: "Reference checks should be the last step in the screening process to confirm evaluations or explore potential problems uncovered in interviews" (p. 12).

Processing Applications and Responding to Applicants

As applications are received, it is a good practice to have a log set up and maintained by the person to whom the applications are addressed. The log represents a chronological tally of responses to the job announcement. Columns can be set up for (1) date application received, (2) name of applicant, (3) application form(s) received, (4) résumé received, and other relevant information that will provide a ready reference for monitoring the completeness of each application. Although it involves extra work and expense, it is advisable that the agency recruiting for the position acknowledge receipt of application materials. A form letter or even a postcard is acceptable. The purpose is simply to let the applicant know that materials have been received and to thank the applicant for considering employment at the agency. These simple courtesies will pay rich dividends in terms of fostering positive public relations for the agency.

Finally, throughout the recruitment process care should be taken to ensure that all recruits and applicants are treated the same. Whatever instructions are given to one should be given to all. If information is provided over the telephone, it is worthwhile to prepare a script for those who are expected to respond to questions about the job opening. If there are afterthoughts about possible additions to or deletions from the job announcement, this type of action must be avoided. Those involved in recruitment and selection must always keep in mind that any changes in the documents or in the process from what was initially advertised have the effect of dividing the recruits or applicants into two or more groups: those that received the original materials and those that received the modified materials. Such actions are likely to be ruled discriminatory and illegal if challenged. That is why it is so important to put the planning efforts up front. Ensure that the process is well planned, and then stay the course through the recruitment, screening, selection, and hiring processes. The College and University Personnel Association (1998) advises: "For a hiring process to be effective, everyone involved must be aware that significant legal limitations restrict an employer's selection decisions" (p. 1).

■ Employee Selection

Over the years, because of the complexity of laws associated with the selection process, employee selection has become a challenging and difficult task. Selection is the process between the recruitment/application phase and the hiring decision. It is a process designed to reduce the list of applicants to a manageable number that will be assessed in a more intensive way in order to have available as much information on the final candidates as possible prior to making the hiring decision.

A critical issue in selection and hiring is fair, equal, and consistent treatment of all applicants. Fair treatment requires that subjectivity be reduced to the lowest possible point and that reliable and valid measures be used to assess a person's qualifications.

The personal interview remains the overwhelming choice as the final step in the selection process (American Society for Personnel Administration, 1983). One study revealed that 99 percent of employers used interviews as a selection tool (Ulrich & Trumbo, 1965). A number of studies have revealed that factors such as physical attractiveness or a likeable personality can affect the interviewer's ability to be objective (Morrow, 1990; Trent, 1987). The challenge, then, is to find the person who possesses the knowledge, skills, and personal qualities that best fit the profile of needs and expectations for the position while minimizing the extent to which interviewer bias influences the hiring decision.

The legal implications of the selection and hiring processes argue strongly for having everyone involved in these processes undergo thorough training on affirmative action and equal employment opportunity law as well as on methods and strategies available for selection. However, the pressure to fill a position in a timely manner often overrides the wisdom of approaching the process in a thorough and systematic way. For this reason, it is important to have selection policies and a well-organized screening system with valid and reliable instruments in place. The screening system is typically conducted in two phases, preliminary screening and secondary screening.

Preliminary Screening

The objective of the preliminary screening process is to select, from the total pool of applicants, a small number, representing the best qualified applicants, who will move to candidate status, the final phase before hiring. During the preliminary screening process, the charge to the recruitment and selection committee is (1) to comply with all affirmative action/equal employment opportunity regulations, (2) to eliminate applicants who do not meet qualifications, (3) to select the applicants whose records indicate that they would be able to perform the position in a highly competent and productive manner, and (4) to select applicants who meet the needs of the organization in terms of its preferred demographic and expertise profile. The challenge to the committee is to accomplish this charge primarily if not exclusively from a review of the application packet submitted. During this phase interviews are not commonly conducted; nor are references typically checked at the applicant stage. The limited amount of data and information available during the preliminary screening process emphasizes the importance of a carefully and skillfully developed application form or supplement as discussed previously. The task at this point for the committee is to review applications and résumés using some type of a scale. The scale is derived from job-related criteria specified in the job announcement and job description and is applied in the same way to all applicants. Each member of the selection committee reviews the application packets separately prior to comparing findings. Figure 11.7 provides an example of some of the criteria that might be used in scoring an application.

FIGURE 11.7

Preliminary Screening Form

Name	Application Responses	Supplementary Application Responses	Education		Experience		Résumé Information
	Complete? Yes/No	Weak, less relevant Strong, realistic 1.............3	Less relevant 1.............3	Highly relevant	Less relevant 1.............5	Highly relevant	Rate any additional positive, relevant information (comment) 1.............3
(1)							
(2)							
(3)							

Based on the scoring system, the pool of applicants is reduced to a number of candidates who will be invited for personal interviews. The number will depend on resources available. If the search is internal or local, and there are no costs associated with travel and lodging, then a larger number can be interviewed. If the search is national, cost will usually be a factor because it is common practice for the employing organization to pay travel, lodging, and other expenses associated with the interview. In addition, the length of time that the position can remain vacant may also be a consideration that will limit the number of candidates.

Secondary Screening

The objective of secondary screening is to secure the best and most relevant information about those applicants who have moved to candidate status so that the organization is in a position to make a well-informed hiring decision. Secondary screening typically involves (1) review of references, (2) testing, if applicable, and (3) one or more interviews.

Review of References

The trend in reviewing references appears to be toward gaining or verifying factual information rather than getting opinions and perspectives about the quality of work. The College and University Personnel Association (1998) recommends that screening committees follow a procedure of (1) obtaining written releases from applicants before checking references or contacting a current employer, (2) collecting information in writing, (3) requesting only job-related information that can be verified such as dates, titles, duties, and so forth, and (4) using information gained only for hiring purposes. It recommends that the employing agency not ask for subjective information (it could be discriminatory), and if it is offered, ignore it.

Bell, Castagnera, and Young (1984) give the following advice to managers who are asked for a reference:

- Don't volunteer information.
- Use qualifying statements.
- Obtain written consent.
- Avoid vague statements.
- Document all released information.
- Clearly label all subjective statements.
- Do not answer trap questions.
- Avoid answering questions that are asked "off the record." (p. 35)

Many personnel experts recommend that the same approach that is used to develop a structured interview schedule for the candidate be used if telephone conversations with references are to be included as a part of the secondary screening process. Factual responses should be recorded for later use in screening the candidate.

Testing

Some types of testing have become controversial because of issues of reliability and validity. Tests must be job related, and those who perform at the highest levels on the test must be those who also perform well on the job. When raters are used, their ratings for the same candidate must be within a prescribed range in order for the instrument used to pass the test of reliability. Organizations have had mixed experiences with testing.

One organization, experiencing high turnover, constructed tests designed to predict job performance characteristics that would likely contribute to a more positive experience and longer tenure. After a few years, the company reported saving more than $300,000 due to reduced turnover and higher productivity (Thomas & Brull, 1993). Schmidt et al. (1992) state that most small human service organizations prefer not to use testing because of the expense of ensuring that tests meet legal criteria. However, they point out, even interviews that involve questions such as "What would you do if/when/about . . . ?" are legally considered to be employment tests and must meet established criteria for testing.

Types of tests include paper-and-pencil instruments that can be scored, performance tests that require a verbal and interactive response, or technical tests such as polygraph or drug testing. Lie detectors have not withstood the test of accuracy over the years (Kleinmuntz, 1985). The College and University Personnel Association (1998) points out that the rights of employers to conduct preemployment drug testing vary by states. "Some states have ruled that drug testing is a violation of a right to privacy under their state constitutions, unless the employer can show a job-related requirement for the test" (p. 14).

Schmidt and Noe (1986) reviewed a number of selection devices and found that validity varies. Devices found to have high validity included work samples, peer evaluations, and assessment centers. Physical ability was found to have moderate to high validity. Those found to have moderate validity included cognitive ability and special aptitude, biographical information, and self-assessments. Those found to have low validity included personality, interest, interviews, seniority, reference checks, and academic performance.

Interviewing

As indicated earlier in this chapter, the interview remains the major source of information used in the final hiring decision. Interviews provide an opportunity to learn how the candidate responds orally to questions that are designed to predict future job performance. The disadvantage of interviews is that people who interview well do not always perform well, and conversely, people who do not interview well may perform at a superior level. This is why all data and information available, including scores from the application form, from the résumé, from testing, and from checking references, should all be reviewed and compiled and made available to interviewers prior to conducting the interview. The College and University Personnel Association (1998) proposes the following steps in preparing for the interview:

1. Review the job description and specifications.
2. Specify information predictive of performance in each area.
3. Develop questions.
4. Select interviewers.
5. Set up the interview; length, schedule, room, and so forth.
6. Review the résumé and the application.

The secondary screening process may consist of any one or a combination of interviews including (1) one-to-one interviews, (2) group interactions, or (3) oral board or panel examinations (Schmidt et al., 1992). Limiting a candidate to a single, one-to-one interview runs the risk of having one person's biases and perceptions affect the hiring decision. Group interactions involve two or more candidates being interviewed by one or more persons at the same time. This type of interaction provides the interviewers with an opportunity to compare and contrast responses, but, as Schmidt et al. point out, "by comparing people with people, the process does not compare candidates with the job qualifications directly" (p. 78).

The panel or selection committee interview is structured to allow those within the organization who are most knowledgeable about the job to solicit oral responses and to rate them using a valid and reliable scale. The multiple ratings can serve as a reliability check and can help to eliminate the bias that might result from the single interview. It is a good practice to have interviewers trained and meet with candidates as a group. "Improper questions, unkept promises, and inappropriate remarks will reflect badly on the institution and might be legally indefensible. If feasible, have all interviewers meet with the applicant as a group. In this way, all the interviewers hear the same information and have a common basis for comparison, promoting productive discussion of each of the applicants" (College and University Personnel Association, 1998, p. 4).

The key to successful secondary screening is creating instruments that are effective in identifying differences between and among candidates while at the same time complying with all aspects of human resource law. Campion, Pursell, and Brown (1988) offer the following advice for conducting a structured interview:

1. Develop questions based on the job analysis.
2. Ask the same questions of each candidate.
3. Anchor the rating scales for scoring answers with examples and illustrations.
4. Have an interview panel record and rate answers.
5. Consistently administer the process to all candidates.
6. Give special attention to job relatedness, fairness, and documentation in accordance with testing guidelines. (p. 25)

Figure 11.8 illustrates a screening instrument that might be used in the selection process for a case manager.

Avoiding Discriminatory Questions   Certain types of questions may not be asked in an interview. Any questions related to gender, age, cultural or ethnic background, religion, national origin, or disability are considered inappropriate for an employment interview. The College and University Personnel Association (1998) has identified sixteen areas in which knowledge of existing local, state, or federal regulations may be needed in order to keep inquiries within the law. They include (1) citizenship, (2) educational background, (3) language proficiency, (4) work experience, (5) marital status or gender, (6) pregnancy, children, and child care, (7) age, (8) sexual orientation, (9) personal appearance, (10) memberships in organizations, religious preference, and names of relatives, (11) credit ratings and reports, (12) discharge from military service, (13) smoking, (14) polygraph examinations and personality tests, (15) prehire drug and alcohol screening, and (16) arrest and conviction records.

FIGURE. 11.8

Sample Screening Instrument Used in the Selection Process

Part 1

Interview Questions	1	2	3	4	5
	Extremely negative Demonstrates little sensitivity or competence ←			→	Extremely positive Demonstrates High sensitivity or competence
1. Describe your experience in working with a homeless client.	1	2	3	4	5
2. Describe a cross-cultural experience in which you dealt with cultural and ethnic issues.	1	2	3	4	5
3. Describe a situation in which you were involved in initiating an organizational or a community change.	1	2	3	4	5
. . . and other related questions	1	2	3	4	5

Part 2

Testing

	1	2	3	4	5
1. Conduct a simulated, 10-minute intake interview with a person playing the role of a client served by this agency.	1	2	3	4	5

Part 3

References

Name of Reference Position Relationship	1	2	3
	Significant reservations ←		→ Exclusively positive comments
(1)	1	2	3
(2)	1	2	3
(3)	1	2	3

The very strong message in current selection and hiring literature is that those who have any contact with applicants or candidates for the position, and especially those that are involved in interviews, rely on their knowledge of the law, the agency's policies, and the job announcement in framing questions and in interacting with applicants or candidates. Good intentions and pure motives mean little if inappropriate questions lead to legal action in the event that a candidate is not selected.

On the positive side, a good interviewing experience can serve as the capstone to a successful recruiting and public relations effort. Sharing information about the strengths of the agency and positive impressions made by existing staff can influence a decision to accept a position. Even candidates who are not selected may leave the experience with a positive feeling about the agency and may apply for a position in the future. The key to successful interviewing, as with the entire process, is careful and detailed planning by knowledgeable and experienced people.

Keeping Candidates Informed   If proper procedures have been followed throughout the recruitment and selection process, several pieces of correspondence will have been sent to each applicant and candidate. When applications are received, they are acknowledged. If the pool is small and the workload manageable, it is also helpful if an applicant is informed when any parts of the application packet have not yet been completed and returned. When the preliminary screening process has been completed, it is proper to notify those who will not move forward to candidate status that they are not among the finalists for the position, and to thank them for their interest. Finalists who will continue in the process are notified, either in writing or by telephone, that they have been selected to participate in the final phase of the selection process.

■ Hiring

When all finalist candidates have completed their interviews, the time has come to make the hiring decision. All of the safeguards proposed throughout this chapter remain in place during this final phase. This is often the point at which the selection committee and others interested in who is hired want to make independent contacts with colleagues or coworkers of the candidates. There is often a sense of urgency about getting good "inside" information about work performance and how a candidate works with others as a member of a team. These temptations must be resisted. Inappropriate contacts or solicitations of information at this stage may not only void the entire recruitment and selection process, it may also result in an expensive lawsuit if a candidate feels his or her employment rights were violated during the hiring process. Although it is rare for a job applicant or candidate to challenge the hiring process in the field of human services, it should be recognized that individuals are becoming increasingly aware of their rights, and it may become more common to challenge careless practices in the future.

Reaching a decision involves a series of final steps prior to making an offer of employment. These steps may include any or all of the following: (1) final evaluation of candidates by the selection committee, (2) final check of references, (3) recommendation by the selection committee to the hiring authority, (4) the job offer, and (5) notification of unsuccessful candidates of their status.

Final evaluation requires a review of each candidate's credentials as they relate to the minimum qualifications and other factors specified in the job announcement. Résumés, application materials, reference letters, and other documents are revisited at the final evaluation session. Strengths and weaknesses or deficits, as revealed by scores emerging from the application materials and interviews, are reviewed in light of the requirements of the job. Care should be taken during this session to ensure that a candidate's characteristics not related to the position do not enter into the evaluation. Unanswered questions should be identified and framed for follow-up checks with references, if needed.

Because reference letters often tend to provide very limited data, it may be useful to telephone references for more detailed information prior to making a formal job offer. This action, however, should be taken only if candidates provide written permission specifying who may be contacted. Questions should be framed carefully prior to making calls to ensure that information requested is job related and that answers given are factual and can be verified if challenged (College and University Personnel Association, 1998).

When all data and information have been compiled and follow-up reference checks completed, the selection committee will have a fairly complete profile on each finalist candidate. At this point the committee members should share their impressions with each other and attempt to arrive at a consensus on a recommendation to the hiring authority. Organizations that use selection committees vary in the way they frame hiring recommendations. Some prefer to rank order, with a rationale provided for each candidate's final ranking. Others prefer that the selection committee present the candidates unranked with a profile of strengths and weaknesses as they relate to the requirements for the position. The former practice has the advantage of presenting a clear preference of a well-informed selection committee to the hiring authority. The latter practice has the advantage of presenting the hiring authority with a choice and avoids the possibility of having to reject the committee's recommendation.

When a decision is made, the person with hiring authority contacts the selected applicant by telephone or in person and makes the formal job offer. All items of information critical to an acceptance or rejection should be clarified prior to making the offer, including but not limited to salary, benefits, working hours, job title, starting date, assistance with moving expenses, and other job-related factors. When the candidate accepts the position, a follow-up letter of confirmation is drafted and sent (College and University Personnel Association, 1998).

Once an offer of employment and its acceptance have been finalized, unsuccessful candidates should be notified that they have not been selected. It is advisable to use neutral language in this type of correspondence. They should be informed that the employer is not able to make an offer of employment at this time, and that the interest the applicant has demonstrated is appreciated. In any case, no mention should be made about the applicant or candidate's ability to perform the responsibilities and tasks of the job at a satisfactory level.

Records should be kept of the entire recruitment, selection, and hiring process. Federal and some state regulations require that records be maintained on all job applicants, including information on race, sex, and ethnic background. It is also important to keep a sample of the application packet and form letters, as well as all documentation relating to interaction with finalist candidates, descriptions of the jobs for which they applied, instruments used to evaluate, and a record of reasons for decisions not to hire (College and University Personnel Association, 1998).

When the new employee has accepted the position and a starting date has been established, current employees should be carefully selected to participate in an orientation to ensure that all goes well in bringing the new coworker on board. First impressions of the new workplace are important and should not be left to chance. Receptionists, personnel, payroll, and other key people should be informed of the hire and told when they should expect to meet with the new employee. A well-planned experience on the starting date will include a tour of the building with an assigned staff person and introductions to all available staff. These orientation activities will be discussed in greater detail in the next chapter.

SUMMARY

1. **The Importance of Sound Recruitment Practices.** A job opening is a valuable opportunity to improve the organization. Many of these opportunities are missed through careless recruitment practices.

2. **Basic Recruitment Concepts and Issues.** Recruitment practices should be based on human resources law, the profile of staff needs, and the job analysis.
   - *Establishing Employment Policies.* Policies should include a statement of nondiscrimination, hiring authority, starting salary approval, promotion from within, hiring of friends and relatives, use of reference checks, use of tests, and recruitment sources used.
   - *Changes in Status.* The status of persons interested in a job changes from potential recruit to recruit to applicant to candidate to employee.

3. **The Preplanning, Recruitment, Selection, and Hiring Processes.** These processes should follow a systematic plan to ensure that all laws and regulations have been followed and that recruits and applicants are provided with necessary and appropriate information.
   - *Preplanning.* This stage includes a review of applicable human resources laws and a review of the job analysis.
   - *Recruitment.* This includes writing of the job announcement, identification of a target audience for recruitment, dissemination of recruitment and application materials, processing of applications, and responding to applicants.
   - *Selection.* Selection includes preliminary and secondary screening processes and interviewing.
   - *Hiring.* This stage includes an offer of employment.

4. **Recruitment**
   - *Preparing the Job Announcement.* This includes position or title, brief description of the job, description of the agency, qualifications, location, starting date, time frame for applications, statement of what to submit (or how to apply), and a statement that the employer is an equal opportunity/affirmative action employer.
   - *Identifying Target Audiences and Potential Recruits.* Potential sources include employment agencies, high schools and colleges, community organizations, newspaper ads, ethnic and specialized newspapers, professional journal and newsletter ads, employee referrals, and contacts with other organizations.
   - *Disseminating Recruitment and Application Materials.* Recruits should be directed as to how to get recruitment and application materials. Applications should require name, address, and identifying information, education, employment history, special honors and achievements, and professional memberships or service activities.
   - *Soliciting Reference Letters.* References should not be requested until applicants reach candidate status.
   - *Processing Applications and Responding to Applicants.* A log should be set up to track applications. All applicants should be treated the same way.

5. **Employee Selection.** The process and the instruments should attempt to reduce subjectivity, especially in interviewing.
   - *Preliminary Screening.* Important decisions about inclusion or elimination from the process are made at this stage. These decisions must be made based on credentials submitted by the applicant without a face-to-face meeting.

■ *Secondary Screening.* This phase involves more detailed analysis of those who have made it through the preliminary screening process.

■ *Review of References.* Screening committees should be careful and conscientious in pursuing information from references. Procedures should include obtaining written releases from candidates, collecting information in writing, requesting only job-related information, and using information only for hiring purposes.

■ *Testing.* Testing is acceptable if there are assurances of reliability (consistency) and validity (relevance).

■ *Interviewing.* A variety of interview formats can be used. Interviews should be structured.

   Avoiding Discriminatory Questions. There are many areas in which questions can raise potentially discriminatory issues. Some of the more common areas are citizenship, educational background, language proficiency, children and child care, age, sexual orientation, credit ratings, military service, and others.

   Keeping Candidates Informed. Applicants and candidates should be informed of their status and notified when they are no longer part of the applicant or candidate pool.

6. **Hiring.** Employers should establish safeguards to ensure that staff do not make their own contacts to solicit information unlawfully. The selection committee reviews all materials and makes a recommendation to the hiring authority, who then makes a job offer.

EXERCISES

Please complete the following sections of your manual based on the content covered in Chapter 11.

Section 11: Recruitment, Selection, and Hiring

11.1 Recruitment. Write a policy statement that lays out the steps for recruiting new employees. Attach a timetable for the completion of the recruitment, selection, and hiring procedures in Gantt chart form, identified as Document 11.1a.

11.2 Selection. Write a policy statement that establishes the organization's expectations of what constitutes a complete selection process.

   11.2.1 Preliminary Screening. Identify the steps included in preliminary screening. Attach a copy of an instrument that will be used for screening, using just résumés and applications.

   11.2.2 Secondary Screening. Identify the steps included in secondary screening. Attach a copy of one or more instruments that will be used for determining the applicant's ability to meet job expectations. At least one sample instrument should be an interview schedule. Label your instruments Documents 11.2.2a, b, and so forth.

   11.2.3 Use of Tests. Write a policy statement on what tests the organization will use in screening potential employees.

11.2.4 References. Write a policy statement on how references are selected, how and when they are to be contacted, and what types of information will be solicited from them.

11.3 Hiring. Write a policy statement on the steps involved in hiring. Add policy statements as needed on:

11.3.1 Hiring Authority.

11.3.2 Starting Salary Approval.

11.3.3 Promotion from Within.

11.3.4 Hiring of Friends and Relatives.

REFERENCES

American Society for Personnel Administration. (1983). *Employee selection procedures* (ASPA-BNA Survey No. 45). Washington, DC: Bureau of National Affairs.

Bell, J., Castagnera, J., & Young, J. (1984). Employment references: Do you know the law? *Personnel Journal, 63*(2), 32–36.

Campion, M., Purcell, E., & Brown, B. (1988). Structured interviewing: Raising the psychometric properties of the employment interview. *Personnel Psychology, 41*(1), 25–42.

College and University Personnel Association. (1998). *Interview guide for supervisors* (5th ed.). Washington, DC: Author.

Dessler, G. (1997). *Human resource management* (7th ed.). Upper Saddle River, NJ: Prentice-Hall.

Jensen, J. (1981). How to hire the right person for the job. *The Grantsmanship Center News.* (May–June), 23–31.

Kleinmuntz, B. (1985). Lie detectors fail the truth test. *Harvard Business Review, 63*(4), 36–42.

Morrow, P. (1990). Physical attractiveness and selection decision making. *Journal of Management, 16*(1), 45–60.

Schmidt, M., Riggar, T., Crimando, W., & Bordieri, J. (1992). *Staffing for success: A guide for health and human service professionals.* Newbury Park, CA: Sage.

Schmidt, N., & Noe, R. (1986). Personnel selection and equal employment opportunity. In C. Cooper & I. Robertson (Eds.), *International Review of Industrial and Organizational Psychology* (pp. 71–116). New York: Wiley.

Thomas, M., & Brull, H. (1993). Tests improve hiring decisions at Franciscan. *Personnel Journal, 72*(11), 89–92.

Trent, S. (1987). The importance of social skills in the employment interview. *Education of the Visually Handicapped, 19*(1), 7–18.

Ulrich, L., & Trumbo, D. (1965). The selection interview since 1949. *Psychological Bulletin, 63*(2), 100–116.

Weinbach, R. (1998). *The social worker as manager: A practical guide to success.* Boston: Allyn & Bacon.

CHAPTER 12

Maximizing Employee Potential through Staff Training and Development

- Making a Positive Transition into Employment
- Establishing Training, Development, and Education Policy
- Orientation
- Training
- The In-Service Training Curriculum
- Steps in Developing an In-Service Training Curriculum
- The Career Development Plan

Upon completion of this chapter, the reader will be able to:

- Prepare a plan for new employee orientation, including an orientation agenda and an orientation checklist.
- Create a framework for a comprehensive staff training and development plan for a human service organization.
- Create a curriculum framework for an in-service training program for a human service organization.
- Establish guidelines for the development of training courses or modules.
- Discuss the elements of a career development plan.

Assumptions

- That well-designed orientation, staff development, and training programs can have a positive impact on overall organizational functioning.
- That human service organizations should develop their own in-service training materials and that they should be updated and reused as new employees come on board.
- That a curriculum framework should be used to develop a comprehensive in-service training program.
- That employees should be encouraged and supported in their career development and education programs, even if it means that their long-range plans will take them to a career outside the organization.

Making a Positive Transition into Employment

In the previous chapter we discussed the importance of carefully planned and thoughtfully implemented recruitment, selection, and hiring processes. Once the employee is hired, a smooth transition into a positive work environment will depend on the quality of the new employee's orientation to the organization, the work unit, and the job. An excellent and highly successful recruitment and selection effort can be wasted if a new employee is brought on board in a careless and offhand manner. When orientation is unplanned and left to chance, it is not at all unlikely that the new employee may become involved in a discussion with a group of workers having a bad day and discussing some of the negative aspects of working for the agency as they perceive them. New employee ideas and enthusiasm, in this kind of environment, can be dismissed or even ridiculed. This is not exactly the way an employer would hope a new employee would be oriented to the agency.

New employees are, in a sense, raw material to the organization. Attitudes and perspectives toward this organization as a place to work usually tend toward being positive or at least open-minded. The employer has a real advantage here in that the new employee is likely oriented toward loyalty and commitment at this point, wanting to make a positive beginning in the new job. A well-planned and timely orientation can take advantage of the new employee's inclination toward the positive aspects of the new place of employment and can help to establish a sense of direction that is productive both for the employee and for the organization. Once a person has been hired, there are a limited number of opportunities in which employee performance can be influenced. Staff training and development is one of those opportunities, and it begins on the very first day of employment with a thoughtfully designed orientation.

Establishing Training, Development, and Education Policy

Training is defined as a knowledge or skill-building activity that is designed to enable the employee to improve performance on the job. *Development* is a more broadly defined term that refers to learning experiences designed to enhance both personal and professional growth but are not necessarily directly related to the job. Education includes learning experiences that are focused on enhancing the ability to advance to a higher level or to take on new and more complex responsibilities in the present job (Gilley & Egglund, 1989).

There are many issues in human resources law that argue in favor of establishing a set of policies and procedures around staff training and development. Organizations are held responsible for employee behavior in the areas of sexual harassment, fair employment, and discrimination. Courts have found that employers are also responsible for employee interactions with the agency's clientele. "Training all staff, especially those who have the most regular and intimate contact with the clients" was referred to in a court case as a "paramount necessity" (Matkin, 1980, p. 136). Employers also are responsible to ensure that all training and development opportunities are provided in a nondiscriminatory manner (Hafer & Riggar, 1981). Finally, staff training and development is an area of organizational life that is sometimes given low priority. Establishing expectations that all employees will make efforts toward continuous growth and development gives training important administrative backing and credibility. For all these reasons, good management planning and practice includes the development of policies on training, development, and education.

Policy statements need not be lengthy. Their focus should be on (1) establishing training, development, and educational opportunities for all employees in a way that is fair and nondiscriminatory, (2) establishing training content (and a monitoring system to ensure implementation) that is considered mandatory for each employee classification, (3) setting aside a percentage of time that each employee is expected to devote to training and development activities, and (4) identifying the resources that the agency is willing to commit in support of training and development activities. The following examples of policy statements on training, development, and education might be used in a human service agency.

Section 12: Staff Development, Training, and Education

12.1 *Employee Orientation.* All employees shall participate in the employee orientation program for the organization, their work unit, and their job as specified in the orientation agenda, beginning on the new employee's first day of work.

12.2 *Staff Training.* All employees shall devote a minimum of 5 percent of their time to training. Each employee shall prepare an annual training plan at the time of performance appraisal, and training completed shall be recorded on the employee's training record.

12.3 *Staff Development.* All professional employees shall be entitled to attend at least one professional conference or workshop each year. Selection shall be made in conjunction with the employee's immediate supervisor.

12.4 *Education.* All employees may be considered for released time and tuition reimbursement for up to six credits per semester to complete a degree in an area of specialization that contributes to the agency's mission.

■ Orientation

The natural tendency of those who plan new employee orientations is to think in terms of what the organization needs to communicate to the employee. Ideally, planners should begin by thinking about how much a new employee can absorb. Simply presenting massive amounts of information does not guarantee that it has been understood or assimilated. It is more useful to take the time to consider learning capacity and spread out the orientation if it increases the likelihood that the new employee can better comprehend the new information and put it into context.

Content and tasks may be organized so that certain objectives are accomplished each day. For example, day 1 might be devoted to some of the more basic aspects of employment such as getting on the payroll, signing up for the various benefit programs, and learning some of the basic personnel policies, such as those having to do with supervision and performance appraisal. Each contact person who explains agency programs and services should have available a packet of information that the new employee can keep for review at a later time because not every benefit, policy, or procedure explained will be remembered or completely understood the first time it is heard.

A second focus for day 1 might be an orientation to the facility and introductions to coworkers. The building floor plan, including the new employee's workstation or office, location of secretaries and receptionists, rest rooms, employee lounge, and other relevant spaces, is typically identified for the new employee at the earliest possible time. Introductions to key employees with whom the new employee will be working are important.

TABLE 12.1	
Three-Stage Orientation	
Organizational Information	**Personnel Information**

Orientation to the Organization

Organizational Information	Personnel Information
1. History and philosophy of the organization	1. Key policies and procedures
2. Goals and priorities of the organization	2. Compensation issues
3. Scope and diversity of activities	3. Fringe benefits
4. Clients served	4. Safety facilities
5. Chain of command	5. Physical facilities
6. Facts about key personnel	6. Unpaid leave, comp time

Orientation to the Department

Organizational Information	Personnel Information
1. History of the department	5. Relevant policies and procedures, rules and regulations
2. Department's role in the organization and relationship to other departments	6. Tour of the physical environment
3. Departmental goals and priorities	7. Introduction to departmental employees
4. Scope and diversity of activities and functions	8. Introduction to clients

Orientation to the Job

Organizational Information	Personnel Information
1. Detailed explanation of job based on job description	6. Instruction regarding the use of any equipment
2. Discussion of common problems and advice on how to avoid them	7. Information regarding supplies, materials, and types of assistance available
3. Review of performance standards	8. Development of weekly schedule
4. Review of supervision practices	9. Provision of keys and supplies
5. Overview of required records and reports	

Source: Schmidt, M., Riggar, T., Crimando, W., & Bordieri, J. (1992). *Staffing for success. A guide for health and human service professionals.* Newbury Park, CA: Sage Publications, p. 90. Reprinted with permission of Sage Publications, Inc.

Selected people should be designated as contact persons, including at least one peer, a supervisor, and one or more persons to go to lunch with the first three to five days (Jensen, 1981).

Schmidt, Riggar, Crimando, and Bordieri (1992), drawing on the work of others (Reed-Mendenhall & Millard, 1980; St. John, 1980), describe orientation as a three-stage process: (1) orientation to the organization, (2) orientation to the department, program, or unit, and (3) orientation to the job. Table 12.1 identifies the types of information that should be provided at each stage of orientation.

Orientation Strategies and Techniques

Teaching methods present somewhat of a challenge in new employee orientation. Traditional classroom instruction usually will not work in a human service organization because few are large enough to bring on new employees in groups. It is more likely that the new employee will be the only one starting work on a given start date. Teaching methods, therefore, must be adapted to individualized learning.

Many organizations have found it useful to develop a standardized orientation checklist. Required meetings with payroll and benefits personnel are listed along with other key personnel. A checklist can also serve the purpose of keeping a record of information and documentation that have been provided to the new employee. Spaces for date and initials or signature by key employees and by the new employee acknowledge that necessary information and materials have been provided. This document can then be filed in the new employee's permanent personnel and training file. Schmidt et al. (1992) describe the value of an orientation checklist in this way:

> Orientation checklists are simply job aids that list all of the components of the orientation that should be provided. They can be categorized by type of activity or person providing the orientation, they can include time frames for delivery, and they can, and should, include places for the signature of both the employee and the person providing the orientation. When well-developed and used consistently, checklists can greatly simplify the task of organizing new employee orientation. (p. 94)

Figure 12.1 illustrates an orientation checklist.

FIGURE 12.1
Orientation Checklist

Orientation Checklist		
Organizational Information	**Initials**	**Date**
1. Viewed video on history and philosophy of the organization	_____	_____
2. Received a copy of the organization's strategic plan	_____	_____
3. Received a copy of the organizational chart	_____	_____
4. Received a copy of the Manual of Policies and Procedures	_____	_____
5. Received a copy of the confidentiality and clients' rights standards	_____	_____
Human Resources Information		
1. Completed payroll information	_____	_____
2. Received a copy of policies on vacation, holidays, sick leave	_____	_____
3. Enrolled in agency's health plan	_____	_____
4. Enrolled in agency's retirement plan	_____	_____
Program Information		
1. Reviewed programs and services with supervisor	_____	_____
2. Received a copy of the Community Directory of Social Services	_____	_____
3. Received copies of all Intake, Screening, and Assessment forms	_____	_____
4. Received copies of job description and performance standards	_____	_____
5. Received a copy of and reviewed the Annual Performance Appraisal	_____	_____
Other		

Another useful document is an orientation agenda. Preparing an agenda individualized to the needs of the new employee will assure the supervisor that all blocks of time are accounted for and that all necessary policies, programs, and other such items have been covered somewhere during the orientation period. In addition, an agenda provides the new employee with at least some degree of independence, so that he or she can proceed comfortably through the orientation process without having to interrupt the work of others to find out where to go next. Finally, a copy of the orientation agenda can be provided to staff members who are affected so that they will know when to expect the new employee and will have reference materials prepared, if needed. An example of an orientation agenda is illustrated in Table 12.2.

Several other techniques have also been found to be useful. Preparing a video, for example, in which the chief executive officer and other key personnel are introduced and briefly describe the agency and selected programs can capture valuable information and allow a new employee to view it at any time. Preparing sample records or a packet of agency forms for use by the new employee provides a good set of reference documents. Combining all written information and documents into a new employee handbook, with a table of contents and dividers for major sections, can serve not only as a useful learning aid throughout the orientation period but also as a handy reference document during the early months of employment.

TABLE 12.2
Orientation Agenda

	Orientation Agenda
8:30	*Program Manager and Unit Supervisor* Welcome and overview of the organization
8:45	*Unit Supervisor* Introductions to departmental staff
9:30	*Training Director* Video—Investing in Human Potential (history of the agency)
10:00	*Break—Host, Unit Supervisor*
10:15	*Program Manager* Organizational and program structure and design
12:00	*Lunch—Host, Coworker*
1:00	*Agency Assistant Director* Overview of the strategic plan and program plans
2:00	*Human Resources Director* Personnel policies, payroll, benefits
3:00	*Unit Supervisor* Review of case management responsibilities; agency data collection forms and procedures
4:00	*Program Manager and Unit Supervisor* Questions, debriefing, planning for the next day

■ Training

The following example illustrates how training can affect not only worker performance but also funding and ultimately can cost an agency director his or her job.

> The Open Door, a sixty-five-bed facility located in the downtown area of a large city, provided short-term shelter for single, homeless men in transition. The shelter was funded through a variety of federal and state grants, along with contributions from a number of corporations whose headquarters were in the city. The shelter was created specifically to meet the needs of temporarily unemployed men, to provide them with a mailing address and telephone number, and to connect them with job training and job placement opportunities. Other shelters were available within the city for long-term homeless with more serious and complex problems.
>
> Funding and regulating sources required that the shelter collect and report statistics on its residents. Of greatest concern was length of stay, participation in employment-related activities, and successful job placement. After several years of operation, end-of-the-year reports indicated that the shelter was not meeting expected objectives for training and placement activities. In fact, success rates went down over a three-year period. A team of management experts was hired to analyze the programs and services provided.
>
> The major finding of the team was that staff members were not adequately trained to deal with the needs of the clientele and the expectations of the funders. Personnel involved in screening were uncertain as to how to determine whether a person requesting services should be admitted and as a result failed to screen out those with drug and alcohol problems as well as some who were seriously mentally ill. Those involved in job training and referral programs were not aware of techniques available designed to assess job skills and interests and were making referrals strictly based on job openings. Partly as a result of poor screening and assessment, morale among workers was low because they did not feel competent to do their jobs. Turnover was high, and most new workers went through the same cycle. Ultimately the board of directors determined that a new CEO, one who was committed to developing a highly trained and competent staff, was necessary to the survival of the shelter.

This example illustrates the kind of impact that poor or nonexistent training can have on an organization. Inexperienced managers sometimes treat staff training and development very lightly and assume that one-to-one contacts with coworkers and supervisors will provide all the job-related information needed. This hit-or-miss approach can have a negative impact, not only on staff knowledge and skill, but also on overall organizational functioning.

A better and more professional approach to staff training and development is to prepare a complete training plan that will help to ensure that staff are performing at the highest levels.

Developing a Comprehensive Staff Training and Development Plan

A plan designed to bring all staff up to the highest levels of productivity possible will include at least four components. Each of these components falls under the heading of either training, development, or education, as follows:

Training
- In-service training
- On-the-job training

Development
- Out-service training and development

Education
- College or university education

Training is defined as knowledge or skill-building activity that is designed to help employees improve performance on the job. Development is defined as learning experiences designed to enhance personal and professional growth but not necessarily directly related to the job. Education is defined as learning experiences that are focused on enhancing the ability to advance to a higher level or to take on new or more complex responsibilities in the same job.

Weinbach (1998) presents a framework that is useful in examining each type of staff training and development activity to understand its purpose, content, and process. These characteristics are presented in Table 12.3.

TABLE 12.3

Purpose, Content, and Process of Training, Education, and Staff Development

	Characteristics of Three Types of Continuing Education		
	Type of Activity		
Distinguishing Characteristics	Training	Education	Staff Development
Purpose	Socialization (orientation to the organization), standardization of activities to meet a standard	Career advancement through advanced study (within context of the profession)	Acquiring and applying new knowledge (to increase professional competence in service delivery)
Content	Specific "how-to" knowledge (application of policy to procedures)	Theoretical knowledge	Emerging knowledge and insights
Process	Instruction in and exposure to needed knowledge	Providing knowledge that is generalizable	Application of new knowledge to a problem situation

Source: Adapted from Weinbach, R. W., & Kuehner, K. M. (1981). Trainer or academician—who shall provide? *Journal of Continuing Social Work Education, I*(3, Summer), 5. Copyright 1981 by the Continuing Education Program, School of Social Welfare, State University of New York at Albany. Reprinted with permission.

	Organization	Program	Unit or Job
TABLE 12.4			
A Framework for Organizing a Comprehensive Staff Development, Training, and Education Plan			

	Organization	Program	Unit or Job
Orientation	History/mission/philosophy of agency Strategic plan; goals and objectives Organizational structure and design Human resources Meet managers/administrators Community orientation	Program purpose, goals, objectives Policies and procedures Services provided Referral sources Meet coworkers	Job expectations/performance standards Supervision Records and reports Supplies, equipment keys, records, computer Meet coworkers
In-Service Training	Planning and delivery of training to meet organizational needs; policies, procedures, regulations	Planning and delivery of training to meet program needs; data collection, budgeting, reporting, evaluation, practice knowledge and skill	Usually handled at the program level; possibly highly specific practice issues planned and delivered at this level
On-the-Job Training			Special "mentoring" relationships are established as learning needs are identified on the job
Out-Service Training and Development	Local, state, and national opportunities to learn more about agency-level concerns Management training	Local, state, and national opportunities to learn more about program and practice knowledge and skill	Usually handled at the program level, although decisions about who will participate may be made at the unit level
Education	Usually administered out of the human resources office for the entire organization May include stipends, tuition, educational leave, or other benefits		

Table 12.4 illustrates a format for incorporating training, development, and education into an overall framework for a comprehensive staff training and development plan.

Types of Training and Development   In-service training is provided by the employing organization, either through the use of existing staff and resources or by contracting with experts in the community to make one or more presentations on a specific topic. This is the program within the agency that bears the responsibility for ensuring that all required information, knowledge, and skill are imparted to staff in some form. The in-service training program must ensure that staff understand the laws and regulations that govern agency programs and services, including human resources laws about sexual harassment, discrimination, and equal employment opportunity.

A plan for in-service training can best be addressed by framing it as a curriculum, in the same way that a community college or university would frame and organize its courses.

However, instead of organizing in terms of mathematics, English, or social studies, the major curriculum themes might be something such as Screening and Assessment, Computer Skills, or Adolescent Growth and Development. Within each category, a variety of courses or training modules can be established, to be completed as employees reach the point when they need the information, the knowledge, or the skills. This curriculum concept will be discussed in greater detail in the next section.

On-the-job training (OJT) refers to learning the job by actually performing its duties and tasks under the supervision of an experienced employee. The experienced employee or "mentor" teaches the new employee using a number of different teaching techniques including job coaching, observation, and feedback. OJT, like other training, needs to be well planned. The supervising employee should begin with an examination of the job analysis to identify the major duties and tasks. Opportunities for hands-on activities can then be designed in a way to ensure that the full range of job-related tasks has been observed and demonstrated. A formal, written on-the-job training plan including learning objectives, types of tasks and skills to be learned, an agenda for implementation, and ongoing evaluation and feedback will very likely lead to a better-quality learning experience than one in which the training simply follows whatever is on the supervising worker's agenda for the day.

Out-service training and development is the term used to describe all those learning activities and experiences developed and sponsored by entities outside the organization. They are attended by staff and either fully or partially paid for by the agency. They are designed to foster professional and personal growth and development. This category would include national- and state-level professional conferences, lectures by experts, workshops, and other learning experiences not directly sponsored or provided by the agency. Knowledge and skills taught in out-service training and development are typically designed to appeal to a wide audience and, therefore, tend to enhance the participant's general professional knowledge. For example, at a professional conference presenters may describe a research project in which they have participated and may discuss the practice implications of their findings. There may or may not be carryover to the specific responsibilities and tasks of the conference participant's job at the time. Many human service agencies include travel, per diem for lodging and meals, and conference registration funding for staff in their annual budgets and consider this to be an important investment in terms of nurturing professional growth.

Finally, when resources permit, some human service agencies will make opportunities available to staff to continue their college or university education and earn a degree. Types of opportunities include paid time off from work to attend classes, tuition reimbursement, book allowances, scholarships, and stipends. When these types of benefits are made available, a strong message is sent that the employee is valued and that the organization is willing in tangible ways to help employees move to the next level in their careers.

■ The In-Service Training Curriculum

Training in human service organizations is often approached on an as-needed basis. When a problem is recognized, a hastily planned training session is designed and presented to those who are seen as needing the information. When the same problem surfaces a year later, the process is repeated. Nothing is captured on paper, and each new episode of training is developed from the beginning.

An alternative to this approach is an in-service training curriculum in which course materials are developed, kept on file, and used as needed. Designing such a curriculum begins with a general framework that can be used to organize the content for each level of staff. For example, the following general categories might be used in a child welfare agency:

- Child welfare policy
- Clinical skills for working with children
- Child growth and development
- Community resources
- Agency policies and procedures

McKenna, Svenson, Wallace, and Wallace (1984) support the concept of a training curriculum using an analogy of architecture:

> Just as an architect designs a building so that each piece considers and contributes to the entire structure, an "architectural" approach to training aims at building a curriculum with individual parts that add up to a logical whole within the context of a given job, a department or an entire organization. (p. 78)

The concept of curriculum implies that it is comprehensive and, as such, should take into consideration all staff, from entry-level clerical to top management. Weinbach (1998) points out that, although managers in human service organizations deal with staff as individuals, it is helpful to understand some of the basic characteristics of each category of staff. His framework is presented in Table 12.5.

TABLE 12.5

Characteristics of Different Levels of Personnel within a Human Service Organization

The Staff Menu

1. Professionals—People who, through extensive formal preparation in a program of advanced study, have acquired a specialized mix of knowledge, values, and skills as well as credentials that allow them to perform certain highly skilled work. Other criteria often must be met for one to be considered a professional (e.g., maintenance of certain ethical standards, decisions not based on self-interest, etc.).

2. Preprofessionals—People who aspire to become professionals and who have met most (but not all) of the prerequisites for becoming professionals. Because they lack the required academic degree or some other credential, they are not allowed to do some of the same work that professionals can do. Most preprofessionals complete the requirements to become professionals one day.

3. Paraprofessionals—People who have undergone specialized education and training that have prepared them to perform some of the tasks once reserved for professionals. They generally do not become professionals.

4. Indigenous nonprofessionals—People who lack the formal education and credentials of professionals and, except in rare instances, of paraprofessionals. However, they have life experiences and/or a cultural identification that makes them especially well suited to relate to certain clients and their problems.

5. Support staff—People who are unskilled or semiskilled employees who perform certain needed tasks within an organization (e.g., secretaries, custodians, maintenance workers, etc.). They do not offer direct services to clients but facilitate the work of others who offer them.

6. Volunteers—People who, for a variety of reasons, offer their time and services without pay. They can be used to perform a wide variety of tasks within an organization depending on their education, experience, and willingness and the needs of the organization.

Source: Weinbach, R. W. (1998) *The social worker as manager* (3rd ed.). Boston: Allyn & Bacon, p. 106. Reprinted by permission.

TABLE 12.6

A Framework for Organizing an Agency's In-Service Training Curriculum

	Policy	Populations	Problems	Practice	Community
Managers and Administrators Supervisors Professional Direct Service Paraprofessional Clerical and Support Volunteers	Content on relevant federal, state, local, agency, and program policies Human resources laws, executive orders, court cases that impact the agency	Knowledge of populations served by agency programs (e.g., children, elderly) Knowledge of cultures, gender issues	Current information and knowledge about existing and emerging social and community problems that affect the agency's programs and services	The latest practice approaches found to be effective with populations served Cultural competence training Management training for supervisors and managers	Working with indigenous community leaders Working with referral sources Community resources Public relations Media relations

Using the categories of staffing presented previously, together with selected categories that might be covered in in-service training, a curriculum framework can be constructed as illustrated in Table 12.6. In this example, the major content areas are policy, populations, problems, practice, and community. Under each of these headings, appropriate courses or training modules would be designed for each level of staff for which the content is relevant. The result of this curriculum design is that each level of staff has a number of required and elective courses from which to choose to fulfill the staff training and development requirement each year, and the agency is assured that important knowledge and information are being made available to staff.

■ Steps in Developing an In-Service Training Curriculum

Developing an in-service training curriculum involves a series of steps, as follows:

Step 1. Identifying training needs.

Step 2. Developing training courses or modules, including objectives, course content, teaching method, and course evaluation design.

Step 3. Monitoring and evaluating the overall training program.

Each of these steps will be covered in the following sections.

Step 1. Identifying Training Needs

There are many sources that can be used to identify staff training needs. The first reference document that should be consulted when planning training for a particular classification or position is the job analysis. This document includes all of the responsibilities and tasks, methods, and the knowledge and skill required to perform successfully in the position. If staff in any particular position demonstrate a deficiency of knowledge or skill in any of the job requirements, training may help to bring performance up to expectations.

A second source for identifying training needs is direct input from staff. A simple memo to staff asking for their ideas about training is not likely to elicit a thoughtful response. A list of topics should be presented for staff reaction, with opportunities for additional suggestions. This is referred to as a training needs assessment and is usually developed by persons responsible for training. This form may draw from the job analysis, from staff suggestions, from supervisory and management input, from ideas generated by outside seminars and workshops, or other sources. The purpose is to develop as comprehensive a listing of potential topic offerings as possible and to survey staff periodically to determine their perceptions of training needs.

McKenna et al. (1984) propose that organizations, in building their training structures, form a curriculum committee. This committee, they suggest, should oversee the design portion of the curriculum-building project. They accomplish this by providing a framework and then consulting staff with specialized knowledge to ensure that training courses that are proposed are those most needed by staff. This design, once completed, could form the basis of a training needs assessment instrument.

In addition to a periodic survey, the instrument may also be used at other times. Periodic surveys do not always reach staff at a time when they happen to be thinking about training needs. As a result, periodic surveys may produce a profile of training needs that leans more toward interesting sounding topics than those that may help improve job performance. On the other hand, there are times when employees are much more receptive to thinking about their training needs. One of these times is when a job-related problem arises. The other is at the time of performance appraisal. The following example provides an illustration.

> A caseworker is working with a difficult adolescent and his parents. The parents explain the behavior problems. The counselor identifies what he believes to be a pattern of rebellion and testing limits. He works with the parents to develop a plan using behavior modification principles in which positive behaviors will be rewarded and negative behaviors punished. After implementing the plan for a two-month period, the parents report that their adolescent child's behavior is worse than ever, and they fear he is about to get into serious trouble with the law. The worker is frustrated with his limited knowledge of adolescent behavior and of parenting techniques.
>
> If a training needs-assessment instrument were available to him at that time, rather than at the end of the year, he may well be able to provide some good insights into training needs for workers who handle cases involving difficult adolescents. This training would not necessarily be in time to help the worker with his current case, but it may help him and other workers to be better prepared to deal with similar problems in the future.

If training needs-assessment instruments are readily available at all times during the year, and if staff are encouraged to complete them and turn them in to the training coordinator, a constant flow of good assessment information can be made available for planning purposes.

Another opportunity to collect good training needs assessment information is at the point of performance appraisal. This is the time when supervisor and employee meet to assess performance for the previous year and is, therefore, a natural opportunity to examine training needs in the light of performance. Bringing training into the discussion, in fact, can help to bring a positive tone into the evaluation by focusing on improving performance in the future rather than merely identifying deficits in past experiences. Performance appraisal also presents an opportunity for supervisors to identify training needs, both for themselves and for their supervisees. Employees do not always perceive and understand their own training needs, and a supervisor's perspective can contribute valuable input. Again, making the needs-assessment forms available allows for data collection at this time and contributes to the regular and timely flow of data and information on training needs.

Rapp and Poertner (1992) argue that all training should be line driven. They go on to explain:

> This means that all content should be directly related to making frontline staff more effective or efficient. Even management and supervisory training must be *explicitly* linked to how it will improve the performance of frontline workers. (p. 169)

Analyzing Training Needs.   Mager and Pipe (1970) were among the first to recognize that every problem or perceived need that prompts staff and management to request training cannot be solved by training. Sometimes training is the answer; sometimes it's not. Take, for example, the issue of properly completing documents and case recording in a timely manner. Some workers may wait weeks before completing dictation on a case, thus jeopardizing the accuracy of the data and information they record. When the recording is finally completed, it may be poorly written and extremely brief, leaving out many important details in case records that may have to serve as evidence in court. Is it likely that these workers need training, or are there other reasons for failing to complete case recording? Mager and Pipe (1970) lay out a series of steps designed to help the planner and analyst understand the nature of a performance deficit. The analytical framework is designed around the following process:

Step 1. Understand the performance discrepancy by:
  a. defining the performance problem (state what the person is doing), and then
  b. describing the desired performance.

Step 2. If it is determined at this point that the problem is not important and not worth investing agency time and resources, the matter is dropped.

Step 3. If it is important, the matter proceeds to further analysis.
  a. The problem can be either a matter of skill,
  b. or it can be a management problem,
  c. or a work design problem.

Step 4. If the performance deficit is a skill problem, it is still too early to conclude that training is the solution.
  a. It may be that the employee needs practice in doing the task,
  b. or needs regular and systematic feedback on performance. For example, a supervisor may ask to see case recording on a weekly basis and provide a critique for each case for a worker until the worker's performance improves.
  c. If practice and feedback will not solve the problem, then it is increasingly likely that training is needed.

Step 5. Consideration should also be given to whether or not this is a management or work-design problem.

   a. It is not unusual to find in some organizations that exemplary performance is punished, and

   b. nonperformance rewarded. This is not intentional, of course, but it often happens by default. For example, workers who conscientiously complete all case recordings in a thorough and timely manner will have less time available than workers who give only minimal attention to this task. Conscientious workers soon find out that they have less time available for lunch or coffee breaks, take work home, and may even have less time for face-to-face contact with clients. They learn that their salaries remain the same as nonperforming workers, and that when there is a difficult case it always seems to come their way. They begin to recognize that the high quality of their work is being punished. Meanwhile, the nonperforming workers are well on their way to creating a country-club environment in the workplace and causing productivity to drop, all without consequences. This is what is meant by a management or work-design problem.

   c. If the performance is important, there should be rewards for compliance and consequences for noncompliance.

Step 6. Finally, when all these analytical steps have been completed, the planner or supervisor is then in a position to propose solutions.

   a. If a small number of workers is involved, solutions might include practice with feedback, on-the-job training, or one-on-one coaching by an assigned mentor.

   b. If many are affected, formal training may be the answer.

   c. If rewards and consequences are skewed, work redesign may solve the problem.

In short, the prescription should fit the diagnosis. This exercise, laid out in a simple format by the authors, can be very useful in matching appropriate solutions to problems and can help avoid the frustration of providing a training solution when the performance discrepancy is not related to a deficit in knowledge or skill.

Step 2. Developing Training Courses or Modules

Because of the structure of formal education, it is likely that when one thinks in terms of a course, the image that comes to mind is sitting in a classroom for several hours each week for ten to fifteen weeks. There are sound reasons for using such time frames as quarters and semesters in the field of education. These reasons, however, do not carry over to staff training and development. The terms *training* and *education* are not interchangeable. As discussed earlier, training is focused on job-related content. Education can be wide ranging from theory to application.

Training, therefore, tends to be more highly concentrated. Units of training can be referred to as either courses or modules and can vary in length from less than an hour to several weeks of full-time study. Police academies, for example, provide full-time training that can extend up to several months. In spite of the wide range in length and content, experts agree that, once needs assessment is complete, the training effort should focus on instructional design (Carolan, 1993; Crimando & Riggar, 1990). Instructional design includes (1) defining learning objectives, (2) identifying content to be covered, (3) specifying teaching and training methods, and (4) designing evaluation instruments.

Defining Learning Objectives   Learning objectives have been an accepted part of teaching and learning for many decades. Gronlund (1970) describes the procedure of preparing instructional objectives:

> The procedure emphasizes the stating of instructional objectives as learning outcomes and the defining of these objectives in terms of student behavior; that is, in terms of the specific types of behavior that students are expected to demonstrate at the end of the learning experience. (p. iii)

Training courses typically include a number of objectives. They are drawn from an understanding of the problem the training is intended to resolve. They form the basis for selecting content, and they provide a focus for the evaluation of learning. In a sense, objectives are the center or pivotal point around which all teaching and learning revolve. Yet they remain the element most frequently overlooked or ignored in the preparation of training courses.

Objectives typically begin with the statement, "Upon completion of this training course, the trainee is expected to be able to. . . ." The statement is completed by defining expectations in terms of performance of skills or tasks or demonstrated understanding of concepts and issues. Objectives must be observable and measurable, so if performance is expected, the trainee must have the opportunity to perform; if understanding is expected, the trainee must in some observable way demonstrate understanding. A training workshop on case recording, for example, might have the following objectives:

Upon completion of this training course,
the trainee is expected to be able to:
- Demonstrate ability to take complete notes from a simulated interview,
- Complete case recording on the simulated interview in a way that meets agency standards and specifications for case recording.
- Critique case recording of other trainees using agency standards and specifications for case recording.

Using these statements as guidelines, training content would focus on topics such as note-taking during and immediately following interviews, mastery of agency standards and specifications for dictation, and case recording techniques. Methods would include in-person, video, or written presentation of correct practices, role-play interviewing, and written exercises in recording and critiquing experiences. Evaluation would be designed to ensure that each trainee achieved an acceptable level of mastery of these skills.

Identifying Content to Be Covered.   Identifying content to be covered follows the defining of objectives. In preparing course materials, the purpose is to compile a packet of resources that is complete enough that it can be used as intended. The basic document should be a course outline that lists major topics and subtopics to be covered. Some courses may be designed in a way that the expectation is that they will be self-taught. In this instance, the content must be fairly complete and comprehensive. If the course is self-taught, perhaps a few journal articles and a list of references may accompany the course outline, with further guidelines about what concepts the trainee needs to master before proceeding on to the next major topic. If the course involves an understanding of agency policy, a copy should be provided, together with any relevant interpretations and possibly some case material that will help the trainee to understand its application.

If a course is to be taught by an instructor who has expertise in the area, a less elaborate content outline will be necessary. Even with experts, however, it is important to establish the principle that training content should follow essentially the same outline for all trainees and should not be left exclusively to the discretion of the trainer. Whether the trainer is an agency employee or is performing a service under a contract, the agency is in one way or another paying for the training and should insist on assurances that the content specified will be covered.

Specifying Teaching and Training Methods.   Methods of training include a number of options, many of which will depend on the number of trainees, the time allotted, and the resources made available. A common format for training is classroom instruction. This has the advantage of having a knowledgeable person present material and answer questions, coupled with trainee interaction and opportunities for role-play and other simulations. Classroom instruction, however, requires at least a minimum number of trainees to make the effort cost-effective.

A less costly method when the number of trainees is small is presenting content through video. Many professionally made tapes are available on a variety of practice-related topics, or videos can often be made by the agency, using its own expertise, at a reasonable cost. An increasingly popular method is the provision of training through the use of computer software. Objectives can be specified, content presented, and an evaluation completed, maintained on a disk, and made available to workers as they need to know the content. Other options include workbooks or programmed learning modules that permit trainees to work through at their own pace and take a brief examination at the end to demonstrate mastery of essential concepts.

Brennan and Memmott (1982) point out some important principles of adult learning that should be considered when decisions are made about methods of training. These principles can be summarized in terms of those relating to the training design, to the adult learner's experience, and to the context in which the learning takes place.

Adult learning is enhanced
when the training design:
- Emphasizes immediate usefulness.
- Is kept simple, yet builds on experience.
- Incorporates problem-solving approaches.
- Uses a variety of teaching and learning methods.

The adult learner's experience
is enhanced when the training:
- Responds to concerns of the learner.
- Is presented in a physical environment that is conducive to learning.
- Lets the learner go at his or her own pace.
- Uses teaching and training media that match the learner's style.
- Provides the learner with focused, immediate feedback.
- Bolsters self-esteem and feelings of competence.

*Finally, the benefits of training
are maximized when:*

- The organizational climate values learning.
- The learning process encourages individuals to reflect on their learning experiences and to incorporate them into their practice.

Designing Evaluation Instruments   Because training often requires an investment on the part of the agency, in terms of financial expenditures as well as in terms of staff time committed to training, it makes good sense to know if training is achieving its objectives. There is a variety of ways to measure the success of training. The following example illustrates alternative approaches to the evaluation of training.

> Sommerset Senior Center provides congregate meals, socialization and recreation, and outreach services to the elderly. It has come to the attention of the program manager that only a small number of seniors is participating in the recreation activities provided. The majority simply sit around and wait for the meal to be served. The program manager decides to bring in an expert on the subject of recreation activities for seniors. The expert is a very entertaining speaker. He organizes a number of activities and gets staff to participate. Many staff comment to the program manager about how much they enjoyed the training session.
>
> As the program manager reflects on this session, what should he evaluate? Staff enjoyed the session. That is certainly better than having them complain that it was a waste of time. Staff commented that they learned a number of new activities. That's important, too. But will this new learning be carried over to the job? Will more seniors participate in the recreation program? These are some of the issues to be considered when evaluating training.

There are four basic approaches to the evaluation of training. Success can be measured in terms of (1) trainee reaction, (2) trainee learning, (3) trainee performance, or (4) results achieved with clients (Carolan, 1993).

Trainee reaction focuses on the participants' experiences during the training session. Did they enjoy the training and did they find it worthwhile? This is probably the most common approach to the evaluation of training because it is easy and relatively inexpensive. Constructing an instrument to measure trainee reaction requires a determination of what it is that the organization wants to know about the training from the trainee's perspective. (For example, was it relevant? Was it understandable?) A generic instrument can be designed to cover all training, or one can be prepared for a particular training session. Trainees are generally asked what they thought of the content, the teaching method, and the trainer. Responses are scaled and an overall sum or mean score calculated for each item on the questionnaire. Room is generally left for comments. Findings from this type of evaluation are useful primarily in deciding whether to use a particular trainer or type of training again in the future. It tells the evaluator very little about the potential of training for solving practice problems. Evaluating only in terms of trainee reaction raises some questions about validity, because it is possible for trainees to enjoy the training and yet it may have no effect on their practice or on the problems that initially prompted it. Figure 12.2 illustrates a typical trainee reaction form.

FIGURE 12.2

FIGURE 12.2

Trainee Reaction Form

Trainee Reaction Form

Please respond to the following questions based on your experience with the training session that you just completed. Circle the answer that most closely approximates your reaction.

	1 Completely	2 Somewhat	3 Not at all
1. The content was relevant to my job.	1	2	3
2. The content was new to me.	1	2	3
3. The content was presented in an interesting manner.	1	2	3
4. I will use what I learned on my job.	1	2	3
5. The length of presentation was appropriate to the subject.	1	2	3
6. The speaker was interesting.	1	2	3
7. I would recommend this training to others.	1	2	3

The second approach to evaluation of training, evaluating trainee learning, attempts to understand the extent to which trainees have been able to master the concepts and to explain, interpret, or apply them in some type of examination upon completion of training. Learning is important, because if knowledge or skills are not learned in a way that they are retained and applied to practice, then the only value of the session was whatever might have happened during the course of training—factors such as enjoyment of training or boosting employee morale. Ideally, when learning is to be measured, training objectives should be stated in terms of learning expectations. A pretest should be administered to determine how much trainees already know about a subject. By administering the same test again as a posttest, it is possible to filter out what trainees knew prior to training, and to determine if the learning that took place was worth the time, effort, and resources invested.

The most common approach to measurement of learning is the paper-and-pencil test, but it is not the only way to measure learning. If training is designed to improve casework skills with the difficult client, role-play situations can be set up in which a trainee interviews a person playing the role of client before training and after training, with an evaluator observing and using a scoring sheet to identify evidence of learning.

The third approach to evaluation of training measures trainee performance. Changes in trainee performance on the job are critical if there is an expectation that training is intended to solve a problem. Measuring changes in performance requires involvement of a supervisor or someone who has knowledge of how the trainee performs on the job. Training objectives should reflect the expectation that training will bring about behavioral or performance changes on the job. Instruments are then designed to be completed by a supervisor or other staff member based on the on-the-job performance of the trainee. The issue here is that, although trainee reaction and learning are important, standing alone they do not provide much benefit to the sponsoring organization if they are not somehow translated into practice. Measuring changes in trainee performance requires a period of time following training to ensure that the trainee has ample opportunity to put newly learned knowledge and skill into practice. It may also require a review of existing practices and supervision within the trainee's unit to ensure that changes in performance are allowed and supported.

The most difficult, yet the most valuable, type of training evaluation is the fourth approach—evaluating for results. Using this approach means that the ultimate test of the value of training will be demonstrated improvements in effectiveness with clients. Evaluating from this perspective requires a review of training objectives to ensure that the training is appropriately focused on achieving positive client outcomes. It also requires that some form of measurement of results or outcomes with clients be in place prior to training to be used as a baseline for assessing change (see Kettner, Moroney, & Martin, 1999).

In the example used previously (attempting to increase seniors' participation in the senior center's recreational activities), measuring results would require a count of the number of participants before and after training. Evaluating training by measuring improved client outcomes must be tied to a specific worker so that the results can be attributed to training. Generalized client outcomes may be the result of any number of factors. What measuring results really means is that the problem or situation originally identified has been impacted in some positive way, and changes can be attributed to training.

The four approaches to evaluation of training can be used in combination. The evaluator should always be clear on what it is that the findings say about the training. Ideally, those sponsoring the training would feel training is most successful when (1) the trainees have a positive reaction to the training, (2) they learn what the training was designed to teach, (3) they carry over what they learned to their on-the-job performance, and (4) the problem that prompted training is resolved.

Step 3. Monitoring and Evaluating the Overall Training Program

Austin (1982) makes a case for the self-evaluating agency. Self-evaluation, he says, begins with the commitment to improve programs in the context of limited resources available to social service agencies. Self-evaluation, Austin argues:

- Is both an organizational principle and an economic and political necessity.
- Allows an agency to become its own best critic by evaluating itself and incorporating results into ongoing program development.
- Puts an agency into a position in which it need not fear outside evaluation.
- Helps to identify questions that will need answers in the future.

Although evaluation generally refers to client-serving programs, many of the same principles can also apply to the agency's staff training, development, and education programs.

Learning about the efficiency, effectiveness, productivity, and quality of these programs requires systematic data collection and aggregation. With a well-designed and maintained record-keeping system, annual reports of training, development, and education activities can be produced and used to help in evaluating their value and cost-effectiveness.

Colleges and universities maintain a transcript of courses completed and grades achieved for each person who has been a student at their institutions. A transcript provides a valuable, cumulative record of progress toward a degree. In the same way, a cumulative training record on every employee can provide a valuable resource to both the agency and the employee. The training record can be used to document both orientation and training completed by each employee. This record may prove valuable should an employee claim ignorance of policies, procedures, or other factors covered in sessions attended by the employee and verified with a signature and date. If the agency provides a series of training courses that is required for all employees, the training record can be used to verify for each employee which courses have been completed and which ones still need to be taken. Records can also provide valuable resources for supervisors when they are asked to write letters of reference. Some of the documents that should be kept in a training record include:

- A copy of the orientation checklist, with signatures of employee and supervising personnel verifying the dates on which each orientation activity was completed.
- A list of required in-service training courses with signatures of employee and training personnel verifying the dates on which each course was completed.
- A list of elective in-service training courses with verifying signatures and dates.
- A copy of the employee's career development plan, including a list of training and education activities planned, dates completed, and verifying signatures.
- A list of professional conferences or other out-service training or workshops attended, with dates and verifying signatures.
- A record of all college and university courses taken that were sponsored or in some way underwritten by the agency, with dates and verifying signatures.

It is reasonable for an agency to expect that a well-designed staff training, development, and education program will pay dividends. The extent to which the agency will be able to measure the effects of the program will be determined by the quality of its cumulative records of staff participation in training, development, and education activities and its thoroughness in evaluating each individual training and development effort as well as the total program. With creative and thoughtful use of available data, these programs can be assessed in terms of effort, efficiency, and effectiveness.

Measurement of effort can be accomplished by aggregating data such as the number of training hours completed by each level of staff each year. Aggregating hours by types of training (e.g., program policy and regulations, improving practice skills, etc.) adds more information to the annual training report. Evaluating efficiency and effectiveness will require the creative use of indicators drawn from a number of sources. Program evaluation summaries may be designed in a way that shows improvement over the years in achieving program objectives. Depending on training provided during this period, there may be a way to make the connection between training and improvement. Performance appraisal systems may indicate aggregated improved performance of staff over time.

Supervisory reports may indicate reductions in client complaints or improved compliance with human resources policies. Collecting data directly from staff in the form of a staff satisfaction survey each year will also indicate how various levels of staff perceive the overall training program and whether their perceptions are becoming more positive over the years.

■ The Career Development Plan

The employer who is in pursuit of excellence will always attempt to consider issues of staff training, development, and education in the context of the agency's and its clients' best interests. However, when it comes to career planning and development, the caring, nurturing employer will also allow for careful and serious consideration of an employee's interests. This may mean that, if an employee's long-term interests lie outside the agency, the employer will support career development activities that will help to achieve these long-term interests. This attitude is difficult to sustain when it affects a highly valued employee, but the alternative—standing in the way of an employee's career development interests—can only result in an unhappy employee who feels that the organization is not supportive of his or her career plans. Conversely, when staff feel supported in their career objectives, morale is likely to be good and employees are likely to perform at high levels.

Career development planning involves a periodic assessment of each employee's short- and long-term career objectives. Employees are encouraged to think through where they would like to be in the short term (one to three years) and also in the long term (five to ten years). Supervisory and coworker input may be helpful in identifying career objectives and reassuring the employee that they are realistic in terms of agency opportunities and the employee's talents and abilities. Once short- and long-term career objectives have been identified, training, development, education, and experience needed are planned in a way that is designed to achieve objectives. These plans are then used to set priorities for development activities for the coming year. It is generally a good practice to complete or update the career development plan at the time of performance appraisal. This provides an opportunity to put the appraisal into a context of identifying employee strengths as well as areas for needed improvement, and to guide the employee toward the kinds of staff development activities that will round out knowledge and skills, and make him or her more competitive for higher-level positions. A sample career development form is illustrated in Figure 12.3.

The position taken from the opening chapter of this book is that the organization and its managers and administrators have a responsibility to ensure that all systems are well designed and structured to work in harmony with each other and to support high levels of performance among staff.

When the agency managers and administrators have fulfilled their responsibilities to build a well-integrated organization, it is then incumbent upon staff members to do their part by performing at the highest levels possible. One measure of staff performance is the annual performance appraisal. Getting the most out of the performance appraisal system is the subject of the next chapter.

FIGURE 12.3
Career Development Plan Form

Career Development Plan

Name _____ Position _____ Supervisor _____ Date _____

In-Service Training Completed

Policy Courses:	Date	Populations Courses:	Date	Practice Courses	Date
Agency Policy	_____	Physical Disabilities	_____	Family Stress	
State Regulations	_____	Development Disabilities	_____	Caregiving	_____
Federal Regulations	_____	Cross-Cultural Concepts	_____	Mobility	_____
Human Resource Laws	_____				

Out-Service Training Completed

Education   Educational Objectives: _____

High School: _____   Credits Achieved Since Date of Employment
Community College: _____   _____ _____
College/University: _____   _____ _____
Advanced Degree: _____

Short-Term Goals to Move Toward Career Objective (Specify Date of Completion)
1.
2.
3.

Training, Development, and Education Designed to Achieve Short-Term Goals (Specify Date of Completion)
1.
2.
3.

Long-Term Goals to Move toward Career Objective (Specify Time Frames for Achievement)
1.
2.
3.

Training, Development, Education, and Experience Needed
Training and Development:

Education:

Experience:

Signatures:

Employee _____ Date _____ Supervisor _____ Date _____

SUMMARY

1. **Making a Positive Transition into Employment.** Attention should be focused on what the new employee needs to know and can absorb. Experienced staff to work with the new employee should be carefully selected.

2. **Establishing Training, Development, and Education Policy.** Training policy should define opportunities for all staff, establish required training content, establish a percentage of time that employees are expected to devote to training and development, and make clear what resources the agency will commit to training and development.

3. **Orientation.** Information should be provided to the new employee in an orderly way with packets of information made available for future reference.
   - *Orientation Strategies and Techniques.* Interviews, checklists, agendas, video, sample records, and a new employee handbook are some of the techniques that can be used for new employee orientation.

4. **Training.** Training can affect employee performance and ultimately overall organizational performance.
   - *Developing a Comprehensive Staff Training and Development Plan.* A complete plan should include training, development, and education.
     Types of Training and Development. Types include in-service training, on-the-job training, out-service training, and college or university education.

5. **The In-Service Training Curriculum.** An in-service curriculum should be modeled after the curriculum design of an educational institution with major categories and course listings under each category.

6. **Steps in Developing an In-Service Training Curriculum.**
   - *Step 1. Identifying Training Needs.* Develop a needs-assessment instrument and use it to survey staff regularly.
     Analyzing Training Needs. Not all performance problems can be solved through training. Some analysis may be needed.
   - *Step 2. Developing Training Courses or Modules.* Materials should be organized in a way that courses or modules can be delivered over and over with a minimum of preparation.
     Defining Learning Objectives. Course materials should specify what the trainee is expected to be able to perform upon completion of the training.
     Identifying Content to Be Covered. Trainers should prepare a course outline and copies of articles or other materials to be used.
     Specifying Teaching and Training Methods. How is the course designed to be taught? In-person instructor, video, computer, other?
     Designing Evaluation Instruments. Training can be evaluated in terms of trainee reaction, trainee learning, trainee performance, or results achieved on the job.
   - *Step 3. Monitoring and Evaluating the Overall Training Program.* The training director should maintain a complete training record on all staff.

7. **The Career Development Plan.** Career development focuses on employee short- and long-term career goals.

Please complete the following sections of your manual based on the content covered in Chapter 12.

Section 12: Staff Training and Development

12.1 Orientation. Write a policy statement that makes clear what orientation activities the agency will provide for a new employee. Attach a sample orientation agenda as Document 12.1a and a sample orientation checklist as Document 12.1b.

12.2 In-Service Training. Write a policy statement that makes clear what in-service training the organization will provide employees and how much of their time employees are expected to devote to training each year. Attach a sample curriculum framework as Document 12.2a for the in-service training program and indicate which courses or modules are required and which are elective for each level of staff.

12.3 On-the-Job Training. Write a policy statement that makes clear who is eligible for OJT, under what conditions, and what elements or components shall be included in an OJT plan.

12.4 Out-Service Training. Write a policy statement that makes clear who is eligible for out-service training, under what conditions, and how much financial support the agency will provide.

12.5 Education. Write a policy statement that makes clear who is eligible for educational benefits, under what conditions, and what benefits are provided.

12.6 Career Development. Write a policy statement that makes clear what should be discussed at a supervisory conference on career development. Attach a copy of a Career Development Form as Document 12.6a.

REFERENCES

Austin, M. (1982). *Evaluating your agency's programs.* Beverly Hills, CA: Sage.

Brennan, E., & Memmott, J. (1982). The information user as adult learner. *The management of information transfer for the employment and training field.* Lawrence, KS: The University of Kansas.

Carolan, M. (1993). Today's training basics: Some new golden rules. *HR Focus* (April), 18.

Crimando, W., & Riggar, T. (1990). *Staff training: An annotated review of the literature.* New York: Garland.

Gilley, J., & Egglund, S. (1989). *Principles of human resource development.* Reading, MA: Addison-Wesley.

Gronlund, N. (1970). *Stating behavioral objectives for classroom instruction.* London: The Macmillan Company.

Hafer, M., & Riggar, T. (1981). Hiring guidelines for rehabilitation facilities. *Journal of Rehabilitation Administration, 5*(4), 155–160.

Jensen, J. (1981). How to hire the right person for the job. *The Grantsmanship Center News* (May–June), 20–31.

Kettner, P., Moroney, R., & Martin, L. (1999). *Designing and managing programs: An effectiveness-based approach.* Thousand Oaks, CA: Sage.

Mager, R., & Pipe, R. (1970). *Analyzing performance problems: Or you really oughta wanna.* Belmont, CA: Fearon Publishers.

Matkin, R. (1980). Supervisory responsibilities relating to legal and ethical issues in rehabilitation settings. *Journal of Rehabilitation Administration, 4*(4), 133–143.

McKenna, D., Svenson, R., Wallace, K., & Wallace, G. (1984). How to build a training structure that won't keep burning down. *Training* (September), 77–83.

Rapp, C., & Poertner, J. (1992). *Social administration: A client-centered approach.* New York: Longman.

Reed-Mendenhall, D., & Millard, C. (1980). Orientation: A training and development tool. *Personnel Administrator, 25*(8), 40–44.

Schmidt, M., Riggar, T., Crimando, W., & Bordieri, J. (1992). *Staffing for success: A guide for health and human service professionals.* Newbury Park, CA: Sage.

St. John, W. (1980). The complete employee orientation program. *Personnel Journal, 59*(5), 373–378.

Weinbach, R. (1998). *The social worker as manager: A practical guide to success.* Boston: Allyn & Bacon.

Supervision, Performance Appraisal, Rewards, and Termination

- Encouraging Optimum Employee Performance
- Supervision
- The Corrective Action Process
- Appraisal Techniques
- Tying Performance Appraisal to Rewards
- Terminating Employees: Voluntary and Involuntary Terminations

Upon completion of this chapter, the reader will be able to:

- Identify and discuss the managerial aspects of supervision.
- Describe the corrective action process.
- Explain the criteria to be used in constructing a performance appraisal system.
- List and give examples of eight approaches to performance appraisal.
- Discuss ways to tie performance to rewards.
- Identify and define four types of terminations.

Assumptions

- That employee performance should be monitored and performance appraisal taken seriously and carried out conscientiously.
- That nonperforming employees should receive special attention and changes in their performance should be monitored.
- That a performance appraisal system should be designed in a way that it is economical, easy to administer, useful for improving employee performance, trusted by employees, valid, and reliable.
- That performance appraisal instruments should be designed with extensive staff input and support.
- That good performance should receive tangible rewards.
- That consistent nonperformers should be terminated.
- That a termination process should be specified in policy, and steps should be followed diligently.

■ Encouraging Optimum Employee Performance

In the previous chapters we have focused on a number of human resource functions—recruitment, selection, hiring, orientation, staff training, and development. The ways in which these functions are planned and implemented can influence the extent to which employees find a niche within the organization and become valued contributors.

The functions to be discussed in this chapter cover the vast majority of day-to-day supervisory activities, ongoing supervision of staff, performance appraisal, allocation of rewards, and, if necessary, termination from the agency. Because these functions are directly tied to daily activities and performance of staff, they can have a profound effect on overall organizational performance and, ultimately, on organizational culture. The following example will illustrate.

> Michelle was an ambitious young woman who had recently received her MSW degree and was employed by Family Dynamics, Inc., a large private, nonprofit agency that provided counseling services to families and children, including a number of contracts with corporations for employee assistance services (counseling for employees of contracted businesses who have personal problems). Her plan was to work for three or four years as a caseworker and then to move into supervision and administration. After about a year and a half on the job, Michelle was beginning to gain recognition as a highly skilled practitioner and was invited to serve on a number of planning committees for the agency. Because of her success with families, some of the most difficult cases were assigned to her. Two of the corporations for which the agency provided employee assistance services specifically mentioned Michelle when they renewed their contracts. It was clear that she was on the fast track to success. Her performance appraisals were glowing.
>
> As each year passed, however, she was finding that essentially all employees were treated the same when it came to performance appraisal and rewards. When coworkers shared with her their evaluation scores and the size of their merit raises, she realized that her exemplary work was valued with words only. Family Dynamics, Inc. was an organization that believed that, in order to reduce turnover, it was necessary to keep employees happy. This philosophy translated into giving high performance appraisal ratings and equal merit raises regardless of performance.
>
> In her third year, a supervisory position became vacant, and Michelle applied for it. Three employees who had seniority over her were short-listed. She knew that the quality of their work was not at a high level, but all of the available documentation indicated that they were superior employees. Michelle decided that loyalty and longevity were the qualities that counted at Family Dynamics, Inc. It was not the type of system in which she felt she could achieve her career goals, and she soon moved on to another job.

This scenario is repeated many times every year. When the culture of an organization values loyalty and longevity over performance, many messages (both direct and subtle) are sent to new and talented employees that the organization is not open to new ideas and change. Nonproductive employees thrive in this type of an environment. The long-range future for such an agency, however, is dismal. Good employees are the lifeblood of a human service agency. A good deal of planning and effort needs to be devoted to designing a system that will keep those who are highly productive and will weed out those who are not.

■ Supervision

Good supervision is intimately intertwined with performance appraisal. In spite of an agency's best efforts in recruitment, selection, and hiring, the true test of an employee's abilities comes in day-to-day performance. When planned and implemented conscientiously, supervision provides an opportunity to help workers continuously improve, to perform at their optimum levels, and to prepare them to move on in their careers to greater responsibilities. Done in a negligent manner, supervision can encourage low levels of performance and can lead to legal problems. Montana and Charnov (1993), in discussing future demands on managers and supervisors, make the following observation:

> There will be a premium placed upon managers with good people skills. *People skills* is a popular term used to describe a group of interpersonal relationship skills (as opposed to mechanical or technical skills, which describe a relationship to machinery) generally assumed to relate to managerial success. These include communications skills, knowledge and application of motivational concepts, goal-setting abilities, and performance appraisal skills. (p. 443)

Good supervision, however, comes with a price. It is time-consuming and requires good planning, teaching, and evaluative skills. Patience, tenacity, and an ability to deal directly and honestly with problems are important supervisory qualities. High ethical standards are expected from those who supervise employees at any level. Lewis (1977) emphasized the importance of ethical behavior:

> One can fail in almost any aspect of administrative judgment and yet retain self-respect. But failure to engage in ethical behavior is to yield to unprincipled practice, and unprincipled practice erodes an administrator's core of personal dignity. (p. 121)

The Code of Ethics of the National Association of Social Workers identifies integrity as a core value. Professionals are expected to be aware of the profession's mission, values, and ethical principles and are expected to act responsibly to promote ethical practices on the part of the organizations with which they are affiliated. Ethical dilemmas are often faced when a supervisor must choose between what appears to be two "right" answers. Thorough study, compliance with existing policies and practices, and elimination of personal bias will contribute to sound and ethical decisions.

Much of good supervision is attitude and experience. The supervisor who is overly concerned with being liked will inevitably run into difficulty. The focus needs to be on establishing work standards, doing whatever can reasonably be done to enable workers to meet the standards, and then rewarding them (or withholding rewards) as performance merits.

In some ways performance appraisal systems operate like grades in a university. When an instructor gives every student an A, the grade loses its meaning. When a supervisor gives every worker a rating of superior, the rating no longer is valued. Honest ratings, backed up by specific examples of performance, and rewards allocated in accordance with level of performance can get an agency on track toward optimum levels of productivity.

Policy on Supervision and Performance Appraisal

The supervisory relationship is a complex one that carries mutual rights and responsibilities. Weinbach (1998) points out that a common perception of supervision is that its function is to provide consultation on cases for the direct service practitioner. This, however, is only one area of supervision. "There exists," he says, "another whole group of supervisory activities that more closely resembles . . . management. It includes the use of management functions as applied to subordinates to shape, support, and enhance the individual's job performance" (p. 153). These management functions of supervision include responsibilities in the areas of (1) accountability, (2) consultation, (3) protection from discriminatory practices, (4) establishing the appraisal format, timing, and process, (5) providing an avenue for appeals, and (6) establishing a relationship between performance appraisal and salary increases or other rewards. Each of these areas should be established in policy that is then used to guide supervisory practices.

Accountability   Schmidt, Riggar, Crimando, and Bordieri (1992) point out that supervisors are responsible for the ways in which those under their supervision carry out their jobs. "The legal doctrine of *respondeat superior* holds that a supervisor is responsible for the acts of his or her subordinates undertaken within the realm of employment" (p. 102). The extent of accountability and the responsibilities of both parties will be better understood if they are stated as part of agency expectations in a policy manual. A policy on accountability might read as follows:

> *Section 13.1   Supervisory Roles and Responsibilities*
> 13.1.1   *Accountability.* All employees of the organization who have responsibility for immediate supervision of subordinates shall be responsible for the acts of their subordinates undertaken within the realm of employment. These acts shall include, but not be limited to, behavior in relation to clients, coworkers, management, and administration, and public comments made about the organization.

Consultation   Regularly scheduled consultation forms the basis of supervisor/worker communication. Some of these sessions need to be formalized, with discussions documented, when important policy and procedure issues are covered. This practice will also help to address the issue of accountability. Policy guidelines will help clarify expectations for consultation and case conferences. The following example illustrates possible wording for a policy on regularly scheduled conferences.

> *Section 13.2   Regularly Scheduled Conferences*
>   The primary source of information about agency policy and practice resides with an employee's immediate supervisor. In order to ensure that lines of communication are kept open to all staff, and in order to ensure that accurate information is disseminated throughout the organization, it shall be the policy of this organization to establish a requirement that each supervisor meet with his or her subordinates on a weekly basis. No length of time shall be specified. Supervisory conferences shall focus primarily on the information and consultation needs of the subordinate.

Protection from Discriminatory Practices   Discrimination and harassment in the workplace are illegal, and supervisors can be held accountable for the behavior of their subordinates. Decisions about employees based on such factors as age, gender, race, religion, or other factors not related to the job are considered discriminatory. It is the job of the supervisor to ensure that decisions are made solely on work-related criteria, and to deal with employees who engage in discriminatory practices (Daughtrey & Ricks, 1989). Employees are also entitled to a work environment in which they feel safe and free from language, displays, or behaviors that can be considered sexually harassing. Employees have a responsibility to report such behavior to a supervisor, and supervisors have a responsibility to intervene and to deal with offending personnel. All of these issues should also be codified into a set of policies and procedures that will define what is meant by discrimination and harassment, make clear that they are not tolerated in the organization, and spell out procedures to be followed should inappropriate behaviors be demonstrated by agency personnel. For example, in its brochure on sexual harassment, Arizona State University provides the following definition, examples, and recourse.

Sexual harassment: unwelcome behavior of a sexual nature that unreasonably interferes with the working/learning environment and creates a hostile, intimidating, or offensive environment, or takes the form of seeking sexual favors in exchange for a promise of a benefit or a threat of a penalty.

You may be the harasser if you assume people are not offended by your behavior of a sexual nature because they neglect to tell you; touch or hug people without their express permission; treat individuals differently based on their gender in professional/educational situations; make personal comments about someone in the middle of a professional/educational discussion; don't think about the impact of your behavior on others.

If you are being harassed, tell the harasser the behavior is unwelcome, say it firmly without smiling or apologizing; keep a log of what happened, when, where, any witnesses or patterns of behavior; seek others who may have received or are receiving similar treatment from the harasser; tell someone about the harassment, talk to a friend or any of the people listed on the following page (Arizona State University, n.d., p. 3).

Establishing the Appraisal Format, Timing, and Process   The format, timing, and process for performance appraisals are very important to the integrity of the performance appraisal system and should be established in policy in a way that ensures that appraisals will be handled in a consistent manner throughout the organization. There is a variety of formats including essay, standardized scales, use of critical incidents, management by objectives, and others. The pros and cons of each format will be discussed in a subsequent section. The timing of performance appraisals can vary. A common approach is to complete the appraisal on the anniversary date of hiring for each employee. This has the advantage of spreading the process over the year and individualizing each employee. Other organizations may prefer that all appraisals be done during the same period of time so that the ratings can be used in decisions about merit increases and other rewards. Brody (1993) suggests that appraisals be conducted throughout the year and that the end-of-the-year appraisal be used as an opportunity to review previous discussions. He further proposes that formal performance appraisal conferences be held semiannually or even quarterly so that corrective action can occur in a more timely manner than if the formal conference is held only once a year.

Processes may also vary. Some prefer a one-way assessment that includes feedback from supervisor to supervisee. Others prefer an interactive process in which both parties complete the appraisal form and then come together to identify points of agreement and disagreement about the employee's performance. Some systems allow for input from peers, some even from subordinates. A recent innovation, called the 360-degree evaluation, is designed to solicit feedback from multiple sources including superiors, coworkers, subordinates, customers, and the person being evaluated (Jarman, 1998). Although single-source evaluations can be dismissed by the employee being evaluated, participants report that multiple-source evaluations have much more credibility.

Whatever practices are selected by an organization, they should be established in policy to minimize differences in the ways that the process is carried out throughout the organization. If flexibility is desired, this can also be made clear with a policy statement. The following example illustrates a policy statement on format, timing, and process of performance appraisal.

Section 13.3	*Performance Appraisals*
13.3.1	*Format.* All employees shall have a performance appraisal completed by their immediate supervisor each year using the job duties checklist in combination with an essay format on the forms provided by the agency for each level of staff.
13.3.2	*Timing.* All performance appraisals shall be completed between June 1 and June 30 of each year.
13.3.3	*Process.* Both employee and supervisor shall complete the appraisal form prior to the scheduled conference. A single document, signed by both employee and supervisor, shall be produced and signed following the conference.

Providing an Avenue for Appeals   Every system also needs to establish a policy about appeals. When assessments are done with conscientious attention to accuracy and detail, it is inevitable that there will be some differences of opinion about performance. Employees may claim that they didn't receive proper instructions, that they were not properly trained, or that their performance was superior to a coworker who received a higher rating. Sometimes these disputes can be resolved through dialog and discussion. Sometimes both parties believe so firmly in their positions that the dispute must be taken to another level. The right of review is fundamental to a fair system.

The process and the makeup of appeals committees should be spelled out in policy. Edwards and Sproull (1985) advise that members of the appeals committee or review board include representatives of protected groups and that they include representatives of peers as well as supervision, so that all parties will feel that their perspectives are reflected in the appeals process. The following example illustrates a policy statement on appeals.

> *Section 13.4*   *Appeals on Performance Appraisal*
> When there are disagreements on matters associated with performance appraisal, they shall be referred to the appeals committee. The committee shall be composed of two persons representing the rank of the employee who filed the appeal, two persons representing the rank of the person who completed the performance appraisal, and one person representing management. Demographic characteristics shall be representative of the organization. The committee shall make a recommendation to the executive director, whose decision shall be final.

Establishing a Relationship between Performance and Rewards   Finally, it is useful to include a policy on the relationship of the performance appraisal to merit increases and other rewards. This is an area that can be difficult to address in a fair and objective manner. There may be budgetary constraints in any given year that may prohibit merit increases. Some supervisors may try to manipulate the system to ensure that their workers get an inordinate share of the benefits regardless of performance. These issues will be discussed further in a subsequent section. The point is that if rewards are not in some way formally tied to appraisal, then one must logically ask two questions: (1) What is the function of the appraisal, and (2) on what basis are the rewards allocated? These factors are absolutely critical to system integrity and have implications far beyond budgetary considerations.

Rapp and Poertner (1992) make the following observation about what happens when rewards are used to reinforce positive behaviors in organizations:

> Positively reinforced behavior slowly comes to occupy a larger and larger share of time and attention and less desirable behavior begins to be dropped. Yet, most managers appear not to understand the power of this concept. The reward structure in many organizations is inadequate. (p. 173)

When an organization can design a system that is successful in rewarding the most productive employees and withholding rewards from the least productive, it will also be successful in shaping its culture in a way that recognizes, values, and respects good performance. That type of organization is well on its way to achieving excellence.

■ The Corrective Action Process

Monitoring and evaluating employee performance and ensuring that communication is clear and well documented are challenging and require careful planning. When conceptualizing the performance appraisal process, it may be useful to think in terms of a worst-case scenario—dealing with the problem employee. The same procedures recommended for the low-performing employee are applicable to the high performer. The difference is that the high performer will understand what needs to be done at an early point in the process and will act on that understanding. The low performer may need to be taken through the full process, perhaps even to the point of termination.

The corrective action process consists of a series of up to five interviews during which the employee receives increasingly detailed instructions about performance, resulting in written agreements about performance targets, time lines, and interim monitoring by the supervisor. For descriptive purposes, the five interviews will be referred to as: (1) the hiring/ orientation interview, (2) the "we've got a problem" interview, (3) the "you've got a problem" interview, (4) the probationary interview, and (5) the termination interview (Umlah, 1976).

The assumption is that, following each interview, the employee knows exactly what performance improvements are expected and when each task or activity is due. During the time frame established, the employee either improves performance and achieves objectives or fails to achieve them. If performance is deemed satisfactory, the series of interviews ends at that point. If it does not improve, the interviews continue, possibly to the point of termination. The performance improvement process is illustrated in Figure 13.1.

FIGURE 13.1

Process for Dealing with the Problem Employee

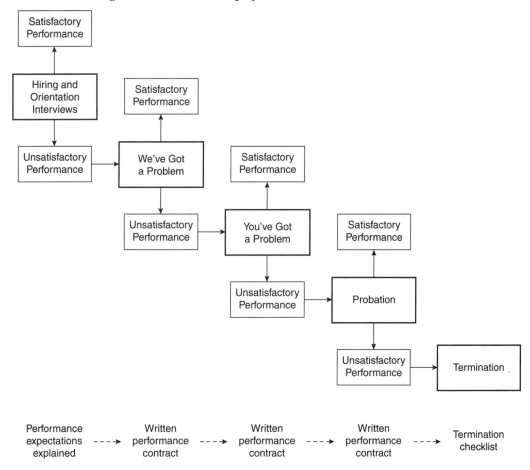

The Hiring/Orientation Interviews

At some point during either the hiring interview, the orientation interview, or both, the supervisor will have an opportunity to meet with the new employee and discuss the position in some detail. This valuable time should not be spent merely getting acquainted, although that is certainly a part of the purpose of the interview. A supervisor should do some advance planning for these meetings and should come prepared with an agenda, a copy of the job analysis, some notes, and perhaps some sample case records, if the new employee will be carrying a caseload. The new employee's résumé should have been reviewed prior to the interview so that the supervisor is in a position to ask informed questions.

When the supervisor describes the responsibilities of the unit and the position, he or she should highlight the major duties and tasks covered in the job analysis, with special emphasis on those functions that are critical to success. Some discussion of the performance appraisal system and accountability is also appropriate. For example, if the agency evaluates its programs and uses client success as a measure of employee effectiveness, it is important that the new employee understand the significance of these evaluation data. This is also the time to ensure that all necessary training has been scheduled. Other topics to be covered would include management or supervisory style, expectations relative to teamwork, requirements for data collection, and other important job-related issues. The interview should end with an understanding that there will be follow-up sessions, and the new employee should be informed about where he or she may go in the event that questions arise. A list of all documents provided, training scheduled, and other relevant orientation materials provided should be placed in the new employee's personnel/training record. On reflection, the supervisor should feel that the new employee has been given every opportunity to start off on the right foot and progress toward an optimum level of productivity.

The "We've Got a Problem" Interview

Very likely the majority of employees will adapt to agency expectations as they become comfortable in their positions and will perform at acceptable or perhaps even superior levels. If no performance problems are identified, employees begin the regular cycle of performance appraisal as described in the policy manual. For those few who have difficulty, it may be necessary to go on to the next structured interview.

The reason for framing the second interview as the *"we've* got a problem" interview is that it is important that the supervisor not make assumptions early in the process about the nature of the problem. This interview should be approached honestly and openly from the perspective that perhaps there were components of the job that were not made clear; perhaps all the necessary training was not completed; perhaps the importance of deadlines for completing data collection and maintaining case records was not fully grasped. By sharing the responsibility, the supervisor creates a supportive environment for the employee and provides an opportunity to share concerns about the orientation, the training, or the nature of the job. This is a good time to discuss the new employee's strengths and to identify the areas in which improvement is needed.

All discussion of performance deficiencies should be based on agency-approved performance standards and specific, documented examples of the employee's failure to meet standards. For example, it is not acceptable to inform an employee that his or her case notes need improvement. Instead, the employee should be handed a copy of the format for case notes, a sample that meets standards, and an example of his or her own work that does not meet standards. A work plan can then be established that explicates how many case records will be brought up to expectations and by what date. The supervisor attempts to remove barriers to successful completion of the work plan, to schedule necessary training, and to help with time management if needed. The work plan is put into writing, signed by both supervisor and worker, and is then used as a monitoring document to ensure that deficiencies are being corrected. Interim sessions may be planned and a follow-up interview scheduled on or after the date when the work plan is to be completed. A performance improvement plan may include some of the components in the following example.

Name: Roger Caulfield   *Supervisor:* Mary Tremaine
Problem Area: Keeping up-to-date on the completion of data collection and documentation on all cases; sixteen of twenty-five case records do not have the necessary documentation.

Performance Objectives: Incomplete records will be brought up-to-date at the rate of two records per week for the next eight weeks.

- Agency format and standards (copies attached) will be used to determine completeness.
- Sample work that meets standards has been provided.
- Interim reviews on the two records brought up-to-date will be held at the end of each week. Barriers to progress will also be discussed.

The "You've Got a Problem" Interview

If the employee's performance improves after the first problem-focused interview, it is not necessary to continue with the series of corrective sessions. Ideally the performance standards were made clear, the employee understood his or her deficiencies, took the necessary remedial steps, and as a result is performing at an acceptable level. At this point the employee moves into the regular cycle of performance appraisal as described in the policy manual. Some, however, may not have satisfactorily corrected their performance deficiencies as of the due date for completion of the work plan. For those employees, the time has come to place the responsibility for the problem on their shoulders.

A performance improvement plan was clearly spelled out and put in writing during the "we've got a problem" phase of the corrective action process. A time line for correcting deficiencies was established. The employee was provided with all the supports needed to successfully achieve work plan objectives, but he or she failed to achieve them. It is now incumbent on the employee to search for answers within himself or herself as to why he or she has been unable to correct the performance problem.

In this interview the supervisor should begin by reviewing the expectations from the last interview to make sure there is agreement on expectations. The supervisor should indicate that there has been insufficient improvement and give the employee an opportunity to present any valid reasons for failure to achieve work plan objectives. Perhaps a bit more time needs to be spent in this interview on analysis and understanding of the causes of the problem. The employee may disagree with agency expectations and, therefore, may not be highly motivated to correct the identified deficiency. Some workers, for example, pride themselves in being strong advocates for their clients and, as such, spend as much time as possible in face-to-face contact with clients or working on their behalf rather than attending to the required record-keeping responsibilities. These workers may resent data collection and case recording as infringements on their time. It may be that values, priorities, and disagreements with agency expectations are appropriate subjects for this interview.

In any case, it is once again incumbent upon the supervisor and worker to come up with a plan for corrective action and a timetable. The supervisor should make clear that failure to meet the objectives of this work plan will result in the worker being placed on probation. Follow-up sessions are scheduled to monitor progress. Supportive services or training needs are addressed. A meeting is scheduled on or after the date when the work plan is to be completed. Following the session, the work plan is put in writing, with copies made available to both worker and supervisor.

The Probationary Interview

If an employee gets to the point in the series of corrective action interviews at which probation is necessary, it is very likely that there are some serious problems with his or her performance. She or he may not be suited for this kind of work, may not have some of the necessary personal qualities such as patience or initiative, or may simply have a profound disagreement with some of the agency's priorities, policies, or practices.

This is an appropriate time to raise for consideration the fit between agency mission and purpose, on the one hand, and the employee's interests and commitments on the other. It is unlikely that the employee, by this time, is not aware of or does not understand the performance deficiencies. Agency expectations and performance standards have been explained at three different points in time. Work plans have twice been developed, specifying precise activities to be completed and due dates. A significant amount of supervisory time has been invested in helping this employee to correct the deficiency. So it is appropriate to consider both the best interests of the worker and the best interests of the agency. If the employee has not already realized the poor fit by this time, a frank discussion may help the employee to rethink his or her position and to look for work elsewhere.

It is always possible, of course, that there is an employee who, in spite of extensive supervision and training, has not been successful in performing up to expectations, yet is strongly committed to keeping the job. When the corrective action interviews have progressed to this point, it is necessary to repeat the discussion of the "you've got a problem" interview. During that session there was a search for an understanding of the causes of performance deficiencies. Perhaps the analysis was incorrect and the working hypothesis for corrective action needs to be adjusted. Once again, the supervisor should have on hand examples that illustrate the performance problem. If more examples of exemplary work will be helpful at this point, these, too, should be made available. A probationary contract should be prepared, again with time lines for completion of each activity. The employee should clearly understand that this is the last opportunity to correct the performance problem. The next interview will focus on termination from the agency. All agreements are documented, signed, dated, and placed in the record.

The Termination Interview

The final interview in the corrective action process, the termination interview, is qualitatively different from the previous four sessions. A decision has been made to terminate. The decision is not up for discussion. The purpose of the interview is to inform the employee of plans to terminate in as direct and straightforward a manner as possible, to make sure that the employee understands all his or her rights as an employee, and to lay out the formal separation process. Applicable employee rights, laws, and regulations will establish the parameters for the termination interview and the process.

Like the other interviews, this one requires a good deal of preplanning. It is important that the supervisor consult with higher-level management personnel to ensure that they are willing to back the decision to terminate. Meetings with human resource personnel and consulting attorneys may also be in order to ensure that all aspects of applicable laws and regulations have been followed. A checklist should be prepared for the employee to ensure that all agency materials such as case records, keys, computer software, and other items are safely returned and the returns are documented with signatures and dates. Documentation of performance discrepancies and work plans should be readily available for reference purposes, but a review of performance problems is not part of the discussion at this point.

The interview itself should be brief. Jensen (1981) suggests that it is best to schedule it late in the afternoon, preferably on Friday. This timing, he says, will help to limit the amount of time the terminated employee remains in the office when emotions are running high. It also provides the opportunity to use the weekend as a cooling-off period, with further discussion to continue the following week if needed. The notice of termination should be given in the first ten minutes; the whole interview should last no longer than thirty minutes. This is not a time for reflection or review of the past. The focus should be on the termination decision and the process. The employee should be assured that all personnel policies and procedures are being followed and that adequate documentation exists to support the decision. Any mention of the performance problems should be completely consistent with the previous discussions and work plans. No advice should be given. No new items should be introduced for discussion. The supervisor should not let himself or herself get baited into any discussion of age, sex, race, disability, or other protected class characteristic, nor should there be discussion of performance in relation to other employees.

It is important that the supervisor listen to what the terminated employee has to say. Allow for ventilation of feelings, within reasonable time limits. Encourage the employee to check with human resources personnel or attorneys if he or she has any questions about violation of his or her rights or due process. Encourage the employee to leave the premises directly following the completion of the interview. Agree to a follow-up meeting. Many questions will occur to the employee over the weekend and there should be assurances that these questions or concerns will be addressed. Remind the employee that there is a checklist that is to be used for verifying that all separation activities have been completed and that this list will be discussed in the follow-up meeting.

Although it is never possible to guarantee that a termination will not be contested, when it is handled in the manner just described, with complete documentation of failure to perform job-related functions, challenges are less likely. Encouraging employees to follow up with their own sources to ensure that they have been dealt with fairly can help them to understand that the agency feels confident in its decision and has nothing to hide. The more thorough the corrective action process and preplanning for the termination interview, the less likely that the employee will contest the termination.

■ Appraisal Techniques

One important purpose of performance appraisal is to provide feedback to the employee. Feedback is highly sought after by employees, and the ways in which it is provided by a supervisor can affect the ways in which it is received and used by the employee. Jensen (1980) suggests that a positive tone be set by observing the following principles:

- Avoid surprises in the interview by providing daily feedback. Saving problems for an annual discussion is apt to overwhelm the employee and trigger a defensive response.
- Show evidence of having listened carefully by repeating what the appraised employee has said about the review.
- Show a flexibility and willingness to change conclusions in the course of the interview after hearing reasonable evidence that such changes are appropriate.
- Assure the confidentiality of what is said and recorded. Revealing the substance of a confidential conversation with others can be a source of embarrassment for everyone concerned.
- Stress an interest in helping the individual's career progress, but not to the point of pushing if the person is not interested. (p. 6)

Designing the Appraisal System

A number of different methods can be used for performance appraisal. Each method has advantages and disadvantages. Carroll and Schneier (1982) surveyed a group of human resource experts on eight different performance appraisal methods. Each method was rated in terms of the following criteria:

Economic Criteria: Cost of development and administration, speed in filling out, ease of use by raters.

Personnel Criteria: Usefulness for research, for allocating merit pay, for providing documentation, for promotion, for identifying training needs, for counseling and development.

Counseling Criteria: Provide job-related feedback, communicate performance expectations and standards, provide guidance on how to improve performance.

Acceptance Criteria: Acceptance to raters and ratees, psychometric soundness.

Usefulness in Different Types of Organizations: Useful in dynamic, loosely structured organizations; useful in formalized, bureaucratic organizations.

Edwards and Sproull (1985) also identify a number of important appraisal system features in their proposal, which they refer to as the *Ten Commandments of Performance Appraisal.* The ten factors include the following:

- *Multiple Raters.* Ensure that performance will be reviewed from a number of perspectives.
- *Rater Feedback.* Provide feedback to raters about their rating skills.

- *Rater Training Based on Feedback.* Provide training for raters.
- *Objective, Observable, and Job-Related Performance Dimensions, Jointly Developed by Management and Employees.* Agreement on performance dimensions is critical to system credibility.
- *Comparability.* Ratings for similar jobs should use similar measures.
- *Professional Procedures.* Be systematic in implementation and guided by policy.
- *Fair Employment Posture.* Keep decisions free from bias.
- *Documentation.* Provide an audit trail that may be used to defend decisions.
- *Systematic Communication of Rating Results to Ratees.* Give every ratee a confidential personal performance profile.
- *Appeals.* Give ratees the option of appealing appraisal results to a higher authority.

All of the foregoing factors may be used as criteria for evaluating appropriateness and comprehensiveness when designing a performance appraisal system.

Appraisal Instruments

Although various authors present their own mix of performance appraisal methods, most include the following options: (1) the essay, (2) the critical incident technique, (3) the trait/behavior checklist, (4) the job duties checklist, (5) behaviorally anchored rating scales (BARS), (6) forced-distribution ranking, and (7) management by objectives (Brody, 1993; Dessler, 1997; Rapp & Poertner, 1992; Schmidt et al., 1992).

Essay   The essay method requires that the supervisor develop from scratch an overall assessment of the employee's strengths, need for improvement, and development needs. This format provides virtually no structure for the supervisor and requires good professional writing skills. It has the advantage of being highly individualized to the person being evaluated. No standardized performance criteria are imposed on the appraisal. Two beginning workers might receive very different types of reviews using the essay method, each raising completely different concerns, because each review would be tailored to each employee's unique profile of strengths and needs. Individualization, however, also has the disadvantage of reducing or eliminating the possibility of comparing employee performances. Comparability is an important feature of a well-designed appraisal system, especially when salary, promotion, or other personnel decisions are involved. The essay format is probably the most time-consuming method and is probably best used in a modified format or in combination with one or more of the other appraisal options. Figure 13.2 illustrates a modified format that uses the essay method.

The Critical Incident Technique   The critical incident technique is one in which the supervisor keeps an ongoing log or record of examples of exemplary and below standard performances for the purpose of providing highly specific feedback to the employee that can be used to take corrective action. This approach has several advantages. It provides the supervisor with actual examples from the employee's work experiences that make a particular point about performance and avoids focusing only on the employee's most recent performance. The supervisor who attempts to recall examples at the time of performance appraisal will be much less likely to come up with good illustrations. Second, the critical incident technique causes the supervisor to be conscious of performance during the entire

FIGURE 13.2
Essay Format Used for Performance Appraisal

Employee Performance Appraisal

Name _____   Position _____

Supervisor _____   Date _____

1. Please describe your employee's performance on the job during the past year.

2. Please list and describe those areas in which the employee's performance exceeded expectations.

3. Please list and describe those areas in which the employee's performance failed to meet standards.

4. What qualities does this employee have that contribute to or detract from effective performance?

Signatures:

Employee _____ Date _____   Supervisor _____ Date _____

year, not just at appraisal time. It lends itself well to providing ongoing feedback to the employee. As Dessler (1997) points out, the critical incident method provides hard facts for explaining the appraisal. Disadvantages are similar to those highlighted for the essay method. The critical incident technique is time-consuming and requires good writing skills and the ability to frame an example in a way that maximizes learning. Used alone, it does not allow comparison to other employees and, therefore, is less useful for making decisions about such issues as salary increases, promotions, or transfers. Critical incidents are most valuable when used in conjunction with an additional appraisal technique. Figure 13.3 illustrates how critical incidents can be used in performance appraisal.

The Trait/Behavior Checklist   The trait/behavior checklist requires that a list of desirable work-related characteristics be developed and used in each appraisal. Characteristics used are those that are generally accepted by the organization and its employees as reflecting positively on performance, regardless of the position held by the ratee. Examples might include such items as "consistently high productivity," "works well under pressure," or "gets along well with others." The scale might use the following values:

1 = Not at all descriptive of this person
2 = Slightly descriptive of this person
3 = Somewhat descriptive of this person
4 = Usually descriptive of this person
5 = Consistently descriptive of this person

FIGURE 13.3

Some Sample Entries from a Critical Incident Log

Critical Incident Log

Employee _____ Maria Rivera _____   Position _____ Child Abuse Investigator I _____

Date	Description of Incident
7/24/XX	Maria returned from a child neglect investigation quite shaken about the condition of the home and the child. Anger at parents tended to cloud her judgment about planning for the children. We discussed the case at length and will follow up on this subject in the future.
8/16/XX	Maria was assigned a high-profile case that involved the death of a child and removal of siblings. She did an excellent job of taking charge and making some critical decisions independently and handled herself in a highly professional manner, including the way she dealt with the media.
10/3/XX	Maria experienced conflict with a colleague over the placement of a child. Differences had to be resolved at the supervisory level. She was commended for the strong advocacy position she took on behalf of her client, but her working relationship with the other worker has been severely damaged. We need to be alert to this issue. Indications are that she may need to focus on developing and maintaining collaborative relationships with colleague and other professionals in supervisory conferences and perhaps a workshop.

Etc.

The trait/behavior checklist has a number of advantages. It is the same for all employees, so it can be used for comparative analysis when making decisions about salary, promotions, or other competitive factors. It produces scores, thereby providing useful data for a number of purposes. It is relatively easy to complete because the checklist presents the supervisor with a structure that can be used as prompts to generate thoughts about the employee's performance. It is somewhat more objective than essay or critical incident techniques and, therefore, may tend to eliminate a bit more bias than those approaches. There are also a few disadvantages. Trait/behavior checklists are not necessarily tailored to reflect job standards and expectations. They reflect personal qualities and can be influenced by personality. A low-producing but cooperative worker may be evaluated more highly than a high-producing but difficult worker. The scores produced by checklists are only as valid as the criteria and the judgments behind them.

Another disadvantage is that employees rarely know how other employees were rated. In the absence of an employee being able to compare his or her rating to an overall mean, it may be difficult to interpret and to understand where one stands in the eyes of management. Like other approaches, trait/behavior checklists are often used in conjunction with other appraisal instruments. Figure 13.4 illustrates a trait/behavior checklist.

The Job Duties Checklist The job duties checklist is in some ways similar to the trait/behavior checklist. Using a scaling approach, some organizations specify a list of duties and tasks drawn from the job analysis or job description and provide an opportunity

---

FIGURE 13.4

Trait/Behavior Checklist Format for a Performance Appraisal

Employee Performance Appraisal

Name _____ Position _____

Supervisor _____ Department _____ Period Covered _____

Please circle the number that best describes this employee's performance in the areas indicated.

	1	2	3	4	5
	Exceptional performance; no improvement needed	Standards are being met above expectations but there is room for improvement	Standards are being met at minimal levels; there is significant room for improvement	Standards are not being met; performance improvement is needed	Standards are not being met; corrective action is needed
Work quality	1	2	3	4	5
Work quantity	1	2	3	4	5
Attendance	1	2	3	4	5
Meeting deadlines	1	2	3	4	5
Relationships with coworkers	1	2	3	4	5
Relationships with subordinates	1	2	3	4	5
Relationship with supervisor	1	2	3	4	5
Initiative in improving	1	2	3	4	5

Comments

Signatures

for a supervisor to rate each duty according to the performance of the employee. A scale might reflect the following range:

1 = Nonperformance
2 = Below acceptable standards
3 = Meets standards
4 = Above standards
5 = Exemplary performance

Duties for a caseworker might include categories such as Intake and Assessment, Client Contracting, Implementation and Monitoring, Case Closure, and Evaluation. A number of tasks listed under each category would be rated using the preceding scale. A cumulative score for performance on tasks may be used to give an overall impression of how competently the employee is able to perform the duty. Like the trait/behavior checklist, the job duties checklist produces scores and can be used for informing personnel decisions. It also has the advantage of being job related, because the duties are drawn from the job analysis and job description. However, quantifying performance is accurate only to the degree that duties listed reflect what is actually expected on the job. Frequent revisions of the job duties checklist (and perhaps the job analysis) may be necessary.

Checklists also may suffer from a halo effect or its opposite, an unwarranted negative overall impression. The halo effect sometimes causes a supervisor, for an employee who is perceived positively, to check the columns representing the highest ratings, without studying each item and giving it independent consideration. The job duties checklist is designed with an expectation that each item will be evaluated individually. The halo effect or negative overall impressions may result in a supervisor's biases entering into the appraisal. When used in combination with the critical incident technique, some of these tendencies can be moderated. Figure 13.5 illustrates a job duties checklist.

The Behaviorally Anchored Rating Scale   The Behaviorally Anchored Rating Scale (BARS) is yet another technique that can be used to help bring more objectivity to the performance appraisal process. Like the two foregoing checklists, BARS uses scaling techniques to produce a performance profile on each employee. A major difference is that a single scale (such as those used in the trait/behavior or job duties checklists) is not specified. Instead, an individualized scale is defined for each item on the checklist. For example, if a caseworker were to be evaluated on the task of intake and screening, the following behaviorally anchored rating scale might be used:

1 = When the client is not forthcoming with important information, the caseworker does not pursue information and leaves the record blank. Gets information only when it is volunteered by the client.

2 = The caseworker attempts to draw out clients by explaining the purpose of the program and by sharing brochures and printed materials. May give up on the most resistant clients.

3 = The caseworker is able to get information by explaining how the benefits will affect the client and fit into the plan. Gets complete and accurate information on most clients.

4 = The caseworker is able to pick up on cues and follow them at the client's pace in order to get the information needed for screening and assessment. Shows patience with resistant clients and usually gets at least basic information.

5 = The caseworker is highly skilled in drawing out even the most resistant clients and consistently turns in files with all necessary information and complete documentation.

FIGURE 13.5

Job Duties Checklist Format for a Performance Appraisal

Employee Performance Appraisal

Name _____ Position _____

Supervisor _____ Department _____ Period Covered _____

Please circle the number that best describes this employee's performance in the areas indicated.

	1 Exceptional performance; no improvement needed	2 Standards are being met above expectations but there is room for improvement	3 Standards are being met at minimal levels; there is significant room for improvement	4 Standards are not being met; performance improvement is needed	5 Standards are not being met; corrective action is needed
Thorough and accurate completion of intake	1	2	3	4	5
Thorough and accurate completion of assessment	1	2	3	4	5
Culturally appropriate assessment of problems, strengths, support system	1	2	3	4	5
Thorough and accurate documentation of assessment	1	2	3	4	5
Establishment and maintenance of a professional relationship with clients	1	2	3	4	5
Use of professional knowledge and skills in developing treatment plan	1	2	3	4	5
Effective use of community resources	1	2	3	4	5

Etc.

Comments

Signatures

As is evident from this example, developing instruments for the BARS approach can be very time consuming and requires great attention to detail. Recommended steps to producing good instruments include (1) interviewing jobholders and their supervisors, (2) specifying the behaviors to be included on the instrument, (3) categorizing or clustering the behaviors into a small number of performance dimensions, (4) use jobholders and supervisors to help develop the descriptors to be used in the scales for each item, (5) circulate among staff for review and comment, and (6) develop the final instrument.

Although this approach offers the advantage of a more accurate and valid appraisal of performance, it suffers from the disadvantages of high cost and a significant investment of time and other resources. BARS is more likely to produce an accurate profile because each item must be studied and rated individually. Thus, it is less likely that a supervisor will be affected by the halo effect (going down one column and using the same rating for every item). Another advantage is that the standards for performance are clear to the employee. Desired behaviors are spelled out and, with effort and the necessary training and development, they can be achieved. Feedback is also more precise. Instead of learning that performance is "average" or "below average," an employee will know exactly how her or his performance is perceived on each dimension of the job.

The Forced-Distribution Ranking   The forced-distribution ranking is not an instrument. It is a technique for comparing employee ratings. Forced-distribution ranking requires that supervisors impose some version of a bell-shaped or normal curve to the ratings awarded their employees. The percentage of each category on the rating scale that can be awarded is prescribed before the performance appraisal process begins. It is built on the assumption that ratings can be reduced to a single indicator that reflects level of performance (e.g., 1 = highest performers, 2 = next level, etc.). In adopting a forced-distribution ranking, the following percentages might be established by an organization:

Overall Grade	Interpretation	Percentage Allocated
1	highest-level performers	15
2	above average performers	20
3	average performers	30
4	below average performers	20
5	lowest-level performers	15

Typically the grade represents a summary of a more detailed appraisal in which employees are rated on job duties, work-related behaviors, or other factors. Ratings of each subsection of the appraisal are totaled, and the totals are translated into an overall grade for the review period. It is also common to use descriptors in connection with each of the grades. For Grade 1 a descriptor might read: "Achieves all objectives and exceeds some. Performance in some way has a measurable impact on the organization." For Grade 5 a descriptor might be worded as follows: "Achieves less than half of objectives. Needs considerable supervision to accomplish job expectations."

The strength of forced distribution is that it demands that supervisors deal with the grade inflation problem. Forced distribution takes away the option of giving every worker a rating of superior or above average. It requires that the rater make finer distinctions between employee performances. The issue of inflated ratings can take on increased importance when the organization commits itself to tie salary increases to performance appraisal scores. If all employees get superior or above average ratings, the budget may not be able to cover the promised salary increases.

The major disadvantage of forced distribution is that it may force raters to give some overall ratings that they believe are not fair or do not accurately reflect the employee's performance. When this happens, it tends to generate bad will among both raters and ratees, and they may develop adversarial attitudes toward management. When performance is rated against standards, employees are more likely to accept feedback about discrepancies. When they are rated against each other, they inevitably feel that subjectivity and personal feelings influence ratings. Employees subjected to forced distribution may feel that every year at appraisal time some staff members must become the designated victims, because the system requires that at least 15 percent be given the lowest rating. Within a high-performing unit, giving mandatory low ratings can have a negative effect on morale and productivity. In order for the system to work effectively, the concept of forced distribution cannot be imposed on small units. If units consist of six to eight workers or less, some of the ratings will be artificial. In smaller organizations, the concept can be applied to the organization as a whole, but this will require a great deal of deliberation and negotiation among managers and supervisors to be sure that standards are applied fairly across all job classifications. Merck and Company, for example, allows supervisors to argue for two of five employees receiving a superior rating prior to final decision making about ratings, when combining several small departments (Dessler, 1997).

Management by Objectives   The final performance appraisal method to be discussed here is management by objectives (MBO). This method is one that has evolved from Drucker's (1954) framework in which he proposed that organizations plan and specify their expected accomplishments at the beginning of the year and that these specifications be used to establish priorities, allocate resources, and measure success. When used in performance appraisal, the concepts of goals, objectives, and activities are carried down to the employee level. Each employee, in consultation with a supervisor, establishes goals and objectives for the coming year. Rapp and Poertner (1992) point out that critical features of an MBO system include:

- The goals are consistent with the person's performance-based task analysis.
- The goals are outcome oriented, positive, realistic, and measurable.
- The goals are established with the person.
- A plan is necessary for how a goal is to be attained.
- A periodic review of the progress toward the goal is required.
- Feedback and rewards are necessary for goal attainment. (p. 163)

An advantage of the MBO approach to performance appraisal is that it tends to ensure that individual employee objectives and performance will be compatible with organizational, departmental, and program goals and objectives. When examined collectively, employee accomplishments relative to their goals and objectives can provide a useful measurement tool for evaluating organizational and program success as well. Another advantage is that an MBO format lends itself to identification of training and development needs. Employees agree at the beginning of the year that they will pursue certain performance objectives. If it happens that they are unable to achieve some of their objectives, a brief analysis should reveal areas in which more training or development activities may be needed.

The major disadvantages cited for MBO are that objectives are difficult to write, and compiling a complete plan for all employees is extremely labor intensive. For example, if a supervisor and worker agree and state as an objective that the worker "will improve skills in case management and referral," it is unlikely that there is a clear mutual understanding about what is meant by "improve." This misunderstanding will inevitably lead to disagreements at performance appraisal time, and much of the value of the MBO system is undermined. A more specific objective, such as "will identify at least ten new referral resources for employment and training, and will meet with a representative from each," is more easily documented. Writing objectives in this precise manner is challenging and time-consuming and is often seen as a disincentive to using the system. MBO also has the limitation that the system may not provide adequate comparability between and among employees to make important personnel decisions.

Table 13.1 summarizes the advantages and disadvantages of each of the approaches to performance appraisal discussed in the foregoing section.

Mixing the Methods   Most organizations find that if they hope to accomplish the multiple purposes intended by performance appraisal, mixing the methods is necessary. Considerations in constructing a system include possible expectations that it will (1) reinforce performance standards, (2) provide accurate and individualized feedback to employees about their performances, (3) be useful in making personnel decisions, (4) be tied to rewards but allow for cost containment, (5) be useful in identifying training and development needs, (6) be efficient from the rater's perspective, (7) be fair from the ratee's perspective, and (8) minimize costs of development and administration.

If the system and the instruments are to reinforce performance standards, some structure must be provided; instruments used cannot be completely open-ended. Some type of checklist (or combination of trait/behavior, job duties, and/or BARS) will be necessary. In addressing the issues of accurate and individualized feedback to employees, management by objectives and the critical incident technique are the methods that are most useful (Carroll & Schneier, 1982).

If performance appraisal data are to be used for personnel decisions, it is necessary that comparable data be produced in a quantified format. This will require some type of scaling in combination with a checklist. If the rating system is tied to rewards, it is important to build in some cost containment features. The forced-choice method will ensure that limits are established for the number of employees who may receive the highest ratings.

In order to help in identifying training needs, a system must be able to reflect performance in relation to standards and to allow employees to recognize their performance discrepancies. Some combination of MBO, the critical incident technique, and checklists will best meet these needs (Carroll & Schneier, 1982). To be considered efficient from the rater's perspective, the instrument must be easy to use. A format that helps to frame the rater's thinking and asks questions that can be rated is generally considered the most user friendly. Space can then be allowed for more elaborate individualized comments.

To be considered fair from the ratee's perspective, the instrument needs to be individualized as much as possible. Incorporation of some of the features of the essay, management by objectives, and the critical incident technique can help to achieve this purpose. Finally,

TABLE 13.1

Advantages and Disadvantages of Selected Performance Appraisal Methods

Appraisal Method	*Summary of Advantages and Disadvantages of Performance Appraisal Methods*	
	Advantages	**Disadvantages**
Essay	Highly individualized Few or no predesigned criteria are imposed	Little or no structure provided Does not permit comparison to other employees Time-consuming to complete Requires good professional writing skills
Critical Incident Technique	Provides highly specific feedback to the employee Uses actual examples of the employee's work Encourages supervisory attention to performance all year	Time-consuming to maintain Does not permit comparison to other employees Requires good professional writing skills
The Trait/ Behavior Checklist	Defines desirable behaviors Easy to complete Produces scores that can be used for comparative purposes	Time-consuming to develop Must be regularly updated May require sharing mean scores to be meaningful Depends on supervisor objectivity and fairness
The Job Duties Checklist	Defines desirable job performance Easy to complete Produces scores that can be used for comparative purposes	Time-consuming to develop Does not reflect job duties and tasks May require sharing mean scores to be meaningful Depends on supervisor objectivity and fairness
The Behaviorally Anchored Rating Scale	Provides a highly detailed profile of job performance and professional behavior Standards are clear to the employee Feedback is precise Produces scores that can be used for comparative purposes Relatively easy to complete	Time-consuming to develop May need periodic updating
Forced- Distribution Ranking	Prevents arbitrary awarding of high ratings regardless of performance Can keep reward system within budget if tied to performance ratings	All ratings may not be fair or accurate, because some will be influenced by forced distribution May force comparison of employees to each other rather than to performance against job standards
Management by Objectives	Requires employees to think about their performance objectives at the beginning of the year and throughout Provides mutually agreed upon standards for appraisal Ensures compatibility with organizational and program objectives	Time-consuming to develop and maintain Objectives are difficult to write Comparisons among employees are limited

to minimize the cost of development and administration, an organization may need to identify experienced staff members and use its own resources in developing a system that meets as many of the foregoing criteria as possible. Checklists tend to require more time and resources on the development side but are more efficient to administer. Conversely, the more individualized systems such as essay, MBO, or critical incidents are less costly to develop but take more time and resources to administer. The ideal is a balanced system that meets the approval of the majority of both raters and ratees throughout the organization.

Tying Performance Appraisal to Rewards

One of the most demoralizing factors of organizational life is salary decisions that appear to be arbitrary. Conversely, employees can become highly motivated and increase productivity if they believe that salary decisions are related to job performance. A number of well-designed performance appraisal and reward systems in business and industry include a series of steps, designed to capture some of the features needed to keep an organization on track to excellence. These steps include:

- Identification of employee objectives at the beginning of each performance appraisal cycle. These objectives must be compatible with organizational and program objectives and delineate the contribution the employee expects to make toward their achievement during the coming year. The relationship between employee objectives and organizational/program objectives is depicted in Figure 13.6.

FIGURE 13.6

Developing an Employee Performance Plan within the Context of Organizational and Program Objectives

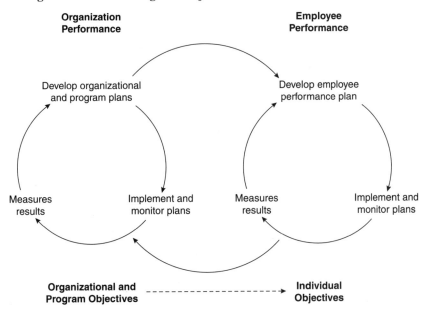

- Establishment of a rating system that translates level of achievement of employee objectives into scores that are comparable across all employees in a given classification.
- Rank order employees in each classification from highest to lowest using ratings similar to the following, based on a more detailed performance appraisal:
  1 = Achievements clearly surpass performance objectives and affect program results
  2 = Achievements surpass expectations for all major performance objectives
  3 = All performance objectives were met
  4 = Major performance objectives were met; some secondary objectives were not met
  5 = Some major performance objectives and some secondary objectives were not met
- Apply a forced distribution ranking that will divide each classification into five groupings, with the largest percentage falling in the middle group and the smallest percentages falling at the extremes.
- Construct a table that specifies the size of salary increase for each employee classification. The table must take into consideration performance assessment ratings.
- Some systems also take the employee's current salary into consideration. This is a controversial practice. When it is done, the practice is based on the following principles:
  (1) If a *high-performing person* is at the *low end* of the salary continuum for his or her classification, there is more room to reward performance and encourage the high-performing employee to stay.
  (2) If a *high performer* is already at the *high end* of the continuum, there is a limit to how high the salary can go, and rewards may increasingly need to be nonmonetary.
  (3) *Low performers,* regardless of their current salary, should not be encouraged by salary increases.

Following these principles related to achieving objectives, forced-distribution ranking, current salary, and cost containment, a table may be constructed that can be used in determining the size of merit increase awards, while also taking into consideration job performance, existing salaries, and budget limitations. Such a table is illustrated in Table 13.2.

TABLE 13.2

Formula for Calculating Salary Increases That Takes into Consideration Individual Performance Objectives, Performance Appraisal Rating, Forced Distribution, and Current Salary

| Performance Appraisal Overall Rating | *Percentage of Salary Increase Tied to Performance Appraisal Rating and Current Salary* | | | | |
	Low End of Salary Range	Step 2 of Salary Range	Midpoint of Salary Range	Step 4 of Salary Range	High End of Salary Range
1	8%	7%	6%	5%	4%
2	6	5	4	3	—
3	4	3	2	—	—
4	2	1	—	—	—
5	No movement in range until performance improves				

A system that includes these features has several advantages. It is uniform and applied to all employees in the same way. It takes job performance into consideration. It rewards talented new employees and sends a message that they are valued. Because salary increases are planned with budget personnel, there can be assurances that total costs will fall within the budget. The forced-choice ranking feature ensures that raters must be careful and conscientious in their appraisals. Disadvantages are that rewards to high-performing, high-salaried personnel may not be commensurate with what they feel they should receive. As always, such a system will be effective and respected only to the extent that the instruments are valid and reliable and are administered fairly and with integrity by raters.

■ Terminating Employees: Voluntary and Involuntary Terminations

Decisions to terminate have been described as being among the most legally complex of all personnel decisions (Schmidt et al., 1992, p. 156). A growing list of court cases for what is perceived to be wrongful termination illustrates its complexity. The law requires that personnel-related decisions such as those affecting salary, promotion, or termination be based on qualifications and specific data about performance. Title VII of the Civil Rights Act of 1964 prohibits discrimination in hiring, discharge, compensation, or the provision of any benefit on the basis of race, color, gender, religion, ethnicity, or national origin (Hart, 1984). Subsequent acts prohibit discrimination (in addition to the foregoing) based on age, disability, or selected diseases such as AIDS, when risk to others is negligible (the Civil Rights Restoration Act of 1987, the Age Discrimination in Employment Act of 1987, the Rehabilitation Act of 1973, the Americans with Disabilities Act of 1990, and the Civil Rights Act of 1991).

In addition to considerations of possible discrimination, all employees are entitled to due process. Due process "implies that persons accused of wrongdoing will be treated fairly throughout the investigation and decision making related to their alleged wrongdoing" (Schmidt et al., 1992, p. 103). The disciplinary process should be progressive and should include opportunities to correct performance as described earlier in this chapter. Documentation of the entire process is critical. Documents may need to hold up to review at higher levels in the organization, to the agency's grievance procedures, to review by the U.S. Equal Employment Opportunity Commission, and to the scrutiny of a court of law.

For all these reasons it is critical that every organization have a complete set of policies and procedures that cover termination. These policies should include (1) a definition of the different types of termination, (2) a description of the process for voluntary terminations, (3) a description of the process for involuntary terminations, and (4) a termination checklist.

Types of Termination

Not all terminations are the same. The first order of business in dealing with a termination is to determine what type it is and then to follow policies and procedures indicated for that type. Terminations fall into four basic categories: voluntary, involuntary, administrative or fiscal necessity, and mutual agreement.

Voluntary terminations include:

- retirement
- resignation

Involuntary terminations include:

- unsatisfactory performance
- misconduct

Terminations for administrative or fiscal necessity include:

- reduction in force
- termination of contract

Mutual agreement involves:

- negotiated terms of separation between employer and employee

Voluntary Terminations   Retirement is defined as "that point when an employee begins to draw income benefits from a retirement plan provided by the agency" (Jensen, 1981, p. 39). Agencies with retirement plans are expected to establish retirement policies. By law there is no mandatory retirement age. Continuation, as for all employees, depends on meeting performance requirements. Retirement policies should include statements about notification, how pensions are calculated, how accrued benefits are to be handled, and retiree rights, if any, to participate in agency benefit programs. General guidelines for notification are two weeks for support staff and one month for professional staff. Calculation of pension amounts are typically based on salary over a period of years prior to retirement and years of service. Accrued vacation time is usually paid in a lump sum at the time of retirement. Some organizations also pay for sick time not used. If retirees are allowed to continue in the agency's health plan at their own expense, that opportunity should also be made clear in a policy statement.

Resignation is a voluntary termination decision that can be made for any reason. Some employees may have plans to move on to another job. Others may choose to stay home and raise their children. Employees are not under any obligation to provide a reason but are usually asked why they are leaving. If a reason for termination is provided, it becomes part of the record of their employment. Accrued benefits are, once again, an issue. Policies should make clear whether or not resigning employees are entitled to be paid for accrued vacation time and/or sick time. Accrued retirement benefits may remain with the agency and be drawn when the resigning employee retires, or they may be portable and eligible for carryover to a new job.

Involuntary Terminations   Unsatisfactory performance involves failure of an employee to meet performance standards (Jensen, 1981, p. 39). A case manager, for example, may regularly fall below the expected number of interviews with clients, may consistently miss case conferences, or may have a long history of complaints from clients. Some form of a corrective action process such as the one described earlier in this chapter must be followed in the case of unsatisfactory performance. The agency must be able to demonstrate that a reasonable effort was made to enable the employee to meet performance standards. Clear notification of performance deficiencies must be documented. Written plans must be on file to document efforts toward improvement. Policies should make clear the rights of the employee and the steps that constitute due process. A statement should also make clear how accrued benefits are to be handled when an employee is terminated under involuntary conditions.

Misconduct can be defined as willful and deliberate violation of the employer's rules (Dessler, 1997, p. 601). Termination for misconduct requires no prior notice or severance pay. There are two types of misconduct: misfeasance and malfeasance. Misfeasance refers to performing a legal act in an illegal or improper manner. For example, if a worker were to consistently prepare the necessary documents for a court hearing in a way that they are incomplete and inaccurate, he or she would be guilty of misfeasance. The act does not involve a crime, but it does involve willful and deliberate violation of the employer's rules. Malfeasance involves deliberate and intentional wrongdoing and may include involvement in illegal acts. A business manager that used agency funds or an agency contractor to make improvements on his or her home at agency expense would be guilty of malfeasance. Documentation is critical when an employee is to be terminated for misconduct. Due process is a right of employees and implies that persons accused of wrongdoing will be treated fairly. Just cause for the accusation must be established. The employee must be given the right to be heard and the opportunity for appeal (Sartain & Baker, 1978).

Terminations for Administrative or Fiscal Necessity   Reduction in force (RIF) involves a separation of employees who have met performance standards but nevertheless are being asked to leave the organization because of budget constraints. Technically a reduction in force may not be a termination because it may include plans for an employee to return to the agency. Separations may be temporary or permanent. Typically there are no guarantees for future employment, but the employer may grant employees in this category rights of first refusal when new positions open up in the future. It is important that agencies have in place a plan for handling a reduction in force that addresses the issues of fairness, avoiding discrimination, and maintaining the ability to continue to provide services with those retained. Jensen (1981) proposes that the following criteria be used in planning for a reduction in force:

- The nature of the job relative to overall success and survival of the organization.
- Relative performance of the individual, as documented in the record.
- Long-range outlook for continued or renewed funding of specified agency activities.
- Seniority of employment with the agency. (p. 42)

The issue of fairness can be addressed through some type of formula that uses such factors as seniority, performance appraisal, and the employee's contribution to critical programs and services. The plan must avoid discrimination by ensuring that reductions will be across the board and that those in protected classes will have equal opportunity to be retained. Selected positions may be designated as critical to agency functioning and may be made exempt. All of these factors must be clearly spelled out in policy, so that it does not become necessary to make reduction-in-force decisions only at the time the actual terminations must take effect.

Termination of contract is, in many ways, similar to a reduction in force. Social service agencies provide many programs and services that are funded through contracts with federal, state, or local governments. Frequently this funding is only for one year with no assurances that the contract will be renewed. Employees hired under these contracts are informed at the time they are hired that their employment will last for the length of the contract. If the contract is renewed, employment may be extended for another year. If it is terminated, the term of employment is over. None of these events should come as surprises to the employee whose position is funded by a specific contract. Rights and benefits of the employee as well as responsibilities of the agency should be spelled out in policy.

Mutual Agreement   The final type of termination is mutual agreement. This happens when both the individual and the organization agree that the employment relationship should be ended for their mutual benefit (Jensen, 1981). If the employee recognizes that his or her talents and skills are not particularly well matched to the job requirements and initiates termination procedures, that is a resignation. However, it may also happen that during the corrective action process described earlier in this chapter, both the supervisor and the employee reach the conclusion that performance in this position is unlikely to improve. Both want the separation to be amicable and mutually agree to terms of a termination, including a reasonable amount of time for the employee to seek other work. Accumulated vacation time and/or compensatory time may be incorporated into a plan that leads to the final separation.

Mutual agreement may also be used when a termination is planned for unsatisfactory performance. Rather than have a termination for cause on the permanent record, an employee may agree to a voluntary resignation. Under these circumstances, it is usually agreed that future employers seeking a reference will simply be provided with basic information, including dates of employment and position held, but will not be informed of the nature of the separation. Allocation of accumulated benefits may become part of the negotiation for termination.

The Voluntary Termination Process

Voluntary terminations usually involve a series of events including formal letters, interviews, and separation procedures. These events should be established in a policy manual. The process may begin with an informal discussion with the immediate supervisor. Plans for resignation or retirement are discussed and the employee is made aware of termination policies and procedures. The employee then writes a formal letter of resignation or intent to retire and addresses it to the person designated in the policy statement, usually the agency director or chief executive officer. A plan is drafted with the supervisor to transfer work responsibilities to other staff. A session is set up with the human resources person to ensure that all forms are completed and processed. For the person who is submitting a resignation, an exit interview may be scheduled with a representative of the management team.

Some employers offer preretirement counseling. The most common practices include:

- Explanation of Social Security benefits,
- Leisure-time counseling,
- Financial and investment counseling,

- Health counseling,
- Psychological counseling,
- Counseling for second careers outside the company, and
- Counseling for second careers inside the company. (Dessler, 1997, p. 612)

In addition to various interviews and counseling sessions, employees who are retiring or resigning will have in their possession a number of items that belong to the agency. Remembering to turn in these items should not be left to chance. The termination checklist will be discussed in a subsequent section.

The Involuntary Termination Process

Because of its complexity and potential legal implications, the involuntary termination process should be broken down into three phases: (1) preplanning, (2) the termination interview, and (3) follow-up. Preplanning involves identifying and defining a clear statement of just cause. Documentation supporting corrective action is compiled during this phase. The plan to terminate for cause is shared with superiors in the organization. The policy manual is reviewed. Human resources personnel and legal counsel may be consulted. Jensen (1981) suggests that the following questions will help to determine whether reasons for termination have been adequately developed:

1. Does any documentation exist that leads to conclusions other than the imminent termination?
2. Who, if anyone, will be surprised by the termination?
3. Was there adequate investigation of alleged misconduct before the action was taken?
4. Is the person's salary record contrary to that of an unsatisfactory employee?
5. Have other employees been treated differently under similar circumstances?

When all questions have been answered, consensus has been achieved among management personnel, and all policy and legal issues addressed, the termination is ready to move forward.

The Involuntary Termination Interview   The termination interview is scheduled by the supervisor at a time when there will be no interruptions. The supervisor should be perfectly clear that the purpose of this interview is not to negotiate. Dessler (1997) recommends a six-step process for termination, as follows:

1. Plan the interview carefully. Have all materials and documents ready.
2. Get to the point. Inform the employee that the purpose of this interview is to inform him/her of the organization's intent to terminate employment.
3. Describe the situation. Be specific about performance.
4. Listen. Don't argue. Restate employee's comments to provide reassurance that they were heard.
5. Carefully review all elements of the severance package.
6. Identify the next step. Explain where to go and whom to contact. (pp. 605–607)

Copies of termination policies should be made available to the employee. The name and number of the human resources director should be provided if the employee does not already know this person. The employee should be given a brief time to consult with experts of his or her own selection but should be made aware of the date the termination is to take effect and that the date is firm.

Ideally, the follow-up interview will be held under conditions that allow both supervisor and employee to interact in a more rational, less emotionally charged manner. During this phase, plans are made to transfer work responsibilities, to complete necessary forms, and to make final separation arrangements with human resources, including receiving the final paycheck. Termination checklist activities are completed, as specified in the following section.

The Termination Checklist   During the course of employment, employees may accumulate many items that belong to the agency. These items may include office keys, keys to an agency vehicle, credit cards, computer software, disks, case records, office supplies, and other agency property. Identifying all these items at the point of separation should never be entrusted to the supervisor's memory. Once an employee has left the agency, whether voluntarily or involuntarily, it may be difficult to retrieve these items. It is, therefore, useful to compile a checklist of items that are to be returned and a list of agency personnel that should be consulted prior to final separation. This checklist should include a place for dates and signatures, verifying that materials have been returned to agency possession, or that appropriate staff have been consulted and agree that all necessary information has been exchanged or forms completed. In preparing the termination checklist, it may be helpful to consult the orientation checklist. A sample termination checklist is illustrated in Figure 13.7.

FIGURE 13.7

Sample Termination Checklist

Termination Checklist

Item	Date Completed	Initials
1. Turn all case records over to supervisor		
2. Turn in all completed dictation	_____	_____
3. Turn in all completed or incomplete reports	_____	_____
4. Turn in all building keys	_____	_____
5. Turn in all desk and filing cabinet keys	_____	_____
6. Remove all personal property from desk and office	_____	_____
7. Turn in agency identification card	_____	_____
8. Other (please list)	_____	_____

SUMMARY

1. **Encouraging Optimum Employee Performance.** The culture of an organization should support high levels of performance and should demonstrate that support in allocation of rewards.

2. **Supervision.** Effective supervision can have an important impact on performance.

   - *Policy on Supervision and Performance Appraisal.* Policies should include six areas, as follows:

     Accountability. Supervisors are responsible for the acts of their subordinates undertaken within the realm of employment.

     Consultation. Regular supervisory conferences will help keep staff current on practice and organizational issues.

     Protection from Discriminatory Practices. Supervisors are responsible for decisions or actions of subordinates as they relate to bias or harassment.

     Establishing the Appraisal Format, Timing, and Process. Supervisors have a responsibility to ensure that supervisees are aware of all parts of the performance appraisal process.

     Providing an Avenue for Appeals. Employees should have opportunities to present their case to others when there are disagreements with superiors, subordinates, or peers.

     Establishing a Relationship between Performance and Rewards. Clear criteria should be established that will ensure that good performance will be rewarded.

3. **The Corrective Action Process.** A process should be spelled out for dealing with the nonproductive employee.

   - *The Hiring/Orientation Interviews.* The first stage of the process should occur during the early contacts with the new employee in which performance expectations are clearly communicated.

   - *The "We've Got a Problem" Interview.* When job-related problem behavior has been identified, the first interview should focus on a sharing of responsibility, assuming that expectations may not have been made clear or explicit. A performance contract is established.

   - *The "You've Got a Problem" Interview.* Once the employee fails to keep the terms of the performance contract, the responsibility for failure to perform belongs to the employee. A new performance contract is established.

   - *The Probationary Interview.* If the employee fails to fulfill the second performance contract, he or she is placed on probation, and a third performance contract is established.

   - *The Termination Interview.* If the probationary terms have not been fulfilled, the final step is termination. Terms and conditions of separation are presented to the employee.

4. **Appraisal Techniques.** Performance appraisal should be made as positive and helpful an experience as possible for the employee.
   - *Designing the Appraisal System.* Researchers have identified five criteria that are helpful in assessing the efficiency and effectiveness of a performance appraisal system: economic criteria, personnel criteria, counseling criteria, acceptance criteria, and usefulness in different types of organizations.

   - *Appraisal Instruments.*
     Essay. Good for individualizing; time-consuming to complete.
     The Critical Incident Technique. Provides specifics from practice; time-consuming to maintain.
     The Trait/Behavior Checklist. Efficient to complete; may not address job functions.
     The Job Duties Checklist. Covers job functions; time-consuming to develop and update.
     The Behaviorally Anchored Rating Scale. Good, precise measures. Time-consuming to develop.
     The Forced-Distribution Ranking. Prevents artificial inflation of ratings. May cause some unfair ratings.
     Management by Objectives. Individualizes expectations. Advance agreement on evaluation criteria.
     Mixing the Methods. Some combination of approaches usually works best.

5. **Tying Performance Appraisal to Rewards.** A systematic approach that establishes objectives at the beginning of the year, translates ratings into comparable scores, applies a forced-distribution ranking, and ties merit increases to existing salaries and incorporates many of the features needed to maintain a fair, objective, and affordable system of rewards.

6. **Terminating Employees: Voluntary and Involuntary Terminations.** The legal complexities involved in involuntary terminations demand a clear set of termination policies and procedures.
   - *Types of Terminations.*
     Voluntary Terminations. Include retirement and resignation.
     Involuntary Terminations. Include unsatisfactory performance and misconduct.
     Terminations for Administrative or Fiscal Necessity. Include reduction in force and termination of contract.
     Mutual Agreement. Negotiated terms of a separation.

   - *The Voluntary Termination Process.* Steps to termination should be established in policy.

   - *The Involuntary Termination Process.* Includes preplanning, the termination interview, and follow-up.
     The Involuntary Termination Interview. Should follow a carefully planned agenda.
     The Termination Checklist. An aid to ensure that those who leave the agency return all agency property and complete all termination contacts and interviews.

EXERCISES

Please complete the following sections of your manual based on the content covered in Chapter 13.

Section 13: Performance Appraisal

13.1 Performance Appraisal Policy. Write a policy statement that makes clear the organization's expectations for performance appraisal. Address at least the following issues:

13.1.1 Frequency and time frame from beginning to completion.

13.1.2 Description of the process and who initiates it.

13.1.3 Format. Attach a sample instrument as Document 13.1.3a.

13.1.4 Appeals.

Section 13: Termination

13.2 Termination Policy. Write a policy statement that defines the types of termination.

13.3 Termination Procedures. Write a policy statement that spells out the steps to termination for each of the following types of terminations. Attach a copy of a sample Termination Checklist as Document 13.3a.

13.3.1 Voluntary Terminations.

13.3.2 Involuntary Terminations.

13.3.3 Administrative or Fiscal Necessity.

13.3.4 Mutual Agreement.

REFERENCES

Arizona State University. (n.d.). *Sexual harassment will not be tolerated.* Tempe, AZ: Author.

Brody, R. (1993). *Effectively managing human service organizations.* Newbury Park, CA: Sage.

Carroll, S., & Schneier, C. (1982). *Performance appraisal and review systems: The identification, measurement and development of performance in organizations.* Glenview, IL: Scott Foresman.

Daughtrey, A., & Ricks, B. (1989). *Contemporary supervision: Managing people and technology.* New York: McGraw-Hill.

Dessler, G. (1997). *Human resource management* (7th ed.). Upper Saddle River, NJ: Prentice-Hall.

Drucker, P. (1954). *The practice of management.* New York: Harper & Bros.

Edwards, M., & Sproull, J. (1985). Safeguarding your employee rating system. *Business, 35* (April–June), 17–27.

Hart, A. (1984). Intent vs effect: Title VII case law that could affect you (Part I). *Personnel Journal, 63*(4), 50–58.

Jarman, M. (1998, April 19). 360-degree evaluations gaining favor with workers, management. *The Arizona Republic,* p. D1.

Jensen, J. (1980). Employee evaluation: It's a dirty job but somebody's got to do it. *The Grantsmanship Center News,* July–August, 36–45.

Jensen, J. (1981). Letting go: The difficult art of firing. *The Grantsmanship Center News,* September–October, 37–43.

Lewis, H. (1977). The future of the social service administrator. *Administration in Social Work, 1*(2), 115–122.

Montana, P., & Charnov, B. (1993). *Management* (2nd ed.). New York: Barron's Educational Series, Inc.

Rapp, C., & Poertner, J. (1992). *Social administration: A client-centered approach.* New York: Longman.

Sartain, A., & Baker, A. (1978). *The supervisor and the job.* New York: McGraw-Hill.

Schmidt, M., Riggar, T., Crimando, W., & Bordieri, J. (1992). *Staffing for success: A guide for health and human service professionals.* Newbury Park, CA: Sage.

Umlah, D. (1976). Dealing with the problem employee. Unpublished monograph.

Weinbach, R. (1998). *The social worker as manager: A practical guide to success* (3rd ed.). Boston: Allyn and Bacon.

CHAPTER 14

Monitoring and Evaluating Organizational Efforts and Accomplishments

CHAPTER OUTLINE

- The Components of Excellence: A Working Hypothesis
- Measuring the Effectiveness of Human Service Organizations
- Identifying Outcome or End-Result Variables
- Assessing Managers' Perceptions of Causal Variables: Organizational Systems and Subsystems
- Assessing Staff Perceptions of Intervening Variables: Opinions on Systems and Processes

CHAPTER OBJECTIVES

Upon completion of this chapter, the reader should be able to:

- Discuss the concept of organizational effectiveness.
- Define causal, intervening, and outcome variables in an organization.
- Develop indicators of success for departments, programs, and/or units.
- Prepare discussion questions for use by a management team to assess the quality of organizational systems and subsystems.
- Prepare survey questions designed to help the management team understand employee perceptions of organizational systems and processes.

Assumptions

- That organizational effectiveness should be measured.
- That indicators should be developed to reflect success at the department, program, and/or unit levels.
- That internal systems and processes should be continuously evaluated to determine their contributions or barriers to success.

■ The Components of Excellence: A Working Hypothesis

This journey toward an understanding of the meaning of excellence began in Chapter 1 with a brief exploration of the variables that, over the years, have been used to define excellence in organizations and excellence in leadership. Chapter 2 examined a number of classical and contemporary theories of management and attempted to develop a theoretical framework for the management of human service organizations based on some of the themes drawn from the history of management thought. Chapters 3 through 6 were devoted to an exploration of the factors within the organization and between the organization and its environment that must be analyzed and adjusted as necessary to ensure that the organization is on track toward optimum performance.

Chapters 7 and 8 focused on the types of data and information that are needed to ensure that programs and finances are being managed in a way that is consistent with organizational mission, philosophy, and the goals and objectives specified in strategic and program planning documents. Chapters 9 through 13 examined the human resources processes and attempted to establish a framework for ensuring that the processes were internally consistent and supportive of the organization's mission.

What the organization of these chapters has attempted to sort out for the budding manager or administrator of a human service organization can be phrased in the following working hypothesis:

If a manager or administrator of a human service agency understands and applies knowledge of:

1. *Theory:* the theoretical principles that form the basis of knowledge about management effectiveness, including ways to achieve optimal employee performance,
2. *The Organization:* the organizational systems and subsystems that must be carefully designed to ensure compatibility with each other,
3. *Data and Information:* the data and information needed to monitor organizational-level activities, programs, finances, technology, human resources, and other important factors, and
4. *Human Resources:* the human resources processes and how to ensure that they are internally consistent and supportive of the organization's mission;

Then the manager or administrator will achieve:

1. *Understanding:* of the meaning of excellence in the management of a human service organization, which is a prerequisite to achieving excellence, and
2. *Steady Progress toward Excellence:* continuous movement of the organization in the direction of excellence, as measured by organizational and program results, smoothly functioning systems, and highly motivated employees.

The pace of progress will depend, to some extent, on agency resources and conditions.

Early Research on Organizational Effectiveness

A number of early researchers on organizational effectiveness attempted to identify the variables that contribute to success. Likert (1961) found that management style influenced productivity. He characterized management styles as falling on a continuum from System 1 through System 4, where the systems were defined as follows:

System 1: Management is seen as having little or no confidence in subordinates in terms of decision making. Input is not valued or used. Planning and decision making are top-down. Information may or may not be shared with workers at lower levels. Fear, threats, and punishment are used to stimulate worker performance. Rewards are limited to those that address physiological, safety, and security needs. Control is highly concentrated at the top.

System 2: Management is seen as having interest in subordinates, but the attention is generally condescending. Major organizational efforts in planning and decision making are restricted to top-level administrators and managers. Some lesser decisions are made at lower levels. Some rewards and some punishments are used to motivate workers. Control is concentrated at the top, but some authority is delegated to middle management and first-line supervision.

System 3: Management is seen as having substantial but not complete confidence in subordinates. Broad policy decisions are made at the top; implementation decisions are made at lower levels. Communication flows both ways, up and down the hierarchy. Rewards, a limited amount of punishment, and some involvement in planning and decision making are used to motivate. Significant aspects of control are delegated downward.

System 4: Management is seen as having complete confidence and trust in subordinates. Decision making is spread throughout the organization. Communication flows up, down, and sideways, from peer to peer. Workers are motivated by full participation in the life of the organization, including strategic and program planning, selection of benefits and rewards, improving methods, and evaluating effectiveness. Control is spread throughout the organization, with accompanying accountability.

Using this framework, Likert asked hundreds of managers to rate their most productive departments and their least productive departments. He found that the closer the management style of an organization approximates System 4, the more likely it is to have a consistent record of high productivity. Conversely, the closer it is to System 1, the more likely the department is to demonstrate low productivity (Hersey & Blanchard, 1988).

Blake and Mouton (1964) also explored organizational effectiveness using a framework based on two concepts—one emphasizing task accomplishment and the other stressing the development of personal relationships. Using this framework, they produced the Managerial Grid, which characterizes five different types of organizational cultures based on concern for production (task) and concern for people (relationship). On the Managerial Grid, production is illustrated on the horizontal axis and relationship on the vertical axis, creating four quadrants and a midpoint. The five organizational cultures are defined as follows:

1. **Impoverished:** (Low relationship, low task). Exertion of minimum effort to get required work done is enough to sustain organization membership.
2. **Country-club:** (Low task, high relationship). Thoughtful attention to needs of people for satisfying relationships leads to a comfortable, friendly organizational atmosphere and work tempo.

3. **Task:** (High task, low relationship). Efficiency in operations results from arranging conditions of work in such a way that human elements interfere to a minimum degree.

4. **Middle-of-the-road:** (Middle task, middle relationship). Adequate organizational performance is possible through balancing the necessity to get out work while maintaining morale of people at a satisfactory level.

5. **Team:** (High task, high relationship). Work accomplishment is from committed people; interdependence through a "common stake" in organizational purpose leads to relationships of trust and respect. (Blake, Mouton, Barnes, & Greiner, 1964, p. 136)

Many subsequent frameworks used to measure the effectiveness of organizations and their leaders have built on concepts and findings developed by Likert (1961) and Blake and Mouton (1964). Most of the research has been focused on for-profit businesses and industries. However, some of the concepts and principles extracted from the findings can be useful in assessing the effectiveness of nonprofit human service organizations as well. Most observers familiar with human services will recognize examples from Likert's four systems and from Blake and Mouton's characterizations of five types of organizations. And it is also likely that most professionals and managers would prefer to avoid being associated with organizations such as those characterized as Likert's "System 1" or Blake and Mouton's "Impoverished." These are not the types of organizations in which one takes pride or looks forward to coming to work.

Variables Useful in Understanding Organizational Effectiveness

How, then, can an organization learn about whether of not it has achieved those high states of commitment, motivation, morale, and productivity? Again, Likert (1967) provides some guidance in assessing organizational effectiveness. He identifies three variables that are useful in understanding effectiveness. He refers to them as (1) causal, (2) intervening, and (3) end-result variables.

Causal variables are those that are under the control of the organization and its management. In research terms they are what would be considered the independent variables. In systems terms they are those organizational components that comprise organizational inputs. Examples include staff and management knowledge and skill, the structure of the organization, job design, or motivation and reward systems.

Intervening variables are those that represent the current condition of the internal state of the organization. Intervening variables are controlled by the employees of an organization and are reflected in the commitment of staff to organizational mission, goals, objectives, teamwork, communication, and other such behaviors.

Output or end-result variables reflect the achievements of the organization. In research terms they would be described as the dependent variables. In systems terms they are considered outputs or outcomes. Output or outcome measures are frequently used to measure organizational and program success. An example of the relationships between causal variables, intervening variables, and output/outcome variables as applied to a human service organization is illustrated in Figure 14.1.

FIGURE 14.1

Relationship between Causal Variables, Intervening Variables, and End-Result Variables

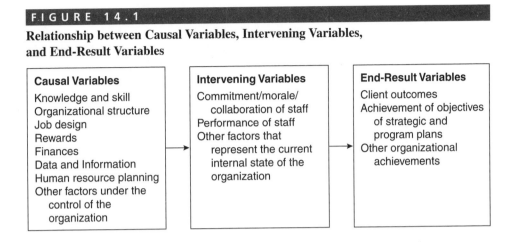

Causal Variables	Intervening Variables	End-Result Variables

Knowledge and skill
Organizational structure
Job design
Rewards
Finances
Data and Information
Human resource planning
Other factors under the
    control of the
    organization
	Commitment/morale/
	    collaboration of staff
	Performance of staff
	Other factors that
	    represent the current
	    internal state of the
	    organization
		Client outcomes
		Achievement of objectives
		    of strategic and
		    program plans
		Other organizational
		    achievements

■ Measuring the Effectiveness of Human Service Organizations

In Likert's terms, the focus of this book has been on causal variables and the intervening variables. The content of all thirteen chapters fits the definition of causal variables: those that are under the control of management. The point has been made repeatedly that management can acquire a sound theoretical and philosophical perspective and can draw on the knowledge base developed about management and organizations to design effective systems and subsystems. By doing this, management enhances the quality of the causal variables.

Furthermore, managers can democratize the workplace and develop their people skills in a way that encourages and supports employees in believing that they make important contributions to the organization. By doing this, management puts itself in a position to influence the intervening variables. If causal variables are managed to achieve the highest levels of quality, and if the intervening variables are influenced toward a commitment to the mission and vision of the organization, then the outcomes or end-result variables should indicate a successful, effective organization.

Organizations interested in periodic assessment of such issues as the quality and appropriateness of the design of their systems and subsystems, the knowledge and skill levels of their personnel, the extent to which organizational structure and job design support optimal functioning, and other such issues can survey selected staff members periodically to determine current perceptions. Staff members may also be surveyed to determine their perceptions of management style and organizational culture. As a guide to evaluating these causal and intervening variables, this chapter will identify questions drawn from each of the preceding chapters that may be useful in helping human service organizations to assess where they are in their journeys toward optimal functioning and the achievement of excellence.

■ Identifying Outcome or End-Result Variables

All well-designed organizational and program evaluations begin at the end. That is, the focus is first on end results and then on the processes that led to the results. Without some measurement of results, it is difficult if not impossible to assess the value, quality, or relevance of the processes.

Chapter 3 explored various types of planning: strategic, long-range, and program planning. Plans establish the outcomes or end results to be achieved, as well as the criteria by which success will be measured. In assessing organizational and program outcomes, it is necessary to return to these concepts. If objectives have been written in outcome terms, and if measurement criteria have been specified, then an annual review might be accomplished using questions such as those in the following sections. The result of this annual review should be to construct a rating system that will produce some comparable data on the organization's departments, programs, services, or task forces so that the management team can evaluate progress and success.

Strategic and Long-Range Planning

It is important to remember that the time frame for strategic planning is five years or more, whereas long-range planning is up to five years. It is likely that an annual review would be used to assess progress toward the achievement of objectives. Questions such as the following might be used in a survey of managers, supervisors, or other involved staff to determine their perceptions on progress.

The agency's strategic plan includes four goals, each with its own set of outcome objectives. Please assess progress toward the achievement of objectives based on your participation in each of the initiatives involved by circling the number that most closely reflects your experience. If you have not participated, please do not rate the objective.

Goal 1: To create new programs and services to meet the needs of newly arriving immigrants

	1	2	3	4	5
	Achieved 20% of the established milestones	Achieved 40% of the established milestones	Achieved 60% of the established milestones	Achieved 80% of the established milestones	Achieved 100% of the established milestones
Objective 1.1	1	2	3	4	5
Objective 1.2	1	2	3	4	5

Etc.

For objectives for which hard data are available, it may not be necessary to survey staff about progress toward achievement of strategic or long-range planning goals and objectives. However, not all efforts produce measurable data each year. The nature of such planning efforts is that they tend to be implemented by task forces made up of staff from different levels. In such instances it might be helpful to direct surveys to task force chairs or members. The point is that some type of structured annual review will provide a rating for the department, program, service, or task force that can be used as a measure of success so that the management team can assess where changes need to be made.

Program Planning

Well-designed programs will regularly produce data and information that can be used to assess outcomes or end results. An overview of program accomplishments can be developed using something such as the following format:

Each program has defined expected outcomes and has tracked its clientele to determine how many achieve success. Please indicate here the rate of success that you have achieved in your program this past year.

Percentage of Clients	Program A	Program B	Program C	Program D
Percentage achieving success as defined by program	————	————	————	————
Percentage still in the program, on track to achieve success	————	————	————	————
Percentage still in the program, not making progress	————	————	————	————
Percentage dropping out of the program	————	————	————	————

Using these or other types of criteria, organizations establish for the total operation and for its programs some measures of success. Each program, service, department, or task force receives a rating that helps the management team to understand and assess annual achievements. If the measures of success are valid and reliable, then the causal and intermediate variables can be assessed to determine if organizational factors or human factors are in any way contributing to or limiting success.

■ Assessing Managers' Perceptions of Causal Variables: Organizational Systems and Subsystems

Causal variables are those that are under the control of the organization and its management. Chapter 2 identified twelve management responsibilities that (it is hypothesized), if carried out in a consistent, conscientious, and ethical manner using the organization's mission and philosophy as a guide, will lead to excellence in organizational operations. Each of these management responsibilities has been the subject of a chapter. Each can now be used as a basis for reviewing and reassessing management knowledge and perceptions about the status of each of these areas of responsibility. The following sections will review each of the twelve areas of responsibility as proposed in Chapter 2 and will suggest questions that might be used to assess management perceptions. These questions could be used in a survey, as a basis for discussion in a management team meeting or a retreat, or in some combination.

Management Responsibility	The Role of the Manager
Analysis of the Entire System	Assess the purpose of the organization, expected outcomes, needed technologies, and state of the art. Define organizational and program inputs, throughput, outputs, and outcomes. Use as an overarching framework the concept of system integrity.

What are your perceptions of the systems and subsystems in this organization (e.g., programs, management, finance, human resources, etc.), not as individual entities, but rather in terms of the ways in which they fit together and are working toward the same ends? What changes, if any, are needed to enable these systems to work together more harmoniously?

Management Responsibility	The Role of the Manager
Establishment of Mission and Goals	Ensure consensus on shared vision. Create a process for ongoing development and refinement of organizational and program goals, objectives, and activities, with input from all stakeholders. Structure the organization and allocate resources to meet goals and objectives. Examine mission, goals, and objectives from the perspective of system integrity.

What are your perceptions of the extent to which our mission and philosophy permeate the organization? Are program goals, objectives, and activities understood and supported by staff? Do they make suggestions for refinements and improvements? Are resources adequate to achieve objectives?

Management Responsibility	The Role of the Manager
Creation of Ideal Structure	Assess existing structure and reporting and control systems. Create "ideal" structure for maximizing efficiency, productivity, effectiveness, and quality in terms of the organic-mechanistic continuum. Consider how the structure is organized to protect the technical core, ensure high quality and competent management, and attend to the needs and demands of the task environment. Examine all components from the perspective of system integrity.

Does our structure support optimal working relationships between and among staff who are expected to work together and collaborate on cases and projects? Does the current structure pose any barriers either to internal collaboration or to work outside the agency? Are informal structures working as intended?

Management Responsibility	The Role of the Manager
Creation of Ideal Job Design	Develop a job analysis for each position within the organization. Create ideal job designs for maximizing efficiency, productivity, effectiveness, and quality, recognizing employee need to use knowledge, skills, and creativity. Evaluate all positions from the perspective of how they fit into the overall system to accomplish stated mission, goals, and objectives. Ensure that there is system integrity.

What duties and tasks are being performed by staff that can be performed by lower-level, less costly staff? What responsibilities can be allocated downward to lower levels, eliminating the need for supervisory approval? What aspects of their jobs do staff like and dislike?

Management Responsibility	The Role of the Manager
Design of Motivation and Reward System	Understand what motivates employees. Design a system that ensures that those who are most successful, work the hardest, and demonstrate the highest levels of commitment to organizational mission, goals, and objectives receive the highest rewards. Incorporate both intrinsic and extrinsic rewards into the system. Check the system against all other components to ensure internal consistency.

What methods and techniques are we currently using to motivate employees? Are they working? What are our assumptions about motivation? Is our reward system fair and equitable? Do our best employees typically receive the highest rewards?

Management Responsibility	The Role of the Manager
Design of a Data Collection and Reporting System	Design a system that will permit collection of data on all phases of implementation and achievement for monitoring, evaluation, and research purposes. Ensure that data and information collected and aggregated are useful in tracking stated goals, objectives, and activities and are used to measure organizational and program success.

Are we currently collecting the data we need to answer the questions we need to have answered and produce the required reports? What information do we need that we do not have? Are reports shared with staff, and do they get feedback on the results of their data collection? How are we using findings from our management information system internally?

Management Responsibility	The Role of the Manager
Establishment of a Budgeting and Financial Management System	Design a system that accounts for and tracks all resources included as agency inputs. Allocate all resources into standard budget formats. Calculate unit costs in a variety of formats in order to track efficiency, effectiveness, productivity, and quality factors. Ensure that budget priorities are consistent with mission, goals, and objectives as well as with principles of the motivation and reward system.

Do our budget priorities reflect our mission and philosophy? Do our budget reports indicate levels of effort and accomplishment that are consistent with projections? Should we consider any changes in the way we allocate resources?

Management Responsibility	The Role of the Manager
Establishment of a Human Resources Plan	Prepare a plan that is grounded in an analysis of the needs of the organization for professional and technological expertise. The plan should include a complete job analysis for each position, together with a plan for recruitment and selection of personnel that is grounded in human resources law and meets the diverse needs of the organization and its clientele.

What are the gaps between our ideal personnel profile and our current staff profile in terms of areas of expertise and demographics? Are we in compliance with all human resources laws, executive orders, and regulations? Do we have a complete job analysis for every position in the organization? Do any need to be updated?

Management Responsibility	The Role of the Manager
Design of a Recruitment, Screening, and Selection System	Establish a system for recruiting a broad and diverse pool of applicants. Design a screening system that will ensure selection and hiring decisions that are consistent with the expectations established in the job analysis for the position. Check against organizational variables to ensure system integrity.

Are our recruiting efforts paying off in terms of attracting the types of applicants that we have attempted to recruit? Are the pools of applicants consistent with our profile of staff needs? Have we experienced any problems with our screening instruments in terms of their validity or reliability? Are we selecting the best candidates from the pool?

Management Responsibility	The Role of the Manager
Establishment of Principles for Supervision, Training, and Staff Development	Ensure that supervision is appropriate to the needs of the employee, taking into consideration what is known about employee needs and motivation in the interest of maximizing performance. Provide training that is appropriate to the employee's need for knowledge and skill. Encourage the employee to focus on his or her career goals and to prepare for advancement toward them.

Is our model of supervision and/or consultation effective? How much time are we spending on supervision? Could any of the functions be better performed in peer consultation? Are our employees keeping up with their training in all aspects of organizational and program operations as specified? What changes are needed in our orientation, training, development, and education programs?

Management Responsibility	The Role of the Manager
Design of a Performance Appraisal System	Design a system for performance appraisal that is consistent with the goals and objectives of the organization and with the job analysis. Ensure that the system accurately measures performance in a way that is comparable to other employees. Reward high levels of performance; do not reward low levels of performance. Check against mission, goals, and objectives, and against reward policies to determine consistency.

Is our performance appraisal system cost-efficient and easy to use by raters? Is it useful for allocating merit pay, promotions, and other rewards? Does it provide job-related feedback and guidance on how to improve performance, and is it accepted by both raters and ratees as being reliable and valid? What changes are needed in the ways we assess performance?

Management Responsibility	The Role of the Manager
Establishment of Policies for Termination	Design a system that will insure that low-level performers, nonperformers, nonproductive employees, and those who commit acts of misfeasance or malfeasance are evaluated in terms of whether they should be continued in employment. Terminate those whose performances do not warrant continuation. Termination policies should be consistent with mission, goals, and objectives and with performance appraisal system.

How many involuntary terminations have we had this past year? How many of these were contested? Do our policies hold up to challenges? Are we utilizing the corrective action process? Are we finding ways to help nonproductive employees to become productive? Do we need any changes in our termination policies?

If these types of questions can be addressed on an annual basis, the management team will be in a very good position to know what needs to be done to improve and strengthen its various systems and subsystems. It is not necessary that such questions all be answered by the same staff, at the same time, or in the same format. It is only important that those who have information and insight into these areas of organizational and program functioning be provided with periodic opportunities to share their knowledge and perceptions.

■ Assessing Staff Perceptions of Intervening Variables: Opinions on Systems and Processes

Intervening variables are those that represent the current condition of the internal state of the organization. Intervening variables are controlled by the employees of an organization and are reflected in the commitment of staff to organizational mission, goals, objectives, teamwork, communication, and other such behaviors.

It is possible that all of the organizational systems and subsystems may be properly designed and interface appropriately with each other, and yet staff may produce at low levels because of their perceptions of the way they are treated within the organization. For this reason it is advisable to survey staff on an annual basis to determine how they perceive the management style and the extent to which they feel they are a valued part of the organization. Questions will again be framed around each of the major systems and subsystems of the organization, but in this exercise, employees will be asked to reflect on their experiences on the job.

The following questions may be used to facilitate such an assessment. Questions are not intended to be exhaustive. They are designed to suggest some of the issues to be explored by management. Some type of scale or continuum (e.g., strongly agree to strongly disagree; consistently to never) should accompany the questionnaire in order to allow staff to express their perceptions using a range of options. If the agency has the resources to analyze written comments, they may be solicited in addition to responding to the designated items.

Annual Staff Survey

Mission, Goals, and Objectives

_____ I am aware of the mission and philosophy of this organization.

_____ I am satisfied with the role that I had in shaping organizational and program goals and objectives.

_____ I feel that management has done a good job of communicating expectations in relation to goals and objectives.

Working Relationships

_____ I find that the structure of my department, program, or unit facilitates and supports good working relationships.

_____ I am able to work in a collaborative way with other staff whenever necessary and do not find organizational or departmental structure to be a barrier.

_____ I find the structures within which I work to be sufficiently flexible and can make changes easily if needed.

Job Design

_____ I enjoy my job.

_____ I feel competent to do my job.

_____ There are parts of my job that I feel could be better done by people with other areas of expertise.

_____ I would like to be able to take on more responsibility for decision making, with accompanying accountability.

Motivation

_____ I am highly motivated to be productive.

_____ I feel that I make an important contribution to my unit, program, department, and agency.

_____ I feel that my input is respected in decision making within my unit, program, department, and agency.

_____ I feel that management is doing a good job of motivating employees.

Rewards

_____ I feel that the reward system rewards employees who work the hardest and deserve the rewards.

_____ I feel that the rewards given are meaningful and worth working for.

_____ I am satisfied with the agency's benefit package.

Data Collection

_____ I feel that the expectations for data collection are reasonable.

_____ I get feedback on data and information produced that affects my work.

_____ I find the feedback that I get helpful in improving my performance.

Finances and Resources

_____ I am familiar with the budget for my program, department, and agency.

_____ I feel that the budget reflects priorities that are consistent with the agency's mission.

_____ I am comfortable with the input and influence I have in the budget process.

_____ I have adequate resources to fulfill the expectations of my job.

Human Resources Law

_____ I consider myself to be knowledgeable about laws and regulations concerning discrimination of all types and harassment.

_____ I feel that the agency does a good job in training employees about all types of discrimination or harassment.

_____ I feel that the agency does a good job in enforcing all provisions about discrimination or harassment.

Human Resources Planning

_____ I am aware of the human resources planning process.

_____ I am comfortable with the input and influence I have had in the human resources planning process.

_____ It appears to me, based on hiring patterns, that human resources planning is worthwhile.

Job Analysis

_____ I have read the job analysis for my position.

_____ I agree that the job analysis for my position accurately reflects the work done and qualifications needed to do the job.

Recruitment, Screening, and Selection

_____ It has been my experience that the recruitment, screening, and selection processes at this agency have produced excellent results.

_____ I am satisfied with the input that I have had into the recruitment, screening, and selection processes.

Orientation

_____ I felt that the new employee orientation program was comprehensive and well designed when I went through it.

_____ I have participated in orienting a new employee this past year.

_____ I was able to achieve my objectives with new employees when I was involved in their orientation.

Supervision and Consultation

_____ The supervisory or consultative sessions I receive from my immediate supervisor are adequate to meet my needs.

_____ I would find peer consultation or other sources of professional consultation helpful.

Staff Training and Development

_____ My overall impressions are that the in-service training program is well planned and worth the time invested in training.

_____ I have been able to take advantage of opportunities to attend statewide or national conferences.

_____ I have been able to take advantage of some of the educational benefits offered by the agency.

_____ I am on track with the objectives in my career development plan.

Performance Appraisal

_____ I have had mostly positive experiences with performance appraisal and have received helpful feedback.

_____ I feel the performance appraisal system is fair and accurately assesses my performance.

_____ I feel the amount of time consumed in performance appraisal is worth the investment.

Termination

_____ I am aware of the termination policies in this organization.

_____ I feel that termination policies have been fairly and consistently implemented.

Interpreting Staff Perceptions

Although it is important to get employee feedback on their perceptions of the functioning of each of the organization's systems and subsystems, other findings are significant as well. Questions can be designed to elicit opinions about management style, using a scale similar to Likert's (1961) Systems 1, 2, 3, and 4, or other such scale. Perceptions about organizational culture, using a framework such as Blake and Mouton's (1964) Managerial Grid, may be helpful, if that is a concern to management. Employee perceptions about their being included in decisions and valued by the organization are important. Any of these types of approaches, or some combination, may be used. Unless there are extenuating circumstances, findings should be published and made available to staff, along with a statement about what will be done to address problem areas.

When an agency's management team, including the chief executive officer, present this type of openness in creating, designing, redesigning, implementing, monitoring, and evaluating organizational systems and subsystems, a new and very positive culture can be created. Employees begin to recognize that instead of complaining they have an opportunity to offer constructive suggestions and become involved in a process of change. The synergy created has the potential to move the organization to a higher level of functioning and to a pattern of continuous improvement that will inevitably lead to excellence.

SUMMARY

1. **The Components of Excellence: A Working Hypothesis.** If managers are well grounded in management theory, if they design good-quality systems, if they collect and make good use of data and information, if they conscientiously implement sound human resources practices, then the organization will be on track to achieve excellence.

   - *Early Research on Organizational Effectiveness.* Likert identified four different managerial styles that contribute or present barriers to organizational effectiveness. Blake and Mouton characterized five types of organizational cultures that affect productivity.

   - *Variables Useful in Understanding Organizational Effectiveness.* Causal, intervening, and outcome variables need to be identified and defined so that the organization can understand its level of effectiveness and can at least speculate about (if not definitively determine) some of the causes of effectiveness or ineffectiveness.

2. **Measuring the Effectiveness of Human Service Organizations.** Management controls the causal variables and can influence the intervening variables.

3. **Identifying Outcome or End-Result Variables.** Outcomes should be defined and produced through some sort of a data collection system first, so that the organization understands which departments, programs, units, or task forces are performing at an acceptable level of success.

   - *Strategic and Long-Range Planning.* Outcomes or achievement of milestones can be measured by reviewing the goals and objectives of strategic and/or long-range plans.

   - *Program Planning.* Program success can be measured by tracking the number of clients who achieve program objectives, including those who remain on track to achieve success.

4. **Assessing Managers' Perceptions of Causal Variables: Organizational Systems and Subsystems.** Organizational systems identified and discussed in Chapters 3 through 13 are reviewed, and questions are posed for management discussion and deliberation in an annual evaluation of organizational efforts and accomplishments.

5. **Assessing Staff Perceptions of Intervening Variables: Opinions on Systems and Processes.** Staff perceptions should be solicited on an annual basis to determine their opinions and experiences with various organizational systems.

   - *Interpreting Staff Perceptions.* Opinions should be solicited on all systems for which management has concerns. Opinions may also be solicited on employee perceptions of management style, organizational culture, and other relevant factors. If there are no serious contraindications, findings should be published and made available to staff, along with proposals to address problem areas.

EXERCISES

Please complete the following sections of your manual based on the content covered in Chapter 14.

Section 14: Organizational Efforts and Accomplishments

14.1 Organizational Review and Assessment. Establish in policy that your organization will conduct an annual review of organizational systems and processes.

14.1.1 Outcome Measures. Identify the departments, programs, units, task forces, or other groups that are expected to develop measures of success that can be used on an annual basis to assess outcomes.

14.1.2 Systems. Identify the systems within the organization that need periodic review. Propose a schedule so that each system to be reviewed will be covered within a three- to five-year period. Propose a format for management team deliberation.

14.1.3 Employee Opinion Survey. Propose a format for an annual survey of staff opinions. Attach a copy of a sample survey instrument, labeled Document 14.1.3a.

REFERENCES

Blake, R., & Mouton, J. (1964). *The managerial grid.* Houston, TX: Gulf Publishing.

Blake, R. R., Mouton, J. S., Barnes, L. B., & Greiner, L. E. (1964). Breakthrough in organizational development. *Harvard Business Review, 42*(6, November–December), 133–155.

Hersey, P., & Blanchard, K. (1988). *Management of organizational behavior: Utilizing human re-*sources (5th ed.). Engelwood Cliffs, NJ: Prentice-Hall.

Likert, R. (1961). *New patterns of management.* New York: McGraw-Hill.

Likert, R. (1967). *The human organization.* New York: McGraw-Hill.

Civil Rights Restoration Act of
1987, 351
Client fees, 197–199
College and University
Personnel Association,
251–253, 258, 269,
270–271, 282, 289,
290–293, 296
Collegial form of organizational
structure, 99–101, 238–239
Color discrimination, 228
Communication, organizational
structure and, 89
Community data collection,
184–185, 186
Compensation systems, 138–148
basic salary structure in,
138–139
bonuses in, 142–143
cost-of-living allowances
(COLA) in, 141–143
employee service benefits in,
147–148
insurance benefits in, 144,
145, 146–147
lump-sum increases in, 142,
143
merit increases in, 139–141
paid time off in, 143–144
retirement benefits in,
145–147
Competence, importance of, 39
Competitors, 170
Computer technology, 124
Constitution, 105–106
Consultation, supervision and,
329
Consumer/client, 170
departmentalization by, 93–94
Context of work, 260
Contingency theory, 36–39, 115,
121
Continuous organizational
improvement, 326–360
appraisal techniques in,
338–349
corrective action process and,
332–338
optimum employee
performance and, 327–328

supervision and, 328–332
terminating employees,
351–356
tying performance appraisal to
rewards, 349–351
Continuous quality
improvement, 45–46
Contracts, 194–197
Contributors, 169
Cook, C., 89
Corrective action process,
332–338
Cost-of-living allowances
(COLA), 141–143
Cost-reimbursement contract,
195
Council on Accreditation
(COA), 5–6
Counseling services, 148
Covey, Steven, 9–10
Crimando, W., 227, 234–235,
241, 242, 251, 252, 259,
264, 266, 267, 282,
292–293, 303, 304,
314–315, 329, 339, 351
Critical incident technique,
339–340, 348
Cross, T., 49, 257
Cross-sectional analysis, 178,
179
Cultural competence, 49,
256–257, 261

Daley, J. M., 103–104, 108, 178,
205, 209, 232
Data and information, 157–189
developing integrated
information systems,
162–186
to ensure organizational
consistency and integrity,
186
importance of, 158
quality of, 158–159
types needed in organizations,
159–161
Data collection, 164–168,
181–185
community, 184–185, 186
for job analysis, 260–265

organizational, 183–184
program, 181–183
Datar, S., 212
Daughtrey, A., 330
Davis, K., 241
Davis, L., 111
Davis, S., 96
Defined-benefit plans, 145
Defined-contribution plans, 146
Deming, W. Edwards, 4, 44
Demographics, 243
Dennis, K., 49, 257
Departmentalization, 91–95
Dessler, G., 125, 145, 146, 148,
227, 228, 230, 232–233,
251–254, 263–264, 266,
267, 284, 286, 339–340,
346, 353, 354–355
Development. *See also* Training
and development
career development plan,
321–322
comprehensive plan for,
307–309
defined, 301
Diaries, in job analysis, 265
Differentiation, 32
Dill, W., 35, 66
Direct solicitation, 200
Disabilities, 229–230
Discrimination
in employment interviews,
293–295
protection from, 229, 330
types of, 228–229
Diversity, 46–50
cultural competence and, 49,
256–257, 261
gender and, 47–48, 49–50,
257
laws governing workplace,
227–233
organizational culture and, 42
in recruitment process,
281–282
valuing, respecting, and
maximizing benefits of,
231–232
Driessnack, C., 259
Drucker, Peter, 4, 28–29, 346